DRIVING CONTINENTALLY

National Policies and the
North American Auto Industry

Edited by Maureen Appel Molot

Carleton University Press
Ottawa, Canada
1993

ISBN 0-88629-197-6 (paperback)
ISBN 0-88629-200-X (casebound)

Printed and bound in Canada

Canadian Cataloguing in Publication Data

Molot, Maureen Appel, 1941-
    Driving continentally : national policies and the North American
    auto industry

Includes bibliographical references.
ISBN 0-88629-200-X (bound) – ISBN 0-88629-197-6 (pbk.)

    1. Automobile industry and trade—North America.   2. Automobile
industry and trade—Japan.   3. Free trade—North America.
4. Automobile industry and trade—Government policy—Canada.
5. Automobile industry and trade—Government policy—United States.
I. Title.

HD9710.N672M65   1993   338.4'76292'097   C93-090188-6

Distributed by: Oxford University Press Canada,
                     70 Wynford Drive,
                     Don Mills, Ontario
                     Canada. M3C 1J9
                     (416) 441-2941

Cover design: Aerographics Ottawa
Layout/Production: Xpressive Designs Ottawa

Acknowledgements

Carleton University Press gratefully acknowledges the support extended
to its publishing programme by the Canada Council and the Ontario Arts
Council.

The Press would also like to thank the Department of Communications,
Government of Canada, and the Government of Ontario through the
Ministry of Culture, Tourism and Recreation, for their assistance.

CONTENTS

FOREWORD

The papers in this volume examine the effects of national policies on the automotive industries in Canada, Mexico, and the United States. They

- analyze the potential tensions or conflicts arising from the effects of national policies on an industry that has become more integrated on a North American and global basis;
- identify the economic and technological forces favouring greater integration of the North American automotive industry through the North American Free Trade Agreement (NAFTA);
- explore the implications for workers and communities of the restructuring and capacity shedding that is occurring in the industry; and
- document the complex web of interests in the auto sector in the three countries.

Some interests favour greater integration, others oppose it, and many wish to impose different, and often contradictory, conditions on the integration process. There are many different agendas in the automotive industry in the three countries, and there are many different visions for how interdependence in the industry ought to be managed. All of these pressures were at play in the NAFTA negotiations, and had an influence on their outcome. These pressures will also influence the debate about the implementation and evolution of NAFTA in the three countries.

The automotive sector is the largest group of manufacturing industries in the three countries and is dominated by enormous multinational firms. In the early 1990s, there are many stresses in the North American automotive sector. Mounting global competition and the introduction of lean technology have induced massive restructuring. The prolonged recession and weak recovery in Canada and the United States have aggravated these stresses and forced capacity shedding, while the Mexican economy has been relatively more buoyant during this period. Some of the sector's structural problems are linked to issues of corporate strategy and management effectiveness. The vitality of the North American automotive sector has long been linked to the fortunes of the Big Three—General Motors, Ford, and Chrysler; their management success or failure reverberates far beyond their corporate boardrooms and shopfloors. For the last decade, these corporate leviathans have been preoccupied with responding to competitive challenges from offshore rivals, particularly the major Japanese automotive firms. The Big Three have substantial investments in all three North American economies and each of the major Japanese firms has significant investments in one or more of the North American economies.

In most industries, one thinks of government policies at the national and subnational level, such as trade and investment policies, subsidies, industrial incentives, and environmental regulation as shaping the development of an industrial sector. However, the automotive sector is so large that developments within it shape government policies, and the interests involved find expression at the level of national and subnational governments.

The automotive sector is the bellwether of North American economic integration under NAFTA. The large economies of scale in production and model design, as well as the economies of scope in the coordination of production in the automotive sector, provide significant potential gains from international specialization, in addition to the specialization gains resulting from differences in labour skills, infrastructure, and other factors influencing relative production costs. Yet realization of these potential economic gains raises concerns about the pace and pattern of restructuring of the North American automotive sector.

The papers in this volume are interdisciplinary, drawing together academics, government officials, and private sector representatives from the three countries. These diverse perspectives were brought together at a conference at Carleton University, Ottawa, in October 1991, just as the NAFTA negotiations were gearing up. Among the disciplines represented are corporate strategy specialists drawn from business schools and firms, economists, labour specialists, lawyers, political scientists, public policy specialists, and trade negotiators. Together they provide many insights into the complex interaction of government policies in an increasingly integrated North American automotive sector.

As the debate about the implementation of the North American Free Trade Agreement proceeds, the stakes are higher in the automotive sector than in any other industry. The prospective implementation of NAFTA would create a new basis for managing interdependence in this sector, but the many interests involved will continue to influence the policy process in all three countries and shape the evolution of NAFTA.

November 1992

Murray G. Smith
Director
Centre for Trade Policy and Law

CONTRIBUTORS

Dennis J. Gayle

Dennis Gayle is Director of International Programs and Activities at Florida International University, Miami, Florida.

Stephen Herzenberg

Stephen Herzenberg is a labour economist with the Bureau of International Labor Affairs, US Department of Labor.

John Holmes

John Holmes is Professor of Geography at Queen's University, Kingston, Ontario.

Andrew Inkpen

Andrew Inkpen is Assistant Professor of International Management in the School of Business and Management at Temple University, Philadelphia, Pennsylvania.

Jon R. Johnson

Jon Johnson is a lawyer with Goodman and Goodman in Toronto, Ontario. He advised Canada's Trade Negotiation Office on the text of the Canada-US FTA concerning provisions on automotive goods and the Auto Pact.

Maureen Appel Molot

Maureen Appel Molot is Professor in the Norman Paterson School of International Affairs and the Department of Political Science at Carleton University in Ottawa, Ontario.

Miguel Angel Olea

Miguel Olea is a partner and Chief Executive Officer with Fondo de Optimización de Capitales, SA de CV, a venture capital fund in Mexico City, and is also a partner in Anàlisis Corporativo, SA de CV, a consulting firm in Mexico City, specializing in financial engineering and international trade operations.

Janice E. Plumstead

Janice Plumstead is a research associate with the US Policy Studies Group in the Faculty of Management at Dalhousie University, Halifax, Nova Scotia.

Simon Reich

Simon Reich is Associate Professor in the Graduate School of Public and International Affairs at the University of Pittsburgh, Pittsburgh, Pennsylvania.

Brian R. Russell

Brian R. Russell is Acting Director of the US Policy Studies Group in the Faculty of Management at Dalhousie University, Halifax, Nova Scotia.

Marc N. Scheinman

Marc Scheinman is with the Lubin School of Business at Pace University in New York.

Helen Shapiro

Helen Shapiro is Assistant Professor of Business, Government and Competition, at Harvard Business School in Cambridge, Massachusetts.

Murray G. Smith

Murray G. Smith is Director of the Centre for Trade Policy and Law in Ottawa, Ontario.

David Stuewe

David Stuewe was Director of the US Policy Studies Group in the Faculty of Management at Dalhousie University, Halifax, Nova Scotia, for four years. He is now Chief Executive Officer of the Workmen's Compensation Board of Nova Scotia and continues as Adjunct Professor at Dalhousie University, Halifax, Nova Scotia.

Glen Taylor

Glen Taylor is Assistant Professor of Management and Industrial Relations at the College of Business Administration at the University of Hawaii.

Kurt Unger

Kurt Unger is Secretario Académico at the Centro de investigación y docencia económicas in Mexico City.

Ronald J. Wonnacott

Ronald Wonnacott is Professor of Economics at the University of Western Ontario in London, Ontario.

Charlotte Yates

Charlotte Yates is Assistant Professor of Labour Studies and Political Science at McMaster University in Hamilton, Ontario.

ACKNOWLEDGEMENTS

A workshop and an edited volume of workshop papers could not have been undertaken without the continuing support of the Centre for Trade Policy and Law (CTPL) at Carleton University and the University of Ottawa. It is a pleasure to acknowledge the assistance, both moral and financial, offered by the Centre's director, Murray Smith, at all stages of this project. Members of the CTPL staff helped in a variety of ways as the project unfolded. Many thanks to Doris Whitteker, Melanie Burston, Lynda Lennon, Isolda Guevara, and Wenguo Cai. Joanne Cousineau, who helped organize the participants and did much of the correspondence, deserves special acknowledgement, as do Chrystine Frank and Cindy Murray, who assisted me with the editing of the manuscript.

Student research assistants at CTPL—Derek Baas, David Hood, Jane Jamieson, and Susan Olsen—undertook a myriad of tasks necessary for a successful workshop and the publication of this book. James Carter of the Automotive Parts Manufacturers' Association of Canada was extremely helpful in suggesting who in the auto industry might want to attend the workshop, and in persuading them to come. The editing skills of Steven Uriarte of Carleton University Press and Jeff Brown, one of my research assistants, did much to improve the quality of the manuscript. Last, but certainly not least, I want to acknowledge the enthusiastic participation of those from the auto industry, government, and academe from Canada, the United States, and Mexico who made the workshop a success.

Maureen Appel Molot

GLOSSARY

Acronyms for *Driving Continentally*

AIF	Annual Improvement Factor
AMC	American Motors Corporation
AMIA	Asociación mexicana de la industria automotriz
APMA	Automotive Parts Manufacturers' Association (Canada)
BEFIEX	Special Fiscal Benefits for Exports (Brazil)
BMW	Bayerische Motoren Werks AG
CAFE	Corporate Average Fuel Economy standards (US)
CAW	Canadian Autoworkers
CIF	Continental Improvement Factor
CKD	Completely Knocked-Down kit
COLA	Cost-Of-Living Adjustment
CTM	Mexican Workers' Confederation
CVA	Canadian Value-Added
CVD	Countervailing Duty
EC	European Community
EIU	Economist Intelligence Unit
EPA	Environmental Protection Agency (US)
FDI	Foreign Direct Investment
FTA	Free Trade Agreement
GATT	General Agreement on Tariffs and Trade
GDP	Gross Domestic Product
GNP	Gross National Product
GM	General Motors
GPT	General Preferential Tariff (US)
GSP	Generalized System of Preferences
GVW	Gross Vehicle Weight
IRI	Instituto per la Riconstruzione Industriale
ISTC	Industry, Science, and Technology Canada
JIT	Just-In-Time (Delivery)
JNAAP	Japan-North America Auto Pact
JOEM	Japanese Original Equipment Manufacturers
LDC	Less-Developed Country
MFN	Most-Favoured-Nation status/tariffs
MNC	Multinational Corporation

MNE	Multinational Enterprise
NAFTA	North American Free Trade Agreement
NAPC	National Air Pollution Control Administration (US)
NIC	Newly Industrializing Country
NSF	National Science Foundation (US)
NUMMI	New United Motors Manufacturing Corporation
OECD	Organization of Economic Cooperation and Development
OEM	Original Equipment Manufacturers
OTA	Office of Technology Assessment (US)
PBES	Pennsylvania Bureau of Employment Security
PRI	Institutional Revolutionary Party (Mexico)
SCEAIT	House of Commons Standing Committee on External Affairs and International Trade
R&D	Research and Development
SIC	Standard Industry Classification
SKD	Semi-Knocked-Down kit
TGR	Things-Gone-Right
TSUS	Tariff Schedule of the US
UAW	United Auto Workers
USITC	US International Trade Commission
VAT	Value-Added Tax
VER	Voluntary Export Restraint
VW	Volkswagen

1 INTRODUCTION

Maureen Appel Molot

The automobile industry is of enormous importance to the economies of Canada, the United States, and Mexico. In each of these countries it employs a significant number of people directly and indirectly through its links with suppliers and producers of raw material inputs. One out of every ten jobs in Canada and the United States is dependent on the automotive industry (US-Canada Automotive Select Panel 1992: 8).

Even before the conclusion of the North American Free Trade Agreement (NAFTA), the economies of Canada, the United States, and Mexico were already closely linked (Cameron, Eden, and Molot 1992). Trade in autos and auto parts constitutes an important part of these connections. Whereas in the early 1960s there were, in effect, three separate auto industries in North America, by the beginning of the 1990s the industry was well on its way toward integration along continental lines. This integration is the result of the interplay between corporate strategies and government investment and trade policies.

The automotive industry has been in the forefront in the introduction of new process technologies and the shift to lean production (Womack et al. 1990; Hoffman and Kaplinsky 1988). These new production techniques have facilitated the rationalization of components production and vehicle assembly across countries. Special bilateral sectoral arrangements, such as the Canada-US Auto Pact signed in 1965, US Tariff Items 806 and 807 (now 9802.00.80), and the Generalized System of Preferences (GSP), which permit the duty-free entry of Mexican exports of auto parts and assembled vehicles into the United States (and parts into Canada), have similarly promoted the de facto continental organization of the auto industry.

The auto industry is also an industry in serious difficulty. The Big Three's—Chrysler, Ford, and General Motors (GM)—share of the North American car market fell from 83 percent in 1978 to 56 percent in 1991, and employment in the industry declined in the same period by about 200,000 jobs (US-Canada Automotive Select Panel 1992: 5-6). Competition from offshore producers and industry overcapacity, combined with the recession of the early 1990s, reduced sales and forced the Big Three producers to develop new strategies they hope will enable them to reassert their dominance in the North American auto industry. Should the current loss of market share continue, a June 1992 report of the US-Canada Automotive Select Panel suggests that the Big Three could lose another 100,000 jobs over the next five years (1992: 6).

This book comprises the papers delivered at a workshop entitled "The Auto Industry: Responding to a Changing North American Trade Environment," held at Carleton University in Ottawa, Canada, in October 1991. The purpose of the workshop was to examine government auto industry policies in Canada, the United States, and Mexico as NAFTA negotiations were unfolding.

Over the last decade, considerable attention has been directed in all three North American countries to new production technologies and their impact on industry investment, organization, rationalization, and supplier relationships[1]. Less analysis has been done on government policies that have promoted, protected, and shaped the auto industry and the ways in which the industry has attempted to shape these government policies. The industry is of such significance to the economies of Canada, the United States and Mexico that it carries considerable political weight. When the industry feels its interests are being threatened, it does not shy away from using its political clout in any of the three capitals.

The policy context for the auto industry in North America is complex, extending beyond national boundaries and involving a variety of stakeholders. Governments need to be attentive to the increasing globalization of production at the same time as they worry about the domestic implications of corporate decisions on investment and employment. In Canada and the United States, both national and subnational governments have adopted policies to promote and regulate the auto industry. Among the policies that affect the industry are tariffs, investment restrictions, domestic content provisions, duty remissions and drawbacks, emission control and safety standards, import quotas, and location incentives. Most of the policies discussed in this volume are national or subnational in form, but some, most notably the 1965 Canada-US Auto Pact and the Canada-US Free Trade Agreement (FTA) are bilateral.[2] Clearly the NAFTA is trilateral.

While it is clearly impossible to disentangle the variety of factors that drive the behaviour of the multinational enterprises (MNEs) in the auto industry, the contributors to this volume were asked to focus on the impact of state policies on industry structure and evolution. This volume is intended to appeal to a wide readership in the industry, policy and academic communities, and among the attentive public in all three NAFTA countries. The purpose of this introduction is to highlight a number of issues that currently confront the North American auto industry and to identify the chapters that address these issues. Given the richness of the papers and the fact that there is inevitably some overlap in the topics covered in each, some chapters may be cited here more often than others. This introduction can only suggest some of the themes addressed by the contributors. As a whole, the volume examines the interaction between government policies and various facets of auto industry behaviour in Canada, the United States, and Mexico.

STATE INTERESTS AND INDUSTRY STRENGTH

Each of the three governments in North America has been attentive to the economic viability of its own auto industry and cognizant of the crucial contribution the industry makes to the health of each national economy. Moreover, each government has had its own priorities for the industry. As Holmes discusses, the Canadian government has historically looked to the auto industry as a source of jobs—primarily assembly jobs—for Canadian workers. There has been less attention given to the nationality of ownership in the auto industry or to the level of Canadian value-added that goes into a vehicle. The Mexican government, as Reich, Scheinman, Shapiro, Taylor, and Unger suggest, has viewed the auto industry as an important agent of industrialization, whether it has seen the industrialization process as import substitution or export-oriented. Through its various Automotive Decrees, the Mexican government has demanded high levels of domestic content in assembled vehicles, as much Mexican production of parts as possible, and a balance between the import and export of parts and vehicles. The US government has sought to ensure a viable industry with maximum production, assembly, and research and development within the continental United States. When the auto industry was initially challenged by Japanese imports, the US government, as Reich, Plumstead, Russell and Stuewe discuss, introduced (as did the

Canadian government) a policy of Voluntary Export Restraints (VERs) that restricted the numbers of Japanese cars imported into North America.

Many authors note that the "traditional" North American auto industry, defined in terms of the Big Three producers in Canada and the United States, is facing challenges from foreign and domestic competition. North American multinationals continue to lead in overall world production of autos; however, since 1978 the combined Canadian and US share of world auto production has fallen from approximately 35 percent to 24 percent, while Japan's has risen from 22 to 28 percent (Flynn 1992: 75).[3] According to the US-Canada Automotive Select Panel, this shift represents the equivalent of lost production in North America of over five million vehicles (1992: 15). The Big Three's share of the North American car market is now less than 60 percent (Flynn 1992:74).

That the economic viability of the auto industry has a direct impact on the overall health of each of the North American economies is to state the obvious. Although other sectors may now be more important than autos in both Canada and the United States in terms of employment and the development of new technology, and even in terms of total value of exports (the film industry in the US, for example), the automotive industry continues to be the largest *manufacturing* industry in North America.[4] The automotive industry accounts for over 4 percent of combined gross domestic product (GDP) of Canada and the United States and for approximately 1.2 million direct jobs (1,050,000 in the United States and 500,000 in Canada) and another one million directly related jobs. The auto industry consumes more than 25 percent of the sales of iron, stampings, machine tools, and semi-conductors, and more than half the sales of lead, rubber, and textiles (US-Canada Automotive Select Panel 1992: 8). The automotive industry is Mexico's second largest earner of foreign exchange, and machinery and transportation equipment comprise nearly half of all Mexican merchandise exports to the United States and the largest component of Mexican exports to Canada (see Unger, Chapter 15).

The importance of the auto industry means that jurisdictions actively compete to lure components and assembly plants. As the chapter by Plumstead, Russell and Stuewe indicates, American states have used a variety of industrial policy incentives to attract new automotive investment. The combination of location incentives and the search for cheaper labour sites has meant the decentralization of the

US auto industry away from the state of Michigan. Plumstead, Russell and Stuewe note the creation of a new "auto alley" extending through Michigan, Ohio, Kentucky, Indiana, and Tennessee; other new automotive investments have been made in Georgia, California, and South Carolina.[5] These new investments frequently mean the closure of older, less efficient plants in other locations. State government subsidies to assembly transplants are estimated to be in the range of US $50-70 per vehicle (OTA 1992: 143).

In Canada, Ontario and Quebec have competed against each other for new auto industry investment, offering (as Quebec did to attract a Hyundai assembly plant to Bromont) a combination of loans and other forms of assistance.[6] Mexico has used its *maquiladoras* (in-bond processing industries), as well as the promise of low labour costs, to entice auto investment to its northern border regions. (See chapters by Holmes, Taylor, and Scheinman on this point.)

Environmental concerns have also led to state regulation of the auto industry. As Gayle's chapter outlines, US attention to air quality and automobile emissions has resulted in Congressional legislation on acceptable auto emissions standards. While this legislation led the Big Three to invest in new technologies, they have also lobbied hard to postpone, if not prevent, more stringent environmental standards. Another piece of US legislation, the Energy Policy and Conservation Act of 1975, while ostensibly aimed at decreasing gasoline consumption, had as its real purpose to ensure that the Big Three would continue to assemble small, fuel-efficient cars in Canada and the United States. Under the legislation, car assemblers producing for the US had to meet two Corporate Average Fuel Economy (CAFE) standards, one for vehicles produced in the United States and a second for imported cars. Although the two-fleet rule was established to slow Big Three imports of small cars, the MNEs found ways to circumvent this provision and brought in Asian-assembled small cars (Hufbauer and Schott 1992: 210-211, 231). There were some modifications to the CAFE regulations under the NAFTA.[7]

THE TRANSPLANTS

If there is one factor that has shaped the current auto industry in North America more than any other, it is Japanese competition. The presence of the transplants in the North American auto industry graphically illustrates the interaction between government policy and the subsequent investment decisions of auto multinationals. Many contributors to this volume, among them Gayle, Herzenberg, Holmes, Inkpen, Scheinman, Plumstead, Russell and Stuewe, are attentive to the role of the Asian transplants in the North American auto industry.

Japanese vehicle producers began with assembly capacity in all three North American economies and have diversified into parts production. Some of the Japanese investments in parts production have been through joint ventures with US and Canadian parts producers, as the chapter by Inkpen discusses. Japanese production techniques of just-in-time production (JIT), zero defect quality, and flexible manufacturing have been emulated by the Big Three.

The transplants originally came to Canada and the United States to circumvent the quotas on imported cars (see Reich's chapter)[8] and to reduce the uncertainties attendant on exchange rate fluctuations. Initially, a number of the transplants (Toyota, Honda, Suzuki, and Hyundai) built assembly operations in Canada to serve both the Canadian and US markets. Canadian governments worked hard to secure this Asian investment, touting the ability to export to the United States provided the North American content requirements were met, as a major attraction of a Canadian location. Transplant investment in Canada, which totalled some $2 billion, constituted 20 percent of total transplant investment in vehicle assembly in Canada and the United States. As Scheinman notes, one out of every three Japanese vehicles sold in the United States is produced in that country and this proportion will increase to one in every two by the middle of the decade. By 1994 the transplant producers will have a capacity of almost three million vehicles, 2.48 million units in the United States, with an additional 345,000 units from Canada and more than 150,000 from Mexico. This combined capacity represents the equivalent output of about twelve standard assembly plants (US-Canada Automotive Select Panel 1992: 8).

Transplant parts suppliers followed the transplant assemblers to North America. There are currently some 400 Japanese or joint venture suppliers in North America, the vast bulk of whom are located in the United States; there are approximately twenty transplant suppliers in Canada, and very few in Mexico (US-Canada Automotive Select Panel 1992: 8). There are at least three reasons why there are so few Japanese or joint venture components producers in Canada: (a) the larger size of transplant assembly plants in the United States made it more attractive for suppliers to locate close to them; (b) governments in Canada could not offer the kinds of location incentives that American states could offer; and (c) the more highly unionized Canadian labour scene was viewed as less attractive to Japanese parts suppliers. Of the 40 joint ventures Inkpen studied, only three were unionized; two of those three were in Canada.

Another reason for transplant supplier interest in a North American location was the possibility of a wider range of potential customers. A North American location would make it easier to attract business from other Japanese companies from whom business might not be secured in Japan, where supplier-assembler relationships were tighter. A North American location might also facilitate sales of components to the Big Three. Concerns about future trade barriers and stricter application of the definitions of North American content[9] have promoted transplant supplier investment in North America.

The transplants, while contributing to the economies of Canada, the United States, and Mexico, will not compensate for the loss of North American owned facilities. The transplants account for only 112,500 jobs in Canada and the United States, less than 5 percent of total automotive jobs in these two countries. The transplants procure most of their high value-added components from Japan and locate most of their research and development there.[10] According to the US-Canada Automotive Select Panel report, *Competitiveness of the North American Auto Industry*, transplant vehicles assembled in Canada and the United States contain "an average of less than 20 percent value-added" from North American components suppliers. The panel suggests that the transplants are not well integrated into the North American industry and represent a parallel and competing industry (1992: 9-10).[11]

LABOUR

Auto industry employment is affected by a number of government policies, including those directly regulating the industry as well as a variety of social policies. Job losses in the auto industry, the age and skill level of autoworkers, and the role of unions are subjects touched upon in this volume. Yates analyzes the impact that government auto policy, most particularly the 1965 Canada-US Auto Pact, has had on the location of assembly jobs between Canada and the United States. The Canadian auto industry was the major beneficiary of the Auto Pact in terms of industry stabilization and employment.[12]

As the chapters by Herzenberg, Holmes, and Yates all note, employment levels in the Big Three have declined in recent years because of the introduction of new production technologies as well as transplant competition. Jobs have also been lost in the parts side of the industry.

There are significant differences between the profiles of autoworkers in the Big Three and transplant facilities, as well as between Canadian or American autoworkers and those in Mexico. The average age of the work force at Chrysler, Ford, and GM (in assembly and component plants) is older than in the transplants. Few workers have less than fourteen years seniority, most have received little on-the-job education, have not learned multiple job skills, and have had little or no involvement in the decisions directly affecting their workplace (De Koker 1992: 26). Job security and pension rights are a major preoccupation of these workers, and recent union contracts with the Big Three reflect these concerns (CAW/GM Report 1990: 3).[13] The age of the Big Three work force also means that these companies carry a significant pension burden for retired workers.[14]

Transplant autoworkers, in contrast, are younger, better educated, and receive significant on-the-job training. Very few of them in Canada or the United States are members of unions. Neither the United Autoworkers Union nor the Canadian Autoworkers Union has had much success in its efforts to unionize the transplant facilities. And because of the age range of their employees, the pension obligations of the transplants are future ones.

The auto labour market in Mexico is differentiated by skill level, with a few plants—such as Ford's Hermosillo facility—operating in a manner similar to plants in the United States or Canada, while most Mexican auto plants are engaged in low-skill, labour-intensive production. The importance of improving the skill levels of Mexican workers to enhance competitiveness is one of the arguments contained in Taylor's chapter. In many Mexican auto plants, employee turnover is very high; on the other hand, labour markets are tighter in northern Mexico, where there are frequently more jobs than workers, and companies compete with each other for labour. Herzenberg, Holmes and Taylor all discuss unions in Mexico, most particularly the Mexican

Workers' Confederation (CTM) and its relationship to the ruling party, the Institutional Revolutionary Party (PRI).

CANADA—US FREE TRADE AGREEMENT (FTA)

Of the various state policies considered in this volume, the Canada-US FTA is one of considerable importance to the auto industry. Chapter 10 of the FTA governs bilateral trade in automobiles and parts. Although, during the free trade talks, the Canadian government insisted that the Auto Pact "was not on the bargaining table" (Doern and Tomlin 1991:83), the Pact was in fact very much under discussion, in large measure because of US dissatisfaction with the Canadian production safeguards and their extension to the transplants in the form of a production-based duty remission waiver.[15] Johnson's chapter addresses the impact of the FTA on the Auto Pact, highlighting both the differences in the way in which the Auto Pact provisions were exercised in Canada and the United States and the changes to the Pact introduced by the FTA.

The FTA altered the Auto Pact in a number of important ways. First, the FTA terminated the duty drawback/remission schemes, which were instrumental in luring the Asian transplants to Canada by 1994.[16] Second, no new firms (with the exception of General Motors' CAMI joint venture with Suzuki) were to be granted Auto Pact status unless they could qualify for such status by the date of implementation of the FTA—namely, January 1, 1989. Since none of them did, the auto industry in Canada now contains "two classes" of producers.[17] Third, the FTA altered the definition of North American content under which vehicles can be imported duty free into Canada or the United States. For a product to qualify as "North American" under the FTA, 50 percent of its manufacturing costs must be incurred in either Canada or the United States. The definition of eligible costs has also been tightened; they are now defined in terms of the value of materials originating in each country plus the direct costs of assembling the product in the exporting country. Thus, overhead and promotional costs may no longer be included in the calculation of direct production costs. This new 50 percent direct cost rule is equivalent to almost 70 percent North American content under the old Auto Pact rules. In sum, the FTA retained Canadian Auto Pact safeguards but changed the rules under which automotive products could enter the United States. In the FTA there is a clear distinction made between North American-owned and transplant producers, and a very definite usage of the trade agreement to protect these North American-owned producers. The rationale for these provisions, as articulated in the foreword to the FTA Auto Chapter, lies in the pressure they place on Asian transplants either to manufacture major components in North American or to purchase them from North American suppliers.[18]

A July 1992, US Customs audit of Ford of Canada cars exemplifies the way in which government policies can conflict with each other. The Ford Crown Victoria and Grand Marquis, which are large, less fuel-efficient vehicles, are assembled using drive train components from Mexican suppliers. They are consciously built this way to side-step the US fuel economy (CAFE) regulations discussed above and, thereby, to be deemed "non-North American" for CAFE purposes. At the same time, Ford wants these vehicles to qualify as North American under the FTA; company officials argue that these cars exceed the 50 percent North American content requirement under the Canada-US trade agreement.[19]

NORTH AMERICAN FREE TRADE AGREEMENT (NAFTA)

The NAFTA provisions on autos and the definition of North American content will influence patterns of auto industry investment in production in the 1990s and beyond. That the auto portions of NAFTA were difficult to negotiate reflects the different perspectives of the various players in the North American auto industry and their assessments of potential gains and losses from further continental integration. The three governments, for their part, adopted bargaining stances that reflected their national economic interests and were the subject of debate until virtually the last stage of the trilateral talks. The chapters by Herzenberg and Olea discuss the interests of the US and Mexican auto industries, while Wonnacott and Smith's chapter addresses the complexities of rules of origin, that is, the definition of North American content.

The Big Three auto producers, sensitive to their weakening competitive position vis-à-vis the transplants, took a protectionist position on NAFTA. Chrysler, Ford and GM all demanded a higher regional-content provision than the 50 percent rule under the FTA; Ford and Chrysler advocated 70 percent, while GM sought 60 percent North American (including Mexico) content. The Big Three argued, moreover, for the creation of a "two-tier" system that would ensure that the five companies which are currently the major players in the Mexican auto industry (themselves plus Nissan and Volkswagen) would enjoy a privileged position in the Mexican market for fifteen years (see Olea, Chapter 14). Under their proposal, performance and other requirements for the Big Three (plus Nissan and Volkswagen) would be reduced more quickly, while those for newcomers to the Mexican market would have a transition period of fifteen years. US parts producers adopted a stance similar to that of the Big Three, although they originally argued for a North American content provision of 75 percent (MEMA 1991: 2).

What underlay the Big Three proposal was their concern that NAFTA would permit "Mexico to establish itself as a platform for major new automotive capacity from third country producers for export to the US market" (*Inside US Trade* September 23, 1991: S-3). Acceptance of the Big Three perspective would mean the reservation of the domestic and import market for assembly firms already established in Mexico, while the tighter rule of origin would make it more costly for non-North American companies to operate in Mexico.

The Canadian subsidiaries of the Big Three took a position similar to their American parents, although the parent firms maintained that their affiliates were being nationally responsive in their stance. The Canadian parts industry, concerned about potential job losses to US as well as Mexican components producers, supported a higher North American content requirement under NAFTA, and the removal of the value-added parts protection afforded Mexican parts producers under the 1989 Automotive Decree. At the outset, the Canadian parts industry advocated a 75 percent North American content requirement with the addition of a 50 percent Canadian value-added content rule to protect Canadian parts suppliers (APMA 1991);[20] but the demand for specific Canadian value-added was dropped when it became clear that this position was not acceptable to the Canadian government (Interview 1992). As Olea's chapter outlines, the Mexican supplier industry opposed both the two-tier proposal and that for higher North American content, preferring the transition period to be structured by the performance requirements of the 1989 Automotive Decree.

Each of the three governments sought to protect its own auto industry. The United States, concerned about the Big Three's competitive strength, demanded that Mexico open its market more broadly to car imports[21] and reduce its strictures on foreign investment, and sought both simplified North American content rules and a level of 60 percent. Canada had three objectives in the NAFTA talks: to improve access to the Mexican market for Canadian auto exports, including parts and finished vehicles; to resolve some of the administrative difficulties with the FTA rules of origin (see Johnson chapter) through the negotiation of more predictable regulations; and the maintenance of the Auto Pact. Canada, sensitive to the situation of the transplants and what attracted them to locate assembly facilities in Ontario and Quebec, did not differentiate amongst auto assemblers as the US did. Canada would have preferred a North American content requirement of 50 percent under which Canada would continue to be seen as an attractive location for new auto industry investment, but was prepared to accept a 60 percent North American content figure. Mexico's goal in the negotiations was to preserve as many of the assembly provisions and domestic content requirements of its 1989 Automotive Decree as it could to ensure its attractiveness as a location for future MNE investment.

Under NAFTA, which has an implementation date of January 1, 1994,[22] intra-regional barriers to trade and investment in the automotive sector are to be dismantled over ten years. NAFTA retains the provisions of the Canada-US Auto Pact and, as Johnson notes in the conclusion to his chapter, continues the prohibition on the extension of Auto Pact status to the transplants. Mexico's 1989 Automotive Decree will be phased out in stages during the transition period; the restrictions on vehicle imports are to be eliminated immediately, with those dictating trade-balancing and national value-added requirements to be eliminated by 2004. By that date Mexico must bring any inconsistent provisions of the Automotive Decree and its implementing regulations into conformity with NAFTA. There can be no new entrants to the Mexican assembly market for ten years, after which new entrants will have free access to all North American markets if they meet the rules of origin requirements. Mexico will also reduce its restrictions on foreign investment under NAFTA so that North American investors can own up to 100 percent of Mexican "national" parts suppliers and up to 49 percent of other automotive parts enterprises, rising over five years to 100 percent (NAFTA 1992: 9). NAFTA also establishes a trilateral automotive group to make recommendations on auto standards and how they can be made more compatible.

As Johnson and Wonnacott and Smith outline, NAFTA will change vehicle content requirements and how they are calculated. North American content provisions have been raised from 50 percent, under the Canada-US FTA, to 62.5 percent for passenger vehicles, light trucks, engines, and transmissions, and to 60 percent for large trucks and buses. These changes will be implemented in two stages over eight years.[23] The measurement of content under NAFTA will be done by tracing the value of imports of automotive parts through the production chain. Although these new rules of origin were designed to resolve a number of the difficulties that arose under the Canada-US FTA (for example, Honda exports to the United States), Johnson suggests that their application will be complex and, therefore, possibly contentious.

With a NAFTA implementation date of January 1994, there can only be modest speculation about the impact of the agreement on the auto industry and, in particular, on the Canadian segment of that industry. NAFTA does provide some breathing space for the Big Three auto producers because of the higher rules of origin, which realistically cannot be met by the transplants without major investments in North American engine and transmission production, and because they have protected status in the Mexican market. Whether this is sufficient time for the Big Three to recover their competitive edge vis-à-vis the transplants remains to be seen. Both the Big Three and parts suppliers in all three countries will restructure—and in the case of Mexico, modernize—as NAFTA is phased in.

One of the concerns about NAFTA is the potential movement of auto industry jobs to Mexico. Although some Canadian and American parts producers have moved labour-intensive production to Mexico, the declining importance of labour as a factor of production makes this strategy attractive only to a specific segment of the auto industry; only for the production of engines and labour-intensive parts do labour costs outweigh the added costs (e.g., transportation) of doing business in Mexico. Mexican parts suppliers are becoming more sophisticated, but so far they have had difficulty simply meeting Mexican content requirements. Mexican-owned parts producers, for the most part, are not competitive in terms of either quality or cost with their Canadian and American counterparts. In the short term, therefore, the US Office of

Technology Assessment suggests that "neither the Big Three nor the transplant assemblers can expect to substantially improve their competitive positions by moving production to Mexico" (OTA 1992: 133, 137). The challenge to the Big Three remains the transplants. Over the longer term, the elimination of Mexican investment restrictions may mean the location of some first-tier suppliers (US and transplant) in Mexico, with a concomitant loss of US jobs (OTA 1992: 149).

The transplants, which favoured a 50 percent regional-content provision and opposed the two-tier system for the Mexican auto industry, labelled NAFTA "a giant step in the wrong direction" (JEI No. 32B: 2).[24] They have eight years to adapt to the new North American content requirements. Transplant firms will have to determine whether, where, and when they will invest in new components production and vehicle assembly capacity in North America.[25] Current market overcapacity may restrain their interest in new investments at least in the short term.

Although NAFTA rules of origin will eventually generate more investment in components production in North America, it is not clear that any of this new production will occur in Canada. Companies planning investments in North America will inevitably be drawn to the largest market—the United States—particularly if there is uncertainty about their ability to meet the 62.5 percent content provision. In fact, the point has already been made that virtually all of the transplant investment in components production is in the United States. Canada is perceived as having a less attractive labour climate, and trade tensions between the United States and Japan provide a political incentive for the transplants to invest in components production in the United States, since parts coming across the border will not be dutiable. Although Canadian parts producers are becoming increasingly competitive, under this combination of circumstances the Canadian parts industry could well see its share of the North American components market decline.

FUTURE MARKETS FOR NORTH AMERICAN AUTO PRODUCERS

The one potential growth market in North America for auto sales is, as Scheinman suggests, Mexico. The robustness of that market is, in turn, a function of continuing economic growth in Mexico. Given the limited prospects for dramatic increases in sales within North America and the large US-Japanese deficit in auto trade, are there alternative market opportunities for North American auto producers?

Mexican auto assemblers have exported some cars to other Latin American economies, and Scheinman sees potential in these markets, particularly as new free trade agreements are signed. There was some hope in early 1992 that Ford of Canada would export 65,000 automobiles to Argentina (Feschuk 1992: A1).[26] However, it is the opening of the Japanese vehicle and parts market to North American producers that is the real challenge. Japan is now the world's second largest vehicle market and the largest parts market. Imports held about 3 percent of the Japanese market in 1990. No other major vehicle-producing nation has an import share below 22 percent, and many of the European producers' import shares are about 50 percent (Flynn 1992: 82). There were suggestions in mid-July 1992 that Toyota, Japan's biggest carmaker, would begin importing US-made cars into Japan in August 1992. Such a strategy is important symbolically as an effort to reduce Japan's trade surplus with United States.[27] Toyota will also begin to import components into Japan in 1994. Nissan said that in 1993 it would start importing into Japan a small station wagon made in Mexico. Honda remains the leader in so-called reverse imports, with average monthly imports of 1,146 units of three different models of the Accord (*Financial Post* 1992: 6). However, the weakening of the Japanese car market in 1992 may force the postponement of some of these import intentions.

FUTURE STATE POLICIES?

Although the contributors to this volume have focused on NAFTA as the state policy of most immediate importance to the auto industry in the coming years, there are other policy issues that demand consideration. Herzenberg, attentive to the continuing North American trade deficit with Japan, which in his view even a 70 percent North American content rule would not reduce, suggests the need to negotiate a Japanese-North American Auto Pact. Reich, whose chapter compares the investment regimes of three European states with those of the three in North America, raises questions about whether a lack of investment restrictions actually redounds to the benefit of nationally owned industries. In

Japan, state regulation of the auto industry has been a major factor in the development of the auto companies' competitive strength.

In other words, although free trade will benefit the auto industry and facilitate continuing continental rationalization of production, it may not be sufficient to ensure the future competitiveness of the Big Three and the North American-based parts producers. In the view of the US-Canada Automotive Select Panel, "industry actions alone will not be sufficient to close the competitiveness gap" (1992: 34). The panel recommends a series of state initiatives that the Canadian and US governments should take separately, bilaterally, and vis-à-vis Japan to assist the auto industry and enhance its competitiveness (1992: 35-42). Although the Panel applauds the moves to freer trade in North America, its suggestions for state action in the areas of market access, improved policy coordination, investment incentives, tax credits to promote research and development, and educational and social policies imply more, rather than less, state support for the industry.

As the experience with the Canada-US FTA illustrates, the conclusion of a free trade agreement does not bring an end to international friction over the auto industry. Nor has it reduced expectations that governments will intervene to assist the industry. Whether any of the Automotive Select Panel's specific recommendations are ever implemented, industry stakeholders will likely pressure national and subnational governments in all three countries to use subsidies and other policies to buttress local auto producers during the phase-in of NAFTA. The degree of competition faced by the North American auto industry at the end of this century and beyond will shape the future demands it makes on all governments.

NOTES

[1] See, for example, Hoffman and Kaplinsky (1988) and Womack et al. (1990).

[2] From time to time these government policies conflict with one another. See below the discussion of the July 1992 US Customs audit of Canadian-assembled Ford Crown Victoria and Grand Marquis cars.

[3] Europe's share of world auto production has remained stable over the 1978 to 1990 period at 38 percent (US-Canada Automotive Select Panel 1992: 5).

[4] According to a recent report by Nuala Beck and Associates, Inc. of Toronto, computer services in Canada now employ more people than the auto industry (Francis 1992: 15).

[5] Plumstead, Russell and Stuewe discuss the competition amongst US states to attract the first BMW plant in the United States and the incentives offered by South Carolina which, in the end, led the company to select a South Carolina location.

[6] In his study of Hyundai's experience in the North American automotive market, Rourke (1989) estimates that the federal and Quebec governments contributed approximately $200 million in subsidies to the construction of Hyundai's $324 million assembly plant in Bromont, Quebec. Moreover, by delaying for two years its 1985 policy to impose the full 9.2 percent tariff on Hyundai automotive imports, the federal government saved the company about $120 million in duties. Putting these two figures together, it could be argued that the two levels of government effectively paid for the construction of the Bromont plant.
Given that the facility is expected to produce only 23,800 cars in 1992, produced only 28,000 in 1991, and has a capacity of 100,000 units, there is speculation that Hyundai may go even further than its current reduced work schedule (the company's 900 employees have been working only three days a week since March 1992) and shut down production completely. There has also been speculation that the Bromont plant was considered early in 1992 by BMW as a possible site for its first North American assembly plant, and that the Quebec government was prepared to turn the plant over to BMW at no charge to the company.

[7] Under NAFTA, the US will modify its fleet definition under CAFE so that vehicle assemblers may choose to have parts and vehicles produced in Mexico and exported to the US classified as domestic. After ten years,

Mexican production exported to the US will receive the same treatment as US or Canadian production for purposes of CAFE (NAFTA 1992: 10). Mexico, which considers CAFE trade distorting, wanted to dramatically alter the CAFE regulations, but the US was not prepared to consider major changes to CAFE.

[8] One of the results of the VERs was to allow the Japanese to move up-market in their auto production, thereby capturing a higher profit on each car sold in North America under the import quotas.

[9] In early 1992, US authorities accused Honda of exporting cars to the United States with insufficient North American content (less than 50 percent) to qualify for duty-free entry. In July 1992, as noted below, US Customs officials investigated the North American content of cars assembled at Toyota's plant in Cambridge and Ford of Canada's facility in St. Thomas (Oxby 1992: F2). Canadian Customs also undertook an audit of two US auto assembly plants, though the plants in question were not named (Saunders 1992b: B2).

[10] These complaints about the transplants, voiced by the US-Canada Automotive Select Panel (1992: 8-9), are not unlike those levelled against practices of the Big Three in Canada by Holmes. A recent report suggests that representatives of US and Japanese auto industry associations will discuss the possibility of Japanese participation in US-based research and development consortia (Pritchard 1992b: B10).
There is a considerable difference in the North American content of transplants (approximately 50 percent) compared with Big Three cars (over 90 percent) assembled in Canada and the United States (US-Canada Automotive Select Panel 1992:8-9).

[11] The American subsidiary of Toyota plans to start buying its first parts from Chrysler Corp. in 1993. The move is part of its effort to ease trade tensions with the UAW and to build a network of suppliers in the US. The American unit, Toyota Motor Manufacturing, will use the parts, canisters containing charcoal used in emission-control systems, at its Georgetown, Kentucky. plant that produces Camrys (*Ottawa Citizen* 1992: D11).

[12] Over much of the 1970s and 1980s the Canadian auto industry was considerably more robust than its US counterpart. The Canadian share of Canada-US vehicle production rose through this period from 7.1 percent of total vehicle production in 1965 to 12.6 percent in 1970, 14.6 percent in 1980, and just over 15 percent in 1989 (Industry, Science and Technology Canada 1990:20, Table 3.1). The later proportions of total Canada-US production are significant because they represent a figure considerably higher than the 9 percent of bilateral vehicle sales for which Canada accounts.

[13] Because GM sources so many of its components internally (70 percent as compared with less than 50 percent for Ford and less than 30 percent for Chrysler), a larger proportion of its workers is employed in components production rather than assembly. The UAW union has been prepared to accept concessions to retain these jobs. Concessions were a major issue in discussions between GM of Canada and the CAW over the future of GM's two Oshawa, Ontario, plants during early 1992 (Pritchard 1992a: B1). One of GM's current strategies to overcome its serious inefficiencies and its deficit is to reduce its in-house sourcing and shed some of its parts producers.

[14] The president of the Automotive Parts Manufacturers' Association of Canada noted that the total cost of employee benefits in early 1992 is nearly $1000 more per vehicle for the Big Three in comparison with the transplants (De Koker 1992: 26). This includes differences in health care costs, another area where government policy has an impact on the auto industry.

[15] For a discussion of the US view on how Canada benefited from the Auto Pact see Hufbauer and Schott (1992: 223-225).

[16] Under NAFTA the termination date for the export duty drawbacks has been extended to January 1996. The production-based duty remissions also terminate in January 1996.

[17] Although the Asian transplants originally supported the negotiation of the FTA, they were extremely unhappy with its auto provisions. The distinction in status among auto assemblers that resulted from the FTA was an interesting precursor to what the Big Three demanded, and got, from the NAFTA auto provisions.

[18] As long as Chrysler, Ford, and GM comply with the provisions of the Auto Pact they will be able to import parts and vehicles duty free into Canada from any other production location, including Brazil, Japan, Korea, and, in the North American context, most importantly, Mexico.

[19] For a discussion on the sourcing of the components in these Ford cars see Saunders (1992a: B1).

[20] The Japanese-owned Canadian auto assemblers wanted North American content rules of 50 percent. This group also wanted the 9.2 percent Canadian external tariff, which encourages domestic content, lowered to at least the US level of 2.5 to 3 percent.

[21] Current Mexican regulations demand that 2.5 cars be built in Mexico for each one imported.

[22] The January 1, 1994, implementation date for NAFTA is predicated on passage of the agreement by the three national legislatures prior to the end of 1993. As of early February 1993, it was not clear when NAFTA would be debated by the US Congress and how long it would take President Clinton to negotiate the side agreements on environmental issues, workers' rights, and import surges that he had promised prior to Congressional consideration of the agreement.

[23] By 1998, North American content requirements for vehicles to move tariff free amongst the three countries will be 57 percent; this will rise to 62.5 percent by 2002.

[24] Nissan is the only Japanese auto producer with assembly facilities in Mexico. As a result, its perspective on NAFTA was different from that of the other transplants. Nissan will take advantage of its protected position in the Mexican market (and its ability to export to Latin America) to open a second assembly plant in late 1992 or early 1993.

[25] Toyota indicated in November 1992 that it was reviewing plans to increase its North American production, including at its Cambridge, Ontario, plant, as well as the feasibility of a new plant in Mexico (*Financial Times* 1992a: 16).

[26] The deal was never confirmed and it appeared that financing was the problem (McHale 1992: B2).

[27] Toyota claimed 42 percent of car sales in Japan. These exports will also help meet the Japanese demand for station wagons. The Toyota wagon will compete against Honda's US designed and made Accord wagon, sales of which averaged 836 a month in Japan in 1992. Toyota has set a sales target of 700 North American-made vehicles per month in Japan.

REFERENCES

Automotive Parts Manufacturers' Association (APMA). 1991. *APMA Proposed Policy Positions for the Automotive Provisions of a North American Free Trade Agreement*. Toronto. October 10.

Cameron, Maxwell; Eden, Lorraine; and Molot, Maureen Appel. 1992. North American Free Trade: Cooperation and Conflict in Canada-Mexico Relations. In *A New World Order? Canada Among Nations 1992-93*, eds., Fen Hampson and C.J. Maule. Ottawa: Carleton University Press.

CAW/GM Report. 1990. *Highlights of the agreement between the CAW-Canada and GM Canada*. Toronto: CAW Communications Department. October.

Congress of the United States. Office of Technology Assessment (OTA). 1992. *US-Mexico Trade: Pulling Together or Pulling Apart?* Washington, D.C. October.

De Koker, Neil. 1992. Turf Wars: The Restructuring of the North American Market. In *Canada's Auto Industry: A Retail Revolution*. Toronto: Financial Post Conferences. February 11.

Doern, G. Bruce, and Tomlin, Brian W. 1991. *Faith and Fear: The Free Trade Story*. Toronto: Stoddart.

Feschuk, Scott. 1992. Ford Canada to fill $550-million order. *Globe and Mail*, March 9.

Financial Post. 1992a. Toyota may expand in North America. November 14.

____. 1992b. Toyota to import its own US-made cars into Japan. July 17.

Flynn, Michael. 1992. Luncheon Address. In *Canada's Auto Industry: A Retail Revolution*. Toronto: *Financial Post* Conferences. February 11.

Francis, Diane. 1992. Another "brilliant" decision by Premier Rae. Financial Post, November 12.

Governments of Canada, the United Mexican States, and the United States of America. 1992. Description of the Proposed North American Free Trade Agreement (NAFTA). August 12.

Hoffman, Kurt, and Kaplinsky, Raphael. 1988. *Driving Force: The Global Restructuring of Technology, Labor and Investment in the Automobile and Components Industries*. Boulder, Colo.: Westview Press.

Hufbauer, Gary, and Schott, Jeffrey. 1992. *North American Free Trade: Issues and Recommendations*. Washington: Institute for International Economics.

Industry, Science, and Technology Canada. 1990. *Statistical Review of the Canadian Auto Industry: 1989*. Ottawa: Minister of Supply and Services Canada.

Inside US Trade. 1991. September 23.

Interview. Automotive Parts Manufacturer Association. 1992.

Japan Economic Institute (JEI). 1992. JEI Report. No 32B.

McHale, Stephen. 1992. Ford's Argentina deal remains unconfirmed. *Globe and Mail*, March 10.

Motor and Equipment Manufacturers Associations (MEMA). 1991. Objectives and Proposed Policy Approaches of the US Motor Vehicles Parts and Equipment Manufacturing Industry for a North American Free Trade Agreement. Washington, D.C. October 14.

Ottawa Citizen. 1992. Toyota to buy Chrysler parts. July 13.

Oxby, Murray. 1992. Ontario car-part audits just routine, US claims. *The Ottawa Citizen*, July 17.

Pritchard, Timothy. 1992a. GM sends unions clear signal. *Globe and Mail*, February 26.

____. 1992b. Japanese may join Big Three in research. *Globe and Mail*, November 13.

Rourke, Philip. 1989. *Hyundai and the North American Automotive Industry*. Masters Research Essay. Ottawa: Carleton University.

Saunders, John. 1992a. Ford Canada, Toyota targets of latest US Customs audits. *Globe and Mail*, July 14.

____. 1992b. Canada audits two US auto plants. *Globe and Mail*, July 18.

US-Canada Automotive Select Panel. 1992. *Competitiveness of the North American Automotive Industry*. June.

Womack, James; Jones, Daniel T., and Roos, Daniel. 1990. *The Machine That Changed The World*. New York: Rawson Associates.

2 FROM THREE INDUSTRIES TO ONE:

Towards an Integrated North American Automobile Industry*

John Holmes

INTRODUCTION

In the early 1960s there were essentially three separate automobile industries on the North American continent. Today, only thirty years later, the momentum toward full continental integration in the automobile industry appears irreversible. With the initialling of a North American Free Trade Agreement (NAFTA), it is likely that by the end of the decade significant progress will have been made toward the creation of one integrated North American automobile production and marketing system spanning Mexico, the United States, and Canada.

The existing level of cross-border integration in the North American auto industry has been achieved in two broad stages. First, the 1965 Auto Pact negotiated between Canada and the United States enabled the North American automakers to move rapidly during the late 1960s and early 1970s toward the rationalization of their Canadian plants and the full integration of the production and marketing of motor vehicles between Canada and the United States. Secondly, a radical shift in Mexican economic and industrial policy at the end of the 1980s signalled that the Mexican auto industry, whose links to the industry in the United States and Canada had been growing throughout the decade as the result of strategic choices made by a number of transnational automakers, was set on a course to become fully integrated into a truly North American auto industry.

---

* An earlier version of this paper appears as "The continental integration of the North American auto industry: from the Auto Pact to the FTA and beyond." *Environment and Planning A* 1992 Vol. 24, 1: 95-119. Pion, London.

The 1980s also saw the development of the Asian transplant sector, which provided companies such as Honda, Nissan, and Toyota with full production capability in North America. Thus, the integration of automobile production and marketing between Mexico, the United States, and Canada is being undertaken not only by Ford, GM, and Chrysler (the so-called Big Three), but also by Japanese automakers and Volkswagen.

The objective of this chapter is to document the recent development and performance of the auto industry in Canada, the United States, and Mexico. It focuses on the continuing process of restructuring and continental integration within the industry, and the challenges that this process poses for autoworkers and their unions. The postwar development and integration of the US-Canada auto industry has been extensively discussed in previous papers (Holmes 1983; 1987; 1991) and will be dealt with only briefly here. The case of the Mexican auto industry, and particularly the degree to which it has recently been integrated into the rest of the North American auto industry, is perhaps less well known and is discussed more fully. In assessing the prospects for the industry during the 1990s, particular attention is paid to the consequences for the industry of the further consolidation of the Japanese automakers' production base in North America, the implementation of the Canada-United States Free Trade Agreement (FTA), and the integration of Mexico as both a low-cost production site and potential market. These recent developments must be situated and understood in the context of the significant shifts that are occurring in the global economy and the international trading regime, and, in particular, the emerging triad of world regional trade and production blocs.

One theme that returns throughout the chapter is the continuing importance of the interplay between corporate competitive strategies and national state policies in shaping the changing structure and geography of the international automobile industry.

THE INTEGRATION OF AUTOMOBILE PRODUCTION BETWEEN CANADA AND THE UNITED STATES

When discussing the postwar development of an integrated US-Canada automotive products industry, it is useful to distinguish four phases.

1. NATIONAL INDUSTRIES IN THE PERIOD BEFORE 1965

Prior to the mid-1960s, production throughout the international automotive industry was organized on an essentially national basis. Most of the advanced industrial countries such as Canada and the United States had a domestic market largely insulated from large-scale imports and supplied by locally-based, although in many cases foreign-owned, producers. During the postwar period this insulation of domestic markets was achieved not so much by de jure trade barriers, but rather by the operation of the fundamental rules of what Dunn (1987) calls the postwar "international auto trade regime". These rules consisted of

> ... a mixture of liberalizing and protecting principles that
> permitted states to develop substantial capacities to manage
> auto trade and investment under a variety of different
> economic conditions...[and] increased trade in autos during
> the 1955-72 period resulted not so much from global trade
> liberalism but rather from the unprecedented demand from
> the North American market coupled with a carefully managed
> set of regional arrangements that permitted trade expansion
> while limiting outsiders 'poaching' in domestic markets to
> tolerable levels (Dunn 1987: 232).

For example, in 1955 less than 2 percent of all new vehicle sales in the world's seven largest markets (the United States, Japan, West Germany, France, Italy, the United Kingdom, and Canada) were imports (Altshuler 1984). Even as late as 1966, vehicles imported from overseas captured only 8 percent of the combined American and Canadian market.

Thus, almost from their very beginnings at the turn of the century through to the early 1960s, the auto industries of Canada and the United States remained organized as essentially separate national operations. In the decades following the Second World War, each of the handful of major automakers produced a broad range of models for domestic consumption within Canada, and there was only very limited trade in finished autos across the border. Sheltered behind tariff barriers and domestic content requirements and severely limited by the scope of its market, the Canadian auto industry suffered declining international competitiveness during the late 1950s, culminating at the beginning of the 1960s in a severe sectoral crisis (Holmes 1983).

2. POST-AUTO PACT INTEGRATION

During the 1960s and 1970s the GATT agreements, the European Common Market, and the Canada-US Auto Pact created the institutional framework that enabled the cross-national integration of automobile production and trade, and marked the beginning of the transition from a collection of national industries to a global automobile industry.[1] Throughout this period, the structure of the North American automotive industry was shaped by the Auto Pact. The Auto Pact resolved the sectoral crisis of the early 1960s in the Canadian industry by forcing the rationalization of the Canadian auto industry and its full integration with the American industry.

One consequence of the Auto Pact was a significant expansion of the auto industry in Canada between 1963 and 1973 (Holmes 1987). Although the Canadian auto industry that emerged in the 1970s from the restructuring triggered by the Auto Pact was relatively competitive and efficient by North American standards, it was one that was decidedly limited in scope. In the reorganization and expansion that followed the signing of the Auto Pact, the relatively low wage rates in Canada attracted a disproportionately large share of the more labour intensive work, such as final assembly and the production of labour-intensive parts, to Canada, while the production of high-value body stampings, engines, and drive train components was concentrated in the United States.

This geographical division of labour led to a distinctive pattern of trade between Canada and the United States under the Auto Pact in which, since 1965, Canada has continuously registered large trade surpluses in finished cars and large trade deficits in parts and components (Table 1). Given the disproportionate sizes of the Canadian and American markets for motor vehicles, the pattern of integration and trade that emerged after 1965 also meant that Canadian assembly plants became highly dependent on the vehicle sourcing decisions of the Big Three, and on the strength and particular composition of vehicle demand in the American market.[2]

The postwar period also saw the development of an integrated and uniform industrial relations system within the US-Canada auto industry. The industry was dominated by a handful of American multinationals that emphasized cross-border uniformity in their industrial relations policies and practices, a uniformity reinforced by the fact that autoworkers in both countries were represented by the United

Table 1

Canada-US Trade in Automotive Products, 1955-90
(in $Can millions)

Year	Canada Imports from US	Canada Exports to US	Total Canada-US Auto Trade	Canadian Auto Trade Surplus/(Deficit)			Canadian Auto Trade Balance as % of Total
				Vehicles	Parts	Total[a]	
1955	361	4	365			(357)	(97.8)
1956	439	4	443			(435)	(98.2)
1957	356	6	362			(350)	(96.8)
1958	324	9	333			(315)	(94.6)
1959	369	17	386			(352)	(91.2)
1960	400	11	411			(389)	(94.7)
1961	371	8	379			(363)	(95.8)
1962	469	9	478			(460)	(96.2)
1963	529	29	558			(500)	(89.6)
1964	637	102	739			(535)	(72.4)
1965	961	250	1211	(59)	(646)	(711)	(58.7)
1966	1487	886	2373	104	(704)	(601)	(25.3)
1967	2042	1520	3562	275	(802)	(522)	(14.7)
1968	2847	2458	5305	605	(974)	(389)	(7.3)
1969	3399	3309	6708	1212	(1270)	(90)	(1.3)
1970	3065	3296	6334	1193	(980)	204	3.2
1971	3810	4040	7850	1215	(990)	230	2.9
1972	4477	4552	9029	1201	(1129)	75	0.8
1973	5739	5299	11038	979	(1356)	(440)	(4.0)
1974	6564	5435	11999	891	(1866)	(1129)	(9.4)
1975	7724	5903	13627	665	(2381)	(1821)	(13.4)
1976	8875	7879	16754	1487	(2531)	(996)	(5.9)
1977	10953	9861	20814	2044	(3127)	(1092)	(5.2)
1978	12582	11543	24125	2688	(3339)	(1039)	(4.3)
1979	14520	11432	25952	1010	(4177)	(3088)	(11.9)
1980	12351	10306	22657	2065	(4195)	(2045)	(9.0)
1981	14452	12724	27176	3230	(5079)	(1728)	(6.4)
1982	13571	16424	29995	7368	(4774)	2853	9.5
1983	17599	20855	38484	7395	(4303)	3286	8.5
1984	23915	29850	53765	10841	(5159)	5935	11.0
1985	28838	33803	62641	10563	(5926)	4965	7.9
1986	29314	34484	63798	10780	(6058)	5170	8.1
1987	28680	32583	61263	8370	(4818)	3903	6.4
1988	31993	35961	67954	12008	(8204)	3968	5.8
1989	29464	35391	64855	12060	(6354)	5927	9.1
1990	27235	35457	62692	14361	(6356)	8222	13.1

a: Also includes tires and tubes

Sources: Statistics Canada Catalogues: 65-202, 65-203.
    Industry, Science and Technology. *Statistical Review of the Canadian Automotive Industry, 1990*. Ottawa: Government of Canada.

NB   These data are for total automotive trade between Canada and the United States and include trade in tubes and tires and aftermarket parts, which are excluded from the Auto Pact.

Autoworkers (UAW)—an international union known for pioneering wage parity and uniform work practices between the two countries—and that the Canadian public policy framework for private-sector labour relations was modelled on the American Wagner Act of 1935 (Holmes and Kumar 1991).

3. RESTRUCTURING THE U.S.-CANADA AUTO INDUSTRY IN THE 1980S

After 1979, the North American auto industry was forced to respond and adjust to changed competitive conditions brought about by the globalization of production and markets in the industry, and, in particular, by the rise of Japan as a major world producer and exporter of automobiles. As a consequence, the 1980s became a decade in which the industry was extensively restructured. Three of the most striking features of this period were the growth of the transplant sector brought about through Asian direct investment into North American assembly and component plants, the growing problem of overcapacity in the industry, and the strong performance of the industry in Canada as compared with the United States.

The Development of the Transplants. In the early 1980s, and really for the first time in their history, North American-based automakers experienced the full force of international competition for their domestic markets. For example, Canada's automotive products trade deficit in overseas trade increased from $259 million in 1979 to $5.38 billion in 1987, mainly as a result of the flood of imported Japanese vehicles and parts (Table 2).

By the mid-1980s, trade limitations on Japanese vehicle imports forced the Japanese companies to build assembly plants in North America;[3] by the end of the decade these plants were able to offer competitive products across virtually all major market segments (the one exception being heavy pick-up trucks, which will be added by the mid-1990s). With investments in engine and transmission plants, the building of a quality North America supplier base (consisting of both Japanese transplant and North American component suppliers), and the establishment of design and research and development facilities in Michigan and California, the major Japanese automakers will have replicated a world scale "top-to-bottom" production system within North America

Table 2

Canada-Overseas Trade In Automotive Products, 1974-90
(in $ Can millions)

Year	Canada Imports from Overseas			Canada Exports to Overseas			Total Trade[c]	Canadian Surplus (Deficit)			Surplus (Deficit) as % of Total
	Vehicles	Parts[a]	Total	Vehicles	Parts[a]	Total[b]		Vehicles	Parts	Total[c] Trade	Total
1974	450	260	710	204	142	346	1138	(246)	(118)	(422)	(37.1)
1975	410	206	616	421	180	601	1314	11	(26)	(82)	(6.2)
1976	522	231	753	427	171	598	1448	(95)	(60)	(216)	(14.9)
1977	592	235	827	614	195	809	1763	22	(40)	(111)	(6.3)
1978	894	262	1156	711	314	1025	2346	(183)	52	(258)	(11.0)
1979	727	365	1092	558	445	1003	2329	(169)	80	(259)	(11.1)
1980	1159	355	1514	634	420	1054	2896	(525)	65	(548)	(18.9)
1981	1599	342	1941	656	556	1212	3821	(943)	214	(435)	(11.4)
1982	1413	379	1792	440	404	844	3167	(973)	25	(647)	(20.4)
1983	1626	613	2241	281	254	535	3114	(1345)	(359)	(1620)	(52.0)
1984	2176	1328	3504	346	280	626	4535	(1830)	(1048)	(2887)	(63.7)
1985	3107	1459	4566	216	307	523	5475	(2891)	(1152)	(4071)	(74.4)
1986	3954	1761	5715	222	418	640	6814	(3732)	(1343)	(5056)	(74.2)
1987	4080	1831	5911	187	382	569	6968	(3893)	(1449)	(5376)	(77.2)
1988	3936	1630	5566	303	346	649	6729	(3633)	(1284)	(4889)	(71.9)
1989	3900	2449	6349	259	369	628	7515	(3641)	(2080)	(5679)	(75.6)
1990	4127	3051	7178	178	329	507	8176	(3949)	(2722)	(6648)	

a: Excludes tires and tubes
b: Excludes re-exports
c: Includes tires, tubes and re-exports

Sources: Statistics Canada Catalogues: 65-202, 65-203.
            Industry, Science and Technology. *Statistical Review of the Canadian Automotive Industry,*
            1990. Ottawa: Government of Canada.

by 1995. It is estimated that, by the end of 1991, thirteen Japanese-managed assembly plants in North America will employ 30,000 workers and have the capacity to produce approximately 2.25 million vehicles a year, including two million automobiles.[4]

Initially, Canada secured a significant proportion of transplant assembly investment, although only a few of the over four hundred transplant and joint venture parts plants built by the Japanese in North America. When, in the mid-1980s, the Asian automakers committed themselves, at the urging of the Canadian government, to build assembly plants in Canada to produce for both the Canadian and American markets (that is, before the negotiation of the Canada-US FTA), four

Asian automakers (Honda, Toyota, Hyundai, and CAMI [Suzuki-GM]) stood to benefit from three aspects of existing Canada Customs Law (MacDonald 1989: 13): (a) the export-based duty remission orders, which allowed importers to earn a dollar of duty-free imports for each dollar of Canadian Value-Added (CVA) exported; (b) the production-based duty remission orders, which were offered to each company building an assembly plant in Canada and allowed them to import an amount of products duty-free, based on the CVA of the products they exported, with the amounts related to the company's progress toward meeting the production-sales and CVA criteria needed to qualify as an "Auto Pact Producer"; and, (c) the general export drawback program under which the government remitted the duty paid on the importation into Canada of materials and components made into products for subsequent export. In the period leading up to the FTA negotiations, the United States argued that these duty remission-drawback schemes constituted blatant subsidies to attract Asian automakers to produce in Canada. Under the terms of the FTA all three categories of duty remission have either been cancelled or will be phased out during the 1990s.

When the American and Canadian governments pressured the Japanese in the early 1980s to build vehicles in North America, the Big Three and the UAW assumed that this would quickly lead to the creation of a level playing field for American Japanese automakers vying for the lucrative North American market. Forced to pay UAW wages and accept traditional North American work practices, the Japanese automakers would lose the cost advantage that they had enjoyed by producing in Japan and exporting to North America. The outcome, however, was very different. With only the odd exception, the Japanese automakers, aided by state subsidies (see Chapter 6), built their plants in the rural small towns of the Midwest, Upper South and Ontario (Mair et al. 1988; Reid 1990). Of all the transplants, only the four Japanese-Big Three joint venture assembly plants and a few components plants have union representation.

Rather than falling into line with existing Big Three production standards and cost patterns, the transplants introduced new standards of performance and competition to the North American auto industry. First, the transplants enjoy a significant production cost advantage over traditional Big Three plants. Even though the hourly wage rates paid by the transplants are only slightly below union rates (Holmes and Kumar 1991), the youthful composition of their recently recruited labour forces means that the transplants enjoy a substantial savings with regard to age-related benefit costs such as pension contributions and health insurance premiums (Howes 1991).

However, from the point of view of changing competitive standards, the new productivity and product quality standards established by the transplants for vehicle production in North America probably hold more far-reaching consequences for the industry than the labour cost advantage they enjoy. The assembly transplants, and particularly New United Motors Manufacturing Corporation (NUMMI),[5] have had an extraordinarily powerful demonstration effect and were both the stimulus and inspiration for the major drive by the Big Three in the latter half of the 1980s to modernize plants, radically reorganize work, and develop more cooperative industrial relations practices (Katz 1986).

Big Three Restructuring and the Problem of Overcapacity. The competitiveness crisis, created by the combination of escalating unit production costs and the large-scale Japanese assault on the North American market, forced the Big Three to develop a variety of new competitive strategies during the 1980s. The two strategies that perhaps have had the most impact have been: first, the global search for sources of low-cost "entry-level" vehicles that the Big Three could "badge" and sell in the North American market at prices that would be competitive with Japanese imports; and, second, the building of new plants and the modernization of existing plants to incorporate new manufacturing process technologies designed to reduce costs and increase productivity.

Initially, in the 1970s, the Big Three developed affiliations and marketing agreements with some of the secondary Japanese producers to supply entry-level products for the North American market (for example, GM's links to Isuzu and later Suzuki, Ford's links with Mazda, and Chrysler's links with Mitsubishi). However, during the early 1980s, as the yen strengthened dramatically against the dollar, the Big Three began to search for products in the new entrant countries.

On strictly geographical grounds, Mexico would appear to have been an obvious choice. It was not pursued for a variety of reasons, including a then highly protectionist and restrictive Mexican state policy with regard to its domestic auto industry and the belief that American consumers would reject "Mexican-built" cars on the grounds of perceived inferior quality. Instead, the Big Three turned to Korea and Taiwan and forged links with companies such as Kia, Daewoo, and Ford Lio Ho.

By the late 1980s, however, it became apparent that this East Asian strategy presented a number of potential problems, including rapidly rising wages and currency appreciation in both Taiwan and Korea, potential import barriers to the United States, and a lack of opportunity for equity control of their Asian suppliers by the Big Three.[6] Later in the paper it will be argued that these factors, coupled with a significant shift in Mexican state policy, led at the end of the 1980s to a reassessment of Mexico as a candidate to fill the role of a supplier of entry-level vehicles to the American and Canadian markets.

The rationalization and restructuring of the domestically-owned North American auto industry during the 1980s resulted in the closure of well over a dozen assembly and major parts plants by the Big Three. It also entailed massive new injections of capital spending to re-equip existing plants and build new facilities. This new investment was tied to the introduction of new forms of automation and the reorganization of work and production in an effort to reduce the competitiveness gap between the Big Three and Japanese automakers. The net geographical effect of the closing of old and the opening of new plants by the Big Three, and the building of the transplant assembly plants, was a reconcentration of assembly plants in the mid-west and southern Ontario. Traditionally, parts production has been heavily concentrated in Michigan, northern Indiana, northern Ohio and southern Ontario. The Japanese transplant suppliers have also concentrated in the US mid-west, but have tended to select sites further south, in southern Ohio, Kentucky, and Tennessee.

With little expectation of the vehicle market in the United States and Canada growing significantly over the next decade, the wave of new investments in North American assembly plants by both Asian and North American automakers during the 1980s raised the spectre of overcapacity. A number of analysts have predicted that by 1992 Asian transplant and joint venture plants will account for 13-15 percent of total vehicle sales in the United States and Canada, and that the Big Three's share will slip to around 60 percent. Even though it may be argued that the vehicles assembled in the transplants are in part being substituted for vehicles previously imported from Japan, if none of the Big Three's existing assembly plants had closed there

Map 1
Location of Automobile and Light Truck Assembly Plants
in North America, 1991

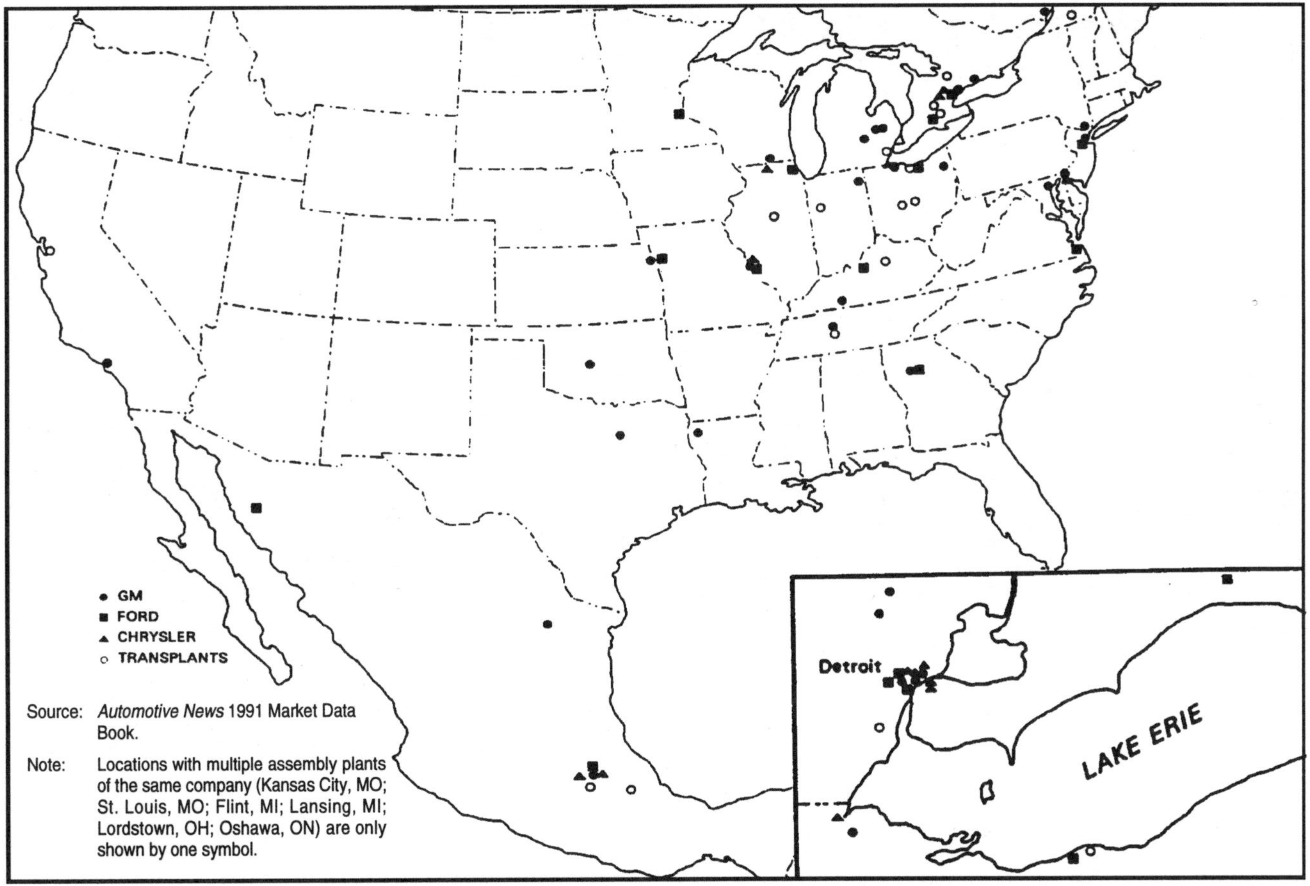

LAKE ERIE

Detroit

• GM
■ FORD
▲ CHRYSLER
○ TRANSPLANTS

Source: *Automotive News* 1991 Market Data Book.

Note: Locations with multiple assembly plants of the same company (Kansas City, MO; St. Louis, MO; Flint, MI; Lansing, MI; Lordstown, OH; Oshawa, ON) are only shown by one symbol.

would have been an annual excess capacity of at least 2.5 million vehicles in North America by 1992. In fact, to date, the problem of excess capacity has been "solved" by the closure of existing Big Three plants in the United States (Womack et al. 1990: 246).

Two further points should be made with regard to the question of overcapacity. The first point, which will be discussed more fully later in the chapter, pertains to the possible incorporation of the Mexican market, which does offer significant growth potential over the next two decades (but would also add additional production capacity). Second, most discussions of potential regional overcapacity are based on the assumption that North America will continue the pattern of the postwar period and not be a significant overseas exporter of motor vehicles. If the arguments regarding the "post-national auto industry" are correct, this assumption needs to be questioned (Womack et al. 1990). In fact, the last couple of years have seen an increase in the export of North American-built vehicles (mainly from the transplants) to both Japan and Western Europe. For example, the total number of automobiles exported from the United States to countries other than Canada rose from 23,395 in 1985 to 214,308 for the period July 1989 to June 1990. Although, to date, the number of units exported remains small, the role of North America as a vehicle exporter could well increase during the 1990s.

The Relative Prosperity of the Auto Industry in Canada. Within North America, the dislocation and adjustment that resulted from restructuring in the auto industry during the 1980s was geographically uneven, with the result that the Canadian portion of the North American automobile industry fared much better than its American counterpart (Holmes 1991). While the industry in the United States failed to regain the peak levels of employment and production attained in the late 1970s, the industry in Canada not only staged a rapid recovery from the deep recession of 1981-82, but continued to go from strength to strength throughout the 1980s, registering record levels of output and employment and racking up significant annual surpluses on its automotive trade with the United States (Table 1, Table 3). Like the United States, Canada attracted significant new investment (over $14 billion in the period 1980-89 [ISTC 1990]) for the extensive modernization of existing Big Three plants and for the construction of new assembly plants by both Asian automakers and

AMC/Chrysler. But, unlike the United States, where over a dozen existing assembly plants were permanently closed during the 1980s, there were no closures of existing Canadian assembly plants during this period.[7] As a consequence, while Canada's share of the total North American market for vehicles remained at around 8 to 9 percent, its share of total North American vehicle production and industry employment each rose to around 15 percent (Table 3).

The strong performance of the industry in Canada during the 1980s can be attributed mainly to the labour cost differential in Canada's favour due to both the lower value of the Canadian dollar against the US dollar and the lower cost to the employer of employee benefits, particularly medical insurance premiums (Figure 1). When it is considered that productivity and efficiency in Canadian assembly plants were generally judged to be on a par with, or higher than, those

Table 3

Automotive Industry Production and Employment, US and Canada, 1965-90

Year	Vehicle Production				Employment			
	US		Canada		US		Canada	
	1000s	% Total	1000s	% Total	1000s	% Total	1000s	% Total
1965	11114	92.9	846	7.1	NC	–	82.8	–
1970	8263	87.4	1193	12.6	NC	–	86.0	–
1975	8965	86.1	1442	13.9	874.5	89.4	103.8	10.6
1976	11486	87.5	1647	12.5	980.5	89.7	112.4	10.3
1977	12699	87.7	1775	12.3	1048.0	89.9	118.3	10.1
1978	12895	87.6	1818	12.4	1091.1	89.7	124.9	10.3
1979	11475	87.6	1632	12.4	1109.6	90.0	123.8	10.0
1980	8010	85.4	1374	14.6	884.1	89.5	104.1	10.5
1981	7941	86.1	1280	13.9	882.4	89.1	107.4	10.9
1982	6985	85.0	1236	15.0	786.8	88.9	98.7	11.1
1983	9226	86.0	1502	14.0	861.3	88.2	115.6	11.8
1984	10924	85.7	1830	14.3	966.5	88.7	123.8	11.3
1985	11648	85.8	1930	14.2	975.7	88.3	129.3	11.7
1986	11317	85.9	1859	14.1	944.0	87.7	132.6	12.3
1987	10908	86.9	1648	13.1	941.0	86.6	146.2	13.4
1988	11197	85.0	1977	15.0	946.0	86.0	153.6	14.0
1989	10851	84.8	1940	15.2	959.0	86.0	156.3	14.0
1990	9878	84.0	1883	16.0	901.0	85.3	155.0	14.7

Sources: DIST Statistical Review of Automotive Industry 1990.
DIST Report on Canadian Automotive Industry in 1986.

Figure 1

Hourly Compensation Costs of Automobile Workers
United States, Canada and Mexico: 1975-1990

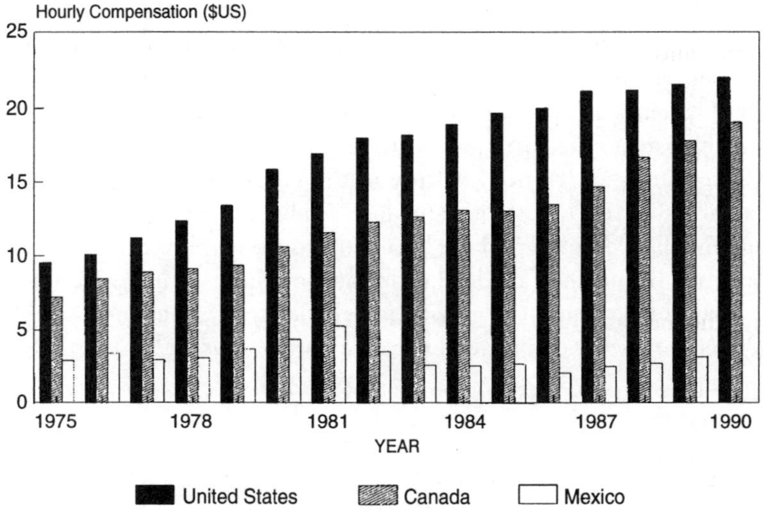

Hourly Compensation ($US)

YEAR

■ United States   ▨ Canada   ☐ Mexico

No Data Available for Mexico for 1990
Source: USDOL, BLS, unpublished data.

in Big Three plants in the United States (Katz and Meltz 1989), these labour cost savings, which by the mid-1980s amounted to about $Can 7.50/person hour worked, gave Canadian plants a significant competitive advantage over American plants.

At the heart of the restructuring undertaken by the Big Three during the 1980s lay the need to lower production costs and increase productivity, and this placed heavy·demand on the traditional auto industrial relations system. After an initial phase of concession bargaining at the beginning of the 1980s, during which management simply sought a reduction in nominal wages, deferment of scheduled cost of living allowance (COLA) increases, and roll-backs on benefits such as holiday entitlements, pressure mounted to restructure the whole compensation system and, particularly, to reorganize work and construct a more cooperative shop-floor and plant-level relationship between labour and management.

The automakers sought to introduce similar new industrial relations practices in both their Canadian and American plants. The responses of the Canadian and American labour movements to these efforts, however, were quite distinct, with the result that there has been a growing divergence in collective bargaining strategies and outcomes as reflected in the labour contracts negotiated in the United States and Canada since 1979.[8]

The first signs of divergence appeared in the unions' response to management's demand for concessions on wages and benefits during the early 1980s when company restructuring strategies were firmly centred on cost-cutting. The 1984 round of contract negotiations, which saw the establishment of a new "pattern" contract in the United States that changed the traditional rules for wage formation in the industry, led to further divergence, a split in the international union, and the formation of the Canadian Autoworkers Union (CAW) (Gindin 1989; Yates 1990; Holmes and Rusonik 1991).

The sharpest divergence between the CAW and UAW since 1985 has been over the nature of the union-management relationship. Whereas the CAW continues to view and treat the relationship as adversarial based on the conviction that the interests of labour and capital are not inherently the same, "cooperation and partnership" between the union and management has become the norm in the United States (Gindin 1989). The UAW has clearly renounced its historical adversarial orientation in favour of cooperation, partnership, and jointness with management. The differences in these positions has been brought into sharp focus by the respective responses of the CAW and UAW to management's efforts to introduce the team concept and other forms of cooperative industrial relations practices. Thus, during the 1980s there was a growing divergence between the two countries with regard to industrial relations practices even during a period when the two countries were moving toward even greater economic integration through the FTA.

4. THE 1990s: THE UNITED STATES-CANADA FTA AND THE AUTO INDUSTRY

Although the United States-Canada FTA does have some implications for the future shape of the auto industry (Holmes 1991), particular sectoral circumstances deriving from the existence of the Auto Pact mean that the provisions of the FTA are likely to have a much smaller impact on the auto industry as compared with a number of other industries such as food processing, footwear, clothing, furniture, and white goods.

There are two notable ways in which the auto industry provisions of the FTA have affected the existing Asian transplants and may influence the potential location of future transplant investment in North America. The first is the elimination of Canadian duty remission-drawback programs that played such a significant role in attracting Asian producers to establish transplant assembly facilities in Canada during the 1980s. The second is the North American content requirement for products to secure duty-free entry, to either country. Under the FTA, in order for a vehicle to qualify for duty-free entry it must contain at least 50 percent North American content as it did under the Auto Pact. However, what may be counted as North American content is much more restricted under the FTA, with only the value of materials originating in each country, plus the direct cost of assembling the product in the exporting country qualifying as North American content.

It is clear from the foreword to Chapter ten of the FTA (the chapter dealing with the auto industry) that the intention of this more stringent definition of North American content is to force the transplant assemblers either to manufacture major components such as body stampings, engines, and drive train components in North America themselves, or to purchase such components from North American-based suppliers. Given the Japanese assemblers' preference for dealing with transplant suppliers rather than traditional North American suppliers, and the fact that virtually all the transplant suppliers are located in the United States, the Canadian parts sector could see its share of the North American component market shrink. This trend will be accentuated if the transplant assemblers continue to capture an increasing share of total North American vehicle production.

Macdonald (1989: 10) has argued that the effect of the FTA's differentiation of Canadian producers into those companies that qualified as Auto Pact producers by the end of the 1989 model year and those (the Asian transplants) that did not, combined with the abolition of the duty remission-drawback orders, will produce a "two-tier automotive manufacturing industry." On the one hand, so long as they continue to comply with the provisions of the Auto Pact, GM, Ford, Chrysler, and CAMI will be able to continue the practice developed during the 1980s of bringing parts and vehicles into Canada duty-free from any country in the world (including such low-cost countries as Brazil, Korea, Taiwan, Thailand, and most importantly Mexico).[9] On the other hand, Honda, Hyundai, Toyota, and any future new producer, "...operating in Canada in the same way as their commercial rivals, will have to pay duty on anything they import from countries other than the United States, no matter how large their production/sales ratio and CVA credits eventually turn out to be" (Macdonald 1989: 15).

More generally, the FTA has afforded the business community the opportunity to press for the creation of a "level playing field" between the two countries with respect to the legislative and institutional framework within which they must conduct business. Canadian autoworkers have feared that in the name of sustaining "competitiveness" and protecting jobs, the political jurisdictions in which they work may be cajoled into accepting the lower employment standards that presently characterize many American states.[10]

MEXICAN INTEGRATION INTO THE NORTH AMERICAN AUTOMOBILE INDUSTRY

At the beginning of the 1990s, the key factor driving both the development of the transplant sector in North America and the progressive integration of Mexico into the North American auto production system is the expectation that the global economy and the international trading regime of the late 1990s will be considerably different from that of the past several decades (Investment Canada 1991; Hart 1990). The emergence of large regional trading blocs is likely to exercise considerable influence on corporate strategic decisions regarding production sites and product sourcing (Ohmae 1985). At the same time, such decisions are also being reshaped by the introduction of new methods of manufacturing, which some argue will result in significantly different geographies of production in industries such as the auto industry (Womack et al. 1990; Hoffman and Kaplinsky 1988).

The precise nature of the role presently played by Mexico in the North American auto industry is not well understood, and many accounts only serve to reinforce the stereotype of Mexico as a producer of only low-value, low-technology parts. Most of these accounts focus on the rapid growth of the low-wage *maquiladora* sector. The maquiladora, or in-bond, industry was established in 1965 as part of

Mexico's Border Industrialization Program. It was designed to attract foreign manufacturing facilities engaged in export-manufacturing processing to a twenty-kilometre strip along the United States-Mexico border, and later throughout the interior of Mexico. The maquiladoras comprise a broad category, grouping together assembly processes from a wide range of industries. Maquiladora plants are exempted by Mexico from paying duties when temporarily importing machinery and raw materials to be used to assemble products or in sub-assemblies for export. Firms manufacturing products destined for the American market also benefit under the outward processing program established by the United States in 1961 under tariff items 806.30 and 807.00 (items 9802.00.60 and 9802.00.80 under the more recent HTS) whereby no duty is applied to the value of US-made components, only to value-added in Mexico.

Although only 140 of a total of 1760 maquila plants in 1989 were in the transportation equipment sector, these plants were much larger than the average maquila plants and the sector was virtually tied with the electronic components sector as the largest sector of maquiladora production in terms of value-added (Shaiken 1990). Most of the auto-related maquiladoras are operated by American companies with subsidiaries of the Japanese automakers a distant second (APMA 1990). GM alone has more than thirty maquiladora plants employing 30,000, which makes it the largest parts manufacturer in Mexico. The APMA report noted only nine Canadian-owned plants among the maquiladoras. This is probably due to the lack of a Canadian counterpart to the American outward processing program.

The reality is far more complex than recent debates focusing on the maquiladoras would suggest. According to Hart (1990: 118), relatively few people appreciate the extent to which "the Rubicon has been crossed and Mexican production is already being integrated into the North American auto industry," or understand that this integration extends well beyond the production of low-cost, low-technology parts in the maquiladoras to include the production of engines, drive train components, and assembled automobiles in world-scale and "world-class" Mexican plants.

The investments made in Mexico by a number of the major automakers over the last decade have already created, in effect, the basis for a de facto trilateral production and trading bloc in the North American auto industry. The continued integration of Mexico, especially with the initialling of NAFTA, as both a production site and as a market, promises to be one of the principal factors that will influence the restructuring and shape of the North American auto industry during the 1990s. The following provides an overview of the development and structure of the Mexican auto industry and a closer examination of the likely consequences of its continued integration into the North American auto industry.

The development of the Mexican auto industry provides an excellent example of how the international and national geographies of global industries, such as the auto industry, are shaped by the interaction between corporations' broader international strategic choices for organizing production and marketing and the changing content of national government policies toward economic development in general, and the auto industry in particular.[11] The APMA (1990) report notes that the changing structure and organization of the Mexican auto industry over the last couple of decades has been shaped by three broad trends: (a) a locational dynamic, which has seen the industry concentrate around Mexico City and along the northern border with the United States; (b) a developmental dynamic, which has resulted in a shift from fragmented production aimed at the limited domestic market toward high-volume, rationalized production aimed at export markets; and (c) the international globalization dynamic, which has led a number of automakers to "rethink" how Mexico fits into the broad context of the world auto industry.

1. A NATIONAL INDUSTRY BASED ON IMPORT SUBSTITUTION: 1962-77

Like other semi-industrialized countries, the domestic market for automobiles in Mexico from the 1920s to the 1960s was served either by finished imports or by assembling imported CKD (completely-knocked-down) vehicle kits in so-called "screwdriver plants." In the postwar period, this led to a proliferation of makes and models, so by 1961, with a total market of under 50,000 vehicles, there were 45 makes and 117 models of vehicles being supplied to the Mexican market by 19 firms from around the world, with twelve companies (Mexican-owned, with the exception of Ford and GM) operating CKD assembly plants in Mexico. These plants were virtually all near Mexico City (Bennett 1986: 17).

Significant changes in Mexican state policy toward the auto industry occurred in the early 1960s and effectively shaped the industry for the next two-and-a-half decades. In 1962, in an effort to promote industrialization, the Mexican government followed the lead of other Latin American governments (Kornish and Mericle 1984; Jenkins 1987) and established by decree a full-scale national automotive industry. This state initiative forced the international automakers either to construct manufacturing plants in Mexico or to leave the country and forfeit the growing Mexican market to their competitors. The fundamental premise of Mexican state automotive policy from 1962 to the late 1980s, which was reflected in the Automotive Decrees of 1962, 1969, 1977 and 1983, was that the most appropriate development path for the Mexican motor vehicle industry consisted of very high levels of domestic content on a product-line basis and as much Mexican ownership of the parts production system as possible.

The 1962 Automotive Decree banned assembled vehicle imports (beyond the US border zone) and required high (60 percent) local content rules for both vehicles and components manufactured in

Map 2
The Automobile Industry in Mexico

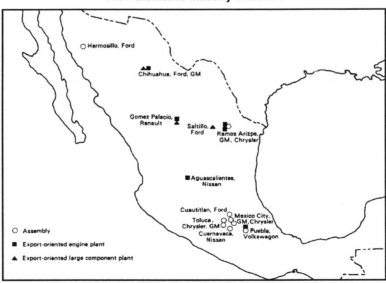

Sources: *Automotive News* 1991 Market Data Book, 1991;
Sources for Table 6.

Mexico. It limited the number of final assemblers allowed to operate in Mexico (by the 1980s the initial seven had been reduced to Ford, GM, Chrysler, Volkswagen, and Nissan) and restricted the manufacturing activities of these companies to final assembly and engine assembly. These companies established final assembly plants that were more sophisticated than the CKD operations but were still significantly smaller and less integrated than those found in the rest of North America. The plants constructed during this period were geographically more decentralized but still concentrated in Central Mexico (Map 2). The local content requirement, coupled with the prohibition on vertical integration (beyond engine assembly) by the assembly firms, assured the creation of an independent autoparts manufacturing industry in Mexico.

As automobile manufacturing expanded rapidly in the area around Mexico City following the 1962 Automotive Decree, most production workers in the assembly plants of the transnational automakers were organized in enterprise and plant-level unions affiliated to the Confederation of Mexican Workers (the CTM).[12] Since the Mexican revolution, the CTM, which is the labour wing of the Institutional Revolutionary Party, has had close political ties with the state. During the 1960s and 1970s, rank-and-file autoworkers challenged both the CTM's established leadership and organizational structure and by 1975 had won more democratic forms of union governance in five of the seven principal assembly plants. This democratization led to a number of the plant-level unions breaking their ties with the CTM, a development which, while progressive from the point of view of creating an independent labour movement, further weakened labour's ability to mount collective action against the automakers as a whole.

Over time, autoworkers in the democratic unions gained some significant measure of control over the production process and restricted plant management's ability to readily adjust to changes in production schedules. The assertiveness of the democratic unions made collective bargaining more adversarial than it had been under the CTM-affiliated unions, and there were more frequent strikes.

Middlebrook (1991: 270) argues that when GM built a new plant in Toluca in 1965, it deployed a strategy to regain managerial control over plant-level labour relations that established a precedent later followed by Nissan at Cuernavaca in 1978 and by the export-oriented auto plants built in the 1980s. By building a greenfield plant outside

Table 4
Motor Vehicle Production and Exports, Mexico, 1960-89

Year	Total Production (1000s of units)	Total Exports		Exports to US	
		Number	% of Prod.	Number	% of All Exp.
1960	50	0	0.0	0	0.0
1965	97	0	0.0	0	0.0
1970	193	0	0.0	0	0.0
1975	361	2938	0.8	0	0.0
1976	325	4172	1.3	0	0.0
1977	281	11793	4.2	0	0.0
1978	384	25828	6.7	0	0.0
1979	444	24756	5.6	0	0.0
1980	490	18245	3.7	0	0.0
1981	597	14428	2.4	3	0.0
1982	473	15819	3.3	623	3.9
1983	285	22456	7.9	203	0.9
1984	344	33635	9.8	13448	40.0
1985	398	58423	14.7	47197	80.8
1986	338	72429	21.4	60466	83.5
1987	395	163073	41.3	140641	86.2
1988	515	173147	34.3	148017	85.5
1989	629	194631	30.9	163000(*)	83.8

Sources: *Automotive News Data Book* 1990.
La Industria Automotriz de México en Cifras, 1988 Edition.
*Automotive News, December 3, 1990.

the traditional auto-making area around Mexico City, GM was not only able to hire workers at lower wage rates, but, by ensuring that the CTM would represent the new labour force, management was able to win back control over various aspects of the production process.

During this period, there was virtually no trade in assembled vehicles either into or out of Mexico (Table 4).[13] However, increased oil export revenues fuelled Mexican domestic demand for motor vehicles, and domestic assembly grew to about 500,000 vehicles a year by the end of the 1970s. As a consequence, there was a substantial increase in the importation of automotive components to Mexico from the United States and Canada to feed Mexican assembly plants. Despite some increase in the value of parts exported, the Mexican trade deficit on its automotive trade increased rapidly in the late 1970s, rising from $231 million in 1970, when it represented just over 20 percent of the

Table 5
Automotive Sector Trade Balance, Mexico, 1950-87
(in $US millions)

Year	Imports	Exports	Balance (Deficit)
1950	55	–	(55)
1955	94	–	(94)
1960	147	–	(147)
1965	203	–	(203)
1970	257	26	(231)
1975	750	122	(628)
1976	719	192	(527)
1977	639	253	(386)
1978	893	334	(559)
1979	1426	377	(1049)
1980	1903	404	(1499)
1981	2519	370	(2149)
1981a.	2639	336	(2303)
1982b.	1301	424	(875)
1983	696	907	211
1984	847	1399	552
1985	1127	1421	294
1986	1805	2072	267
1987	1373	3060	1687

Sources: 1950-81, Samuels (1990) Table 5.1.
            1981-87, Womack (1989) Table 3.

total Mexican trade deficit, to over $2 billion in 1981, accounting for over 57 percent of the total deficit (Table 5).

2. TOWARDS THE EXPORT-ORIENTED PRODUCTION OF ENGINES AND VEHICLES: 1977-1989

In response to the worsening trade balance, the Mexican government issued a new Automotive Decree in 1977 that required each assembler to achieve a trade balance on its own operations within four years. The collapse of oil revenues and the severe debt crisis that confronted Mexico in the early 1980s had two effects on the automotive industry. The need for Mexico to eliminate the chronic automotive trade deficit became imperative, so, despite extreme opposition from and prolonged bargaining with the international automotive corporations, the Mexican state stuck to its 1977 Automotive Decree trade balance demands and effectively forced all the parent companies to significantly increase their investments in Mexico as well as their auto parts purchases from their Mexican subsidiaries and other Mexican parts suppliers.[14]

Most of the companies achieved the trade balance requirements by building world-scale engine plants in northern Mexico from which to export large volumes of engines, mainly to their parent assembly plants in the United States and Canada (Table 6 and Figure 2A). As Samuels (1990: 113) notes, the investments associated with the automotive subsidiaries' compliance with the 1977 Decree "...led the country into a new era of export promotion...[and ensured that] as a major sourcing location within the global strategies of the automotive MNCs, Mexico would have the much-coveted access to international markets." In

Table 6
Mexican Export Engine Production

Company	Plant Location	Start Date	Capacity 1988	Target Export (1000s)	Exports 1988 Share (%)	Destination of Exports (1000s)
GM	Ramos Arizpe	1982	450	90	543	US/Canada, Europe, Australia
Ford	Chihuahua	1983	400	90	312	US/Canada
Chrysler	Saltillo	1982	270	85	242	US/Canada
Nissan	Aguascalientes	1983	192	80	54	Japan, U.S.
VW	Puebla	1980	440	80	211	Europe, US (until 1989)
Renault	Gomez Palacio	1984	350	80	133	US/Canada, Europe

Other Engine Plants (mainly for domestic market): GM (Toluca); Ford (Cuautilan); Chrysler (Toluca); Nissan (Cuernavaca, Toluca).

Sources: Samuels (1990) Table 6.1.
Shaiken and Herzenberg (1987) Table 1.
Economist Intelligence Unit (1989) *The Automotive Industry in Developing Countries* Table 38.
APMA (1990), Table IV-1.

Figure 2A
**Exports of Vehicle Engines from Mexico to the United States
and Canada, 1980-89**

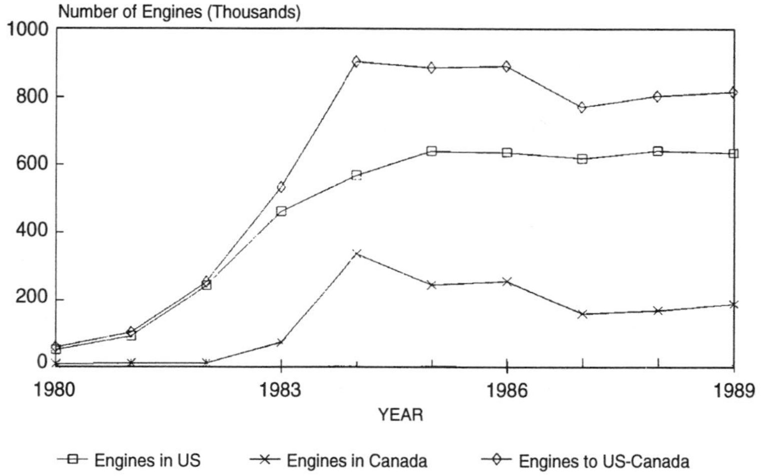

Number of Engines (Thousands)

Source: USITC ASI 2044-37; Statistics Canada Cat. 63-203.

fact, with a planned capacity of 3.5 million engines, Mexico became, and remains, one of the world's major sources of auto engines. This is a far cry from the usual image of Mexico as a producer of low-technology, labour-intensive parts. A recent comparative study of engine plants in Mexico, Canada, and the United States (Herzenberg and Shaiken 1990) has shown that the Mexican engine plant (Ford's Hermosillo facility) achieved levels of efficiency, labour productivity, and quality comparable to the Canadian and American plants.

The second consequence of the collapse in oil revenues was that Mexican domestic demand for automobiles collapsed, and the production levels of assembled automobiles, which had jumped from around 281,000 units in 1977 to over 597,000 in 1981, tumbled to 285,000 in 1983 (Table 4). Mexico, was still bedeviled by "...too many manufacturers (seven in 1981 [GM, Ford, Chrysler, VW, Nissan, AMC, Renault]), too many makes (nineteen) and too many models (forty-seven)" (Bennett and Sharpe 1985: 274). Even in the peak year of 1981, the automakers produced an average of only 13,000 units per line in their Mexican assembly plants, as compared with an average of between 100,000 and 150,000 units per line in their plants in the rest of North America, Japan, and Western Europe. Thus, a further Automotive Decree in 1983 sought to rationalize the structure of the automobile industry by requiring assemblers to reduce their range of product offerings. By 1987, each firm was to be limited to one make and five models and could only produce an additional model if over half its output was for export. The hope was that higher production volumes of individual models would help achieve both an increase in local content to 60 percent and revive the domestic market by reducing prices.

Until the early 1980s, annual exports of assembled automobiles represented less than 8 percent of total Mexican production and were mainly in the form of exports by VW, Renault and Nissan to other Central and South American markets. No vehicles were exported to either Canada or the United States. After 1982, this picture changed, with a rapid increase in the total number of vehicles exported and with most of the increase taking the form of automobile exports to the United States and Canada (Table 4 and Figure 2B).[15] Although Mexican policy, in the form of the 1983 Automotive Decree, may have played a minor role in stimulating this growth in the export of assem-

Figure 2B
Exports of Motor Vehicles from Mexico to the United States and Canada, 1980-89

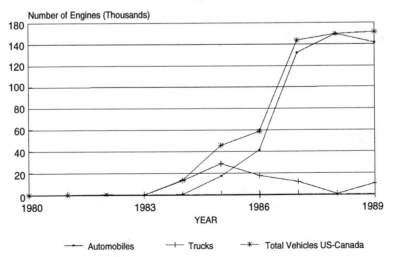

Source: USITC ASI 2044-37; Statistics Canada Cat. 63-203.

bled vehicles, the prime cause was the Big Three's reassessment of Mexico as a low-cost source of entry-level vehicles in light of flaws that appeared in their East Asian strategy during the mid-1980s.

For example, in order to circumvent the Voluntary Export Restraints (VERs) that had been imposed in the early 1980s on the import of vehicles directly from Japan, in 1986 Ford opened a new greenfield assembly plant at Hermosillo in northern Mexico to assemble a vehicle for sale in North America from parts mainly from sources in Japan. Under the provisions of the 1983 Automotive Decree, Mexico allowed Ford to assemble an extra model with only 30 percent domestic content on condition that at least 80 percent of the output would be exported (Womack et al. 1990; Shaiken 1990). At Hermosillo, Ford uses advanced Japanese-style production-management and work-organization techniques to build a variant of the Mazda 323, which sells in the United States and Canada as the Mercury Tracer, an entry-level vehicle. The plant has attained high levels of productivity and, in a recent worldwide assembly plant survey, achieved a product quality rating higher than the best volume assembly Japanese plants or the best North American transplants (Womack et al. 1990: 87).[16]

With the strengthening yen, however, it became increasingly difficult for Hermosillo to meet its cost targets while importing 65 percent of the parts used in assembling the Tracer from Japan. It became increasingly apparent toward the end of the 1980s that, if Mexican assembly for export was to be successful, there was a need to switch the sourcing of components from Japan to North America, and probably supplement the existing engine plants in Mexico with stamping and plastic injection moulding plants producing body parts. In part, this explains the maquiladora investments made by a number of Japanese parts companies.

Thus, during the 1980s, Mexico went some significant way to becoming integrated with the remainder of the North American auto industry as an important source of vehicles and parts. The parts included not only low-cost, labour-intensive parts, such as wiring harnesses and radios produced in the maquiladoras, but also a substantial flow of engines to the American and Canadian assembly plants of the Big Three and Nissan. In fact, the Mexican auto industry presently consists of three segments: (a) a segment centred on Mexico City, which consists of indigenous Mexican suppliers that have traditionally supplied parts for domestic assembly and who operate at relatively inefficient levels;

(b) the maquiladora segment, which is located predominantly along the northern border and takes advantage of low-cost Mexican labour to supply high-quality parts to North American assembly plants; and, (c) the still-forming group of export-oriented assembly and engine plants in northern Mexico, which is now being joined by other major component plants.

The shift in the 1980s toward export-oriented production, first of engines and then of assembled automobiles, resulted in a new locational pattern to the Mexican auto industry (Map 2). Most of the new plants were built in northern Mexico. Besides facilitating the integration of Mexican production with auto production in the United States by placing the new plants within rail or truck reach of just-in-time delivery, this location again afforded the companies lower wage rates and the opportunity to regain managerial control of the production process by encouraging CTM-affiliated unions to represent workers in the new northern plants (Middlebrook 1991: 283).

As a consequence of these developments, there are significant differences in wages, benefits and work practices between the new northern export plants and the older established plants in central Mexico. The CTM-controlled northern plants have lower wages and have introduced many of the Japanese-inspired new work practices that have been introduced in the United States (for example, Ford Hermosillo). The stance taken in many of the older plants by independent unions has generally been in opposition to the introduction of new work practices on grounds similar to those espoused by the CAW in Canada. The absence of a unified national automobile workers' union in Mexico and the heterogeneity of CTM affiliates means that the auto unions in Mexico remain plant-level or enterprise unions, which are geographically dispersed and divided by ties to rival national labour organizations.

3. THE FURTHER INTEGRATION OF MEXICO INTO THE NORTH AMERICAN AUTO INDUSTRY: 1989 AND BEYOND

Two sets of circumstances conspired at the end of the 1980s to ensure that Mexico would likely play an important role in shaping the continued restructuring of the North American auto industry during the 1990s. First, there was the continued intensification of world competition in the auto industry, particularly for the North American market. The fashioning of new production and marketing strategies in recognition of the emerging triad of regional trading blocs led the multinational auto-makers to re-evaluate the future role of Mexico within the North American auto industry, not only as a low-cost production location but also as the one geographic sector of the regional bloc with the potential for signifi-cant market growth over the upcoming decades. Forecasts suggest that the Mexican auto market will expand from 275,000 vehicles in 1989 to around 675,000 in 1994 (see Scheinman, Chapter 13). Second, just as Mexico's role was being reassessed by the automakers, the newly-elected Salinas administration was engaged in a radical rethinking of Mexico's entire approach to economic and industrial development, particularly in the context of Mexico's 1986 decision to join the GATT. This rethink-ing resulted in the abandonment of the state-protected and regulated import-substitution approach that had dominated since the early 1960s, in favour of the promotion of an export-led, market-oriented Mexican economy integrated into the world economy (Hart 1990).

The 1989 Mexican Automotive Decree reflected the more general shift in state policy.[17] It certainly represented a dramatic shift in govern-ment policy toward the auto industry, and was designed to raise the Mexican auto parts industry to "world class" standards. The 1989 Automotive Decree significantly reduced the domestic content require-ments from the previous level of 60 percent to 36 percent for assem-blers and 30 percent for parts producers. In another change, the Decree relaxed the restrictions on imported assembled vehicles by allowing assemblers with production facilities in Mexico to import automobiles of their own manufacture to supplement or complement their domes-tic Mexican production, while still maintaining the requirement that automakers export at least as much as they import.[18] These imports will enable the auto assemblers to expand the product lines they can market in Mexico while concentrating on producing fewer models, which will improve economies of scale and probably lead to greater exports. In order to be able to import vehicles, for every $1.00 worth of goods imported the assemblers must export $2.50 of goods in 1991, $2.00 in 1992, and $1.75 in 1993. In the wake of the 1989 Decree, a number of automakers announced significant expansion plans for their oper-ations in Mexico (Table 7). A number of these investments by both the Big Three and Japanese transplants are explicitly designed to further increase the level of integration of auto production between Mexico, the United States and Canada.[19]

Table 7

Recently Announced Major Investments in Mexican Auto Industry

Company	Investment	Source
Nissan	$1 billion over five years. New 200,000 unit assembly plant at Aguascalientes to build Sentras for export to US and increase component supply to Smyrna, Tennessee plant.	*Automotive News*, April 23 1990. *Automotive News*, January 29 1990.
VW	$1 billion over five years. Modernization of Pueblo assembly plant and increase capacity from 220,000 to 300,000. Aims to export 150,000 vehicles to US/Canada by 1993, increase engine exports to Europe.	*Automotive News*, August 20 1990.
Ford	$700 million to expand Chihuahua engine plant to become sole North American source for new Zeta four-cylinder with capacity at 500,000 engines. $300 million to enlarge and retool Hermosillo assembly plant to produce 160,000 Escorts and Tracers for export.	*Automotive News*, January 21 1991. *Automotive News*, October 15 1990.
Chrysler	$100 million for new plant at Toluca to build Shadow convertibles for export.	*Automotive News*, October 15 1990.

CONCLUSION

The purpose of this chapter has been to describe the development of the present-day structure and geography of the North American automobile industry. One theme has been the seemingly inexorable trend over the last quarter century toward the full continental integration of the industry. I agree with those such as Womack et al. (1990) and Hart (1990) who argue that the negotiation of NAFTA will likely make relatively little difference to the auto industry because Mexico is already in the process of being fully integrated into the North American auto industry. For a decade or more, the Big Three have brought parts, and more recently assembled cars, and imported them duty free into Canada from Mexico under the terms of the Auto Pact. In addition to the parts manufactured in the maquiladoras, many Mexican-built engines enter the United States under outward processing programs and are assigned relatively low levels of duty. The Japanese assemblers in

Canada are paying only 6.2 percent GPT on their imports from Mexico.

Therefore, it is difficult to disagree with the view that NAFTA will simply smooth and facilitate a process already set in train by the strategic choice made by automakers and by the 1989 Mexican Automotive Decree.[20] In the case of the auto industry, there is a common set of multinational vehicle-assemblers and component manufacturers with manufacturing facilities in all three countries (in marked contrast to sectors such as steel or food processing, where ownership and present organization of production is much more nationally centred). These companies are likely to strongly support the full integration of the North American industry under NAFTA because it will enable them to rationalize and integrate their own corporate activities. A similar feature certainly facilitated the integration of the Canadian and American auto industry under the Auto Pact in the 1960s.

What then will be the likely impact on the present industry in Canada and the United States of its full integration with Mexico? On this question, opinions remain divided. Womack et al. argue that, with this new step in Mexican state policy and the development of new strategic corporate plans by the automakers,

> ...a new configuration for the entire North American region could emerge. GM, Ford, Chrysler, Nissan, and VW might assemble in Mexico —for sale to the entire North American market—cheap entry-level cars and trucks that use parts (engines, transmissions and body stampings) produced by production complexes in northern Mexico near the assembly plants. At the same time, larger cars and trucks for Mexican customers might be supplied by plants in the US and Canadian Midwest (1990: 226).

They optimistically predict that such a full integration of Mexico into the North American auto industry would result not only in a substantial trade surplus in automotive products for Mexico, but also in a net gain for the auto industry in Canada and the United States. This would be so because they would gain from their exports of assembled vehicles to Mexico (allowed for the first time since 1962) and the Mexican-built entry-level vehicles that they would import would displace "captive imports" rather than vehicles presently assembled in North America. Elsewhere, Womack (1989) and others have suggested that Mexico could well become the "Spain of the North American

Region," with rapid growth of the Mexican motor vehicles industry during the 1990s fuelling the growth of an internal domestic market that, if it were to parallel the experience of Spain in the 1970s and 1980s, could grow to over two million units a year by the year 2010 (compared to 338,000 in 1988).

Others are less sanguine. Mexico's full integration will lead to a new geographical division of labour within the continental industry in which Canada will lose the competitive advantage that it has enjoyed over the last two-and-a-half decades by virtue of its lower production costs vis-à-vis the United States. Given the relative size of the Canadian and Mexican auto industries as compared to that of the United States, Canada is likely to be much more sensitive to expanded investment and production in Mexico than the United States, particularly in the automotive components sector.

A secondary theme running through this chapter has been the consequences for autoworkers and their unions of the restructuring and progressive integration of the North American auto industry. There is considerable concern within the ranks of the Canadian and American labour movements that formal economic integration with Mexico could lead to a highly polarized pattern of development within the continental economy and increasing segmentation within the labour market (Shaiken and Herzenberg 1990). At the same time, it would likely lead to significant downward pressure on "market-determined" wages and working conditions in the Canadian and American sectors of the industry. The gap in real wage costs between Mexico and the rest of North America is enormous (Figure 1), and recent investments in Mexico, such as Ford Hermosillo, have been in technologically advanced plants with high rates of productivity. The momentum toward economic integration in industries such as the auto industry is irreversible. To avoid being placed in competition and played-off against each other within a regional production and trade bloc, Canadian, American, and Mexican workers need to fashion a progressive vision of economic development and continental integration and push for a harmonization of labour standards and industrial relations practices that protect workers' interests across the continent.

NOTES

[1] At the same time that industry integration was occurring across national boundaries in Europe and North America, many semi-industrialized countries (including Mexico) and countries such as Australia, for whom integration was geographically impractical, embarked on programs of increased protection and high domestic content requirements.

[2] It is argued that one reason the industry in Canada fared so well during the 1980s relative to its counterpart in the United States was that Canadian plants were oriented to the production of light trucks and large cars, market segments in which there was weak or non-existent offshore competition.

[3] Besides the threat of protectionist sanctions, other important factors that led the Japanese to establish the transplants should be noted. These include: the Japanese companies' own long-term corporate strategies for growth in profits, given the fiercely competitive nature of the Japanese domestic market; the appreciation of the yen against the other OECD currencies; and, as a central element of the process of globalization, the evolution of a marketing/production strategy within the world auto industry that is predicated upon the recognition of the formation of a triad of world regional market blocs—North America, Europe, and the Western Pacific Rim.

[4] This makes the transplant sector as large as the total Canadian assembly industry and several times larger than the present production capacity of the Mexican vehicle industry.

[5] The significance of NUMMI, the first of the transplants, stems from the direct comparison that was made between it and the former GM-Fremont plant that had stood on the same site. With essentially the same plant, technology, workers, wage rates, union, and union leaders, NUMMI demonstrated that Japanese production management practices were transferable to North America, and that American workers could achieve levels of productivity and quality that significantly exceeded those of every other GM plant, and even compared favourably with Toyota's home Takaoka plant in Japan.

[6] There is a significant difference in the timing of these closures among the Big Three. Ford and Chrysler closed six of their existing 21 assembly plants between 1980-83. For GM, most closures came later in the decade. Between 1987 and 1990, GM closed five of its 31 assembly plants, and in December 1991 it announced that it would be closing a further 21 plants, including six assembly plants. One consequence of this difference is that in the late 1980s Ford was operating at much higher plant capacity rates than GM.

Chrysler's overall plant capacity utilization rate has been low in the last couple of years due to its integration of the plants acquired in its takeover of AMC.

[7] In 1991, it was announced that GM would cease assembly operations at the old Scarborough Van Plant, and the future of other GM Canada plants was uncertain in the wake of the December 1991 announcement of further GM closures. Chrysler is phasing out its older Brampton plant while expanding production at Bramalea.

[8] See Holmes and Rusonik (1991) and Holmes and Kumar (1991) for a detailed analysis of these contracts.

[9] This is an accidental by-product of the way Canada chose to implement its side of the Auto Pact. In order to avoid having to obtain a GATT waiver, Canada treated the Auto Pact as applying to a multilateral setting (unlike the United States, which interpreted it as strictly applying only to bilateral trade) such that qualified producers could import components or vehicles duty free into Canada, not just from the United States, but from anywhere in the world for direct sale in Canada, or for assembly into a vehicle in Canada for subsequent sale in Canada or export to the United States. It must be remembered, however, that, with the exception of the duty on full-sized pick-up trucks, most duties on imports from these countries to the United States are already relatively low (4 to 8 percent range) due to most-favoured nation status (Weintraub 1990) and, therefore, this feature of the Auto Pact may well have become relatively inconsequential.

[10] The recent response of the Big Three to the proposed changes to the Ontario Labour Relations Act lends some credence to these fears (see Galt 1992: B1).

[11] See Bennett and Sharpe (1985) and Samuels (1990) for excellent discussions of the development of Mexico's automotive policy through to the mid-1980s.

[12] This discussion of the organization of union structure in Mexico relies heavily on the excellent English-language accounts by Kevin Middlebrook (1989; 1991).

[13] Jenkins (1987: 211) shows that, in the period 1972-83, vehicle exports from Mexico rarely exceeded 20,000 units and accounted, on average, for only 4.1 percent of Mexican vehicle production. Virtually all of these exports were by one company, Volkswagen. Since all the principal assemblers in Mexico were foreign-owned, they had no incentive to make an aggressive export push at the expense of production facilities elsewhere in their worldwide manufacturing system. In this regard, Mexico was quite different from Taiwan and South Korea where the principal automakers,

such as Hyundai, KIA and Daewoo, were domestically owned and there was a clear incentive to establish an export-oriented industry.

[14] Clearly there were two routes by which the assemblers could meet the requirements of the Decree: by increasing local content, or by increasing their exports.

[15] Of the 194,631 vehicles exported in 1989, 163,000 were exported to the United States—61,701 by Chrysler, 40,292 by GM, 39,580 by Ford, and 21,427 by VW (Automotive News 1990: 26). Only Nissan continued to export solely to other countries in Central and Latin America. In the first nine months of 1990 Mexico exported 1,987,026 vehicles.

[16] In fact, Womack et al. (1990) argue that the Ford Hermosillo plant demonstrates that Japanese-inspired "lean production" can be introduced successfully anywhere in the world. See Shaiken (1990) for a detailed discussion of production organization and labour relations at Ford Hermosillo. The anonymous Universal Motors discussed by Shaiken is clearly Ford Hermosillo.

[17] For the full Spanish text of the decree, see Diario Oficial, vol. CDXXXV, no. 7 (December 11, 1989), pp. 2-10; for an English translation, see Booz, Allen and Hamilton (1990), Appendix A. The whole tenor of the Decree is the liberalization of trade and the opening up of the Mexican auto parts industry to international investment and competition in order to produce a rationalized and internationally competitive industry. However, the measures contained within the Decree can probably be best characterized as constituting a policy of "guided liberalization" because it does contain measures to ensure that Mexico retains certain guaranteed levels of auto production. In this sense, the Decree might be appropriately compared with the "managed trade" provisions of the US-Canada Auto Pact. The measures are more clearly export-related than the production-to-sales ratio requirements of the US-Canada Auto Pact. The latter credited manufacturers with all Canadian production for ratio purposes whereas the Mexican requirement only gives credit for automotive products that are exported from Mexico to other countries.

[18] The assemblers are allowed to import up to 15 percent of total domestic sales by unit in 1991-92 and up to 20 percent in 1993. In addition, the automakers are allowed to count 30 percent of their investment in new or modernized Mexican plants toward export earnings that will permit them to import more assembled vehicles.

[19] It is also significant that both the Ford and GM Mexican subsidiaries now report directly to Detroit with GM's Mexican operations being fully integrated into GM's Chevrolet-Pontiac-Canada Group.

[20] However, some of this smoothing could still be quite significant. For example, it will result in the immediate reduction, and eventual removal, of the existing 25 percent tariff on full-size pick-up trucks entering the United States—a fact that helps explain why the bulk of Mexican and Japanese vehicle imports to the United States are automobiles rather than trucks. Of perhaps even greater significance is the North American automakers' need to have "Mexican content" count as "North American content" in order to use the Mexican-assembled entry-level vehicle strategy and still be able to meet their CAFE (Corporate Average Fuel Economy) requirements. A couple of years ago, Ford, out of concern for meeting its CAFE requirements, actually moved to reduce the North American content of the full-sized cars being assembled in Canada in order to have them reclassified as non-North American built cars while increasing the North American content of the Tracer being built in Mexico.

REFERENCES

Altshuler, A., et al. 1984. *The Future of the Automobile*. Cambridge, Mass.: MIT Press.

APMA. 1990. *The Mexican Auto Industry: A Competitor for the 1990s*. Toronto: APMA.

Automotive News. 1990. December 3: 26.

Bennett, D.C., and Sharpe, K.E. 1985. *Transnational Corporations versus the State: The Political Economy of the Mexican Auto Industry*. Princeton, NJ: Princeton University Press.

Bennett, M. 1986. *Public Policy and Industrial Development: The Case of the Mexican Parts Industry*. Boulder, Colo.: Westview Press.

Booz, Allen, & Hamilton Inc. 1990. *A Comparative Study of the Cost Competitiveness of the Automotive Parts Manufacturing Industry in North America*. Toronto. March 26.

Canada, Industry, Science and Technology. 1990. *Statistical Review of the Canadian Automotive Industry: 1989*. Ottawa: ISTC.

Dunn, J.A. 1987. Automobiles in international trade: regime change or persistence? *International Organization* 41,2: 225-52.

Galt, Virginia. 1992. Big Three assail changes to Ontario labour laws. *Globe and Mail*, January: B1.

Gindin S. 1989. Breaking away: the formation of the Canadian Auto Workers. *Studies in Political Economy* 29: 63-89.

Hart, M. 1990. *A North American Free Trade Agreement: The Strategic Implications for Canada*. Halifax: Institute for Research on Public Policy.

Herzenberg, S., and Shaiken, H. 1990. Labor Market Segmentation in the North American Auto Industry. Paper delivered at CIRRA Annual Meeting, Victoria, B.C.

Hoffman, K., and Kaplinsky, R. 1988. *Driving Force*. Boulder, Colo.: Westview Press.

Holmes J. 1983. Industrial reorganization, capital restructuring and locational change: an analysis of the Canadian automobile industry in the 1960s. *Economic Geography* 59: 251-71.

____. 1987. The crisis of Fordism and the restructuring of the Canadian auto industry. In *Frontyard/Backyard: The Americas in the Global Crisis*, eds. J. Holmes and C. Leys. Toronto: Between the Lines Press.

____. 1991. The globalization of production and Canada's mature industries: The case of the auto industry. In *The Era of the New Competition*, eds., D. Drache and M. Gertler. Kingston: McGill/Queen's Press.

Holmes, J., and Kumar, P. 1991. Divergent Paths: Restructuring Industrial Relations in the North American Automobile Industry. Queen's papers in Industrial Relations, 1991-94.

Holmes, J., and Rusonik, A. 1991. The break-up of an international labour union: uneven development in the North American Auto Industry and the schism in the UAW. *Environment and Planning A*: 23,1.

Howes, C. 1991. The Benefits of Youth: the Role of Japanese Fringe Benefit Policies in the Restructuring of the US Motor Vehicle Industry. *International Contributions to Labour Studies* 1: 113-32.

Investment Canada. 1991. *The Opportunities and Challenges of North American Free Trade: A Canadian Perspective*. Working Paper 7. Ottawa: Investment Canada.

Jenkins, R. 1987. *Transnational Corporations and the Latin American Automobile Industry*. London: Macmillan.

Katz, H.C. 1986. Recent Developments in U.S. Auto Labour Relations. In *The Automobile Industry and its Workers: Between Fordism and Flexibility*, eds. S. Tolliday and J. Zeitlin. Cambridge, Mass.: Policy Press/Basil Blackwell.

Katz, H.C., and Meltz, N.M. 1989. *Changing Work Practices and Productivity in the Auto Industry: A US-Canada Comparison*. Paper presented at the annual meeting of the Canadian Industrial Relations Association. Quebec City. June 1989.

Kornish, R., and Mericle, K.S. 1984. *The Political Economy of the Latin American Motor Vehicle Industry*. Cambridge, Mass.: MIT Press.

MacDonald, N.B. 1989. Will the free trade deal drive a gaping hole through the Auto Pact? *Policy Options* 10,1: 10-17.

Mair, A.; Florida, R., and Kenney, M. 1988. *The New Geography of Automobile Production: Japanese Transplants in North America*. Working paper. School of Urban and Public Affairs. Pittsburgh, Pa.: Carnegie-Mellon University.

Middlebrook, K. 1989. Union democratization in the Mexican automobile industry: a reappraisal. *Latin American Research Review* 24: 71-93.

____. 1991. The politics of industrial restructuring: transnational firms' search for flexible production in the Mexican automobile industry. *Comparative Politics* 23,3: 275-97.

Ohmae, K. 1985. *Triad Power: The Coming Shape of Global Competition*. New York: The Free Press.

Reid, N. 1990. The spatial location of Japanese automobile production in North America. *Industrial Relations Journal* 21: 49-59.

Samuels, B. 1990. *Managing Risk in Developing Countries: National Demands and Multinational Response*. Princeton, N.J.: Princeton University Press.

Shaiken, H. 1990. *Going Global: High Technology in Mexican Export Industry.* Monograph Series 33. San Diego: University of California, Center for US-Mexican Studies.

Shaiken, H., and Herzenberg, S. 1987. *Automation and Global Production: Automobile Engine Production in Mexico, the United States and Canada.* Monograph Series 26. San Diego: University of California, Center for US-Mexican Studies.

Womack, J. 1989. The Mexican Motor Industry: Strategies for the 1990s. IMVP International Policy Forum.

Womack, J.; Jones, D.T.; and Roos, D. 1990. *The Machine that Changed the World.* New York: Rowson Associates.

Yates C. 1990. The internal dynamics of union power: explaining Canadian autoworkers' militancy in the 1980s. *Studies in Political Economy* 31: 73-106.

3 NAFTA, FOREIGN DIRECT INVESTMENT, AND THE AUTO INDUSTRY:

A Comparative Perspective

Simon Reich

INTRODUCTION

This chapter examines the degree of complementarity among the policies of Canada, Mexico, and the United States toward each country's auto industry. There is discussion of their treatment of foreign direct investors, the policy impetus that NAFTA will generate in that sector, and the implications that the agreement will likely have for each country's economy.

In performing this evaluation of the prospects for the North American economies, I will rely on an historical and comparative perspective that reflects contrasting treatments of potential or actual foreign direct investors, drawing from the experiences of the major European auto-producing countries. I will then note the comparable and distinct features of state policy in the United States, Mexico, and Canada compared to Britain, France, Germany, and Italy with a view to speculating on a North American agreement's likely economic effects on each signatory.

The chapter therefore focuses on the ways in which state regulations have historically established the parameters within which the auto industry has organized production, how it does so today, and the subsequent effects of those regulations. My intention is to establish lessons drawn from the various European experiences with a view to informing the present North American context, the purpose here being to offer two arguments. The first claim is that the varied treatment of foreign direct investors has traditionally rewarded those European states that have pursued selective discriminatory policies against foreign capital and that the terms of the NAFTA agreement will largely nullify the capacity of its members to pursue such policies. States will thus have a reduced ability to influence the investment patterns of foreign capital. The second, more specific argument is that the agreement's policies concerning foreign direct investors will prove the least rewarding for Canada, which will not attract significantly more foreign investment in the context of a regional free market. Indeed, it will also probably dilute the domestic manufacturing base by encouraging Canadian firms to realize new opportunities by investing in the United States and Mexico. In contrast, Mexico will benefit from a policy of nondiscrimination through the influx of investment capital in the absence of its own domestic producers. Mexico has lacked a substantial domestic manufacturing base, and so will largely benefit from the arrival of non-NAFTA firms seeking easy, non-tariff access to the US market. Although the Americans will also suffer from a dilution of their domestic manufacturing base as production moves to Mexico, and will no longer be able to use trade barriers to encourage foreign direct investment, the United States will still retain a relatively large domestic production base by virtue of two factors: its status as the largest North American market, and the sunk cost of both domestic and foreign capital already invested there. In the United States, however, as in Canada, the adjustment costs will be disproportionately borne by organized labour.

Finally, both of these claims, and indeed any discussion about foreign direct investment, confronts the question of "who is us?" initially raised by Robert B. Reich (1990). Reich suggests that "us" is determined by where a corporation invests in research and development (R&D) and manufacturing facilities. He concludes that foreign investors who have such facilities located in the United States contribute more to American competitiveness than, for example, notable American corporations that invest in production in East Asia (Reich 1990: 53-54). In an age of globalized competition, "us" is "the American work force, the American people, but not particularly the American corporation" (Reich 1990:54). Reich's claim is debatable by virtue of his selection of criterion—location of employment rather than ultimate location of profits. But a more direct criticism may be that he did not recognize a third possibility, that "us" is a corporation both owned by Americans and investing in America. In this chapter, I specifically contrast foreign direct investment with domestic ownership and production. I begin from the premise that the domestically-owned firm that produces at home is "us" because that firm employs domestic labour, invests in domestic R&D, and contributes to an economy's competitiveness and balance of trade. Robert Reich's article largely avoids that point.

WHY FOREIGN DIRECT INVESTMENT MATTERS TO THE NAFTA PROPOSAL

Perhaps the foremost feature of the NAFTA agreement is the way it is defined by its advocates as a "stepping-stone" toward globalization and liberalization, rather than one toward regionalism and protectionism. The way in which the present process is defined is, therefore, steeped in ideological baggage, as integrative developments like the formation of the European Community (EC) and NAFTA are considered part of the present triumph of neoclassical liberalism and democracy.

Proponents of such a view cite evidence concerning the absence of internal barriers between member states, rather than the presence of barriers against nonmember states as crucial.[1] Advocates of NAFTA assume that these enlightened founding members of the trading zone will be joined by adjacent states once the benefits of membership become transparent. They point to the steady expansion of the EC to justify this claim. The first significant disagreement, therefore, exists between classical liberals, who support the formation of regional trading blocs as a path to global liberalization, and critics, who see the formation of trading blocs as a stage in the return to the protectionism of the 1930s.[2] Robert Kuttner is critical of the claim that bilateral or trilateral agreements such as NAFTA and the principle of free trade are consistent when he states that "preferential trade deals are clearly inconsistent with universal free trade, and the Mexico deal could come back to haunt the Bush Administration when it argues against similar preferential regional deals designed by other aspiring 'mother nations' in Europe and Asia" (1991: 18).

The second disagreement, along similar lines, is between those same liberals who see the benefits of such institutions as NAFTA or the EC in absolute terms and as positive-sum, and critics from both the left and the right who generally see the benefits as relative and zero-sum. The United States, Japan, and Germany are the primary beneficiaries in their respective North American, Asian, and European trading zones. Cutler et al. provide an example of this critical view when reflecting on the distribution of benefits generated by the EC with the statement that "Apologists for free trade believe that the Community owes its prosperity to being a free trade area; but a study of the pattern of trade reveals that the Community under free trade is a German 'co-prosperity' sphere in which prosperity is divided unequally" (1986:26). They then go on to suggest that these potential imitators could not match the German pattern of prosperity because that prosperity was built on an economic domination of these countries (Cutler et al. 1986: 5).

The contemporary economic policies of the United States, Japan, and the European states suggest that they could establish a consensus amongst themselves that legitimates a limited form of economic closure by combining a "soft" form of regionalism that allows or encourages foreign direct investment while discouraging the free flow of finished products. Unlike the 1930s, when closure included constraints on foreign direct investors, the 1990s promise to accelerate both the absolute and relative rates of foreign direct investment.[3] Foreign direct investment will be permissible, indeed often encouraged, and will provide a "safety valve" for much of the potentially worst trade friction.[4]

Second, while trade will take place between these zones, it will be limited in a period of capital scarcity and cyclical manufacturing downturn. Furthermore, this process of closure will be largely negotiated and limited rather than unilateral and comprehensive.[5] In this scenario, Japan will sustain its critical American and limited European markets through increased investment in local production facilities while enlarging its ASEAN markets; the United States will complete the codification of its North (and later Latin) American free trade zone;[6] and the European integration process will be completed, not by 1992 but relatively soon thereafter.

American fears of, for example, "Fortress Europe," whereby they get locked out of European markets, will therefore not materialize in the way Americans fear, because US firms will compensate for the constraints placed on finished products by sustaining their tendency over the last five years to accelerate their direct European investments through the formation of affiliates, joint ventures, or acquisitions.[7] The dawning realization by American business that foreign direct investment is an alternative way of sustaining the profits of manufacturing firms, but is not a way of sustaining the profits in the agricultural sector, largely explains why the American government has been relatively more pressured by, and responsive to, domestic agro-business rather than domestic manufacturers.

Yet defining the unique features of the present relationship between trading blocs does not address a second concern that divides liberals and their critics: the likely distributive effects within trading blocs. Certainly, the EC here provides the precedent for those considering the likely outcome of NAFTA cooperation, and views about the outcome of that three-decade-old experiment differ considerably.[8] Similarly, Japan's efforts to expand its raw material and manufacturing base among the ASEAN states can be alternatively seen as the extension of liberal free trade values by its advocates or an attempted return to the economic subjugation of a series of dominated satellites by the Japanese who, critics claim, are the only ones who stand to prosper from such arrangements.[9]

I will suggest, however, that what links these two issues—the consistency between bilateralism and free trade and the redistributive effects of FTAs—is a concern about the pattern of foreign direct investment and how state policies define that pattern. In the section that follows, I will initially focus on the specifics of the auto industry, then outline the major forms of state policy historically pursued by European governments in this respect, and finally discuss the effects of those policies on the structure of the industry. This will involve a discussion of the conflict among EC member states on Community policy that will demonstrate how the residue of traditional policies clearly results in contemporary entanglements and disagreements. I will then consider the pattern of state policies toward the auto industry in North America, with a bias toward consideration of American and Mexican policies and, most importantly, how the legacy of traditional state policies toward direct foreign investment, the likely structure of new arrangements, and the evolving global context will combine to affect each country's auto sector.

THE AUTO INDUSTRY IN EUROPE

The *modus vivendi* of the auto industry globally has never included the concept of free trade. Protection, whether the product of structural impediments or state policy, has always existed in each major producing country and has dominated the way in which the major manufacturers plan corporate strategy. Indeed, it could be argued that the advent of the notion of the "world car" in the 1970s, with its deliberate division of labour, was as much a product of the political impetus of state policy toward protected markets as it was a response to economic concerns about the development of economic efficiency through economies of scale.[10]

One major distinction, therefore, has not been between states that pursue free trade policies and those that pursue protectionist ones, but, as the empirical evidence reveals, between those where structural factors constrain free trade and those where such constraints are the product of state policy. A second, perhaps more important, distinction has been between how states have traditionally treated foreign investors; that is, whether they have been welcomed, abused, or simply refused the opportunity to compete. The following section attempts to delineate briefly the three major combinations that state policy in Europe has taken in regard to the treatment of foreign investors, and to consider the state's purpose and the economic implications in each case.[11]

UNQUALIFIED PROTECTION: THE EXAMPLES OF FRANCE AND ITALY

Among major European producers, France and Italy represent the clearest examples of states that have, historically, effectively barred both the import of foreign products and foreign direct investment. In France, the government imposed tariff levels of between 70 percent and 220 percent dating from 1916. Ford set up production facilities in response to these tariffs, and the broad market insulation for struggling domestic firms, combined with new Ford production, boosted aggregate domestic production from 18,000 automobiles in 1919 to 254,000 in 1929 (Fridenson 1981: 133-134). Domestic concentration and rationalization ensued, with four firms—Renault, Peugeot, Citröen, and Simca—as the major producers and challenged only in their own market by this growing Ford presence.

Ford of France's prospects seemed bright in 1945 with the construction of a new plant at Poissy (Wilkins and Hill 1964: 342). Yet it encountered consistent political hostility in the postwar period from the new French state, which proved fundamental in the parent company's decision to sell its French operation to Simca in 1954

(Wilkins and Hill 1964: 393). Ford's attempt to reenter the French market in 1964 failed when it was denied permission to build a plant by President Charles de Gaulle (Jones 1981: 36).

Chrysler, however, did successfully gain entrance to the French auto market, purchasing Simca in 1963 by exploiting a legal loophole. However, once purchased, Chrysler found its attempts to integrate the company into its European operations thwarted at every turn by successive French governments. GM proved even less successful, its initial application to build in France being rejected by the government in 1964 (Roos 1984).

Daniel Jones characterizes the postwar period in France as one in which "hostility to foreign firms has been a continuous feature of car industry policy." Even after joining the EC, the French government retained the right to limit foreign investment. Until 1980, all foreign firms had only the right to purchase up to 20 percent of the shares of a French firm without Ministry of Finance approval. This ministry had the power to veto any acquisitions it considered "harmful to French interests or contrary to the government's industrial strategy" (Jones 1981: 37). These rules were only relaxed in 1980 for acquisitions made by firms whose ownership is in other EC states. Ford's efforts to build an assembly plant in the depressed Lorraine region was rejected as late as the early 1980s. The French market has thereby been sealed off from foreign imports and investors to as great a degree as possible as a result of state policy.

Even with the liberalization of intra-European trade as a result of the EC, it has been the French who have been at the forefront of the battle to exclude non-European (primarily Japanese and American) imports from Europe's market and to disqualify cars built within the EC by those same non-European firms from a definition of acceptability as European-built products.[12] The purpose of French policy has therefore been consistent throughout the twentieth century: to stress French national autonomy and the welfare of its generally inefficient firms at a cost to the French consumer. French cars have been relatively uncompetitive but, in an insulated market for the first six decades of the twentieth century, French auto firms were major employers despite their lack of contribution to France's trade balance beyond the "Franc Zone." The stress of state policy has therefore been on autonomy and producer welfare rather than efficiency and consumer welfare.

State policy toward the Italian auto industry represents a case similar to the French one. After the fascists seized power in 1922, the Italian state instituted measures designed to insulate its inefficient producers. Tariff duties on imported autos were introduced, ranging between 122 percent and 142 percent, depending on the size of the car's engine, supplemented by a quota system that limited foreign producers to a total of 3 percent of market share. In tandem, these measures outlasted the fall of the fascist regime and its replacement by a liberal democratic one until well into the 1960s, and gave domestic producers a virtual monopoly on sales in Italy from the 1920s onwards (Prodi 1974: 57).

New state policies were then also designed to preclude all future foreign direct investment and to drive existing foreign direct investors out of Italy (Jones 1981: 113). Citröen was the largest foreign direct investor, while Ford had been the only American producer to establish a subsidiary in Italy in the pre-fascist period. Ford initially hoped that its Italian subsidiary could coexist with a fascist regime, despite Mussolini's calls for autarky, but these hopes proved illusory.

The issue of Ford's presence in Italy finally came to a head in 1929 when the company signalled its intention to expand its share of the Italian market rapidly, first by purchasing a large area of land at Livorno as a site for an assembly plant, and then by opening a variety of new sales offices. Fiat's part-owner and president, Giovanni Agnelli, immediately protested Ford's actions to Mussolini, who advocated that the two sides negotiate. The lethargic efforts in this direction by both sides soon petered out and the fascist government then forbade the construction of the Ford plant. Efforts by General Motors to build production facilities in Italy met with a similar response (Roos et al. 1984: 10). Mussolini then announced that "it was not the desire of the Italian Government to permit any big volume of imported automobiles, but rather to foster a 100 percent Italian manufacture thereof" (cited in Wilkins and Hill 1964: 230). Ford officials interpreted this as a directive that they should buy a domestic firm and so entered into negotiations with the firm of Isotta Fraschini over a possible merger or purchase. Isotta Fraschini's owners were delighted by this approach, but Mussolini vetoed the merger. Faced with Mussolini's intransigent discrimination, Ford succumbed to increased governmental pressure to abandon the Italian market while Fiat's percentage share of the Italian market grew. Further government restrictions forbade Ford to liquidate the company by threatening that such an act would require the forfeiture of all assets. Faced with this choice, Ford decided to sustain the cost of its sales network. Ford's Italian operation remained in existence, consistently registering a loss, until 1939 when Ford finally forfeited its assets (Wilkins and Hill 1964: 230, 260). Ford did not attempt to return to Italy as a producer until 1969 when it tried to take over Lancia. As had been the case four decades earlier, Ford's plans were frustrated by the Italian government's intervention, which denied it the right to purchase an Italian firm (Jones 1981).

Just as in France, the Italian government's aggressive treatment of foreign firms proved effective in enclosing the domestic market in a vacuum, assuring local producers a monopoly that raised their profit levels. This money was used to finance both domestic capital investment and the formation of foreign subsidiaries, contributing to increased economies of scale, the best example being that of Fiat.

The fascist period had consolidated the formation of Fiat as a national champion and, therefore, the primary target and beneficiary of the government's auto policy (Wells 1974: 234). Giovanni Agnelli, majority owner of Fiat and a fervent supporter of Mussolini, welcomed this close relationship and cultivated it as intensely as he could in order to spread his influence (Sarti 1971: 40). The government used the newly established Instituto per la Ricostruzione Industriale (IRI)[13] to acquire a 50 percent ownership in Fiat from the Agnelli family, while it also assumed complete control of Alfa Romeo. As a result of this change, Fiat and Alfa benefitted from exclusive access to the Italian state and its resources (Michalet 1974: 107-109; Sarti 1971: 109). Fiat became the dominant Italian producer under fascism and, therefore, naturally assumed the mantle of "national champion" after 1945. While its fascist past was discredited in the postwar period, the structure of relations between firm and state was sustained despite often strained relations with the Agnellis (Jones 1981: 53).

Fiat's virtual monopoly as the only firm selling mass-produced cars in Italy was maintained, providing significant profits but encouraging product stagnation until its monopoly on the Italian market was broken by EC membership. This increased competition severely affected Fiat's profits and the government responded to the crisis of the early 1980s by allocating extensive funding over a three-year period that provided the basis for Fiat's reemergence in the late 1980s as one of Europe's most competitive producers (Jones 1981: 53).

The pattern in Italy, therefore, closely matches that found in France: market insulation and concentrated producer benefits. Italy's domestic industry, however, has responded better to the adjustments enforced by intra-European trade, largely because the existence of only one mass producer allowed the government to concentrate its exhaustive financing in a period of crisis. Integration has opened up the Italian market, but state policy has nevertheless focused on ensuring that a degree of autonomy is maintained by sustaining a national champion. It is therefore not surprising to discover that the Italians are the greatest supporters of the idea that exports from Japanese-owned plants in Britain should be curtailed by instituting a formal domestic content requirement at 80 percent (*Automotive News* 1988d).

QUALIFIED PROTECTION: THE CASE OF GERMANY

Traditional German state policy represents an interesting and subtle contrast to Italian and French policy. Pre-fascist German policy combined protectionism against imported finished products with a willingness to tolerate foreign direct investment and treat foreign firms equitably in the context of a relatively noninterventionist state. American firms, such as Opel (owned by General Motors) and Ford, dominated the German market as a result. The German auto industry consisted of a number of small German producers such as Wanderer, Horch, Audiwerke, and Zchopauer, which merged in 1932 to form Auto-Union. There were also specialist producers such as Daimler-Benz and BMW that were struggling to survive as they sought to create market niches and sign lucrative government armaments contracts. Indeed, Daimler-Benz was only able to remain in existence in the 1920s and early 1930s because it was continually subsidized by the Deutsche Bank.[14] The resulting German structure was one in which foreign firms thrived and domestic firms were overwhelmed by the effective competition that they faced (S. Reich 1990: 246).

Nazi policies represented a significant departure from that combination, with an emphasis on market insulation coupled with explicit and extensive discrimination against foreign direct investors.[15] The state initially tolerated Opel far more readily than Ford because Opel was responsible for so much of Germany's production, repeatedly accounting for over 50 percent of car sales.[16] Because of its size, Opel, for example, could dictate the terms of the German standardization of auto parts in the early years of the Nazi regime (Palumbo 1948). In both Ford and Opel's cases, however, the Nazis used their investments to enhance German security interests, create jobs, and improve the German balance-of-payments situation while ensuring that the flow of material resources and government contracts rehabilitated their own domestic producers (S. Reich 1990: 147-202). Opel's production became increasingly dispensable as the state's own Volkswagen plant was constructed and commenced manufacturing operations, and the Nazis adopted more coercive means to implement their discriminatory policies, using state decrees on certification, standardization, resource allocation, and market access to ensure that foreign firms either economically stagnated or were abandoned completely by their owners. In contrast, a select group of domestic firms—either owned or co-opted by the state—thrived, benefitting from conditions that included a guaranteed market, discriminatory access to resources, cheap (often slave) labour, and a lack of competition from imported products or foreign direct investors. This latter list included BMW and Daimler-Benz, for whom the Nazi period proved to be the turning point in their subsequent successful economic development (S. Reich 1990: 253-261).

Despite the defeat of fascism and the supposed institution of reforms by the allies in the embryonic liberal democracy, this combination of discrimination against imported products combined with a tolerance for, but simultaneous discrimination against, foreign direct investors persisted in the German auto industry in the postwar period, at least as documented during the first two decades of the Bonn Republic. Ironically, Allied officials often consciously reinforced this process of discrimination during the occupation as they sought to get the German economy back on its feet so Germans could earn scarce foreign currency (S. Reich 1990: 171-173). This same form of reasoning motivated state officials after the formation of the Bonn Republic. Although many of those involved in the decision-making processes were explicitly anti-Nazi, they often invoked similar justifications and implemented similar policies, albeit in a much milder, more subtle form, systematically favouring domestic firms and discriminating against foreign firms trying to operate their subsidiaries. Officials of the new German state were a lot less subtle in their protection of ailing domestic firms against prospective foreign buyers, often explicitly organizing the purchase of these firms by other domestic manufacturers. They were also quick to rehabilitate convicted war criminals such as Friedrich Flick, a member of Hitler's elite and former owner of the huge Flick armaments combine, of which Daimler-Benz was one component. Flick's 39 percent holding in Daimler-Benz was restored to him, and with it his former position as the firm's dominant shareholder (*New York Times* 1975: 27).

In contrast, the sustained discrimination of the state during the Nazi occupation, and then early Bonn periods, ensured that the foreign subsidiaries never reestablished their prominent position in the German market. Opel had accounted for between 40 percent and 52 percent of the German market before 1939. This figure fell to 19 percent in the late 1940s (compared to Volkswagen's share at that time of 25 percent) and bottomed-out at 11.7 percent in 1952 (Ford Industrial Files). The Allied and embryonic Bonn government refused to provide any comparable financial support to that accorded to Volkswagen, so General Motors then provided the funding to begin the process of Opel's reconstruction (Wilkins and Hill 1964: 391). However, the vacuum created by Opel's lost output had been filled by Volkswagen, and Opel never again approached its prewar market share, even trailing behind the formerly much smaller Ford in the 1950s (Nevins and Hill 1962: 402).

The result of these policies provided the "best of both worlds" for the Germans: an influx of needed capital investment and hard currency coupled with the maintenance of a vital, highly profitable set of domestic producers such as Volkswagen, Daimler-Benz, and BMW, whose reemergence had begun under fascism (S. Reich 1990: 253-261). Although discriminatory policies became less systematic, less coercive, and increasingly subtle over time, traces of this discriminatory treatment of prospective foreign investors still occasionally emerge. Notable examples include the Deutsche Bank's intervention to thwart the Iranian purchase of Daimler-Benz in the mid-1970s (an attempted purchase that resulted in the passage of national legislation to protect "strategic firms" from foreign purchase), and the late 1980s case of Continental Tire, Germany's major tire producer, in which the German state went to great lengths to see that the firm maintained domestic ownership.

In the German case, state policy tended toward unqualified protection against imported goods coupled with an unqualified but increasingly subtle protection of domestic firms against foreign direct investors.

This combination had the cumulative effect of creating a remarkably prosperous set of domestic firms that were well placed to compete with the opening of markets caused by EC membership. As this analysis would predict, periodic crises at German auto companies resulted in state intervention designed to protect and rehabilitate these firms, and thus maintain a vibrant, durable sector.

EGALITARIAN COMPETITION: THE CASE OF BRITAIN

The case of Britain shares the characteristics of the other European countries already discussed in that state policy included the introduction of protectionist measures designed to stem the import of finished products. Unlike these other countries, however, the measures in Britain were combined with others designed both to encourage foreign direct investment and to treat those investors equitably. Equitable treatment in practice often meant that foreign firms had an advantage over their domestic rivals because the British state felt that foreign affiliates, unlike their domestic counterparts, faced a realistic option to leave if they were dissatisfied. Ironically, state ownership in Britain, therefore, did not mean state sponsorship. Rather, British firms such as BMC, British Leyland (in its various incarnations), and then Austin-Rover, did not benefit from discriminatory policies despite state ownership, while privately owned firms in France, Germany, and Italy often did, despite their lack of a formal link to the state.[17]

This policy combination in Britain was not accidental. The British state was committed to this policy largely as a product of its ideological proclivity toward liberalism (S. Reich 1990: 31-38). It was the conscious choice of an interventionist state convinced that unimpeded, unrestricted investment was to the aggregate benefit of the British economy, as measured in terms of employment levels and Britain's balance of payments. The result, however, was the steady, unrestrained demise of Britain's indigenous producers and eventually the whole indigenous industry, as domestic firms were destroyed in direct competition by the affiliates of foreign direct investors that had superior resources and better access to foreign markets.

This description of British policy as externally protectionist and internally egalitarian was consistent with that found in Germany, France, and Italy before the onset of fascism. The McKenna duties, introduced in 1915, were the British automobile industry's first protectionist measures, imposing a tariff of 33.3 percent on imported cars. These duties were designed to limit competition from imported finished goods but, at the same time, encourage postwar foreign direct investment. The measures succeeded on both scores after the recession in the auto industry of the early 1920s, as a number of major British mass producers like Austin, Morris, Standard, and Wolesley were joined as manufacturers by Ford and Vauxhall, the latter being General Motors' British subsidiary.

Indeed, Ford's decision to build a manufacturing plant at Dagenham, modelled on its River Rouge plant in Detroit, signalled the company's intention to compete seriously in the British market. Construction of what was to become, not only the largest manufacturing plant in Britain, but also the then largest Ford plant outside North America, commenced and was completed by the beginning of the 1930s. Ford was thereafter well placed to assume a market dominance with any surge in domestic demand.

General Motors sought a different route, preferring to purchase an existing British company and its facilities rather than to build a new plant. After unsuccessful attempts to buy Austin, GM purchased Vauxhall, a much smaller company, reflecting a decision to focus its resources on its German affiliate, making it GM's primary European export base, and to use the British affiliate to concentrate on purely domestic sales (Church 1979: 62).

The 1920s and 1930s proved to be a turbulent time for firms in the British auto industry, but the British state steadfastly refused to favour even those British firms like Austin that had worked so hard to assist the national cause during World War I. This major bifurcation in state policy between Britain and the other European producers in their treatment of foreign direct investors only slowly emerged as the full effects of fascist state policies in France, Germany, and Italy became transparent. With the onset of war, the significance of this divide accelerated, as foreign investors were coopted into the planning process of the British state, with the executives of foreign affiliates being appointed to important bureaucratic positions at the heart of Britain's strategic decision-making apparatus (S. Reich 1990: 82-92). Foreign firms were awarded important government contracts and, in contrast to the European mainland, where their efforts were stymied, expanded their facilities in the wartime period.

The end of World War II brought raw material shortages. The allocative mechanism provided the perfect opportunity for the British state to discriminate against foreign subsidiaries with the purpose of giving its domestic firms a competitive advantage. Yet successive British governments of the Left and Right refused to do so, sustaining a scrupulously unbiased allocation process that resulted in affiliates such as Ford often receiving as many or more resources than their major domestic competitors (S. Reich 1990: 238). When the government formed the Politics and Economic Planning Group, composed of academics, industry, and government officials, the purpose of which was to make suggestions for the auto industry's future, it appointed a Ford executive to head the committee.

Analyzing the situation from the perspective of the early 1950s, the general thrust of state policy seemed justified by the results. Foreign direct investors had made a major contribution to the defeat of fascism, the aggregate growth in production, exports, employment, and the balance of trade in the postwar period. The subsequent withdrawal of investment over the next two decades as the political and economic context changed, however, subsequently encouraged a more critical perspective. This withdrawal was made all the more dramatic by its rapidity, dating from the late 1960s. By this time, American firms had asserted their dominance over their British rivals, partly as a result of their greater capital investment due to their superior access to resources, but also as a product of a high dividend policy by British firms that was stimulated by a fear of impending nationalization in the 1950s. The successive merging of British firms—organized by the state—proved of no value in the absence of either enforced rationalization of the new amalgam or its being given discriminatory advantages over foreign direct investors. The successive incarnations of BMC, Leyland, British Leyland, British Leyland (1975) Ltd., Austin-Rover, and the Rover Group all tended to couple prosperous firms with uncompetitive ones and let the latter drag down the former. The result was that the domestic section of the industry stagnated and then shrank as foreign direct investors enlarged their market share.

None of this concerned British governments until the exodus of foreign investment began in the late 1960s. Successive British governments had hoped that EC membership would encourage foreign direct investors to use Britain as their export base to Europe. The opposite, however, was the case, and firms such as Ford steadily converted their British facilities from manufacturing to assembly plants or abandoned British production altogether. In reference to the American firms, for example, Stephen Wilks suggests that "the industry's success, since the mid sixties, has become inseparable from the success of these companies" (1984: 87) but that "the American companies had taken the strategic decision to supply continental Europe with cars from their continental factories and could not be relied on to take advantage of the opportunities theoretically offered by membership of the EEC" (1984: 112).

Between 1968 and 1982, the market share of imported cars grew from 8.3 percent to 57.7 percent, and "captive imports" accounted for over 20 percent of sales (Wilks 1984: 70 and 237). By that time, Ford had converted its position from that of Britain's largest exporter to its largest importer, with a net trading deficit in 1982 of £265 million. Chrysler, having bullied the British government into a series of loans and subsidies in 1975, in exchange for its promise to maintain British production, promptly sold its British subsidiary two years later to PSA/Talbot, which scaled it down to an assembly plant, retaining 25 percent of the labour force.

Wilks describes the decline of the British auto industry, dating from the late 1960s, as being of "a unique order of magnitude" (1984: 71). Domestic production halved in the 1970s and halved again in the 1980s. When the Americans abandoned their British manufacturing facilities, there was no real domestic firm capable of filling this production void. What was left of British industry was too small and uncompetitive to seriously consider expansion in the context of a global recession.

Yet the British state's response to this situation was characteristic. They sought alternative foreign direct investors by both attracting new firms to Britain and selling off what remained of British domestic industry to the highest bidder. Despite their own strenuous efforts to avoid foreign purchase, firms such as Jaguar were sold off to foreigners while the Japanese companies replaced their American counterparts as Britain's new producers. Nissan, Toyota, and Honda all invested in British production facilities in the 1980s as a way of combatting domestic content restrictions. Margaret Thatcher openly courted this investment, earning Britain the ire of some other EC members, most notably France, which tried to have exports by Japanese companies produced in Britain excluded from the EC by raising the standard of domestic content requirements (Greenhouse 1989). The domestic British automobile industry, once the largest exporter in the world, had therefore all but disappeared by the start of the 1990s. A sign of its decline is that Nissan, with a single plant, is projected to be the largest exporter of cars from Britain, in a country that now produces fewer autos than Spain *(Economist* 1988b: 10).

IN SUM

State policy toward domestic firms and foreign direct investors has varied tremendously within Europe with a characteristic trade-off between autonomy and capital flows. Interestingly, the trade-off has not been between autonomy and efficiency or prosperity, because it is the British who have been the most open to capital flows and have fared the worst. Indeed, it is the Germans who have managed foreign direct investors so carefully and who have formed the most effective foundation for a sustained competitive industry.

Of course, accession by these states to EC membership has largely nullified their importance in the regulation of dollars. This fact, coupled with the legacy of traditional state policy, creates a clearly discernable pattern of problems or benefits for each national industry. It is the traditionally protectionist French and Italians who continue to pursue protection against Japanese producers, whether those products are primarily produced within or outside the EC. Their inability to sustain those restrictions is an indication of how effectively integration can, in the appropriate context, assail national sovereignty. Interestingly, the Japanese have their highest market share in Germany amongst EC states (15 percent) but, conversely, it is the Germans who have the least to fear from further liberalization because they have allowed the Japanese to compete against their products.

It would, therefore, appear that European states have tended to pursue consistent policies, allowing for the adjustment caused by integration, dating from the early 1930s or before. While pure protectionism is no longer possible in the context of European integration, some states that have traditionally sought to limit foreign direct investment and the importation of finished products still seek to do so. These contrasting policies have led to conflicts about the treatment of foreign direct investors that are still playing themselves out in negotiations between the EC member states in the early 1990s.

BETWEEN A ROCK AND A HARD PLACE: THE US, CANADA, MEXICO AND NAFTA

The history of the North American auto producers and the contemporary issues concerning foreign direct investment reflect some significant parallels to the European examples. The following section highlights these issues as they relate to the US, Mexico, and Canada and then discusses the likely effect of a free trade agreement on the structure of the industry in each country.

BETWEEN STATE AND STRUCTURAL PROTECTION: THE UNITED STATES

The United States provides an interesting case to juxtapose with the European ones. The United States, unlike Europe, has long believed itself to be the historical bastion of free enterprise, following the rejection of Hamilton's principle of infant-industry protection in favour of Locke's principle of open trade. The history of the auto sector, however, reveals a pragmatic alternation between state protectionism and de facto structural protectionism, dating from the second decade of the twentieth century, and an insulation from foreign direct investment until the 1970s.

More than just a strategic industry, the American automobile producers created both a new production mix and form of industrial relations characterized by some as "Fordism." Fordism synthesized mass-production methods and high-salaried anti-unionism (Meyer III 1981). Yet, despite the development of unprecedented levels of economy of scales, successive administrations were willing to implement a series of tariffs dating from the Dingley tariff of 1897, which protected the infant American auto industry from rival European producers by classifying their products as manufactured steel, thus ensuring that they were subject to a 45 percent tariff (Wilkins and Hill 1965: 37).

By the 1930s, a number of factors had rendered protection largely a redundant policy. The first consisted of the combination of peculiar market conditions in the United States, where cheap gas, varied climatic conditions, and huge geographical distances encouraged the production of exceptionally large, "gas-guzzling" cars and produced a unique form of consumer demand. The second factor was the rapid development of a competitive and quickly concentrating industry.

European producers, who had initially represented the greatest threat to the domestic auto industry, lacked the resource base either to produce a suitable model in large enough numbers to achieve competitive economies of scale or to create the extensive service base such sales would require.

Together, these factors amounted to structural constraints that inhibited the import of finished products and foreign direct investment just as effectively as the protectionist state policy codified by the Dingley tariffs had done. Both state protectionism and structural impediments functioned to achieve the same outcome: an insulated market in which the process of unabated domestic competition led to increasing concentration among a few profitable firms that manufactured markedly similar products at comparable prices, and which consistently generated high profits. The eventual outcome was a market structure composed of the "Big Three" of GM, Ford, and Chrysler. The only actual state policy evident in this period of insulation, stretching from the 1930s to the 1970s, was the state's consistent implementation of anti-monopoly legislation designed to ensure that GM did not destroy its two remaining competitors. This market structure, however, excluded competition from imported products and foreign direct investors just as effectively as French or Italian state policy did.

This insulation was rudely disturbed, however, by the two oil shocks of the 1970s, which together shattered the structural influences that had combined to insulate the market from foreign products or investors, and had thus secured the position of American firms. But the short-sighted response of those firms had predictable results: record losses and the eventual bankruptcy of Chrysler by the end of the decade. By 1980 the "Big Three" had collectively lost $4 billion (*Economist* 1988a: 69).

The American state's response was predictable: the reintroduction of overt protectionist policies through the thinly disguised and supposedly self-imposed Voluntary Export Restraint (VER) Agreement in 1981 to replace the de facto protectionism that had existed for the previous four decades. There were a series of major distinctions between this and measures enacted in the US earlier in the century. First, the VER was bilaterally negotiated rather than unilaterally imposed by the US, although it maintained the pretence of having been unilaterally-imposed by the Japanese state on its own producers. Second, it was bilateral (dealing with only the major Japanese competitors to domestic firms) rather than multilateral, unlike earlier American protectionist policies. Third, it amounted to a quota rather than a tariff on the import of finished products, with specified limits on the number of cars imported each year. Finally, the purpose of the VER was to discourage the import of finished products, but simultaneously encourage foreign direct investment by firms that now, unlike in earlier periods, had the resources to invest in manufacturing and servicing facilities in the United States.[18]

Yet, despite these differences, the more important aspect is the similarity in terms of the overt retreat to protectionism, albeit under the guise of sustaining fair trade as a stage in establishing free trade. Scepticism on this point seems to have been justified by intervening events, whereby the temporary restriction has shifted from a formal to an informal status, but has nevertheless been maintained in only a slightly modified form with a growth from 1.68 to 2.3 million per annum in the number of cars allowed into the United States under the terms of the VER.

The results of the introduction of VERs are reminiscent of the phrase that you should never wish for anything in life because your curse may be that you might just get it! The first effect has been that Japanese investment has flooded into the United States, designed to help the balance of trade and employment levels in a threatened industry. This investment, however, has also had an unforeseen consequence: a political backlash resulting from concerns about possible threats to national autonomy (S. Reich 1989: 545; Tolchin and Tolchin 1988: 25). The subsequent debate has only contributed to the growth of, rather then the reduction of, trade friction.[19]

The second effect of VERs was to create a time period between the reduced levels of import competition and the construction of American plants by Japanese firms, in which American firms could take advantage of market conditions to generate "false" profits that would give them additional capital for reinvestment and thus make them more competitive.[20] Yet, despite generating these profits, American efforts at reinvestment have been both lacklustre and unimpressive. No better example of this exists than the case of GM's Saturn car, which was originally planned in grandiose terms, only to shrink visibly over time. An additional factor was a return to the inequitable distribution of company profits. Executives were rewarded for their apparent patience and there was a smug—and incorrect—belief that the Japanese firms would not provide the same overwhelming competition when constrained by having to relocate production in the United States.

Once located in the United States, these foreign firms have been accorded equitable status in the same way as they were in Britain, a state policy conventionally termed one of "national treatment," whereby foreign direct investors in the US are guaranteed all the rights and privileges of domestic firms (and in practice have few of the obligations). With the breakdown of structural insulation, American policy has therefore most closely come to resemble that of Britain's: protectionism, the encouragement of foreign investment, and the equitable treatment of foreign firms.

This market distortion ended within a period of five years, and the gamble of American firms and the American state has proven to be incorrect. In the context of an American state policy of national treatment, the result has been the sustained undermining of the competitive position of American firms, without the ultimate protection of tariff barriers.[21] No longer can the American state impose protectionist measures as a means of creating "breathing space" while domestic firms generate "artificial" profits through market distortions. American firms, therefore, no longer have anywhere to hide, and popular estimates suggest that Japanese producers will be responsible for in excess of 45 percent of production through combined American-built autos and imports by the mid-1990s (*Economist* 1988b: 8). James Womack outlines the economic implications of this policy with the comment that

> [t]he key question, therefore, is not whether the US auto industry will be revitalized, but whether traditional domestic producers can introduce new techniques rapidly enough— burdened as they are with sunk investments and outdated social systems—to avoid losing much of the market to Japanese producers with new plants in the heartland of the United States. Although the prospect of a Japanese-dominated North American motor vehicle industry is startling, it should be clear that it is a real possibility within the next twenty years. Four Japanese-owned or managed assembly plants are now operating in the United States and Canada, and six more are under construction. More than two million units of Japanese assembly capacity will therefore be in place

in North America by 1990, at a direct investment cost exceeding $5 billion. The scale of this enterprise comes into focus
when one realizes that, in less than eight years, a new
Japanese-US motor industry will have emerged with nearly
four times the assembly capacity of the entire Mexican motor
vehicle sector (Womack 1987: 106-107).

In addition, Womack estimated in 1987 that the Japanese would
own 129 component plants by 1990, with the combined effect that
"the entire motor vehicle industry in the United States and Canada
will be rebuilt before the end of the century" (Womack 1987: 107).

It is not simply the number or size but, more profoundly, the
productivity of these new Japanese plants that poses a problem for
American firms. As Womack notes, "[i]nitial experiences at the new
Honda, Toyota-GM, and Nissan facilities in the United States make it
clear that best practice can and will be transplanted, with Honda's
Ohio plant having a 40 percent higher productivity rate per hour and
far fewer quality defects than a typical GM plant in the United States
(1987: 106).

American proponents of NAFTA suggest that it is imperative that
it be instituted because it provides them with a "life-belt" now that the
Japanese can compete directly, free from discrimination, and so effectively in the US manufacturing environment. According to the representatives of American firms, NAFTA will provide American firms with
a significant advantage over these new Asian foreign direct investors.
American auto corporations have already invested heavily in Canada
and Mexico, and can therefore better utilize the major comparative
advantages that production in those markets has to offer: a highly
skilled labour force in Canada and a cheap one in Mexico. They further
suggest that the job losses to Mexico as a result of new American
investment there is mitigated by five factors. The first is that those
jobs would have been lost to Asia anyway, as American firms increase
their percentage of "captive imports" in order to stay competitive.
Second, that this loss of low-paying jobs complements American interests by creating more high-paying manufacturing and servicing jobs
for the industry. Third, that the creation of new Mexican jobs will
contribute toward alleviating the problem of illegal Mexican immi-
gration to the United States. Fourth, that, under the terms of NAFTA,
Mexican wealth generated by these new jobs will be spent primarily on
American goods, while Asian money would not. And finally, that the

Mexican border (*maquiladora*) expansion that is likely to accompany the signing of NAFTA will reap significant regional benefits for the long-depressed American Southwest (Weintraub 1991; *Business Week* 1990a: 40-41; 1990b: 112-113).

American critics of NAFTA are largely the representatives of labour and environmental groups. Labour advocates stress that job losses will not be balanced by job creation and that those losses will occur preponderantly among unskilled workers, who will be permanently displaced from the work force, damaging not only the economy but also the social fabric of society. Richard Rothstein notes, for example, that US manufacturing shrank as a percentage of the work force, from 23 percent of domestic employment in 1979 to 18 percent in 1990 (1991: 32). These critics also stress that the claim that the losses will be exclusively in unskilled, low-paying jobs is inaccurate. Harley Shaiken and Stephen Herzenberg's analysis of productivity rates at comparable US, Canadian, and Mexican plants concludes that the differential in skills and productivity rates is shrinking, which suggests that the argument that the export of American jobs will be confined to low-skilled ones seems unlikely in the long term (Shaiken and Herzenberg 1987).

The relationship between foreign direct investment and NAFTA in the United States is, therefore, an important but reasonably complex one. An egalitarian principle of national treatment has allowed Japanese firms to overcome successfully American protectionist measures and threaten to dominate the American market, just as the Americans formerly did in Britain. Half-hearted attempts to generate higher rates of productivity by the American firms in the interregnum period between the introduction of VERs and the establishment of Japanese production facilities have left them with a dilemma from which, they believe, their only beneficial escape is the NAFTA with Mexico (and Canada). Thus, American firms have responded by significantly increasing their investments in, and exports from, Mexico in recent years. In 1983 they collectively exported 2,388 vehicles; by 1989 that figure had grown to 153,259 *(Business Week* 1989: 32).

Yet a question remains as to whether this new policy of Mexican investment is a short-term or a long-term solution. As the following discussion of Mexican policy reveals, Mexico now also employs an egalitarian principle in its treatment of foreign direct investors, and it only appears to be a matter of time before these investors follow American firms in the building of extensive Mexican production facilities, as recent activities by Nissan and Honda seem to indicate (*Business Week* 1989: 32). While the principle of national treatment predominates, Mexican investment is the last and quickly disappearing hope of the American manufacturers to seize a comparative economic advantage in the absence of a state-induced political one.

MEXICO: A REVOLUTIONARY REVERSAL OF POLICY

Mexico is, therefore, possibly the key component in deciding the future of the US auto industry, making state policies worthy of close scrutiny. Traditional Mexican policy toward foreign direct investors tended to reflect aspects of French and German policy, depending on which segment of the industry is examined. There were never any major indigenous auto manufacturers, and so the choice for the state was simply between allowing a free flow of imports or choosing an import-substitution strategy. It consistently chose the latter in the postwar period, with successive state decrees, dating from 1962 to 1977, designed to reverse the flow of imports by instituting ever more rigorous domestic content and export regulations on foreign direct investors (Bennett 1986: 25-28).[22] Foreigners, the Big Three, Volkswagen, and subsequently Nissan (*Automotive News* 1988c), did generally sustain investment, despite the relatively small size of the domestic market. These firms, however, confined export only to those circumstances where it was suitably profitable for them, assisted before the 1977 decree by the lack of a government mechanism capable of regulating their sales.

Yet this German-style management of foreign investment (albeit with a significantly heavier hand than the Germans used after 1945) was complemented with an approach in the auto parts segment of the market that made the French and Italians look as if they were the height of warmth and sensitivity to foreigners. Here the Mexican state zealously guarded the interests of a number of domestic producers to ensure that they were free from foreign competition. Mark Bennett outlines the comprehensive nature of relevant government policy:

> In summary, the Mexican auto parts industry is subject to a set of public policies that includes local content and compensating export requirements and limitations on foreign equity participation. A special government commission administers these requirements; it also controls the issuance of technology

> licenses, the addition of new product lines, and the entry of
> firms into the parts industry. The industry is concentrated,
> with high barriers to entry that appear to be created and
> enforced in part by public policies (Bennett 1986: 42).

This combination of relatively heavy-handed management in the manufacturing segment, coupled with explicitly interventionist behaviour
in the parts segment, had the effect of creating surplus capacity among
underutilized assemblers in a small market and a set of inefficient,
bloated parts manufacturers whose interests were better served by selling to the domestic market, where prices were artificially high, than
exporting to competitive markets with correspondingly lower prices
(Bennett 1986: 47).

The domestic market grew at a conservative but consistent pace
until the late 1970s, when the oil boom briefly offered what proved to
be the illusionary promise of richer rewards. Reality soon followed
with the onset of the debt crisis, which saw a stunning decline in
demand from a sales level of 600,000 in 1981 to 360,000 in 1987,
and a comparable decline in the number of car dealerships from 1,253
to 914 (*Automotive News* 1988b). The response of then President de
la Madrid's government was a characteristically interventionist decree
in 1983 that sought to improve efficiency for export purposes by limiting the number of makes (one) and the number of models (five) that
each firm could produce. This was to be achieved by raising domestic content levels to 60 percent, and by placing a renewed emphasis on
exports. This stress on exports was resisted by the multinational corporations until the contraction in domestic demand forced them to focus
on it; aggregate car exports rose from 15,819 in 1982 to 155,983 in
1987, and engine exports increased from 320,301 to 1,431,733 in
the same period (Middlebrook 1991: 280).

The significance of this brief review of state policy is to contrast
it with the revolutionary shift in state policy following the succession
of de la Madrid by Carlos Salinas de Gortari. Rejecting both the import-
substitution policy and the more interventionist version of export-led
growth policies pursued by his predecessors, Salinas has pursued more
traditionally neoclassical liberal policies designed to attract foreign
investment, with major implications for the negotiation of the policy
with which he has become most closely associated—the NAFTA.[23]

Salinas' reforms reflect much more traditional British policies
toward foreigners than French or German ones because they seek to

maximize relatively unconstrained foreign direct investment. Indeed, they go further toward free trade than any other national policy, because they have eliminated all protectionist measures, as well as the formerly cumbersome domestic content requirements that often served to deter rather than attract investment to this relatively small market.[24] The logic of Salinas' approach is simple, reflecting the belief that Mexico's flexible, industrious, and, above-all-else, cheap labour force, coupled with its proximity to the enormous US market, will expand old and attract new investment from the US, Japan, and Europe in the form of "greenfield" sites, especially to the border maquiladoras region, where traditional union influence is nominal (*Business Week* 1989: 32; Middlebrook 1991: 281-285). As Kevin Middlebrook suggests,

> [t]he combination of significant (and, in all likelihood, persistent) hourly wage differentials between the United States and Mexico and extensive managerial flexibility through contracts negotiated with CTM-affiliated unions may considerably extend Mexico's competitive edge in the global automobile industry (1991: 291).[25]

Early indications are that these reforms have resulted in a growth of foreign direct investment, reversing the trend of the mid-1980s when multinationals such as Ford closed plants, and Renault left Mexico altogether. These indications also suggest that Salinas' reassurances to advocates of Canadian and American labour that this investment will result in a reduction in the differential between Mexican wages and their own are unsubstantiated. The result so far has been the opposite, as new plants, built away from traditional urban labour strongholds, pay workers substantially less and thus increase the differential.[26]

Furthermore, Salinas, desperate to accept foreign capital without regard to its source, has given no indication of any willingness to discriminate against non-American multinationals seeking to supply the American market. His reforms have therefore replaced the old discriminatory principles with new nondiscriminatory ones predicated on the concept of national treatment. NAFTA may expand American sales and investment opportunities, but it will also eventually do the same for the more competitive Japanese foreign direct investors. Without state intervention to "stack the deck" in favour of American firms, it will not be long before Japanese firms respond to this new situation with predictable results. This view is supported by early evidence of Nissan's and Honda's expanded investment (*Business Week* 1989: 32).

CANADA: LOTS TO LOSE, LITTLE TO GAIN

Much to the chagrin of Canadian nationalists, the history of Canada's foremost manufacturing industry reflects the general state of relations between Canada and the United States. The Canadian auto industry has largely been confined to the role of assembler for the American multinational affiliates and domestic parts producers located along the border region, with no independent national producer to support. This production has overwhelmingly been intended for export, with only 20 percent of the average production of 1.8 million being retained for domestic sales (ISTC 1988: 2). The traditional policy employed has, de facto, had to be one of national treatment, integrating Canadian production into the American system. This informal system was recognized and institutionalized on a formal basis under the terms of the US-Canada Auto Pact, signed in 1965.

Like Americans, Canadians have enjoyed the questionable benefit of transplanted foreign direct investment, most notably from Japanese firms, albeit on a much smaller basis (ISTC 1988). Now, however, Canadians are threatened with even these meagre benefits under the proposed NAFTA's terms. Canadian production has no equivalent of the significant advantages offered by the other two North American countries to prospective investors: namely, cheap labour in Mexico and proximity to markets in the case of the United States. All the qualities that Canada can offer to present or potential investors, such as an educated work force or a modern infrastructure, are available in the United States. Moreover, with a population of only approximately 28 million people, there appears little likelihood of Canada sustaining or attracting more foreign investors, since NAFTA allows unimpeded investment and trade. Indeed, even domestic Canadian parts firms have recognized the inescapable impediments associated with sustaining a Canadian manufacturing base in the context of an open North American trade and investment market, including more expensive land, tighter labour regulations, and higher taxes in Canada and have started to relocate production south of the border in increasing numbers. For example, between January 1989 (when the Free Trade Agreement with the United States was implemented) and

February 1991, Canada lost 289,000 manufacturing sector jobs. Even Canadian government officials acknowledge that these losses are permanent (*Macleans* 1991a: 36).

This problem is exemplified in the auto industry, where Ford and GM have already transferred jobs to Mexico and Canadian auto parts representatives concede that domestic parts suppliers are likely to relocate to Mexico with the signing of NAFTA (*Macleans* 1991b: 43). Perhaps the biggest Canadian fear during the NAFTA negotiations was that, added to these structural impediments to sustaining Canadian investment, would be an institutional factor if the 1965 Auto Pact was scrapped. Its terms protected Canadian jobs through domestic content requirements (*Macleans* 1991b: 43).[27] This fear did not materialize, although there is still reason for worry as the realities of the North American car market, which is dominated by the US, mean that the US is a more attractive location for new investment. There is always the potential for additional job loss or foregone investment in Canada. As auto assembly is Canada's largest direct and indirect manufacturing employer, this is a very real concern.

In the North American context, therefore, Canada faces a situation comparable to, if not potentially worse than, Britain's in the European context. There are advantages to maintaining an open admission of foreign direct investors when a country has strong domestic firms and the state "manages" those foreign producers as the Germans did. The result was the creation of a stable base for those domestic firms so that they could eventually compete in a more open environment. There are, conversely, advantages to protection where a state insulates its domestic firms, which thereby generate artificial profits such as in France and Italy. At least when companies like Fiat and Renault eventually had to compete, they could organize the transition to a more competitive base, which Fiat, for example, did successfully in the early 1980s.

The structure of the Canadian industry, however, more resembles the contemporary British one because Canada has no major indigenous producer to protect and is, therefore, fully reliant on foreign investors. Canada does, like Britain, have a traditionally competitive domestic parts sector but, in the new investment climate created by NAFTA, those firms are likely to come under serious challenge because of the labour advantages offered by relocating to Mexico, and the infrastructural and market-access advantages offered by investing in the United States. At least Britain offers certain distinct linguistic characteristics that some investors might find advantageous in the EC. But there are no features to Canadian investment that are not replicated more competitively in the United States.

CONCLUSION

This chapter has outlined three forms of state regulation of foreign direct investors in the European context, and the implications of the resulting policies, as a way of contemplating the present North American situation. The European examples highlighted some of the advantages and disadvantages of allowing free access by foreign direct investors. The British permitted unimpeded access. This generated significant employment and balance-of-payments benefits for an extended period (at a cost to Britain's autonomy), but eventually generated a crisis when those investors withdrew their manufacturing base and there was no domestic firm left to replace them. Some of this lost British employment was transferred to other advanced industrial states because they had what business defined as "more reasonable" labour regulations and a closer proximity to markets. Much of this employment, however, moved to semi-peripheral countries in the context of the EC, such as Spain, which has annually manufactured more cars than Britain since the early 1980s.

Canada now faces a comparable problem. In North America, it is the "semi-peripheral" Mexicans who will be the primary beneficiaries of NAFTA if purely market forces are left to determine investment decisions regarding location. Although these jobs may not be the type that the Mexicans ideally want in the short term, because they will be primarily low-skilled and low-paid, they do represent export-oriented employment, which is critical to a country with both a burgeoning population and a budget deficit. These jobs will certainly be created by US firms transferring jobs from Canada, probably by Japanese firms, and quite possibly by European firms seeking a North American manufacturing base for US sales. Indeed, such European firms may follow Volkswagen's example by exporting components from Mexico to Europe as well as the United States (*Automotive News* 1988a). To the Mexicans, who lack an indigenous producer, foreign investment is therefore better than no investment, even if it involves sacrificing a degree of national autonomy.

Comparably, the Americans may benefit from increased foreign investment because of infrastructural advantages and market proximity, although I reiterate that the term "benefit" has a rather more ambiguous meaning here because foreign investors are likely to eventually displace the market share of domestic firms. The pattern of investment to date suggests that traditionally conservative Japanese firms are likely to expand their US facilities, because the high productivity rates at those plants means that they can compete with Mexican production by the Big Three, despite the disparity in wages.

The behaviour of the Canadian state, however, represents an example of the triumph of ideology over rationality—in this case liberal ideology—that defines economic interaction as positive-sum.[28] Evidence and logic indicate that an unbridled trilateral free trade agreement provides little of benefit in the automotive sector, and reduces Canada to a narrowly defined role in the provision of raw materials. With a relatively small domestic market and only Auto Pact guarantees for its manufacturing employment in the auto sector, the situation might become one where Canadians look back with fond memories to the time when their industrial base was described as an American subsidiary. Advocates applaud the potentially rehabilitative effects of integration; while it may bolster the Mexican economy by creating investment and employment in its auto sector (despite admittedly reducing Mexico's autonomy by increasing its propensity toward dependent development) and may give the US auto firms a short-lived boost, it holds little of promise for Canada's auto industry. Unless the Canadian state wants to create a new, indigenous, and highly mechanized auto manufacturer that can compete against other firms, as the Germans, Italians, and French once did, it risks the disappearance of its manufacturing base in a pivotal sector.

NOTES

1. See, for example, Keohane's comments on why American decision-makers sponsored the formation of the EC (1984: 149).

2. See, for example, Conybeare (1992). For a more popularized, pessimistic view on the implications of the breakdown of the GATT negotiations and the possibility of a return to the situation of the 1930s, see Farnsworth (1990).

3. For an extensive analysis of state policies toward foreign direct investment in the first half of the twentieth century, see S. Reich (1990).

4. For an example of trade restrictions designed to encourage foreign direct investment, see S. Reich 1989a.

5. Such a view obviously contrasts with many of the assumptions of regime theory, where the primary purpose of trade negotiations is to sustain free trade arrangements rather than organize their restraint in an orderly manner. See, for example, Lipson (1983: 236).

6. It is interesting to note that in the fall of 1990, in the middle of the Gulf War Crisis, George Bush attached enough importance to the issue of a regional trade zone to conduct an extensive visit to several Latin American states specifically to promote the extension of a hemispheric trade zone incorporating Latin America.

7. See, for example, *Economist*, 1990a: 61; 1990b: 63.

8. The classic liberal books on the positive effects of integration include Haas (1958), and Lindberg and Scheingold (1970). For a more critical assessment of the distributive effects of unification, see Markovits and Reich (1991).

9. The liberal view was expressed to me in an interview I conducted on 13 May 1990 with Schunichi Hiraki, an official in the Japanese Treasury who was on leave and working as Director of Planning and Research at the Foundation for Advanced Information and Research (FAIR) in Japan. This view was more formally expressed in the "Final Report of the Research Group on the Economies of Asian Countries," Committee for Asia-Pacific Economic Research, FAIR, May 1991. For more critical responses, see, for example, Widyahartono (1987: 63-74), Hoong (1987: 1102-1103), and Robinson (1985: 195-225).

10. For an expression of the latter view, see Roos et al. (1984: 181).

11. This section draws heavily on prior research work discussed more extensively in S. Reich (1989b).

[12] See, for example, *New York Times* (1988 Section IV 4) and *Automotive News* (1988d).

[13] For a description of the role and financial structure of the IRI, see Posner and Woolf (1967: 43-53). For a succinct description of IRI origins and functions under fascism, see Allen and Stevenson (1974: 217-222).

[14] For a discussion of the fiscal relationship between Daimler-Benz and the Deutsche Bank, see Pohl, Habeth and Breninghaus (1986). For a discussion of the political implications of this relationship, see Roth (1986: 28-40).

[15] This controversial claim is the subject of extensive analysis and its validity is documented in S. Reich (1990).

[16] See "Organizational and Management Basic Data Book: Ford of Germany," Cologne, Germany, Fordwerke AG 1951-1952, AR-75-63-430:93, Ford Industrial Files. In the late 1920s, Ford and General Motors occupied positions in the German market that were opposite those they each held in the British market, where Ford was a more significant force as a producer and General Motors' subsidiary was of relatively minor importance.

[17] For a systematic comparison, see S. Reich (1990: 246-303).

[18] For a more extensive discussion of these points, see S. Reich (1989a).

[19] For a fuller discussion of this point, see Krauss and Reich (1992).

[20] Note that the exception to this comment is the case of Honda, which had earlier invested in the US, ironically in an effort to reduce MITI's influence on the company rather than from any consideration about prospective protectionism.

[21] For a full examination of the effects of a policy of national treatment on prosperity in the auto industry, see S. Reich (1990).

[22] See also chapters by Holmes and Shapiro in this volume, which discuss the Mexican auto decrees. For an extensive discussion of the history of the Mexican automotive industry, see Bennett and Sharpe (1985), USITC (1990), and Jenkins (1977).

[23] See Salinas (1991).

[24] See *Business Week* (1989: 32). Note the mitigating fact that Mexico has no major domestically-owned manufacturing producer, only parts producers, unlike all the other major manufacturing nations that employed protectionist measures.

[25] For a discussion of historical labour policy in the auto industry, see Roxborough (1984).

[26] For figures, see Middlebrook (1991: 283-284).

[27] For a description and analysis of the terms of the Auto Pact, see Beigie (1970).

[28] For a discussion of the role of ideology in decision-making, see S. Reich (1990: 30-54).

REFERENCES

Allen, Kevin, and Stevenson, Andrew. 1974. *An Introduction to the Italian Economy.* London: Robertson.

Automotive News. 1988a. Mexico to Supply VWs for US. February 15.

Automotive News. 1988b. 7-Year Slump Strangles Mexico. September 26.

Automotive News. 1988c. Mexico Expects Boom in Exports to Continue. March 7.

Automotive News. 1988d. Britain, France Battle over Nissan Local Content. October 10.

Beigie, Carl. 1970. *The Canada-US Automotive Agreement: An Evaluation.* Washington, D.C.: National Planning Association.

Bennett, Douglas C., and Sharpe, Kenneth E. 1985. *Transnational Corporations versus the State: The Political Economy of the Mexican Auto Industry.* Princeton N.J.: Princeton University Press.

Bennett, Mark. 1986. Public Policy and Industrial Development: The Case of the Mexican Auto Parts Industry. Boulder, Colo.: Westview Press.

Business Week. 1989. A Free-for-All for Carmakers South of the Border. October 16: 32.

Business Week. 1990a. Inching toward a North American Market. June 25: 40-41.

Business Week. 1990b. Is Free Trade with Mexico Good or Bad for the US? November 12: 112-13.

Church, Roy. 1979. *Herbert Austin: The British Motor Car Industry to 1941.* London: Europa Publications.

Conybeare, John. 1992. The International Political Economy of 1992: Free Trade or Fortress Europe? Paper prepared for The 1992 Project and the European Community.

Cutler, Tony; Haslam, Colin; Williams, John; and Williams, Karel. 1989. *1992—The Struggle for Europe: A Critical Evaluation of the European Community.* New York: Berg.

Economist. 1990a. Bids and Deals. February 10: 61.

Economist. 1990b. Business this Week. March 17: 63.

Economist. 1988a. The American Car Industry's Own Goals. February 6: 69.

Economist. 1988b. Motor Industry Survey. October 15.

Farnsworth, Clyde. 1990. Planting the Seed of a Trade War. *New York Times*: December 10.

Fridenson, Patrick. 1981. French Automobile Marketing, 1890-1970. In *The Development of Mass Marketing*, eds. Akio Okochi and Koichi Shimokawa. Tokyo: University of Tokyo Press.

Greenhouse, Stephen. 1989. Europe's Agonizing over Japan. *New York Times*: April 30.

Haas, Ernst. 1958. *The Uniting of Europe: Political, Social and Economic Forces, 1950-1957*. Stanford: Stanford University Press.

Hoong, Khong Kim. 1987. Malaysia Japan Relations in the 1980s. *Asian Survey* Vol. XXVII, 10: October.

Industry, Science and Technology Canada (ISTC). 1988. *Industry Profile: Light Motor Vehicles*. Ottawa: Minister of Supply and Services.

Jenkins, Rhys Owen. 1977. *Dependent Industrialization in Latin America: The Automotive Industry in Argentina, Chile and Mexico*. New York: Praeger.

Jones, Daniel T. 1981. *Maturity and Crisis in the European Car Industry: Structural Change and Public Policy*. Lewis, Sussex: European Research Centre.

Journal of Commerce and Commercial. 1990. Allure of US Sites is Tough to Resist. June 13.

Keohane, Robert. 1984. *After Hegomony*. Princeton, N.J.: Princeton University Press.

Krauss, Ellis, and Reich, Simon. 1992. Ideology, Interests and the American Executive: Towards a Theory of Foreign Competition and Manufacturing Trade Policy. *International Organization* 46,4: 857-97.

Kuttner, Robert. 1991. A Vote for Free Trade with Mexico is a Vote against Free Trade. *Business Week*, May 6: 18.

Lindberg, Leon, and Scheingold, Stuart A. 1970. *Europe's Would be Polity: Patterns of Change in the European Community*. Englewood Cliffs, N.J.: Prentice Hall.

Lipson, Charles. 1983. The Transformation of Trade: The Sources and Effects of Regime Change. In *International Regimes*, ed. Stephen Krasner. Ithaca, N.Y.: Cornell University Press.

Macleans. 1991a. Giving Up, Moving Out. March 18: 36.

Macleans. 1991b. Reopening the Trade Wounds. March 18: 43.

Markovits, Andrei S., and Reich, Simon. 1991. Modell Deutschland and the New Europe. *Telos* 89, 1: 45-64.

Meyer III, Steven. 1981. *The Five Dollar Day: Labour Management and Social Control in the Ford Motor Company 1908-1921*. Albany, N.Y.: State University of New York Press.

Michalet, Charles-Albert. 1974. France. In *Big Business and the State: Changing Relations in Western Europe*, ed. Raymond Vernon. Cambridge, Mass.: Harvard University Press.

Middlebrook, Kevin. 1991. The Politics of Industrial Restructuring. *Comparative Politics*, 23,3: 275-97.

Nevins, Alan, and Hill, Frank E. 1962. *Ford: Decline and Rebirth 1933-1962*. New York: Scribner.

New York Times. 1975. January 15: 27.

New York Times. 1988. English-Made Nissans in Dispute. November 7.

Palumbo, E.J. 1948. Germany 1948: Economic and Political Review, Survey of German Vehicle Industry. Appendix Exhibit B, 15 April, AR-75-63-430:86, Ford Industrial Archives: 4-12.

Pohl, Hans; Habeth, Stephanie; and Breninghaus, Beate. 1986. *Die Daimler-Benz AG in den Jahren 1933 bis 1945*. Stuttgart: Zeitschrift für Unternehmensgeschichte, Franz Steiner Verlag.

Posner, M.V., and Woolf, Stuart J. 1967. *Italian Public Enterprise*. London: Duckworth.

Prodi, Romano. 1974. Italy. In *Big Business and the State: Changing Relations in Western Europe*, ed. Raymond Vernon. Cambridge, Mass: Harvard University Press.

Reich, Robert B. 1990. Who is Us?. *Harvard Business Review* 68, January-February: 53-64.

Reich, Simon. 1989a. Between Production and Protection: Reagan and the Negotiation of the VER for the Automobile Industry. Pew Foundation Case Studies in International Negotiation, No. 10, Graduate School of Public and International Affairs, University of Pittsburgh.

____. 1989b. Roads to Follow: Regulating Direct Foreign Investment. *International Organization*: 43, 4: 543-84.

____. 1990. *The Fruits of Fascism: Postwar Prosperity in Historical Perspective*. Ithaca, N.Y.: Cornell University Press.

Robinson, Wayne. 1985. Imperialism, Dependency and Peripheral Industrialization: The Case of Japan and Indonesia. In *South East Asia: Essays in the Political Economy of Structural Change*, eds. Richard Higgott and Richard Robinson. London: Routledge and Kegan Paul.

Roos, Daniel et al. 1984. *The Future of the Automobile*. Cambridge, Mass: MIT Press.

Roth, Karl Heinz. 1986. Der Weg zum guten Stern des "Dritten Reichs": Schlaglichter auf die Geschichte der Daimler-Benz AG und ihrer Vorläufer (1890-1945). In *Das Daimler-Benz Buch: Ein*

Rüstungskonzern im Tausendjährigen Reich. Nördlingen: Delphi Politik.

Rothstein, Richard. 1991. Exporting Jobs and Pollution to Mexico. *New Perspectives Quarterly*, 8, 1: 32-35.

Roxborough, Ian. 1984. Labour in the Mexican Motor Vehicle Industry. In *The Political Economy of the Latin American Motor Vehicle Industry*, eds. Rich Kronisch and Kenneth Mericle. Cambridge, Mass.: MIT Press.

Salinas de Gortari, Carlos. 1991. North American Free Trade: Mexico's Route to Upward Mobility. *New Perspectives Quarterly*, 8, 1: 4-9.

Sarti, Roland. 1971. *Fascism and the Industrial Leadership in Italy 1919-1940.* Berkeley, California: University of California Press.

Shaiken, Harley, and Herzenberg, Stephen. 1987. *Automation and Global Production: Automobile Engine Production in Mexico, the United States, and Canada.* San Diego: University of California, Center for US-Mexican Studies.

Tolchin, Martin, and Tolchin, Susan. 1988. *Buying into America.* New York: Times Books.

US International Trade Commission Publication 2275 (USITC) 1990. *Review of Trade and Investment Liberalization Measures by Mexico and Prospects for Future United States-Mexican Relations: Phase I: Recent Trade and Investment Reforms Undertaken by Mexico and Implications for the United States.* Washington, D.C.

Weintraub, Sidney. 1991. A Vote for Free Trade is a Vote against Protectionism. *New Perspectives Quarterly* 8,1: 26-28.

Wells, Louis T. 1974. Automobiles. In *Big Business and the State: Changing Relations in Western Europe*, ed. Raymond Vernon. Cambridge, Mass: Harvard University Press.

Widyahartono, Robert. 1987. Indonesia-Japan Relations in the 1980s. In *Asian Survey* 37,10: 1102-03.

Wilkins, Mira, and Hill, Frank. 1964. *American Business Abroad: Ford on Six Continents.* Detroit, Mich.: Wayne State University Press.

Wilks, Stephen. 1984. *Industrial Policy and the Motors Industry.* Manchester: Manchester University Press.

Womack, James. 1987. Prospects for the US-Mexican Relationship in the Motor Vehicle Sector. In *The United States and Mexico, Face to Face with New Technology*, eds. Cathryn L. Thorup et al. New Brunswick: Transaction Books.

4 THE DETERMINANTS OF TRADE AND INVESTMENT FLOWS IN LDC AUTO INDUSTRIES:

The Cases of Brazil and Mexico*

Helen Shapiro

INTRODUCTION

The automobile has become a symbol of national competitiveness and conflict in international trade. The automobile industry was one of the first manufacturing industries to open offshore assembly plants and to be characterized as a global oligopoly. In the last decade, it has also come to symbolize globalization in the sense that manufacturing and sourcing have become cross-national; firms now penetrate each other's national markets to an unprecedented degree. Firms of different national origins have formed strategic alliances, blurring the definition of a national car, and products and performance standards have become more universal.

The voluminous literature on the industry has focused on the implications of this globalization process for the dominant firms and their home bases in the United States, Japan, and Europe, which account for the largest markets and the bulk of international trade and investment. At the same time, however, a less heralded but no less portentous shift in trade patterns has taken place between these countries and Brazil and Mexico, the two largest motor vehicle

* Portions of this paper appear in "From Import Substitution to Export Promotion in Brazil," in David B. Yoffie, ed., *Beyond Free Trade: Firms, Governments, and Global Competition.* Boston: Harvard Business School Press, May 1993. Copyright 1993 by the President and Fellows of Harvard College; all rights reserved. Reprinted by permission of Harvard Business School Press.

producers in Latin America. By the late 1970s, it became increasingly common to find Brazilian- or Mexican-made engines under the hoods of cars manufactured in the United States or Europe. These engine exports were soon followed by finished automobiles manufactured by Fiat, Volkswagen (VW), and Ford, among others.

While transnational auto companies have been manufacturing motor vehicles for the domestic market in both Brazil and Mexico since the early 1960s, only in the 1970s and 1980s did they begin to export significant volumes from these production sites. At the end of the 1970s, Brazil was producing over 900,000 automobiles, but exporting less than 10 percent of them. Over the 1980s, exports as a share of car production grew, albeit erratically, peaking at 41 percent (279,530) in 1987 and settling at 18 percent (119,409) of the 663,383 cars produced in 1990. By 1990, Mexico was the largest exporter of engines to the United States and exported 211,640 cars, predominantly to the United States and Canada.

This chapter will document the shift in the volume and direction of these trade flows in small cars and engines and assess the relative impact of variables relating to firm strategy, government policies, and underlying country characteristics in determining these patterns. It will explore why firms chose these countries as export platforms for these particular products and whether increased exports reflect a structural shift in these national industries or simply a short-run strategy to compensate for weak domestic demand. It will also suggest how firm-specific factors explain the observed variation among firm strategies.

Understanding the changing trade patterns of the Brazilian and Mexican auto industries is important for a number of reasons. They are two of the largest in the periphery, and include most of the industry's major transnational players, several of which have subsidiaries in both countries. Brazil has been home to the world's tenth largest automotive industry. For General Motors (GM), Ford, Volkswagen, and Fiat, which produce virtually all of Brazil's passenger cars, it has also been home to their largest subsidiaries outside of the United States and Europe. Volkswagen established its first offshore facility there in 1954, and Brazil is now the only less-developed country (LDC) in which Fiat produces cars. General Motors, Ford, Chrysler, Volkswagen, and Nissan dominate Mexico's automobile industry, which has been one of the world's fastest growing in recent years. The industry is becoming increasingly integrated into the North American operations of some firms. Today, Mexico is Volkswagen's only production site in North America and the home of Chrysler's only foreign subsidiary. For Brazil and Mexico, the industries are major sources of jobs and foreign exchange; automotive exports accounted for a large share of both countries' record-breaking trade surpluses in the 1980s. Understanding the sources of this export boom is an important step toward explaining how these countries effected such dramatic structural transformations of their economies more generally.

The Brazilian and Mexican experiences also shed light on what may happen to national industries when the domestic and external conditions under which they were originally established change, and how the legacy of previous investment and government policy might influence firm strategy with respect to new investments and global sourcing patterns. Both of these auto industries were initially established under import-substitution strategies to serve protected domestic markets. Foreign investment flowed into domestic production at a time when firms remained multimarket, rather than globally inte-grated, operations. The conditions that allowed these countries to attract foreign investment have since changed. The industry's structure and the nature of international competition have been transformed. Foreign subsidiaries potentially become part of a global strategy and no longer only serve individual, unconnected national markets. On the domestic front, market stagnation accompanied the debt crisis in Brazil and Mexico, forcing both debtor nations to become net exporters in the 1980s, thereby reversing recent historical trends.

Due to the "stickiness" and long-run nature of investment in the auto industry, investments made in one time period affect the deci-sions firms make about exports in the next. Since firms do not auto-matically view these investments as sunk costs, their subsequent strategies might be different than they would be in the absence of these prior investment decisions. Would firms have chosen Brazil and Mexico as bases for export in the 1970s and 1980s if they were not already participating in the local market?

A comparison of Brazil and Mexico also illustrates how the legacy of specific government policy might influence the manner and extent to which national industries become integrated into global trade flows. Within similar protectionist frameworks, each country initially adopted different policies with respect to domestic-content requirements and regulations on foreign ownership and vertical integration. These policy regimes played a role in shaping the ultimate structure of the domestic industries and in determining the types of products manufactured. They also led to different incentive systems for exports. Therefore, subsidiaries in each country were in a different position to confront the domestic and external changes discussed above. In this context, the overall regulatory regime, and not simply trade policies, must be included among other country-specific factors such as location, macro-economy, and market size as potential influences on the nature and direction of trade.

The chapter begins with a brief overview of the auto industry's changing global structure from World War II to the present. This is followed by an account of the process by which the Brazilian and Mexican industries were established in the 1950s and 1960s. After a brief comparative summary, the major trends in the two industries since 1973 are analyzed, with special emphasis on firm strategies. The chapter concludes with some remarks on the implications of this study.

COMPETITION AND TRADE IN AUTOMOBILES SINCE WORLD WAR II

In the late 1940s and early 1950s, US and European automobile companies faced sellers markets at home as a result of the repressed demand that had accumulated during the war. Competition intensified by the mid-1950s, when the repressed demand had been satisfied and profits on domestic operations fell. Firms in the United States and Europe placed greater emphasis on overseas expansion, either through exports, expanding existing subsidiaries, or creating new ones. In the United States, changing market conditions bankrupted the independents, leaving GM, Ford, and Chrysler in control of 95 percent of the car market by 1955 (Jenkins 1987:29). In Europe, the creation of the European Economic Community and the gradual reduction of tariffs on imported vehicles created additional pressures on the slowing of demand growth and increased production capacity; the volume of intra-regional trade in motor vehicles nearly quadrupled between 1958 and 1965 (Bennett and Sharpe 1985a:58). Although national markets still remained remarkably segmented, with imports accounting for a small share of total sales, this period witnessed the first cross-penetration of producer-country markets; before the war, most exports had gone to non-producing countries. The protected, relatively faster-growing European market also became more significant for US firms, which had first invested in local manufacturing capacity in the 1920s and 1930s when European countries established tariffs to protect their national automotive industries.

The recovery of the European industry also led to increased competition in the US market. Imports jumped from less than 1 percent of sales in 1955 to 10 percent in 1959. This was due to reduced productivity differentials and European firms' ability to fill the small car market niche vacated by the independents. The import share would decline when the Big Three introduced their own compact models in the early 1960s, but would bounce back to 10 percent by 1968 (Jenkins 1987:30-31).

Competition also increased for third-country markets. Trade patterns changed as colonial preferences were eliminated and geographical proximity became less important. Heightened interest in these markets also reflected the expectations firms had of their future profitability, and their attempts to maintain a presence in markets where domestic manufacture was being considered. In addition to Brazil and Mexico, many importing countries, including Argentina, India, Australia, and South Africa, began to restrict auto imports in the 1950s and 1960s. Coming at a time when competition for foreign markets was intensifying and when the dominance of US firms was being challenged, these countries had relatively more bargaining power to force firms to set up manufacturing facilities within their borders.

The auto industry of the 1950s was characterized by nationally based firms that competed in third markets via exports of finished vehicles, with the exception of US firms that had established overseas manufacturing or assembly operations. Most national industries were protected with high tariff walls, and markets and products were distinct. Over time, tariffs began to fall, and the 1960s witnessed mergers and industrial concentration in Europe, accompanied by growing commercial links among European firms.

On the eve of the first oil shock, rebalanced competition had been established between US and European firms. Trade and investment in automobiles had increased within Europe and across the Atlantic. Regional blocks had developed, and firms still followed multimarket strategies.

This relatively stable oligopoly was challenged in the 1970s by rising oil prices and the emergence of powerful new competitors from Japan. At the same time, by 1973, as a result of the 1962 GATT negotiations, the tariff on autos was down to 10.9 percent in Europe, 3 percent in the United States, and 6.4 percent in Japan. While Japanese exports to the United States in the early seventies had come primarily at the expense of European small cars, that situation changed as Japanese cars became increasingly competitive and took away market share from US firms. They posed an increasing threat in Europe as well.

Countries responded to Japan's growing share of world production and trade by imposing either fixed or voluntary export caps on Japanese imports. In Europe, this occurred first on a country-by-country basis, and was followed by a European Economic Community agreement on the rate of growth in Japanese imports. Firms responded by restructuring their operations in an attempt to cut costs and downsize their product lines.

The search for low-cost production sites, combined with the emergence of new product lines, led to a new wave of foreign direct investment in peripheral producing countries such as Spain and South Korea. Firms began to integrate their global operations and products became more standardized. These restructuring and globalization processes would open new opportunities for Brazil and Mexico as well.

INSTALLATION OF THE BRAZILIAN AND MEXICAN AUTO INDUSTRIES

In the 1950s and 1960s, a combination of sector-specific government policies and the dynamics of oligopolistic competition led to the creation of domestic auto production capacity in Brazil and Mexico. Through the installation of domestic productive capacity, both countries hoped to save on the costs associated with imports. Each faced recurrent foreign exchange constraints, with automotive products appearing at the top of their import bills. The costs of imported cars and trucks included not only scarce foreign exchange but the rents paid to the importing firms and the positive production and technological externalities associated with the industry.

In each case, the auto programs were part of general import-substituting industrialization efforts in which the industry was to play the role of leading sector by attracting foreign capital and technology and generating linkages to complementary sectors. The government planners also hoped that the transnational firms would transfer technology and skills to the still incipient industrial work force. In effect, they hoped that the auto firms would be forced to create the factors that would increase the productivity of their industrial sector as a whole and attract new investment to the country.[1]

BRAZIL 1956-1973

Brazilian planners did not expect auto firms to invest voluntarily in manufacturing capacity. Foreign firms had been assembling completely- or semi-knocked-down kits (CKDs or SKDs) in Brazil since the 1920s. Even though the Brazilian market was the largest in Latin America, accounting for 25 percent of the 2.7 million vehicles in circulation in 1955 (Guimarães 1980:173),[2] these firms had resisted Brazilian attempts to significantly increase the domestic content shares of their imported vehicles and move into full-scale manufacturing. The Brazilians concluded that they would only do so if given no alternative but to abandon the market.

A five-year plan was promulgated through executive decree in late 1956 and early 1957. Its basic approach was effectively to insulate the sector by closing the market to finished vehicles and guaranteeing it subsidized access to foreign exchange to import necessary components and pay off foreign financing. In exchange for these foreign exchange and tax subsidies, which amounted to 48 percent of the total invested in imported equipment and components (Shapiro 1993), firms had to meet an exceptionally ambitious domestic content schedule. The requirements increased annually, and, by July 1960, trucks and utility vehicles were to contain 90 percent domestic content, and jeeps and cars 95 percent.

Eleven firms ultimately participated in the plan. Three were controlled by Brazilian capital, two were fifty-fifty joint ventures, and six were controlled by, or were wholly-owned subsidiaries of, foreign firms. Total investment by the terminal sector in imported capital equipment within the five-year program came to US $145 million. By 1962, five years after the plan had gone into effect, 191,194 vehicles were rolling off Brazilian assembly lines annually. By 1961, the share of domestic content in vehicle production had reached 93 percent of weight and 87 percent of value.

A disaggregation of the industry's performance reveals that US and European firms initially responded to Brazil's auto program in different ways. Chrysler, facing hard times at home, chose to stay out of the market altogether. Despite appeals by the Brazilians, Ford and GM submitted projects to produce trucks but not automobiles. These were the firms with the longest history in the country; Ford opened the first assembly plant in 1919 and dominated car sales before World War II. European cars only gained a foothold in the market after the war as a result of Brazil's dollar shortage and European government pressure on auto companies to export. Apparently, Ford was only concerned with matching the investments of GM and Chrysler, its US competitors, and not those of the Europeans (Shapiro 1991).

No European company had assembly capacity in Brazil until after 1953, when the import of assembled cars was prohibited. After that date, all vehicles had to be imported as CKDs or SKDs. Volkswagen responded by setting up an assembly plant in 1954. At the time of the 1956 plan, VW did not have manufacturing facilities anywhere outside of Germany and was financially weak. As a special property of the German government, it was forbidden from raising capital through public shares until 1959, but it was also the recipient of various forms of state support. The company was the market leader at home and was seeking new markets abroad. The Brazilian subsidiary (in which a Brazilian partner held 20 percent) submitted plans to produce a minivan and the Beetle. With Ford and GM out of the picture, VW had virtually no competition in the automobile market. By 1968, its share of car sales was almost 80 percent.

The industry entered a period of crisis and consolidation in the early 1960s. Firms had built ahead of demand and the industry was plagued with overcapacity. The investment that was initiated under the five-year plan was coming on-stream. The repressed demand from the 1950s had been satisfied. Future growth would now depend on replacement demand and new demand resulting from increased incomes, population growth, etc.

The expected demand did not materialize in the short run, however. The market shrank with the downturn in overall economic activity in 1963 and 1964, and disintegrated when the military implemented an austerity program after the coup of 1964. Smaller, financially weaker firms, which had been able to survive until that point due to protection, repressed demand, and rationed market shares (through foreign exchange rationing), did not survive these lean years.

By 1968, the original eleven firms had shrunk to eight. Only those controlled by transnational capital remained. It was at this time of consolidation that Ford and GM entered the passenger car market by investing in new production facilities and absorbing existing firms. They became the second and third largest automobile producers after Volkswagen.[3] They aimed their products at the replacement market for the growing middle class. Production became even more concentrated. In 1960, the four top firms—Willys-Overland, VW, General Motors, and Ford—produced 78.5 percent of all vehicles. By 1968, VW, GM, and Ford controlled 89 percent of the market; VW's share alone was 55 percent.

The newly-structured industry, growing at rates of over 20 percent a year, led the Brazilian "economic miracle" of 1968-73. Demand for cars boomed in response to income concentration and new consumer credit instruments; wage compression and the repression of trade unions reduced labour costs. A new wave of investments accompanied this growth spurt. The projects approved by the Industrial Development Council from 1967-73 anticipated investments of US $ 1.3 billion, more than half of which was approved in 1973 alone (Guimarães 1988:5). Exports were virtually nonexistent, amounting to only 2.5 percent of automobile production in 1973. Firms had invested exclusively to serve the domestic market.

Attracted by Brazil's estimated market potential of 1.5 million vehicles by 1985, Fiat entered the market in 1973 and began production in 1976. Fiat overcame the disadvantages of being a late-comer to the Brazilian market by negotiating an attractive incentive package with the state of Minas Gerais, which had been trying unsuccessfully to attract an auto plant since the 1950s. The entire auto complex was concentrated around the city of Sao Paulo. The state government of Minas guaranteed the necessary infrastructure, provided fiscal incentives, and participated in loan offerings to Fiat. The company did receive some incentives from the federal government, but the state subsidies were decisive.

MEXICO 1962-1973

Motivated by similar concerns for industrial development, Mexico issued its automotive decree in 1962. The Brazilian and Mexican auto plans had much in common. Nevertheless, several important differences between the two countries led to some variation in strategy and outcome. To begin, as the "first mover" in Latin America, Brazil had established a precedent for the rest of region. That experiment not only provided valuable data for the Mexican government but influenced the strategies of firms in Mexico as well. Second, Mexico's long border with the United States presented the country with different constraints. Unlike Brazil, its import substitution process took place in the context of macroeconomic stability and a fixed and unified exchange rate regime, which precluded the use of exchange rate differentials and overvaluation as a means of subsidizing the industry. Third, with a smaller population and per capita income level, Mexico did not possess the market potential of Brazil. Finally, the starting points of their respective industries were different. On the one hand, unlike Brazil, some Mexican-owned firms had a strong market presence. Fabricas Auto-Mex, for example, had been assembling vehicles under licence from Chrysler since 1938. It remained a wholly-owned family business until 1959, when Chrysler bought a third of its stock. In 1960, its market share was 25 percent. On the other hand, the only foreign firms assembling vehicles were from the United States; no European or Japanese firm had yet entered the market. In general, Mexico took a more nationalistic posture toward foreign capital.

The first Mexican Automotive Decree was issued on August 23, 1962. Besides protecting the market from imported vehicles, the government offered fiscal incentives such as exemptions from taxes and from import duties on imported equipment and components. Mexico relied more heavily on quantitative restrictions than did Brazil and imposed quotas on imports and production. The terminal sector was exempted from Mexico's standard foreign investment regulations, which restricted foreign firms to minority ownership positions. A requirement of majority domestic ownership was imposed on the supplier industry, however. In addition, firms were restricted to assembling vehicles, fabricating engines, and manufacturing components that they had produced prior to the decree; further vertical integration was prohibited.

Domestic content requirements were less stringent than in Brazil. As of September 1964, 60 percent of a car's value, based on direct cost, was to be manufactured in Mexico. The power train (the engine and transmission) was to be included in this 60 percent. By setting domestic content levels at 90-95 percent of a vehicle's weight, Brazil had ensured that body stamping would be done in the country. In general, the Mexicans were more concerned about relative costs and inflation, and the largest economies of scale are in the stamping process. Moreover, with so much contact with the United States, Mexican consumers were exposed to the frequent model changes made in Detroit. A domestic content level of 60 percent allowed for body stampings to be imported and facilitated frequent model changes. This benefitted US firms, who relied more heavily on annual body changes than did the European and Japanese firms at the time.

All together, eleven firms had received permission to produce automobiles by 1964. These included three wholly-owned subsidiaries of foreign firms, one joint venture with Mexican majority ownership, and six Mexican firms, one of which was state-owned. By 1970, the ownership structure of the industry had considerably changed. The foreign-owned subsidiaries of Ford, GM, and Nissan remained. Of the five privately-owned Mexican firms, three had ceased operations. A fourth, after getting permission to manufacture Volkswagens, was bought by the German company in 1964. The last one was divided between American Motors (40 percent equity) and the Mexican government (60 percent). The joint venture remained under Mexican control, but Chrysler increased its equity share from 33 percent to 45 percent in 1968. As in Brazil, the consolidation and denationalization of the industry resulted from the differentiated access of firms to financing and technology; in the Mexican case, easier access to imported parts was also a contributing factor (Bennett and Sharpe 1985:128).

Nevertheless, the Mexican industry had not consolidated to the same extent as the Brazilian manufacturers had by this time. In 1976, the top three firms accounted for 57 percent of all vehicles produced in Mexico; the top four for 70 percent. (The corresponding figures in Brazil were 90 percent and 95 percent.) The difference is due to such factors as: the severe recession in Brazil, which exacerbated the cyclic fluctuations in the industry and forced many financially weak firms to shut down or sell out; the Mexican production quotas, which guaranteed firms some market share; and the Mexican government's commitment to prop up domestic firms as counterweights to the foreign subsidiaries.

US companies played an active role in the establishment of the Mexican auto industry. Ford in particular showed an early willingness to begin domestic production in Mexico when it appeared that the government would close the market to imports. In contrast to

Table 1
Mexico's Motor Vehicle Production
1950-1989

| | Units | | |
| | | Commercial | |
Year	Cars	Vehicles	Total
1950			21,575
1955			32,275
1960			49,807
1961			62,563
1962			66,637
1963			69,135
1964			90,752
1965			96,654
1966			113,807
1967			126,365
1968			143,478
1969			165,164
1970	133,218	59,623	192,841
1971	153,412	57,428	210,840
1972	163,005	66,761	229,766
1973	200,147	85,366	285,513
1974	248,574	102,181	350,755
1975	237,118	123,560	360,678
1976	212,549	112,430	324,979
1977	187,637	93,176	280,813
1978	242,519	141,609	384,128
1979	280,049	164,377	444,426
1980	303,056	186,950	490,006
1981	355,497	241,621	597,118
1982	300,579	172,058	472,637
1983	207,137	78,348	285,485
1984	244,704	98,994	343,698
1985	297,064	101,128	398,192
1986	208,660	132,392	341,052
1987	277,398	117,860	395,258
1988	353,900	158,843	512,743
1989	438,633	202,643	641,276

Source: AMIA.

Brazil, both Ford and GM went into car production immediately in Mexico.

The Mexican motor vehicle industry grew at an average annual rate of 18 percent from 1962-74, almost twice as fast as the manufacturing sector as a whole. In 1973, it exported 9 percent of all cars produced and 7 percent of total vehicle production. Although these export shares were greater than Brazil's, they were not enough to compensate for the sector's imports which, due to the relatively low domestic content requirements, increased along with production volumes. A government resolution issued in 1969 tried to address the growing trade deficit by rewarding exporting firms with larger production quotas. While exports showed some growth, reaching 16 percent of imports by 1975, they came nowhere close to the 50 percent target set for that date (Moreno Brid 1988:6). A 1972 Decree reconfirmed the timetable for compensating imports with exports and added the additional caveat that, by 1974, 40 percent of a firm's exports would have to consist of components supplied by Mexican suppliers with 60 percent Mexican capital. This too failed to bring the sector's trade into balance.

SUMMARY

By the mid-1960s, both Brazil and Mexico had halted virtually all vehicle imports and firms that had previously supplied these markets through exports now did so through local production. Their success in attracting foreign direct investment was due in great part to the nature of oligopolistic competition in the industry at the time. Both countries restricted auto imports when competition for foreign markets was intensifying, particularly in Europe. Firms responded by following each other to these new markets. Brazil and Mexico would have had less bargaining power vis-à-vis the transnational firms if they had faced a "tighter" oligopoly or had they still been confronting the virtual duopoly of Ford and GM that prevailed before World War II.

Outcomes were not completely determined by oligopolistic firm behaviour, however. Government policy was critical for risk reduction. Subsidies not only significantly reduced the cost of capital investment, but guaranteed a return if the market had not materialized. Most importantly, these government automotive programs set the timing of firm investment. A firm's failure to invest during the initial period would have meant sacrificing the financial subsidies and being relatively disadvantaged were it to enter the market at a later date. The extent to which government policy accelerated firm entry is not a trivial point. Timing was everything from the governments' point of view, given the larger objective of jump-starting industrialization and generating productive linkages, rather than protecting domestic firms. In addition, as will be seen, these investments of the 1960s would have ramifications for trade flows in the 1970s and 1980s.

Moreover, structural characteristics unique to each country, combined with distinct industrial policies that partly reflected those characteristics, led to differences in firm investment strategies and industrial structure and would ultimately create variations between the countries' trade patterns. Brazil had a more sophisticated industrial infrastructure and greater market potential. Its trading partners and sources of capital flows were relatively diverse. Mexico's foreign trade was tied to the United States and its economy was subject to macroeconomic constraints that Brazil evaded. As a result, Brazil was in a stronger position to require firms to build cars with very high levels of domestic content. The market size would allow for greater economies of scale, and the inflationary impact of high-priced automobiles could be accommodated, at least in the short-run. In Mexico, however, firms were less willing to incorporate such high levels of local content. The government was also more concerned about the impact on prices. In addition, the proximity of US firms to suppliers at home made them even more inclined to fight against higher nationalization levels.

Due to these differences, Brazil built up a larger and more sophisticated supplier network. The auto companies were accompanied to Brazil by many of their suppliers from home. High domestic content requirements, combined with policies that banned the import of components and parts for which there were domestically-produced equivalents, insulated the domestic industry from the world. As a result, cars on the street tended to be antiquated as firms changed models infrequently in order to amortize tooling costs. Mexico's lower domestic content allowed firms greater flexibility in production, particularly by allowing metal stampings to be imported. This was important for US firms, for which frequent model change was an important competitive strategy. On the other hand, Mexico's lower domestic content levels also meant that the sector continued to generate trade deficits that grew proportionally with the numbers of vehicles produced.

Mexico's micro-level industrial policies also affected the extent to which firms were willing to substitute local production for imports and the way in which firms competed. Firms were constrained from vertically integrating and could only be minority partners in any independent supplier firm. Some US firms claim that there are some small components that they may have produced in Mexico had they been allowed full control. (Brazil had no limitations on either vertical integration or on foreign investment in the automotive parts sector. As a result, its supply base was more representative of international standards.) These industrial policies also made US firms even less willing to balance trade by increasing domestic content levels. Mexico's decrees also influenced market structure by allocating production quotas and by limiting the vehicle class firms could enter. This limited a firm's ability to compete and increase market share through product diversification.

In 1973, producing over 560,000 automobiles, Brazil appeared to be the one LDC whose industry had a chance of becoming a global competitor. Mexico's industry was trivial in comparison, producing little more than a third as many cars. By 1991, however, Mexico's production would skyrocket and its exports would outstrip Brazil's.

THE SHIFT TO EXPORTS

BRAZIL

At the time of the first oil shock in 1973, 80 percent of the oil consumed in Brazil was imported. Concerned with the balance of trade, the government looked to the auto industry as a potential source of foreign exchange. It shifted the incentive structure toward export promotion, with the aim of generating a positive trade balance at the industry level.

While some export incentives were introduced in the late 1960s, export promotion only gathered steam in the early 1970s under the Special Fiscal Benefits for Exports (BEFIEX) program, which was not unique to the automobile industry. BEFIEX incentives included exemption from taxes on imported capital goods, parts, components, and raw materials. Federal and state value-added and sales taxes were waived on exports. Firms also received a credit equal to these waived taxes that could be used toward taxes due on goods produced for the domestic market. Various drawback schemes were also introduced that allowed firms to import goods for the production of exports that would otherwise be banned.

Each major auto company participated in the BEFIEX program. As a result, investment levels were sustained despite the slowdown in domestic market growth compared to the "miracle" years. Firms adopted different export strategies. Generally, US firms, as represented by Ford and GM, responded to the challenges of the 1970s by automating in the United States and by adopting "world car" strategies. They sought to increase economies of scale and spread research and development costs over more vehicles by increasing product standardization worldwide and by using low-wage production sites as export platforms for engines and components. European firms such as Fiat and VW looked to LDCs as low-cost export bases for finished vehicles to other low-income countries. Vehicle exports by all firms in Brazil were directed primarily to regional markets. Ford and GM fulfilled their BEFIEX obligations by exporting engines to the United States. European firms exported both engines and finished vehicles. GM, Ford, and VW all committed exports to US $ 1 billion over a ten-year period; Fiat committed US $ 550 million (Mericle 1984).

Despite the growth in exports, they remained a small percentage of production, and the industry continued to focus on the domestic market. Brazil adjusted to the oil shock by adopting a debt-led growth strategy rather than by recessing the economy. Total vehicle production topped the magic million mark in 1978 and future demand projections were optimistic. Production costs had fallen and the World Bank characterized the industry as a successful infant industry on the verge of maturity (World Bank 1983:116).

The optimistic projections of internal demand did not materialize in the 1980s as the full impact of the debt crisis hit. Firms looked to exports as an alternative. Brazil's export success in the 1980s depended partly on fortuitous timing. The export capacity was available from investments planned in the 1970s, when projections for internal demand were optimistic and firms made BEFIEX commitments. The BEFIEX program also came at a time when new product lines, particularly in engines, were coming on stream. However, the initial BEFIEX plan was to build upon a growing domestic market to attain economies of scale. For some firms, exports came to substitute for, rather than complement, domestic sales.

The direction of exports began to shift as Brazil's LDC markets also contracted. In the early 1970s, nearly 90 percent of finished vehicle exports went to other Latin American countries. By 1984, this share was reduced to 60 percent; by 1989, 60 percent of vehicle exports went to the United States, Canada, and Europe.

INDIVIDUAL FIRM STRATEGIES

Ford relied almost exclusively on exporting engines and components to the United States. The decision to produce engines came at a time when Ford was downsizing and needed new capacity. A more sophisticated, four-cylinder engine of the same family was being built in Lima, Ohio. If the engine had not been produced in Brazil, it would have been produced in Lima.

Ford did experiment briefly in the mid-1980s with exporting Escorts to Scandinavia when Ford-Europe was capacity-constrained and relative exchange rates favoured Brazil over England and West Germany. The export program was short-lived since Brazilian Escorts became less cost-competitive when the exchange rate situation reversed itself, European unions protested, and Ford began to turn its attention to East Asia as a potential export source (Silva 1991:89). Brazil was also chosen as the primary source of the Cargo—a truck—for the North American market.

Volkswagen used Brazil as a low-cost production site for vehicles to other LDCs. When Latin American markets collapsed in the early 1980s, VW Brazil shifted its exports to the oil-exporting nations of Africa and the Middle East.

Volkswagen and Ford formed the holding company of Autolatina in 1987 to rationalize operations in both Argentina and Brazil. VW Brazil also introduced the passenger car, the Fox, in 1987 and began to export almost exclusively to the United States and Canada. Although the car received positive reviews when first introduced into the US market, it quickly lost its competitive edge to Japanese imports. An increasingly overvalued exchange rate and internal cost increases were critical in its price-sensitive market niche. VW could not raise prices sufficiently to cover its losses. Overall uncertainty in Brazil, as well as an aging product, were also contributing factors.

Autolatina had effectively cancelled all export programs by 1990, with no plans to replace them. Ford had been exporting over 100,000 engines a year. This engine had received the highest quality ratings of all Ford engines, but the model was phased out. The new Ford engine program will not be located in Brazil.

After General Motors began its first "world car" program in the mid-1970s with the introduction of the "J" car series (Chevy Cavalier,

Opel, and Monza), GM Brazil lobbied Detroit to introduce the J car in Brazil. The subsidiary needed a new product line to compete in the Brazilian market. The domestic market, however, could not justify the large investment needed to build the new engines, which had to be manufactured in Brazil to comply with domestic content requirements. GM decided that GM Brazil should provide the "family-two" engine for the US Pontiac division as well as for the domestic market.

Although producing engines in Brazil was cost-effective for GM, the company did not need to build a new plant. It could have supplied engines from its engine plant in New York state. Nevertheless, according to GM managers, domestic market conditions in Brazil forced the decision to produce J cars and export engines.

GM Brazil never considered exporting vehicles to either the United States or Europe. Like the overall industry, its product line was antiquated. In addition, Brazilian models had followed European product lines, with a lag, and so could not be easily placed in the US market. The cars that were exported from Brazil went to GM assembly plants in other Latin American countries, which had begun to clamour for cars made by GM's Japanese partners. As of 1991, GM Brazil had no new export proposals, although it continued to export engines.

Fiat initially considered exporting cars to other Latin American countries from Brazil. Its Brazilian product was always akin to that produced in Europe, so when Latin American markets collapsed it could shift its exports to Italy. In most years since 1982, exports accounted for 40-50 percent of Fiat's annual production, most of which went to Italy. This export performance made Fiat Brazil's largest private exporter. Fiat Brazil benefitted from rapid growth of the Italian market and Fiat Italy's capacity constraints. In the face of increasing costs and the slowdown of the Italian market, Fiat's export performance will be hard to maintain.

The Brazilian auto industry's overall capacity to export has fallen. Exports in the 1980s were based on earlier investments; firms hit capacity constraints before the deep recessions of 1990 and 1991. Virtually no capacity was added over the decade. Firms made marginal investments to maintain their competitive position in the domestic market. Moreover, due to the collapse of many of its LDC export markets, Brazil must compete in the more difficult markets in the developed countries. This will be virtually impossible without new investments, which are unlikely given the stagnant domestic market and the excess capacity of firms in their home markets.

MEXICO

Mexico's difficulties in adjusting to the oil shock led to increasing economic disequilibrium and a balance of payments crisis. In 1976, the peso was devalued by 50 percent for the first time since 1954 and austerity measures were adopted. The domestic recession hit the auto industry particularly hard. The discovery of vast oil reserves at the end of 1977, and with it easy access to foreign loans, promised to eliminate any balance of payments constraints on future economic growth. With real Gross National Product (GNP) growing at an annual average rate of 8.4 percent from 1978-1981, prospects for the domestic auto market brightened considerably.

It was in this context that the government issued the 1977 Automotive Decree. The decree marked the first serious attempt to leverage firm access to the domestic market for increased exports, since new investments would be required to make existing capacity more competitive and to initiate new export projects. It mandated firms to eliminate their trade imbalances by 1982 by increasing either domestic content levels (set at a minimum of 50 percent) or exports. Firms' import bills were broadened to include the imported portion of domestically purchased parts and components, as well as royalty and interest payments abroad. In an attempt to modernize the domestic supplier industry, at least 50 percent of a firm's export requirement had to be supplied by local auto parts producers. If firms failed to balance their trade, they would sacrifice various subsidies and tax exemptions, as well as risk loss of market share due to reduced access to imports.

Although the auto firms did not immediately respond, they all ultimately complied with the decree by building new engine capacity for export. After first increasing exports of wire harnesses from a *maquiladora* plant on the border, GM announced plans to build new engine plants and a new assembly plant in 1979. At the time, the US $ 250 million investment was GM's largest one-time investment in a single site (Samuels 1990:132). By 1988, the plants were exporting 412,000 engines to GM subsidiaries around the world, making GM's Mexican subsidiary the largest engine exporter in Latin America.

In defensive fashion, the other automobile producers followed suit. All together, the plants increased Mexico's annual productive capacity in engines to almost two billion (Womack 1989b:19). With the exception of VW, which concentrated all facets of production in its Puebla facility, the firms built these engine plants in north or north-central Mexico, far away from their manufacturing operations near Mexico City. All of the engines were aimed at the US market, except for Nissan's, which were to be divided equally between the United States and Japan.

The motivating factor behind these new investments was the 1977 Automotive Decree. None of the firms would have built new engine capacity in its absence. Increasing exports was required to protect or increase domestic market share in Mexico, which, at the time of the decree, was booming. While each firm was in a slightly different position, all needed the additional capacity as they restructured their global operations, a necessary condition for the decree's efficacy. Mexico had no evident cost advantage as a production site, although it was not clear that it had a serious cost disadvantage; in fact, these plants proved to be both cost and quality effective.[4]

The position of individual firms also helps to explain their responses. In the absence of the decree, GM and Ford would probably have built the engines in the United States by increasing capacity at existing facilities. Potential, yet uncertain, cost advantages did not drive their decisions. Labour and political volatility, in their view, were still mitigating factors against using Mexico as an export base. GM also needed additional capacity for its Mexican operations. Although Ford, in particular, cites UAW pressure at the time, the fact that the US market was growing made the Mexican investment less controversial. Additionally, engines made in Mexico were less conspicuous than finished vehicles.

In the late 1970s, the Chrysler Corporation was struggling to survive and was closing many subsidiaries. Its Mexican subsidiary was the only Latin American operation that was not a financial drain. In fact, at the time of the decree, the Mexican subsidiary was exporting capital to support the parent. Therefore, despite Chrysler's financial weakness, protecting its Mexican operations was critical. As in the cases of Ford and GM, the alternative production site would have been the United States rather than a third country.

Since its vehicles had more local content, VW's trade deficit was not as severe as that of the US firms. In addition, Volkswagen began exporting Beetles from Mexico in 1977, after shifting all production to Mexico and Brazil from Germany. VW needed the new engine capacity to supply its US plant as well as its Mexican operations. With fewer production sites worldwide or in the Americas, and facing higher transport costs, VW began to integrate Mexico into a North American strategy before Ford and GM.

While all firms wanted to protect their domestic market position in Mexico, it is unlikely that any would have complied with the decree if the additional capacity had not been necessary. In effect, the decree did not really test the importance of the Mexican market to these firms, as no existing facilities elsewhere had to be shut down in order to comply. In interviews, industry executives made clear that they would not close a facility down if its product still had a viable market. Even with accelerated depreciation, the financial blow of closing down an operation can be significant. Exit costs include not only the losses posted on the firm's balance sheet, but contractual arrangements with workers as well as union and community opposition. VW is subject to German law that forbids firms from relocating production abroad if it results in layoffs. The decree did demonstrate that, at the margin, the Mexican government could compel firms to choose Mexico over alternative sites when building new capacity.

While this new export capacity was coming on stream, the sector's overall trade deficit skyrocketed along with domestic sales, hitting US $ 2.1 billion in 1981. This represented 58 percent of the total trade deficit and made the automotive industry the largest private sector contributor to Mexico's trade imbalance (Samuels 1990:128). The government responded in 1981 by insisting on stricter compliance with the 1977 Automotive Decree, but to little avail.

The Automotive Decree of 1983 was an attempt to rationalize the industry and to improve its overall balance of payments position. By 1987, firms would have to generate their own foreign exchange to cover all imports and service payments. They would also have to reduce their product lines down to one make and five models. Additional makes would only be allowed if they were self-sufficient in foreign exchange. Self-sufficiency could be accomplished either by exporting half of the units produced or the equivalent value of components used in their manufacture. Moreover, production of V-8 automobiles for the domestic market was prohibited, as were imported components for luxury cars. Some flexibility was allowed with respect to domestic content, especially for makes that were self-sufficient in foreign exchange. The decree hit US firms especially hard, since it placed severe limits on their ability to compete via product diversification. In addition, their fastest growing and most profitable lines during the oil boom had been in luxury and sports cars.

Unlike the 1977 decree, the 1983 decree was announced during a time of deep economic recession. The debt crisis had exploded in Mexico the year before. Domestic auto production had fallen by 15 percent in 1982 and would fall another 30 percent in 1983. Several firms had built up large dollar-denominated debts during previous expansion plans and the maxi-devaluation of the peso was financially catastrophic.[5] Ford and GM seriously considered pulling out of the Mexican market altogether. Although the Mexican subsidiary was a small part of GM's total operation, its losses negatively affected the firm's overall balance sheet for 1982.

In 1986, production was still over 40 percent less than in 1981. One estimate of industry losses over these years was US $ 1.5 billion (*Automotive News* 1987). The French firm, Renault, gave up and pulled out of Mexico's vehicle market in 1986. Growth resumed in 1987 when the domestic market began to recover. In the years from 1985-87, the industry's performance would have been even poorer if not for growth in automobile exports. Nevertheless, while growing in percentage terms and as a percentage of total production, only a small number of vehicles were exported. Ford's new Hermosillo plant was responsible for the bulk of them. With few exceptions, the government did not succeed in getting firms to invest in major new export projects. Nor did it succeed in getting firms to substitute vehicle exports for engines; the engine plants still generated the lion's share of sectoral exports.

From 1983-89, the industry overall showed a trade surplus for the first time, due initially to the reduced demand for imports in the face of severe contraction in domestic vehicle production, and subsequently, to export growth. Auto companies became the country's biggest exporters and importers. After PEMEX, the state-controlled oil company, GM and Chrysler switched top billing for exports and were the most outwardly-oriented of the auto firms, with exports accounting for 45-58 percent of sales from 1983-85. Exports as a share of sales grew in importance for all firms in 1986 due to the steep drop in the domestic market. During these years, GM and Chrysler maintained positive trade balances, while Ford and VW had more scattered performances and Nissan showed perpetual deficits. In 1986, the auto industry accounted

Table 2
Mexico Motor Vehicle Exports
1973-1989

(Units in Thousands)			
Year	Cars	Trucks and Buses	Total
1973	17,962	2,179	20,141
1974	16,280	2,837	19,117
1975	1,083	1,855	2,938
1976	648	3,524	4,172
1977	5,132	6,611	11,743
1978	18,306	7,522	25,828
1979	19,085	5,671	24,756
1980	13,293	4,952	18,245
1981	9,296	5,132	14,428
1982	14,142	1,677	15,819
1983	20,768	1,688	22,456
1984	30,397	3,238	33,635
1985	49,856	8,567	58,423
1986	40,216	32,213	72,429
1987	135,481	27,592	163,073
1988	144,000	29,147	173,147
1989			195,999

Source: MVMA World Motor Vehicle Data

for 20 percent of Mexican exports, the most important sector by far after oil, and registered a trade surplus of US $ 13.7 billion.

In 1989, the Salinas government issued its Automotive Decree. It mirrored more general moves to liberalize the economy. Restrictions were removed on product lines and, for the first time, the government allowed auto firms manufacturing in Mexico to import finished vehicles. A firm had to generate 2.5 dollars of exports for every dollar spent on imported vehicles. Over time, the ratio would be reduced. In an effort to build up the local supplier industry, 36 percent of any car produced would have to include parts and components supplied by the domestic parts sector. After the decree was issued, the domestic market boomed and firms had trouble meeting demand.

INDIVIDUAL FIRM STRATEGIES

The 1983 decree would have forced GM to reduce its product offering to one line. In retrospect, company executives insist that GM would not have created a new export niche simply to be able to add an additional line to maintain domestic market share. Conveniently, the Chevrolet El Camino and the GMC Caballero pick-up were being phased out in the United States. The vehicle upon which they were based was defunct and production was shifted to Mexico until market demand disappeared altogether. The Ramos Arizpe assembly plant, which had been built along with the new engine plants to assemble the generic "A" body cars for the domestic market, had considerable excess capacity. Small runs of these vehicles were assembled there, sourced almost exclusively from the United States. As low volume niche vehicles, they could be handled cost effectively in Mexico.

In 1987, GM Mexico moved from the International Group to the Chevrolet-Pontiac Canada group. GM also announced its intention to shift some production of certain A cars from the United States to its Mexican plant. In response to UAW complaints, the firm claimed that these cars would eventually be phased out and that 95 percent of their components would be imported from the United States. The assembly plant is now operating at full capacity, but for ten years operated at 20 percent capacity. According to top management, it would never have been built without government pressure.

Products in Mexico and the United States are updated at the same time. The cars produced for the Mexican domestic market are virtually the same as those produced for export, except for domestic content levels. The subsidiary is used to fill in when US or Canadian facilities cannot meet demand. At the end of 1991, the focus was on satisfying the booming domestic car market and engine exports swamped vehicle exports. In the early 1980s, GM had studied the costs of leaving the Mexican market. In 1991, GM's Mexican subsidiary was its most profitable in the Western Hemisphere.

Ford was the last auto firm to respond to the 1977 decree. Its engine plant in Chihuahua came on stream in 1983 when the domestic market was depressed and the company was considering whether or not to stay in Mexico. In 1986, it opened a plant in Hermosillo to assemble Mazda-designed Mercury Tracers for export to the United States and Canada. In Japanese fashion, it was the first Ford plant to house stamping and assembly operations under one roof and Ford's only stamping facility in Mexico (which, according to Ford executives, will remain the case). Since the plant was devoted exclusively to export, the government did not object to the fact that 60 percent of the vehicle's content was sourced from Japan, 30 percent from Mexico, and 10 percent from the United States.

Ford built the Hermosillo plant to fulfil the government's foreign exchange requirements. Only afterwards did it use the plant to negotiate government approval to produce the Taurus line for the domestic market. Some have speculated that the prime motivation for building the plant in Mexico was to evade US constraints on Japanese imports. This seems implausible since the vehicle, though sourced from Mazda in Japan, had been assembled in Taiwan and would not have been considered a Japanese import.

The Hermosillo plant was closed for six months in 1989 to retool for a new Escort/Tracer. Eighty percent of the new model's content is sourced from the United States. The reason behind the model switch evidently had to do with US regulations. For Corporate Average Fuel Economy (CAFE) purposes,[6] the original Tracer was counted as an import because of its low US content. Fortuitously, the appreciating yen lessened the pain of the switch by raising the relative cost of Japanese sourcing.

Hermosillo is still a relatively small-scale assembly plant, but production has been growing. Eighty-nine thousand units were exported in 1990. Still, due to the sluggish demand for automobiles worldwide, the plant is not running at full capacity. Ford Mexico has considered using the plant to source the more buoyant domestic market, but it is concerned about running into foreign exchange problems. Furthermore, it is more profitable for the company to export small cars and to sell luxury cars in Mexico.

Chrysler began to export small volumes of vehicles to Puerto Rico in 1983, making use of its excess capacity. In 1985, in response to capacity and financial constraints in the United States, the company started to produce K cars in Mexico for export. Today, except for local content, Mexican products are the same as those manufactured in the United States. Certain models are produced in Mexico exclusively. Within Mexico, the company has reduced its product offerings, which has cost it market share but not profits. It is the only firm in Latin America to produce automatic transmissions, and it no longer produces cars with manual transmissions in Mexico.

Volkswagen is in a unique position. Until the 1970s, it produced a single model in Mexico, which facilitated producing at high levels of domestic content. Unlike the US firms, it started stamping in Mexico even before building engines. The distance from its parent company also worked in favour of higher domestic content. However, the firm also had a harder time adapting to export promotion because it did not have easy access to its primary market, as did the US firms. In 1974,

VW stopped producing Beetles in Germany and started exporting them from Mexico in 1977. Germany was no longer an economical production site and European demand was small. Today, the Beetle is only produced in Mexico.

VW is committed to spend US $ 1 billion over five years to modernize and expand capacity in Mexico, where production for all of North America is now concentrated. The domestic product line has been broadened to include Golfs and Jettas, and production of Jettas and Golfs for the US market has now been shifted to Mexico. By 1991, about 500,000 engines a year were being exported to Germany. Unlike the United States, Canada bought only Golfs from Mexico and Jettas from Germany. Starting with the 1992 model, both will be sourced from Mexico.

The primary reasons for shifting production to Mexico from Germany were the lack of capacity in Europe and the need to reduce exchange rate risk. VW's market share in Europe has grown, so it needs Mexican capacity to meet demand. The weak dollar has also hurt VW sales in North America; it competes in a price-sensitive market niche. Unlike the US firms, exchange rates have helped shape VW's trade strategy. The firm has tried to balance trade with Europe by exporting engines and increasing local content. At current exchange rates, Mexican production is cost competitive with Germany.

VW has shown the fastest growth and now controls almost 40 percent of the Mexican market. Car exports climbed from practically nothing in 1988 to 46,000 in 1990. In 1991, it sold more cars in Mexico than in the United States.

CONCLUSIONS

While an oligopolistic structure has prevailed since the auto industry's early years, the introduction of new technologies, new entrants, and changing market conditions have meant that the nature of oligopolistic competition has changed over time, and that the relative impact of government policies, firm strategy, and country-specific characteristics on investment and trade flows has varied as well. Brazil and Mexico were able to take advantage of the shake-up occurring in the industry after the war. Even if their industrial infrastructure, administrative capacity, and domestic markets had been as developed before World War II, it is unlikely that similar policies could have induced

either Ford or GM, the industry's giants, to invest in domestic manufacturing. Brazilian and Mexican attempts to increase exports in the
1970s were also coincidental with another shake-up in the industry, as
US and European firms were forced to restructure and reduce costs
in response to the oil shock and the Japanese challenge. This time,
however, the story was complicated by the fact that the firms were
already present in these markets. Therefore, firms moved not only to
protect access to these markets, but also to protect their past investments, which they did not treat as sunk costs. Indeed, firms were
reluctant to close down a plant until it had been written off or until its
product was obsolete. Given the large investments and long time-
horizon in the industry, trade and investment strategies do not immediately change in response to variation in relative costs.

The findings of this study indicate that while internationally
competitive production costs might be a necessary condition for a firm
to begin exporting from a country, it is not a sufficient one. Auto
companies do not randomly survey the globe in search of low-cost
production sites, despite the images conjured up by the notion of a
"world car strategy." While this may be an accurate portrayal of firm
strategy in labour-intensive industries that can be easily relocated to
exploit low wages and government incentives, it is less so for industries
such as autos that require large fixed investments, distribution
networks, industrial infrastructures, and skilled labour.

The fact that firms were forced to consider these countries as
production sites when they otherwise might not have had to speaks
to the success of import-substitution policies. Once the initial investments were made, firms took these sunk costs seriously. Moreover,
these investments increased entry costs for new entrants or for those
firms that might consider re-entry after leaving the market, thereby
increasing the risk of temporarily opting out of a potentially growing
market. While this study does not attempt to calculate the full domestic
resource costs of these national industries, its findings about firm
behaviour do raise questions about how best to assess costs and benefits. They suggest that the initial investment's impact on future investment, foreign capital inflows, and exports must be considered in the
calculation.

The study also shows that government policies were fundamental
in prompting firms to export from both Brazil and Mexico. A comparison of the two countries also reveals how differences in policy regimes
and macroeconomic performance affected the way in which their

respective industries were integrated into world trade and the degree to which their governments could leverage access to the domestic market in exchange for exports. Consequently, the overall regulatory regime, and not simply trade policies, must be included among other country-specific factors such as location, macroeconomy, and market size as potential influences on the nature and direction of trade.

While it has long been understood how trade regimes can affect industrial structures and exports, it is less clear how particular industrial policies toward a sector in which transnational firms operate may affect trade patterns. The auto industries of Brazil and Mexico demonstrate how they can affect trade by influencing the type of product produced. The fact that Mexico was producing more up-to-date vehicles that were based on international standards made it easier to increase exports and to integrate into global production plans. Firm strategy with respect to vehicle type may also have been a factor in positioning these two national industries. Ford and GM in Brazil started producing European-designed car models in the 1970s. Cars produced there have little relationship to those sold in the United States. VW also produces different vehicles in each country. Autolatina does not produce Golfs and Jettas, but cars of its own design. VW Mexico, like the US subsidiaries, takes its product lines from the parent. As a result, Mexico and Brazil do not compete for the same export markets, even if they are the largest producers in Latin America.[7] Brazilian exports would face tough competition in the European market. There are other low-cost producers such as Spain, where Ford, GM, and VW also have subsidiaries. If trading blocs do form around locational proximity and common currency, Brazil will be in a difficult position.

Apparently, Brazil and Mexico have seldom competed as potential sites for investment in new capacity. When US export programs were cancelled in Brazil, they were relocated to the United States. The alternative to engine production or vehicle assembly in Mexico was also the United States. This was true for GM and Ford, which have many alternative sites, and for Chrysler, which has much fewer.

High domestic content policies left a problematic legacy in Brazil, not only because they isolated the industry and led firms to have longer production runs. By moving to high domestic content levels so quickly, the Brazilian government sacrificed trade policy as an instrument to shape firm behaviour. Since firms had invested to produce at 95 percent domestic content levels, preferential access to imports was not an issue.

When Brazil wanted to promote exports, it could only offer subsidies and a limited drawback scheme as carrots, but had virtually no sticks to discipline firms for not participating. Access to the domestic market was unaffected because vehicles were sourced locally. To force firms to export and/or become more competitive, the government must threaten to open the market to finished vehicles and risk reductions in employment. Moreover, reducing domestic content levels is politically difficult since the supplier network that arose to support the industry will be affected, as will the auto firms themselves, which built relatively integrated facilities.

Mexico, on the other hand, was in a weaker bargaining position vis-à-vis the transnational auto companies and originally adopted lower domestic content requirements. It has been able to use access to imports, however, as both a way to structure the industry and force firms to export. Given the changing nature of oligopolistic competition, policies that were adopted out of weakness were turned into a strength.

This study also underscores the importance of the Brazilian and Mexican domestic markets in explaining export performance and the leverage each country had over foreign firms. Cost and locational considerations alone were not sufficient to induce investment for export in the absence of domestic market potential. In Brazil, it is the domestic market potential that keeps firms there and that will determine the role Brazil assumes in international trade. As long as foreign firms decide to maintain a presence in Brazil, despite stagnant demand, they will make marginal investments to maintain their competitive position in the domestic market. In the absence of domestic market growth, even if the market is opened, it is unlikely that firms will commit new capital inflows, as they have done in Mexico.

Mexico's strategy of reducing domestic content, increasing imports, and integrating its domestic industry more closely with that in the United States carries some risk. With the domestic market growing at a rapid clip as compared to the worldwide slump, future growth in the industry (as for the economy as a whole) could become foreign-exchange constrained. When NAFTA is implemented, there will be an adjustment period in which the sector will still have to meet trade balancing requirements. It has been shown that the government cannot get the auto companies to invest on command, and indeed, the US firms have been unwilling to do so given the excess capacity in the United States. On the other hand, Mexican facilities could benefit from a consolidation of the US industry, as was seen in the recent GM restructuring. While Mexico (and Brazil) may have had less ability to regulate the behaviour of transnational firms than they would have had over domestic firms, the integration of the North American economies under NAFTA may tend to blur these national distinctions.

NOTES

Research for this chapter was sponsored by the World Trade and Global Competition Project, Harvard Business School. I would like to thank Miguel Lengyel, Phyllis Dininio, Antonio Botelho, and Clemencia Torres for valuable research assistance; Professors David Yoffie, Lou Wells, and other members of the World Trade and Global Competition Project for their feedback; and Maureen Molot and other Auto Industry Workshop participants for their comments.

[1] As strategic trade theorists have shown, economic rents are not competed away through free trade in oligopolized industries such as autos, which are characterized by economies of scale and other barriers to entry (see Krugman 1986). The existence of such market imperfections may justify government protection of domestic industries. Given the nature of motor vehicles and the political economies of Brazil and Mexico, domestic production was to be controlled by foreign, rather than domestic, capital, as is typically assumed in the literature on strategic trade. Therefore, the issue would not simply be rent distribution between nations, but the internal distribution between the firms and the state (see Shapiro 1993).

[2] The next largest countries of Argentina, Mexico, and Venezuela each had only 200,000 vehicles in circulation.

[3] This process of concentration appeared to have the government's blessing. Secretary of Planning Roberto Campos encouraged mergers. According to a *Visão* interview, he viewed concentration as "an inevitable international tendency" that would reduce industrial costs and propagate competitive pricing.

[4] These observations are based on extensive firm interviews. Samuels (1990) and Womack (1989b) come to similar conclusions.

[5] The Mexican Central Bank eased the debt burden of firms by allowing them access to dollars at a subsidized rate.

[6] See discussion of CAFE regulations in Chapter 7 by Gayle.

[7] One minor exception was a case of a four-cylinder marine engine produced by GM in Mexico and Brazil. Both subsidiaries competed for the US market of about 30-40,000 units a year. According to GM Mexico, Brazil's BEFIEX subsidies put GM Brazil in a preferential position.

REFERENCES

Almeida, José. 1972. *A implantação da indústria automobilística no Brasil.* Rio de Janeiro: Fundação Getúlio Vargas.

Automotive News. 1987. February 9.

Baranson, Jack. 1969. *Automotive Industries in Developing Countries.* World Bank Occasional Staff Papers, No. 8. Washington, DC: The World Bank.

Baumgarten Jr., Alfredo Luiz. 1972. Demanda de autómoveis no Brasil. *Revista Brasileira Econômica.* 26: 203-97.

Behrman, Jack N. 1972. *The Role of International Companies in Latin American Integration: Autos and Petrochemicals.* Lexington, Mass.: Lexington Books.

Bennett, Douglas C., and Sharpe, Kenneth E. 1985a. *Transnational Corporations versus the State: The Political Economy of the Mexican Auto Industry.* Princeton: Princeton University Press.

_____. 1985b. The World Automobile Industry and its Implications. In *Profits, Progress and Poverty*, ed. R. Newfarmer. Notre Dame: University of Notre Dame.

Bergsman, Joel. 1970. *Brazil: Industrialization and Trade Policies.* Published on behalf of the Development Centre of the Organization for Economic Co-operation and Development, Paris. London: Oxford University Press.

Bloomfield, Gerald. 1978. *The World Automotive Industry.* Newton Abbot, London: David and Charles.

Bonelli, Regis, and Werneck, Dorothea F.F. 1978. Desempenho industrial: Auge e desaceleração nos anos 70. In *Indústria: política, instituções e desenvolvimento*, ed. Wilson Suzigan. Rio de Janeiro: IPEA/INPES.

Carrillo, Jorge V., ed. 1990. *La neuva era de la industria automotriz en México.* Tijuana: El Colegio de la Frontera Norte.

Caves, Richard E. 1982. *Multinational Enterprise and Economic Analysis.* Cambridge: Cambridge University Press.

CEPAL (Comisión Económica para América Latina). 1984. México: Sector automotriz y comercio exterior. April.

Edelberg, Guillermo S. 1963. "The Procurement Practices of the Mexican Affiliates of Selected United States Automobile Firms." Doctoral dissertation, Harvard Business School.

Evans, Peter. 1979. *Dependent Development: The Alliance of Multinational, State, and Local Capital in Brazil.* Princeton: Princeton University Press.

_____, and Gereffi, Gary. 1978. Foreign Investment and Dependent Development: Comparing Brazil and Mexico. In *Brazil and Mexico: Patterns in Late Development*, eds. Sylvia Ann Hewlett and Richard S. Wienert. Philadelphia: Institute for the Study of Humane Issues.

Fishlow, Albert. n.d. "Foreign Trade Regimes and Economic Development: Brazil." Manuscript.

_____. 1986. "A Tale of Two Presidents: The Political Economy of Brazilian Adjustment to the Oil Shocks." Working Paper No. 202, University of California, Berkeley, Department of Economics, February.

Gordon, Lincoln, and Grommers, Engelbert L. 1962. *US Manufacturing Investment in Brazil: The Impact of Brazilian Government Policies 1946-1960*. Cambridge, Mass.: Harvard University Press.

Guimarães, Eduardo Augusto de Almeida. 1987. *Acumulacao e crescimento da firma*. Rio de Janeiro: Editora Guanabara SA.

_____. 1980. "Industry, Market Structure and the Growth of the Firm in the Brazilian Economy." Ph.D. dissertation, University of London.

_____. 1988. "A politica governamental e a industria automobilistica." World Bank Paper. October.

Hymer, Stephen. 1976. *The International Operation of National Firms: A Study of Direct Foreign Investment*. Cambridge, Mass.: MIT Press.

Jenkins, Rhys Owen. 1977. *Dependent Industrialization in Latin America: The Automotive Industry in Argentina, Chile, and Mexico*. New York: Praeger Publishers.

_____. 1987. *Transnational Corporations and the Latin American Automobile Industry*. Pittsburgh: University of Pittsburgh Press.

Knickerbocker, Frederick T. 1973. *Oligopolistic Reaction and Multinational Enterprise*. Boston: Harvard University School of Business Administration.

Krugman, Paul R. 1984. "Import Protection as Export Promotion." In *Monopolistic Competition and International Trade*, ed. H. Keirzkowski. Oxford: Oxford University Press.

_____. ed. 1986. *Strategic Trade Policy and the New International Economics*. Cambridge, Mass.: MIT Press.

Latini, Sydney A. 1984. *SUMA Automobilística*, Vol. I. Rio de Janeiro: Editora Tama Ltda.

Maxcy, George, and Silberston, Aubrey. 1959. *The Motor Industry*. London: George Allen and Unwin.

Mericle, Kenneth. 1984. *The Political Economy of the Brazilian Motor Vehicle Industry*. In The Political Economy of the Latin American Motor Vehicle Industry, eds. Rich Kronish and Ken Mericle. Cambridge and London: MIT Press.

Moreno Brid, Juan Carlos. 1988. "Mexico's Motor Vehicle Industry in the 1980s." World Employment Programme Research Working Paper No. 21, International Labour Office, Geneva. August.

Newfarmer, Richard, ed. 1985. *Profits, Progress and Poverty: Case Studies of International Industries in Latin America*. Notre Dame: University of Notre Dame Press.

Oliveira, Francisco, and Popoutchi, Maria Angélica Travolo. 1979. *El complejo automotor en Brasil.* ILET Mexico City: Editorial Nueva Imagen, SA.

Orosco, Eros. 1961. *A indústria automobilística brasileira.* Rio de Janeiro: Consultec.

Reich, Simon. 1990. *The Fruits of Fascism.* Ithaca and London: Cornell University Press.

Roos, Daniel, and Altshuler, Alan. 1984. *The Future of the Automobile.* Cambridge, Mass: MIT Press.

Samuels II, Barbara C. 1990. *Managing Risk in Developing Countries.* Princeton, N.J.: Princeton University Press.

Shapiro, Helen. 1991. "Determinants of Firm Entry into the Brazilian Automobile Manufacturing Industry, 1956-68." *Business History Review* 65, 4: 876-948.

____. (1993). *Engines of Growth: The State and Transnational Auto Companies in Brazil .* Cambridge: Cambridge University Press.

Shaiken, Harley. 1990. *Mexico in the Global Economy.* San Diego: Center for US-Mexican Studies, University of California.

Shaiken, Harley, and Herzenberg, Stephen. 1987. *Automation and Global Production.* San Diego: Center for US-Mexican Studies, University of California.

Silva, Elizabeth Bortolaia. 1991. *Refazendo a fabrica fordista.* Sao Paulo: Editora Hucitec.

Ventura Dias, Vivianne. 1975. "The Motor Vehicle Industry in Brazil: A Case of Sectoral Planning." Masters thesis, University of California, Berkeley.

Visão. Quem é quem na economia brasileira. Various years.

Wells, Louis T. Automobiles. In *Big Business and the State,* ed. Raymond Vernon. Cambridge, Mass.: Harvard University Press.

White, Lawrence J. 1971. *The Automobile Industry since 1945.* Cambridge, Mass: Harvard University Press.

Wilkins, Mira, and Hill, Frank Ernest. 1964. *American Business Abroad: Ford on Six Continents.* Detroit: Wayne State University Press.

Womack, James P. 1989a. *The Mexican Motor Industry: Strategies for the 1990s.* International Motor Vehicle Program, Massachusetts Institute of Technology, International Policy Forum. May.

____. 1989b. *Seeking Mutual Gain: North American Responses to Mexican Liberalization of its Motor Vehicle Industry.* Prepared for the 44th Annual Plenary Meeting, Mexico-US Business Committee, Orlando, Florida. November 9.

World Bank. 1983. *Brazil: Industrial Policies and Manufactured Exports.* World Bank Country Study. Washington, D.C.: The World Bank.

5 JAPANESE JOINT VENTURES IN THE AUTOMOTIVE INDUSTRY:

Implications for North American Suppliers

Andrew Inkpen

T he North American automotive industry is undergoing significant structural change. The North American Free Trade Agreement (NAFTA) and the emergence of the Japanese car producers as leading international competitors have created new demands for North American automakers and suppliers. The focus of this chapter is on the increasing Japanese presence in the North American automotive industry.

In 1981, there were no Japanese assembly plants in North America. By 1991, there were nine Japanese-operated assembly plants in the United States and three in Canada. These plants produced 1.78 million units in 1990, more than 20 percent of total North American production (Miller and Winter 1991). By the end of 1990, the North American Japanese assembly plants, or Japanese original equipment manufacturers (JOEMs), had combined capacity in place or announced to make 2.3 million vehicles per year. The JOEMs, plus imports from all countries, accounted for more than 40 percent of the units sold in North America. With the growth in JOEM capacity, some industry observers were projecting that North American automobile capacity could exceed demand by three million units or more during the 1990s (for example, see Smith 1989).

The three largest JOEMs in North America, Honda, Nissan, and Toyota, have been called the "other Big Three." These companies are steadily becoming full-fledged North American producers capable of designing, engineering, and assembling vehicles entirely in North America. Toyota, for example, had an objective of 75 percent North American content in its cars by 1992. Nissan was in the process of completing a modern engineering centre near Detroit that would employ six hundred by 1992. Honda was sourcing about 75 percent of its parts and components and 25-30 percent of its tooling and equipment in North America. In 1990 Honda, for the first time, sold more domestically built cars in North America than it imported from Japan.

Along with Japanese investment at the original equipment manufacturers (OEM) level, an increasing number of Japanese automotive suppliers have invested in North America. This chapter examines the implications of the large number of joint ventures between North American and Japanese-North American automotive suppliers. An examination of joint ventures provides an excellent opportunity to observe the interplay between Japanese and North American companies in an industry undergoing significant structural change. There are three primary goals of the chapter: (1) to identify the factors motivating North American firms to enter joint ventures with Japanese suppliers, and to consider the longer-term implications for the competitive strategies of the North American firms; (2) given that many joint ventures are viewed as unsuccessful by the North American partners, to discuss the question of whether domestic suppliers should continue to rely on joint ventures to gain access to the JOEMs; and (3) to develop insights into the potential effects of the increasing Japanese presence in the automotive industry. The principal data for the chapter come from field observations of 40 North American automotive suppliers involved in joint ventures with Japanese firms.

AUTOMOTIVE SUPPLIERS

Several trends characterized the automotive supplier industry of the late 1980s. First, OEMs were increasing their outsourcing of parts through the establishment of multi-tiered supplier arrangements. Second, automakers were pushing their suppliers toward just-in-time (JIT) delivery systems and increased investment in design and engineering capabilities. Third, mergers were becoming prevalent in the supplier sector, largely because of heavy demands for research and development, new equipment, and employee training. Finally, of direct importance to this chapter, suppliers were moving away from their traditional focus on home markets toward foreign investment. Specifically, more than 250 Japan-based supplier firms established operations in North America, and most arrived in the 1987-88 period.

By the late 1980s, the implications of foreign investment in the automotive supplier industry were clear: similar to the situation with automaking capacity, excess capacity at the supplier level was becoming a reality. The overcapacity and competition from foreign-based component suppliers were creating increasingly difficult conditions for North American automotive suppliers, conditions that were forcing North American suppliers to adapt to a new competitive environment. A statement by a senior manager in a US component supplier reflects the new environment:

> The next five years are going to be horrible. With the new Japanese companies coming in, with peripheral capacity, and with component integration and the car companies all chasing the same market . . . a lot of suppliers are going to fall out (Smith 1989: 37).

Japanese investment in the North American automotive industry included a large number of Japanese-North American joint ventures. Most of these joint ventures comprised joint-manufacturing activities; few involved basic or applied research or the introduction of new types of products with new technologies. The joint ventures were primarily at the manufacturing end of the research-development-manufacturing continuum and involved the transfer of management methods from one location to another (Womack 1988: 329).

THE RESEARCH STUDY

This chapter reports results from a larger study of Japanese-North American joint ventures in the automotive supply industry. The focus of the study was on North American[1] firms and their involvement in joint ventures with Japanese firms. A joint venture is defined as a means of performing activities in combination with one or more firms instead of autonomously. A joint venture occurs when two or more legally distinct firms (the parents) pool a portion of their resources within a jointly-owned legal organization. This definition excludes other forms of cooperative agreements such as licensing, distribution and supply agreements, research and development partnerships, or technical assistance and management contracts.

Joint ventures have become increasingly popular in recent years and, for many firms, have moved to the mainstream of domestic and international corporate activity. A variety of strategic objectives have been suggested to explain the motives of firms for forming joint ventures (Contractor and Lorange 1988; Harrigan 1985; Hennart 1988; and Porter and Fuller 1986). The objectives include the reduction of risk, economies of scale, access to technology or markets, and the search for legitimacy.

Following Koh and Venkatraman (1991), there are also potential costs of joint venture strategies. First, there are the costs of coordinating the often divergent interests of the partners (Porter and Fuller 1986). Second, joint ventures can create an adverse bargaining position when one partner captures a disproportionate share of the value created by a joint venture (Hamel 1991; Koh and Venkatraman 1991). Third, when proprietary expertise and market access are transferred to partner firms, joint ventures have the potential to create competitors. This third cost will be examined in more detail later in the chapter.

It was against the background of a changing automotive industry and the recent wave of Japanese-American supplier joint ventures that this study was carried out. The study focused on various aspects of the joint venture relationship, including the motives for joint venture formation, joint venture performance, and the interaction between the North American and Japanese partners. The primary data collection method was field interviews with senior managers involved in joint venture management. The majority of managers held positions such as joint venture president or joint venture general manager. Interviews were conducted with 58 North American managers associated with 40 joint ventures.

All sample joint ventures were automotive suppliers located primarily in the US midwest and upper south. More than three-quarters of the ventures were manufacturers of parts and components while the remainder produced materials such as paint, steel, glass, and chemicals. With the exception of two cases, the joint ventures were startup or greenfield organizations. A joint venture was classified as a greenfield venture if an organization was created where none existed before (Lewis 1990).

Interestingly, only three joint ventures were located in Canada, even though both Toyota and Honda have established Canadian assembly plants. Several reasons may account for the small number of Canadian joint ventures. For one, it appears that the US states had more advanced systems in place to attract foreign investment.[2] Tax and training incentives were often important location factors for joint ventures. At the provincial level, it is unlikely that the Canadian provinces can compete with their US counterparts. Second, my observations suggest that the Japanese partners perceived the Canadian labour climate as more uncertain than that of the United States. Finally, with the bulk of the Japanese OEM investment in the United States and the lessening of trade restrictions between Canada and the United States, a US location could probably support Canadian markets.

The predominant equity relationship was equal ownership. The number of years the joint ventures were in operation ranged from one to six years. Two-thirds of the cases were between three and four years old, and only two joint ventures were as old as six years. More than three-quarters of the joint ventures were first-tier suppliers. The joint ventures ranged in size from eight to 920 employees. The mean number of employees was 206 and fifteen joint ventures had between 150 and 300 employees.

Most of the joint ventures comprised single plants geographically separated from the American parent's facilities. An important factor contributing to the geographical separation was that, generally, both partners wanted a union-free company. The American partners were predominantly unionized and located in heavily unionized areas. By establishing the joint ventures in smaller, less-industrialized areas, the partners could usually operate a union-free organization. Generally, new plants and equipment were built or acquired specifically for the joint ventures.

American partners initiated about the same number of joint ventures as Japanese partners. For one-third of the joint ventures there was no clear initiator. When there was no initiator, the joint ventures typically evolved out of several years of discussions about possible collaborative relationships.

THE JOINT VENTURE FORMATION

For three-quarters of the sample joint ventures, the primary motivating factor in the American partner's decision to form a joint venture was access to the North American JOEM market. All but five joint ventures supplied JOEMs and eleven supplied a single JOEM. The prevalent opinion of managers involved with JOEM customers was that the access of American firms to the JOEM market would not have been possible without a Japanese connection. A Japanese joint venture partner was viewed as the most effective and timely means of acquiring the connection.

If the joint venture was supplying JOEMs, the joint venture product was generally identical with products produced by the Japanese partner in Japan. Given that the primary joint venture motive was market access, it is not surprising that, in most cases, the joint venture products were functionally similar to products produced by the American partners. Thus, the joint venture provided the American partners with exposure to a Japanese firm producing a functionally similar product for a different customer market. Accordingly, a secondary objective for many American firms was access to the skills and capabilities of their Japanese partners.

Four American firms sought access to manufacturing technology and the capital necessary to implement the technology. In three of the four cases, the Japanese partner possessed proprietary, leading-edge technology. In the fourth case, the technology was not proprietary but was outside the American partner's product line focus. Access to capital was critical in all four cases because, without an infusion of capital from the joint venture partner, the American firm would have been unable to invest in the technology, even if it was purchasable.

In five cases, the primary motive was access to technology that would allow the American partner to broaden its product line and give the Japanese partner entry into the North American market. Unlike the previous four cases, access to Japanese capital was not an important factor in the joint venture formation. In other words, the American firms were not faced with capital shortages, but needed access to a specific technology possessed by their Japanese partners. In four of the five cases, the joint venture gave the American partner entry into a related product line. The Japanese firm was already competing in that product line and, therefore, was experienced in the manufacturing processes and product technologies. As an American manager commented, "We had the market access through our own plants and the administration talent to run the business. We did not have the manufacturing expertise." The fifth case was slightly different in that the American firm wanted access to two very specific manufacturing processes in which the Japanese partner was a world leader. Access to the technology would allow the American firm, through its joint venture, to compete in some new niche markets.

In one case, the two partners wished to enter the North American automotive market with a product both firms manufactured outside North America. The joint venture allowed the partners to combine forces and share the risk of entering a new market. Finally, in one case the formation of the joint venture was motivated by the desire of the American partner to collaborate with a Japanese firm because "everyone else was doing it." This motive could be called a legitimacy motive (Oliver 1990) because the American partner was motivated to appear in agreement with the prevailing norms in the automotive industry. Other managers indicated that forming a joint venture with a Japanese partner was a very "fashionable" thing to do during the period 1985-90.

A common theme expressed by many managers was that access to the JOEM market comprised the American firm's first step toward becoming a more international firm. American firms recognized that the automotive industry was rapidly changing and wanted to partic- ipate in that change. However, the objectives of JOEM access and inter- nationalization often took precedence over economic reasons for forming an alliance. Several managers indicated that "faith" drove the joint venture formation process: both the American and Japanese firms entered the joint venture with little more than faith in each other. In these cases, neither partner communicated its objectives and little effort was made to prepare financial forecasts. Not surprisingly, many joint ventures subsequently experienced problems because of the lack of communication during the formation process.

JAPANESE FIRM JOINT VENTURE MOTIVES

In forming joint ventures in North America, the Japanese partners were motivated by several factors. Many of the Japanese firms were, as one American manager put it, "internationally naive." A large number had no foreign investments other than in Korea or Taiwan. Therefore, an American partner helped ease the uncertainty about operating in North America and, in particular, about dealing with an American work force. As a manager explained, "The Japanese partner wanted some handholding. We got them their houses, got their kids in schools, etc." A second factor was pressure from the JOEMs. As Hoffman and Kaplinsky (1988) suggested, joint ventures with American firms helped to offset increasing protectionist sentiment against "screwdriver" assembly plants. Indeed, Womack (1988) reported that Toyota actively encouraged its suppliers to form joint ventures with American firms when investing in North America. A third factor, and one that will be explored later in the chapter, is that the Japanese firms saw the joint ventures as transitional arrangements that preceded wholly-owned subsidiaries.

JOEM ACCESS

As indicated, JOEM access was the American partner's primary joint venture motive in most of the joint venture cases. The following short case[3] illustrates an American firm's decision to form a joint venture. Alpha Corporation (Alpha), a large American tier-one supplier, sought access to the JOEM market segment but had made little progress. Alpha saw a joint venture as an opportunity to gain access to a growing segment of the automotive market.

CASE 1

For thirty years, Alpha had maintained a sales office in Japan. The office was established by a non-automotive division that had since been sold. Alpha kept the sales office open primarily to maintain contact with the Japanese market. In the mid-1980s, Alpha became interested in developing business with the growing JOEM market in North America. Alpha's objective was to be a major player in the world's largest markets, but it lacked a significant Japanese presence.

Alpha considered forming a joint venture and used its sales office in Japan to review the industry for potential partners. Three companies were identified as potential joint venture partners. Alpha was considering its next step when Toyota's North American purchasing department asked Alpha to quote on a product for its new Georgetown, Kentucky plant. Alpha's vice-president of manufacturing remarked, "At that point we were still naive enough to believe that we might be able to get some transplant business without a Japanese connection."

After the quotation was submitted, Toyota contacted Alpha about forming a joint venture to supply its new plant. Toyota was informed that Alpha was interested; this led to a trip to Japan arranged with Toyota's assistance. Several senior Alpha executives met with two potential joint venture partners, the number one and two suppliers for Toyota in Japan. The meetings were very formal and, according to Alpha's vice-president, "We only saw their conference room."

The next step was to have the potential Japanese partners come to North America. Both companies visited in May 1986 and "we only showed them our conference room." Neither Japanese company was interested in a wholly-owned North American investment because of their unfamiliarity with the North American business environment.

Alpha management concluded that there was a better "chemistry" with the larger supplier, Hito Ltd. Hito was one of the largest automotive suppliers in Japan and a long-standing member of Toyota's supplier association. They also thought that Toyota was very supportive of Alpha as a joint venture supplier and wanted to see an Alpha-Hito joint venture. Alpha's vice-president commented, "I am not really sure of the extent to which Toyota influenced the joint venture formation but I think that Toyota and Hito worked together to make it happen."

The joint venture was formed in December 1986, about one year after the first meetings in Japan. The joint venture investment was $15 million and, initially, 100 percent of the joint venture's business was with Toyota. Several years later, the joint venture developed a small amount of work with General Motors and Ford.

An initial problem in the formation process was that Hito wanted majority ownership. Alpha's vice-president suspected that Hito sought majority ownership because that was what Toyota wanted. They also may have wanted to protect their technology. Alpha management knew they could not get majority ownership but held out and were successful in negotiating a fifty-fifty joint venture. After 10 years, the joint venture agreement will be reviewed.

BARRIERS TO ENTRY

The Alpha case illustrates the perception held by most of the managers interviewed, i.e. that the JOEM market is not open to American firms. While the JOEMs vehemently deny that the situation is so, there is no question that much of the JOEM business goes to wholly-owned Japanese suppliers or Japanese-American joint ventures. In reference to the

JOEM market, several managers made comments such as: "the market is rigged in favour of Japanese firms," and that "the Japanese firms are arrogant and unwilling to trust the quality of American suppliers."

Why have American firms had difficulty penetrating the growing JOEM market? American firms wishing to supply the Japanese automobile JOEMs face several significant barriers. First, they are often unfamiliar with the rigours of Japanese JIT systems and demands for flexible production. As a manager explained, the JOEM supplier-manufacturer relationship was radically different from that between domestic OEMs and suppliers:

> The typical domestic automaker's relationship with its suppliers is adversarial. With the JOEMs, the relationship is supportive if you can deliver the product. JOEMs will work with their suppliers and help them when there is a problem. They also expect complete commitment. With our main JOEM customer, if there is one problem, there is one phone call; we are expected to fix the problem immediately. . . . Business is much faster with the JOEMs; the rules that bind the other [American parent] plants would not work here.

Another joint venture used its American parent as a supplier. As a first-tier supplier to a JOEM, the joint venture was under pressure to extend its Japanese-style JIT system to its upstream suppliers. However, the joint venture management was frustrated by the inability of the American parent to meet its quality and delivery demands.

> They [the American parent] are our largest supplier and we have had a lot of problems with them. When they started they were shipping us about 20 percent rejects. They got it down to about 2.5 percent and thought that was great. We expect much better because our rate with our customer is one-half of 1 percent. The parent's reaction is "you want too much." They even put a man in our plant with the job of inspecting the parent product as it arrives. They pay him but it still costs us because he is using our facilities. Why can't they inspect it before it leaves their plant?

For most managers in the study, dealing with a JOEM customer was a new experience that was both frustrating and enlightening. The general agreement was that the JOEMs were more demanding customers than the domestic OEMs. Given that the majority of managers had previously been involved with domestic automaker suppliers, this reaction is of particular interest. As one respondent said of the JOEMs, "their expectations about quality are relentless. They overemphasize quality concerns so much that they make you do much better in other ways. To meet their quality demands we have to be a lot better in all respects." Many managers emphatically stated that the quality of the joint venture product was far superior to anything produced by their American parent. A joint venture executive compared the joint venture with its parent that made a similar product for the domestic OEMs:

> They [the American partner] are light years behind in terms of their defect rate, their production equipment, their delivery capabilities, etc. For example, the American partner has an on-time delivery record of about 70 percent. Their target is 80 percent. The joint venture has a delivery record of 99.9 percent. It is not perfect because occasionally we have been early. . . . They don't have the engineering talent to make changes. To them, making is a craft. The engineer makes a drawing and gives it to the operators. The operators are the craftsmen. In the joint venture, the manufacturing process is an engineering process. Quality is engineered into the process rather than inspected in.

A second and perhaps more formidable barrier is the relationship between Japanese manufacturers and their suppliers. In Japan, an extensive network of inter-corporate agreements exist between many firms; Kester (1991: 76) referred to this as an "intricate network of largely implicit reciprocal trading agreements." Trust and loyalty play a key role in creating an environment of voluntary forbearance and long-term relationships. Unlike North American manufacturers, Japanese companies rarely change suppliers.

The Japanese automobile industry illustrates how a network of high trust relationships can evolve into an institutionalized arrangement. For example, Toyota's first-tier suppliers are organized into a group known as Kyoho-kai, which translates as a "club for co-prospering with Toyota" (Dodwell Marketing Consultants 1990: 36). This group has remained almost unchanged since the 1950s. Many Japanese suppliers are partially owned by the automakers and therefore have a stronger relationship than a typical North American supplier-manufacturer relationship. The president of Nissan's US operations explained:

> Nissan's mix of US suppliers and Japanese suppliers is not
> likely to change much. Given our philosophy, once you
> become our supplier you're our supplier forever on that part,
> unless you mess up so bad we can't fix you (Miller and Winter
> 991: 29).

The existence of Japanese automotive supplier groups is perhaps
the fundamental reason American suppliers have been largely unsuccessful in capturing a large share of JOEM business. Because of the
implicit reciprocity in the Japanese networks and the norms and expectations that have developed over many years, it is logical that the
JOEMs would prefer to deal with the same suppliers in North America
as in Japan.

Many Japanese suppliers have made their North American investment because of their position in a supplier association or group. As a
member of a supplier association, suppliers are expected to do what
is necessary to meet the needs of their primary customers. If the JOEMs
build a plant in North America, the suppliers must follow or risk upset-
ting their relationship with the JOEMs. Thus, much of the investment by
Japanese suppliers in North America did not follow the Western notion
of capital investment. It is very unlikely that the Japanese suppliers
treated the potential return on investment from a North American facility as the primary decision-making criterion. Instead, the Japanese
JOEMs expected their suppliers to follow them to North America and
the suppliers recognized that they had little choice.

It is important to recognize, however, that Japanese manufacturers do not guarantee business to their long-term suppliers. Japanese
firms strive to maintain a tradeoff between long-term relationships
and competition between suppliers. Consequently, the Japanese supplier
investment in North American is not without risk. Several of the joint
ventures in this study were formed with expectations of OEM contracts
that have yet to materialize. While many suppliers expect JOEM business because of their existing relationship in Japan, it is not guaranteed. Nevertheless, one of the keys to the JOEMs' success in North
America has been the willingness of Japanese suppliers to invest in
North America to support new assembly operations.[4] Many of those
investments have been made without any formal commitments from
the JOEMs and, given the findings of this study, it is likely that many
of the non-joint venture Japanese suppliers have suffered significant
operating losses over the first four to six years of operation.

A second important point is that Japanese suppliers in North America may be free to compete for business outside their primary customer segment. While several joint ventures in the study were explicitly tied to a single JOEM, and effectively prevented from seeking additional customers, most ventures were actively developing new business. Indeed, a goal of many Japanese firms was to become supplier to domestic OEMs. A link with an American firm was often perceived as a key factor in achieving that goal.

AMERICAN PARTNERS AND THE JAPANESE NETWORK

By forming a joint venture with a Japanese firm that is part of a complex network of relationships, the American partner becomes part of that network. The unfamiliarity of most American managers with the Japanese form of supplier-manufacturer relationships and contractual governance often creates a sense of frustration for the American partners. A joint venture executive describes the relationship between the Japanese partner and the joint venture:

> Gradually, we realized that our partner had a hidden agenda that we would never be able to understand. They [the Japanese partner] saw the joint venture as advertising; they were willing to lose money to maintain their Japanese relationship. That relationship was beyond anything we could get a handle on.

In our study, an area that was particularly difficult for American managers to understand was pricing decisions. A dissatisfaction with the pricing structure of the joint venture products was a major source of conflict between the joint venture partners, particularly when the joint venture only sold to JOEMs. When the joint venture customers were JOEMs and the products sold by the joint ventures were duplicates of products made in Japan (the majority of the cases in the sample), most of the American managers indicated that they had limited knowledge about how initial prices were determined for the joint venture products. Usually, the price was based on an agreement between the Japanese partner and the JOEM using the price in Japan as the target. This price, at least initially, would not necessarily be related to the cost of manufacturing the part in North America. Or, the price may have been low-balled by the Japanese partner to ensure that the joint venture got the

US business. In any event, the US partners usually found themselves excluded from any discussions about price and profit margins.

Armed with little or no knowledge about how the initial product prices were determined, and a profit situation deemed unsatisfactory in most cases, a typical reaction by the US partner was "we need to renegotiate the price." The American partner's only link with the JOEM was through the joint venture. There were few opportunities to bene-fit through adjustments other than price. The Japanese partners, on the other hand, generally had a myriad of relationships in Japan to consider, and the last thing they needed or wanted to do was force a confrontation over price. As Kester (1991) explained, price adjust-ments are not the way Japanese companies usually solve conflicts. Forcing a confrontation about a pricing issue may be relatively com-mon in North America, but in Japan it would rarely happen between manufacturers and long-term suppliers. As a manager noted:

> In Japan, our Japanese partner does not compete head-to-head. Head-to-head competition takes place between "mother" [the JOEM] and the other JOEMs. Mother tells the sibling to be good and we will take care of you. Getting involved in tough price competition in the US was something new for our partner and made it hard for them to take the pricing issue seriously. In Japan the price is set gentlemanly.

Nevertheless, several American managers in the study forced confrontations because they felt that the prices negotiated in Japan were unrealistic in an American environment. Without a price increase, they argued, the joint venture could not survive. There is now some indication that negotiating directly on price issues is becoming more common between JOEMs and their North American suppliers.

AMERICAN SUPPLIERS AND JOINT VENTURE STRATEGIES

Given the large number of existing Japanese-North American joint ventures, this section considers the implications of the joint venture strategy, particularly as it relates to the objective of gaining access to the JOEM market.

JOINT VENTURE PERFORMANCE AND STRATEGIC IMPORTANCE

Most informants indicated that, at least initially in the joint venture process, the venture was considered very important by the American partners. For several reasons, American firms considered their Japanese joint ventures strategically important, perhaps even disproportionately important given their size and contribution to overall firm results. First of all, many American firms saw access to the JOEM market as critical because of the JOEMs' increasing market share. A joint venture could help the American firm overcome barriers to entry in the JOEM market and, hopefully, the American parent could develop its own JOEM business. Furthermore, in most cases, the joint ventures represented the American partner's first close relationship with a Japanese firm. Since Japanese firms were viewed as a genuine threat to American automotive suppliers, a joint venture would give the American parent an inside look at the reality of Japanese competition. As well, the joint ventures were often the result of an attitude of, "if we can't beat them, join them." As one executive said, "The joint venture was essentially a defensive move. I could not improve the company by myself. I had to find a partner who could help me." Finally, while many American parents had international experience, competition from international competitors in North America was relatively new. Forming a joint venture was, to some degree, an admission that international competition in North American was here to stay and that American manufacturing was not necessarily world class.

Given the high levels of strategic importance, many joint ventures were formed with unrealistic expectations concerning both profitability and market share. As one executive commented about anticipated joint venture performance, "We thought we were well positioned to get transplant business. The joint venture would be a piece of cake; the transplants were like ducks on the pond." Other executives indicated that, initially, no major differences were expected between supplying the JOEMs versus supplying the domestic automakers; a typical attitude was, "JOEM business must be good business."

When the joint ventures failed to become a panacea for the American partner, the joint ventures lost some of their lustre. Although the joint venture may have been performing adequately, initial expectations were so high—and the reality so different —that many American partners reconsidered the strategic importance or centrality of their joint ventures. With the reconsideration of importance came the realization that selling to the JOEM market and managing a joint venture were very difficult tasks. Together, they presented a formidable challenge that some firms eventually decided was too great.

Most American partner firms were unprepared for the level of profit margins their joint ventures experienced as suppliers to the JOEMs. The financial performance of more than half the joint ventures (52 percent) was unsatisfactory from the perspective of the American partners. As evidence of the dissatisfaction with joint venture performance, 13 of the 40 joint ventures in the sample have, or likely will be, terminated, and that number probably will increase over the next few years. Concerns about joint venture performance were the major cause of joint venture termination. The American partners were generally unwilling to absorb losses to the same extent as their Japanese partners. Granted, the Japanese firms were often in a position of having no choice but to remain with the joint venture firm because of their relationship with the JOEMs.

Managers often expressed concern that the American parent was primarily interested in performance issues and failed to grasp that the joint venture was producing a world-class product. A related view was that the Japanese firms tended to place their emphasis on areas such as market share and quality control. As an executive explained, "The Japanese are not interested in return on investment; they are interested in looking for voids, departures from the plan."

As well, the American partners tended to view the joint venture as a profit centre rather than as part of a larger organization. As a separate profit centre, the joint venture should survive as a stand-alone company. In that sense, the American partner was trapped in what Hamel and Prahalad (1989) referred to as the strategic business unit mindset. The Japanese partner often had a different perspective, viewing the joint venture as an integral component of a larger organization. The following case illustrates the often unrealistic expectations of American joint venture partner firms.

CASE 2

In 1984, the Japanese firm, Noro Inc., was encouraged by its primary Japanese customer to establish a plant in North America. Noro had some experience with joint ventures and decided a joint venture would be the best strategy for a North American investment. Noro management made several trips to North America in search of a suitable partner.

Meanwhile, Sigma Ltd., an automotive supplier based in Detroit, had been scouting Japan for potential joint venture partners and sales contracts. Sigma was then involved in a small, low-tech job for Noro's main JOEM customer's North American division. Noro, aware that the JOEM was satisfied with its relationship with Sigma, contacted Sigma about the possibility of forming a joint venture. A joint venture agreement, with Sigma holding a 60 percent interest, was signed and the joint venture began operations in 1985. The joint venture was established initially to supply a single JOEM, Noro's main Japanese customer. The partners agreed that Noro would supply all the technical resources and Sigma would take care of the management.

After two years of operations, Sigma became very concerned that the joint venture was still losing money. According to the joint venture general manager, "Sigma wanted to make a quick buck; they were sceptical of making long-term investments. They saw the joint venture as a way to make some money and expected a profit in two years." Noro, however, had a very different perspective. "Noro expected the joint venture to lose money for about five or six years. Unfortunately, they never communicated this to Sigma and no explicit business plan was prepared."

Despite continuing to lose money, the joint venture was increasing its market share and attracted several new customers, including Ford and General Motors. When an expansion became necessary, Sigma declined to contribute any new capital. Thus, Noro financed the expansion and increased its joint venture interest from 40 percent to 45 percent. After a second expansion a short time later, Noro's interest increased to 49 percent. Sigma, in the meantime, was most concerned about the joint venture's losses. The general manager explained:

> Sigma was going berserk because the joint venture was losing much more money than was anticipated. They were also concerned that Noro did not seem nearly as upset about the financial situation as they were. Sigma did not really understand Noro's expectations about the business.

In 1990, it became obvious that a major expansion would be necessary. Over the previous four years, sales had increased from $7 million to more than $40 million. Plans were put in place to add another building that would double the size of the company from 300 to 600 employees. Sigma, however, was gradually withdrawing from the joint venture. With the latest expansion, Sigma's joint venture interest decreased to 30 percent and the general manager anticipated that the joint venture would soon be terminated. The general manager described Sigma's attitude toward the joint venture:

> Sigma is in a different business than Noro. They are in the commodity business. Machines are run until they wear out. There is no capital reinvested. Noro is in a dynamic business in which capital must be reinvested to compete. There is always pressure to lower costs and to improve the product.
>
> Because Sigma is in a different business than Noro, it's hard for them to understand the joint venture business. Sigma would have liked to get involved with the joint venture but they don't understand what the joint venture does. They got in over their heads financially. Even if they knew what they had to do to change, they could not afford to do it.

JOINT VENTURE TERMINATION AND THE CREATION OF COMPETITORS

Where serious conflicts between partners made termination of a joint venture inevitable, the Japanese partners were usually willing to buy out their American partners. Of the 13 joint ventures that have or will likely be terminated, there was only one case where the American partner acquired full ownership. In this case, the informant indicated that the Japanese partner had not abandoned the North American market and was probably planning a re-entry in another form. The other 12 joint ventures have or will become wholly-owned subsidiaries of the Japanese partners.

For the terminated joint ventures that were JOEM suppliers, the American partners usually seemed willing to concede the JOEM market to their Japanese partners. In contrast, the Japanese firms were committed to their North American investments and, rather than dissolving the joint venture organization, preferred to become its sole owner. However, by transferring its share of the joint venture to the Japanese partner, the American firm was often creating a new competitor. Compounding the problem, this competitor had a state-of-the-art plant, a young work force, and an owner that was willing to lose substantial amounts of money in order to gain a foothold in the North American automotive industry.

In several cases, the implications of creating a competitor were recognized by the American parents only after the joint venture relationship became unmanageable. Some American firms recognized the risks involved, but still decided that, because of the joint venture's superior capabilities, the venture should be used as the basis for targeting new domestic OEM business. A joint venture executive explained the dilemma facing an American partner:

> The American partner is losing some of its domestic OEM business. They are starting to consider how they might be able to use the joint venture to manufacture for their domestic OEMs while not turning over the business to the joint venture. The American partner does not want to create a monster that becomes a potential competitor in the event of a breakup.

In several terminated joint ventures, managers indicated that they suspected the Japanese partners may have entered the joint ventures with the goal of full ownership several years later. Along these lines, Kogut (1991) developed the perspective that joint ventures may be investments that provide firms with expansion opportunities. Faced with uncertainty and a desire to learn, firms may prefer a joint venture to an acquisition. If one partner has the option to purchase the other's equity in the venture, that partner can utilize the joint venture as a means of acquiring complex knowledge about the business. Once the party with the option to buy has acquired (i.e., learned) the skills of the partner firm, further investment in the venture may not be warranted. At this point, the buy option may be exercised. Even if there is no explicit purchase option, the success of a joint venture in transferring knowledge may shorten the life of a joint venture partnership by making one associate less essential over time (Kanter 1989).

The American partners in this study may have underestimated the speed with which their Japanese partners would adapt to the North American environment. Similarly, Badaracco (1991) suggested that perhaps General Motors underestimated the risks involved in forming a joint venture with Toyota. The NUMMI (New United Motors Manufacturing Corporation) joint venture was managed by Toyota, thus forcing Toyota managers to learn how to work with American workers and labour unions. Toyota was then able to deploy its new knowledge in a wholly owned plant in Georgetown, Kentucky.

To move beyond a North American joint venture to wholly-owned operations, Toyota and the other Japanese firms in this study had only to learn how to transfer an existing management process to North America. While many of the Japanese firms in the sample were initially uncertain about operating in North America, several years of involvement in a joint venture would probably allow them to acquire the necessary knowledge to compete on their own. The American firms, on the other hand, were faced with what Hamel and Prahalad (1989) referred to as the difficult-to-unravel strengths of their Japanese partners. Thus, it is not surprising that, so far, none of the American partners studied has been able to mount a genuine competitive threat to its Japanese joint venture partners.

IMPLICATIONS FOR AUTOMOTIVE SUPPLIERS

Just as the presence of the JOEMs in North America has pushed the domestic OEMs to higher levels of quality and customer satisfaction, the Japanese suppliers will undoubtedly have the same impact on North American suppliers. To make inroads into the growing JOEM market, American suppliers must re-evaluate their attitudes toward supplier-manufacturer relationships. For example, one area that is particularly difficult for American managers to appreciate is the JOEMs' assumption that annual cost-downs or price decreases from suppliers are standard practice. The JOEMs realize that price increases for costs, such as labour and material, are sometimes unavoidable and, therefore, generally accept increases in those areas. However, there is an expectation that suppliers will make an overall effort toward decreasing prices. Cost improvements will be shared between the supplier and the customer as part of the long-term relationship. One supplier was told by its JOEM customer, "Each year you will give us back three percent or you may lose the business. In return, you will be given priority for future contracts." Clearly, a JOEM supplier under that type of pressure will try to exert the same sort of pressure on its American suppliers. However, as an American manager explained:

We cannot do the same with all of our suppliers. Sooner or

> later you get back to the Mom and Pop rivet manufacturer.
> They don't know anything about Kaizen and annual cost-
> downs. Therefore, the three percent has to come out of my
> conversion cost.

The results of this study indicate that the Japanese joint venture partner firms in North America have quickly adapted to a new environment and, generally, are not content to remain solely JOEM suppliers. Both the suppliers in this study and wholly owned Japanese suppliers have made significant inroads into the North American automotive industry and are well-positioned to capture an even greater market. Although it is too simplistic to describe Japanese management as long-term oriented and American management as short-term oriented, the Japanese partner firms in this study appeared more willing than their American partners to focus on customer satisfaction and product quality rather than profit performance. The Japanese firms seemed less constrained by issues of share price and impatient boards of directors than their American counterparts.

For an American supplier, gaining access to the JOEM market will undoubtedly remain difficult, given the reasons discussed earlier. Thus, a joint venture will remain an attractive option, at least in terms of the speed and timing of market entry. Nevertheless, there were indications in this study that, as the JOEMs gain confidence in their existing American suppliers and add American managers, there will be greater emphasis on developing a domestic supplier base.

Moreover, American suppliers have one key advantage over their Japanese competitors that may play a role in future supplier negotiations. The American suppliers are generally much larger than their Japanese competitors and therefore may be able to capitalize on cost advantages. An American executive explained:

> The Japanese joint ventures typically have much lower
> volumes than their American parents and although they might
> be able to outperform them on quality, delivery, and service
> it is questionable whether they can outperform them on cost.
> Our joint venture can never be competitive with the tradi-
> tional sources because of its higher cost base. It will be difficult
> for the joint venture to be competitive with us. The joint
> venture product is higher quality but it also has a higher cost.
> The quality is higher because: 1) the design is different; and
> 2) the manufacturing process is superior.

NORTH AMERICAN FIRMS AND JOINT VENTURES

Despite the many problems encountered by North American firms in their joint ventures with Japanese partners, a joint venture strategy can be effective when the American partner has realistic expectations and understands its partner's objectives. The joint ventures that were successful met these conditions. The American partners in the success- ful joint ventures usually had at least some prior knowledge of the JOEMs and the reality of supplying JOEMs. These firms also recognized that the automotive industry was changing and that the assumptions of a few years ago no longer held true. Realizing the implications of cooperating with a potential competitor, several American partners took steps to limit the likelihood of that occurrence. In several of the successful joint ventures, American partners restricted the joint venture to supplying JOEMs; as part of the joint venture agreement, domestic OEMs could not be supplied by the joint venture.

Another key element in successful joint venture strategies was the use of the joint venture as a learning opportunity. Joint ventures can provide companies with a window to their partners' capabilities. There were two main ways in which this window was valuable to the American partners in the study. First, the opportunity to supply JOEMs had the potential to be a major learning experience. Second, the major- ity of joint ventures provided the American partners with first-hand access to their partners' skills and capabilities. All but five joint ventures were involved as JOEM suppliers and, in most cases, manufactured products similar to products made in Japan. Because the Japanese partner was usually responsible for implementing the manufacturing process and supplying the product technology, the joint venture plant was often a virtual copy of a Japanese plant. The equipment usually came from Japan with a team of Japanese engineers responsible for the joint venture's startup. Consequently, the joint ventures provided the American partner with a unique opportunity to study a new, state- of-the-art organization. The opportunity would not have been possible without a collaborative relationship.

However, poor joint venture performance seemed to create a barrier to learning because it shifted managerial attention away from the learning objective. In the poor-performing joint ventures, the American firms seemed fixated on improving performance. With this fixation came two types of reaction: first, resources that might have been committed to staff development or other learning efforts were directed toward improving joint venture performance; and second, loss of interest in the joint venture. For example, a manager explained the implications of poor joint venture performance:

> The [American partner's] emphasis on the profitability of the joint venture clouded their judgement. They just could not see past the startup period. The losses distorted the attitudes of the American partner. Learning was never allowed to surface. Their attitude became: the Japanese partner doesn't know anything so how can we learn from these people?

THE CHANGING TRADE ENVIRONMENT

The changing trade environment in North America has contributed to the development of a North American-based Japanese automobile industry. With movement of Japanese suppliers to North America, Canadian and US suppliers have come under increasing competitive pressures. Now industry is faced with the prospect of the implementation of NAFTA.

NAFTA will certainly have competitive implications for North American automotive suppliers, especially those firms involved in products with low engineering content. Should the JOEMs choose to establish operations in Mexico, their supplier base will probably be drawn from their existing North American suppliers. However, the Japanese OEMs have shown some reluctance to invest in Mexico, suggesting that their base of operations in North America will remain Canada and the United States. An additional factor is the geographic constraints of JIT production. None of the tier-one businesses in this study was more than six or seven hours from its OEM customers. Thus, establishing supplier operations in Mexico may not be consistent with a JIT environment that has OEMs in Canada and the United States.

CONCLUSION

The 1980s introduced North American automotive suppliers to a new set of competitive demands. Judging from the speed with which Japanese and other international firms have made inroads into the North American automotive industry, pressures for lower costs and higher quality will continue to escalate. One aspect of the changing industry structure is the large number of Japanese-North American joint ventures at the supplier level. Many North American firms, recognizing the implications of a growing JOEM presence, have seen a joint venture with a Japanese firm as the only means of gaining access to this growing market segment.

While the joint ventures have often performed far below expectations, a joint venture strategy offers the advantages of timeliness and efficiency in market access. The JOEMs' market share will undoubtedly continue to grow and firms that gain access now will be well-positioned for future growth, especially with NAFTA and JOEM investment in Mexico. Access without a Japanese connection will continue to be difficult for many North American firms, but not impossible if the supplier is capable of meeting the stringent demands of the JOEMs. Evidence from this study suggests that the JOEM market is not impenetrable but, rather, structured very differently from the domestic industry. A Japanese connection helps because of the network of long-term relationships that effectively creates a barrier to entry for outsiders.

Besides the network of relationships in the Japanese system, JOEM expectations in areas such as pricing, JIT delivery, monitoring of suppliers, information-sharing between suppliers and customers, and product design input are often unfamiliar to North American suppliers. Unfortunately, as this study found, many North American firms are not prepared to enter into supplier relationships with JOEMs that depart from the norms of traditional supplier-manufacturer relationships. For those firms that are willing to make the effort to modify their behaviour, the experience can be very positive and even enlightening. The experience may also prepare firms for the increasingly competitive North American trade environment. For example, the vice president of a large North American supplier described the firms's reaction to its initial joint venture experience:

> Initially, we thought there was nothing to learn from our partner. We thought we were better than anybody. When we first went to Japan we thought our partners wanted a joint venture so they could learn from us. We were shocked at what we saw on that first visit. We were amazed that they were even close to us, let alone much better. We realized that our production capabilities were nothing [compared with the

Japanese firm's]. We realized that we were not world class. Our partner was doing many things that we couldn't do. For example, they had excess equipment capacity that gave them more flexibility. We can't do that because of our short-term pressures. . . . We were spoiled from being number one in the industry. It wasn't until the mid-1980s that we began to get serious about quality and things like JIT and inventory control.

NOTES

[1] Although there were two Canadian firms in the sample, for brevity I will use "American" rather than "North American" in future references to the sample of firms.

[2] For a discussion of US state investment incentives see chapter 6 by Plumstead, Russell, and Stuewe.

[3] The names of joint venture partners and companies have been disguised.

[4] Several managers commented that the Japanese companies were surprised by the level of competition between Japanese companies in North America. According to one manager, "With all the new plants and potential business in America, nobody wants to risk missing a piece of the action. So they all come over even if they don't have any guarantee of getting the business."

REFERENCES

Badaracco, Joseph L. 1991. *The Knowledge Link.* Boston: Harvard Business School Press.

Contractor, Farok J., and Lorange, Peter. 1988. Why should firms cooperate: The strategy and economics basis for cooperative ventures. In *Cooperative Strategies in International Business*, eds. Farok Contractor and Peter Lorange, pp. 3-30. Toronto: Lexington Books.

Dodwell Marketing Consultants. 1990. *The Structure of the Japanese Auto Parts Industry.* Tokyo: Dodwell Marketing Consultants. Referenced in W. Karl Kester. *Governance, Contracting, and Investment Time Horizons.* Paper presented at the conference Time Horizons of American Management, Harvard Business School.

Hamel, Gary. 1991. Competition for competence and inter-partner learning within international strategic alliances. *Strategic Management Journal* 12 (special issue): 83-104.

Hamel, Gary, and Prahalad,C.K. 1989. Strategic intent. *Harvard Business Review* 67, May-June: 63-76.

____, Yves L. Doz, and Prahalad,C.K. 1989. Collaborate with your competitors—and win. *Harvard Business Review* 67, January-February: 133-39.

Harrigan, Kathryn Rudie. 1985. *Strategies for Joint Ventures.* Lexington, Mass.: Lexington Books.

Hennart, Jean-François. 1988. A transactions costs theory of equity joint ventures. *Strategic Management Journal* 9: 361-74.

Hoffman, Kurt, and Kaplinsky, Raphael. 1988. *Driving Force: The Global Restructuring of Technology, Labour, and Investment in the Automobile and Components Industries.* London: Westview Press.

Kanter, Rosabeth Moss. 1989. *When Giants Learn to Dance.* New York: Simon and Schuster.

Kester, W. Carl. 1991. *Japanese Takeovers: The Global Contest for Corporate Control.* Boston: Harvard Business School Press.

Kogut, Bruce. 1991. Joint ventures and the option to expand and acquire. *Management Science* 37, 1: 19-33.

Koh, Jeongsuk, and Venkatraman, N. 1991. Joint venture formations and stock market reactions: An assessment in the information technology sector. *Academy of Management Journal* 34, 4: 869-92.

Lewis, Jordan D. 1990. *Partnerships for Profit: Structuring and Managing Strategic Alliances.* New York: Free Press.

Miller, Edward K., and Winter, Drew. 1991. The "other big 3" are becoming all-American. *Ward's Auto World* 27, 2: 24-51.

Oliver, Christine. 1990. Determinants of interorganizational relationships: Integration and future directions. *Academy of Management Review* 15, 2: 241-65.

Porter, Michael E. and Fuller, Mark B. 1986. Coalitions and global strategy. In *Competition in Global Industries*, ed. Michael E. Porter, pp. 315-43. Boston: Harvard Business School Press.

Smith, David C. 1989. Whatever happened to teamwork? *Ward's Auto World* 25, 7: 3-44.

Womack, James P. 1988. Multinational joint ventures in motor vehicles. In *International Collaborative Ventures in US Manufacturing*, ed. David C. Mowery, pp. 301-48. Cambridge, Mass.: Ballinger.

6 THE NORTH AMERICAN AUTOMOTIVE INDUSTRY:

State Government Response to a Changing International Environment

Janice E. Plumstead
Brian R. Russell
David Stuewe

INTRODUCTION

This chapter discusses the nature and pattern of support provided by American state governments to the domestic auto industry. In the context of international trade agreements and global economic developments, the chapter provides several examples of the types of support available and the consequences that may follow. Government assistance programs play an increasingly important role in determining the future of the industry. The technological and financial challenges faced by a North American auto industry confronted with intense foreign competition have been a significant factor in determining the nature and extent of government support to business.

Confronted with increasing budgetary restraints, governments have been forced to evaluate program targets and objectives in order to obtain maximum benefits per dollar spent. This has resulted in increased emphasis on programs designed to foster research and development, labour-force training, and infrastructure expansion. Throughout the 1980s, state governments established numerous industrial development programs in an effort to maintain existing employment levels. By the mid-1980s, technology development and dispersion programs, such as the Michigan Modernization Program and Ohio's Thomas Edison Program, were in place and being supported by an array of employee-training and skill-development programs.

Though the US federal government typically denies that it has an overall industrial policy, there are similarities in approaches to state economic development across the United States. These state initiatives are supported by, and in many cases built upon, federal government direct spending and transfers for research and training. Individual states thereby give substance to the national policy by direct spending or joint venture support with industry or the federal government. The US position at the General Agreement on Tariffs and Trade (GATT) talks is that research should be an allowable subsidy.

Since 1989, the authors, in conjunction with the US Policy Studies Group at Dalhousie University, have undertaken several studies of the business assistance activities of eleven states representing over 50 percent of US gross national product (GNP). The eleven states studied to date are: California, Georgia, Illinois, Massachusetts, Michigan, Montana, New York, Ohio, Pennsylvania, Texas, and Washington. In addition, extensive research was undertaken in Washington, DC, examining the nature and extent of federal industrial support to business.

This study of US state government support to business in the late 1980s indicated that states are now concentrating more on enhancing and maintaining indigenous business rather than smoke-stack chasing (trying to attract large manufacturing firms). States will, however, continue to compete fiercely for new firms or firms thinking of relocating.

This research also showed that the expanding focus for encouraging economic development is through knowledge creation and dispersion. A broad range of industries benefit from this approach because technology and materials development have wide-ranging applications. The proliferation of this emphasis on research and development programs and worker training, while not constituting a coherent industrial strategy, nonetheless indicates a pattern of policy initiatives that reflect overarching concerns and responses.

THE APPLICATION TO AUTOS

As noted in other chapters in this volume, the automotive industry has been one of the mainstays of the US economy and international business. This predominant role eroded quickly in the 1970s and 1980s. Hastened by a series of external economic shocks, the oil crisis, the rise of the newly industrializing countries (NICs), and generally increasing foreign competition based on low wages and high technology, new state assistance programs were developed to increase research and development funding and improve the skills of the US labour force. Given the importance of the auto industry in the overall

US economy, some of these programs were designed specifically to benefit the industry and respond to its difficulties. Others were directed at more general problems that afflicted many industries, including autos.

Additional motivation for the rapid increase in state support for economic development was provided by the need to fill a vacuum caused by the cuts in direct federal business support programs. Despite the trend toward downloading by the federal government, the amount of federally directed support aimed specifically at research and development increased. Much of this support required the partnering of private, state, and university resources.

FOREIGN DIRECT INVESTMENT IN THE U.S. AUTOMOTIVE INDUSTRY AND NATIONAL POLICY

State and local economic development policies provide incentive packages for large plant locations in-state. While most studies indicate that state incentive programs do not heavily influence the decisions of automakers to build new capacity, such programs may, all things being equal, influence where new capacity is built.

In the 1970s and early 1980s, state governments began to shift their focus to attract foreign direct investment to create employment and encourage business growth. Table 2 lists the major foreign auto plants set up during this period. In addition to these incentives, US trade policy provided added motivation for direct US investment. For foreign auto producers, US locations provided a means of reducing some of the protectionist sentiment caused by the perceived loss of American jobs to offshore production. In fact, jobs created by foreign firms expanding US production do appear to have helped reduce protectionist feelings amongst American labour.

US capacity expansion resulted in some lessening of the pressure from US trade officials and politicians to reduce foreign imports. In response, much of the new auto capacity in the US is the product of foreign direct investment, primarily that of Japanese firms. These direct investment strategies have provided some relief from politically sponsored protectionist trade arrangements. To some extent, offshore auto manufacturers have been able to reduce calls for tighter Voluntary Export Restraints (VERs) and other trade barriers through direct investment in plant facilities within the United States.[1]

Despite some success with this strategy, national policies have served to protect American auto manufacturers when their market share has come under attack by competitors. The following policies are the most commonly used:

1. VERS. Japanese auto exports to the US are currently limited by agreement to 2.3 million units annually;

2. Domestic content regulations. For example, the Auto Pact, the fta, and nafta; and

3. Investment Control Policy. This approach is most commonly used in developing countries. In the US, there has been some concern that the interpretation of "national security," as presented in the 1988 Exon-Florio Amendment, could be extended beyond this specific restriction of foreign mergers, acquisitions, and takeovers to include foreign investment generally (Godfrey 1989: 14). This interpretation could restrict foreign investment by Japanese automotive transplant companies.

Existing VERs have, arguably, worked primarily to the advantage of Japanese manufacturers through the effects of limited supply. American consumers have been willing to pay a premium for imported automobiles, which on a relative basis, were viewed as being more technologically advanced and reliable. Demand has exceeded supply, which was constrained by VERs, and, as a result, prices have risen. Further, the number of jobs saved through this protective trade practice appears to have been relatively small. In a study done for the OECD, Willig and Dutz (1987) estimated that between 20,000 and 35,000 jobs were saved. Their study also estimated that, due to automobile price increases, these jobs cost consumers between $93,000 and $250,000 each. Both the additional premium and the benefits of direct investment have increased profits for Japanese manufacturers (Willig and Dutz 1987: 36-38).

SUBSIDIES AND TRADE

Overall, US trade policy works aggressively toward eliminating foreign trade practices that may create competitive disadvantages for domestic companies both at home and abroad. Under the GATT, government support for business (in the form of subsidy arrangements to specific firms, groups of firms, or sectors) is proscribed unless such assistance falls outside the indicated restrictions.

Subsidy use is symptomatic of the conflict between economic nationalism and global gains from trade theory. Although most export subsidies are illegal under GATT rules, domestic subsidies are widely argued to be a legitimate tool for developing national economic policy. It is contended that, within its national boundaries, a government may provide any type of business support it wishes, as long as this financial assistance is not directed specifically at increasing or supporting exports, a practice that is usually in clear contravention of GATT Article XVI.

Unfortunately, these domestic subsidies can have a significant distortionary effect on the costs of internationally traded commodities. This can occur in at least two ways:

1. Domestic subsidies may distort competition within the home market between domestic and foreign producers. Domestic producers receiving subsidies through economic assistance programs may, as a result, enjoy a cost advantage over foreign producers who do not receive the subsidies.

2. Domestic subsidies, while not specifically targeted at exported products, often result in a cost reduction either to upstream inputs to exports or various factors of production in exported products. Again, this may result in a cost reduction to the exporting producer who can then sell below the unassisted market price of producers in the export market.

If these cost reductions translate into price reductions, this combination of import replacement activity and export cost reduction confers advantages on recipient producers who are not part of the cost structures of competing firms not receiving these benefits. These types of programs are offered by all levels of government in the US.

TRADE ARRANGEMENTS

Several international trade agreements impact directly on the North American auto industry. As noted, GATT attempts to reduce tariff barriers between countries while also providing rules and procedures for addressing grievances.

The Canada-US Auto Pact is a bilateral agreement, concluded in 1965, that removed many duties on trade between the two countries in new motor vehicles and original-equipment parts.[2] From the US perspective, the objective of the Auto Pact was to "achieve unrestricted free trade in the North American automotive industry." In 1965, the US received a waiver from its obligations under Article I of the GATT (the MFN clause) in order to implement this agreement.[3]

Under the Canada-US Free Trade Agreement (FTA), tariffs and many trade barriers between the two countries were eliminated. The Agreement also provides for a consultative framework for resolving future trade disputes between the countries. The FTA continues and expands on the provisions of the Auto Pact and provides rules of origin that establish a 50 percent Canada-US content rule for vehicles to qualify for preferred entry treatment under the agreement. The FTA establishes a Working Group on Subsidies but does not directly address the substantive issue of subsidies.

Now, a North American Free Trade Agreement (NAFTA) has been negotiated and awaits final ratification in Canada, Mexico, and the United States. This treaty deals at some length with the trade rules now in place for the automotive industry. The agreement provides, in Chapter 3, Appendix 300—A.1(1), for the continuation of the Canada-US Auto Pact. Under the agreement, new vehicles produced in each country with sufficient North American content would qualify for phased-in tariff-free trade within the continent. By 2004, Mexico is required to remove those provisions of its highly restrictive Automotive Decree that are inconsistent with NAFTA. Furthermore, all parties agree to "review, no later that December 31, 2003 the status of the North American automotive sector...to determine actions that could be taken to strengthen the integration and global competitiveness of the sector" (Government of Canada 1992).

Rules of origin provisions have been expanded significantly in Chapter 4 of the Agreement and attempt to remove ambiguities that resulted in differing interpretations of the provisions for determining content levels under the FTA. As well, the North American content requirement has been raised to 62.5 percent for most vehicles. With respect to subsidy provisions, NAFTA follows the FTA example and does not deal with substantive subsidy issues, other than to continue provisions for consultation.

The Uruguay Round GATT negotiations have yielded proposals for a substantial tightening of subsidy disciplines and explicit inclusion of rules on domestic subsidies. It has been suggested that these proposals, if approved multilaterally, would be incorporated into NAFTA. One element of these proposals, contained in the "Dunkel draft" of

December 20, 1991, provides that government assistance for basic and applied research will be identified as an allowable—or "green-lighted"—subsidy, subject to specific limits on the extent of this exclusion. In order to qualify, assistance:

1. must be provided to firms, or to higher education or research establishments under contract to firms; and

2. must not cover more than 50 percent of the costs of basic industrial research, or 25 percent of the costs of applied research.

Clearly, the definition of the terms "basic" and "applied" will be crucial in influencing the future development of these types of programs in the US and elsewhere. This is of particular importance to the auto industry, which benefits extensively from research and development assistance programs. Not only is it important to know the extent and impact of this support, but the boundaries of the exclusion must also be carefully monitored. Definitions provided in the footnote are helpful, but obviously not determinative. The text provides that these definitions "shall be reviewed in the light of work in other relevant international institutions" (GATT 1991). This is a reference to OECD endeavours in this area, which is an obvious starting point for future discussion. Given the nature and extent of the programs revealed by our research, the ability to delineate this exemption will be a crucial test of the success of the subsidy provisions of the agreement.

Many other provisions of the draft agreement could affect the extent and nature of subsidies available to the auto industry. Of particular note is Article 2.2, which would appear to limit the ability of subfederal units, such as US states, to provide programs that are generally available within their respective jurisdiction. This would clearly impact on the ability of states—or provinces—to design and fund economic development programs within their own boundaries and could necessitate a major change in assistance policy and strategy.

STATE POLICIES AND INDUSTRY RESPONSE

As discussed above, the GATT Subsidies Code does not explicitly deal with domestic subsidies. The incentives provided by state governments for auto plants locating within their jurisdictions are generally not treated as actionable within GATT guidelines.

Under Article XI of the GATT Code,

> [s]ignatories recognize that subsidies other than export subsidies are widely used as important instruments for the promotion of social and economic policy objectives and do not intend to restrict the right of signatories to use such subsidies to achieve these and other important policy objectives which they consider desirable (GATT 1980).

Accordingly, public policy options available to entice industry to locate within a particular state are extensive. In the 1970s and early years of the 1980s, state governments competed for new plants using an extensive array of support provisions. Industrial support policies at the state level which act as incentives for attracting in-state investment are:

1. Enterprise zone status;

2. Tax incentives;

3. Give-aways, e.g., land;

4. Infrastructure improvements;

5. Provision of services, e.g., applicant selection, worker training, plant site tours, etc.; and

6. State financing, e.g., grants, low-cost loans, industrial development bonds, loan guarantees.

The competitive position of a firm or industry can be affected by government subsidization. Whether or not they are recognized in trade law, these practices can have real economic effects. Our research on governmental assistance to industry reveals that the auto sector benefits from government assistance activities are currently ignored within the scope of existing GATT subsidy provisions. In one example, the Illinois Technology Challenge Grant Program awarded $469,000 to a consortium composed of the University of Chicago, Ford Aerospace, and Ford Motor Company.[4] The project will, "help scientists study and visualize in 3-D the impacts of the changing cloud formations, with potentially marketable spin-offs from massive information storage, retrieval and visualization techniques" (Illinois 1990). The grant was contingent on receiving a National Science Foundation (NSF) Science and Technology Center Grant of $7.5 million. The long-term derivatives of this and other types of research may well contribute to automated driver systems or other auto-related applications.

There are also a number of grey areas that have benefitted the industry. Under most national countervailing duties statutes, generally available benefits are not countervailable, while specific support targeted at industries or firms is prohibited. By disguising the nature of specific assistance programs, a government can assist firms and provide support for new plants located in its jurisdiction. Sometimes this support is directed through an individual or an educational institution. In other instances, funds are given directly to the firm where there has been a major investment in the local area.

An example of this process in relation to worker training is provided by the incentives package given to Diamond-Star Motors in Illinois. A revised amount of $30 million was allocated as a budget line item for job training in 1990 under the Illinois Industrial Training Grant Program. Under this program, which was nominally available, Diamond-Star Motors received over US $ 3.9 million to train individuals for 708 new jobs. Arguably, this was a de facto specific subsidy of a type which, if practised by foreign governments and detected, would attract countervail under US law. Historically, however, countervailing duty (CVD) action has been largely the purview of US producers, and the threat of action by other countries is regarded as low.

One weakness in these types of incentives can be seen in Kentucky. In 1987, the total amount allocated for government economic development support was used for job training related to one Toyota plant. When the costs of industry attraction become as large as in this case, and require such substantial allocations from general funds for one specific project, government is unable to respond to other economic issues or pursue additional economic development objectives through available loan, grant, and assistance programs.

A useful illustration of state incentive programs used to attract automotive plant investment is shown in Table 1. Diamond-Star Motors was a joint venture between Chrysler and Mitsubishi Motors developed to manufacture Eclipse automobiles. The companies received a combined incentives package of US $96 million from the State of Illinois and local government units in McLean County. Diamond-Star Motors considered these incentives "a given in its negotiations with state and local governments" (Lind and Elder 1986: 23).

The process of attracting new capital investment, commonly known as "smoke-stack chasing," has been documented in a number of cases. One of the more notable examples of an auto plant chase was the competition for the first foreign plant to be built in the United

Table 1

Incentives to Diamond-Star
(All figures in millions of US dollars)

Incentives given to Diamond-Star	State of Illinois	Cities of:		Other[a]
		Normal	Bloomington	
Land to Diamond-Star	5.59	.96	.96	
Infrastructure	29.57	.55	.55	2.04
Tax and Fee Abatements	9.05	1.18	1.18	1.66
Services Job Training	41.14			
Cost reductions Reduced Utility Fees				1.20
Financing IDB	.40			
Total	**$85.75**	**$2.69**	**$2.69**	**$4.90**

a. Includes: county, township, sewer district, airport authority, school and private utility concessions.
Source: Lind and Elder (1986: 23).

States. The Commonwealth of Pennsylvania provided US $ 71 million in government support to attract and retain the Volkswagen (VW) plant. Overtures by a number of US states to secure the Volkswagen (VW) investment started as early as 1973. There have never been guarantees, however, that foreign investment would be successful. After ten years of operation, the Westmoreland plant in Pennsylvania was closed and Volkswagen production moved to Mexico.

Corporate executives at Volkswagen had anticipated that production in the United States would resolve the issues of foreign exchange and import restrictions. Relying on market analysis suggesting that American consumers wanted high-quality, fuel-efficient, smaller vehicles, Volkswagen invested in a North American plant facility dedicated to the Rabbit model. It is reported to have initially cost VW US $ 250 million to start up (*Business Week* 1978: 106), and another US $ 100 million to retool in 1984 (Fulton 1988: 36).

Volkswagen's decision to invest in the United States was also prompted by the quota arrangements that had been established against some foreign automotive competitors. By locating in the United States, Volkswagen was able to avoid import quotas that would have restricted

Table 2

**New Auto Plant Expansions Receiving
State Assistance: Cost per Job**

Company	Location	Cost per Job	No. of Jobs	Investment (millions US$)
VW (Rabbit/Golf) 1976-1987	New Stanton, Pa.	$14,200	5,000	$350
Nissan USA (Trucks/Sentra) 1980	Smyrna, Tenn.	$11,000	2,900	$660
GM (Saturn) 1985	Spring Hill, Tenn.	$26,000	6,000	$3,500
Toyota (Camry) 1988	Georgetown, Ky.	$30,000	3,000	$800
Diamond-Star (Chrysler/Mitsubishi) 1987	Normal, Ill.	$30,000	2,900	$650
Fuji/Isuzu (Subaru) 1989	Lafayette, Ind.	$50,000	1,700	$500

Source: Fulton 1988: 32-39.
               Business Week, May 30, 1988: 45.

its US market share. The company sought to insulate itself from the familiar argument that import quotas protected the domestic auto industry from foreign competitors who enjoyed an unfair competitive advantage resulting from government subsidization. (At that time, Volkswagen was 40 percent owned by the German government).

Throughout the 1970s and early 1980s, smoke-stack chasing continued to benefit the auto industry. The trend continues to grow in the 1990s. The per job price extracted for each plant has increased significantly during this time. Table 2 shows the per job cost for several of these new plant investments. This table also highlights the new "auto alley," which extends through Michigan, Ohio, Kentucky, Indiana, and Tennessee.

There appears to be a positive correlation between the building of foreign-owned or joint venture auto plants and the increase in the cost of government assistance to industry. This has resulted in competition between states, and between communities within states, to serve as sites for new plants. The GM Saturn and Nissan plants, which eventually were located in Tennessee, were hotly competed for by several other states.

Georgia, which on paper does not have many direct industry giveaway programs, was one of those in the bidding war for the Saturn plant. It seriously pursued the plant with an incentives package that included tax expenditures, training, and the favourable pricing of land. One Georgia official from the Department of Industry, Trade and Tourism commented in an interview that Georgia decided not to continue with the bidding when it became clear the cost would outweigh the conceivable potential benefits.

Firms seeking a plant location will generally consider a site more favourably if there is support from the local government. This complements the state government policy of encouraging economic development, especially in depressed areas.

The continued location of plants in the mid-west states is not just due to the large incentive programs offered by these state governments. Site location specialists often choose states in this area for their favourable access to transportation routes, which inevitably decreases freight costs. Transplant firms also want the flexibility of starting up plants without unionized labour membership. Some plants have been located in "right-to-work" states. Out of twenty other states that bid for the Nissan plant, Nissan chose Tennessee largely because it is a right-to-work state, where union membership is not required (*Economist* 1985: 61-62).

In June 1992, the German auto manufacturer Bayerische Motoren Werks AG (BMW) announced a $400 million investment in a new plant to be located in South Carolina. In an effort to enter the proposed North American free trade area and compete with US-produced Japanese luxury models, the company felt a need for a US manufacturing operation. An extensive competition for the investment ensued among states. South Carolina emerged the victor for a number of, by now, familiar reasons: the proximity of major transportation links, a low level of unionized labour, and a substantial package of state incentives. These state inducements included the donation of a 360-hectare plant site, airport and road upgrading, tax reductions, and the provision of worker-training programs, among others. The value of the total package is estimated to exceed $130 million. BMW estimates that by the year 2000, through doubling their initial investment, the facility will employ some 2,000 workers and produce 60,000 units per year. Assuming this to be correct, this yields an average cost per job of $65,000 in public funds.

Other factors for site location have been suggested. Milward and Newman concluded in their paper on site location factors that, aside from state incentives, transportation, a positive business climate, the degree of involvement at the state government level, and the state tax regime all have significant weight in the investment decision (1989: 203-222). Our research indicates that incentives provided through the state and federal tax systems are the largest sources of government financial support to US business.

Additional assistance available to companies locating in some states also includes pre-screening of employees. The state of Tennessee did the initial sorting of 130,000 applicants for the first 2,000 jobs that the Nissan plant generated (*Forbes* 1984: 99). Similarly, the Pennsylvania Bureau of Employment Security (PBES) was involved in preliminary job screening for Volkswagen. This service included initial interviews, aptitude testing, and measurement of manual dexterity. After the initial process was completed, the PBES served as a referral service (*Business Week* 1978: 106).

Underlying the acceptance of foreign investment in autos is the hope that overall domestic content will increase, thereby expanding employment and facilitating technology and knowledge transfer. State economic development specialists believe that, as domestic content increases, the number of suppliers surrounding the plant will increase. To this end, states offer incentives for new plant investment in the hope of obtaining significant spin-off effects. Federal and state programs encourage productivity enhancements through small- and medium-sized businesses. These are often the firms that become suppliers to the large auto plants. Specific monetary set-asides exist for small- and medium-sized businesses in most research and development programs. States will often assist with the development of a firm's Small Business Innovation Research application to the federal government.

In Tennessee, Nissan gets many of its parts, such as shock absorbers, tires, and exhaust systems from the local supplier base (*Forbes* 1984: 106). Until recently, Honda promoted its vehicles as

"American" made (*Business Week* 1991: 105). Now, questions have been raised as to the accuracy of that statement. A study by Massachusetts Institute of Technology economist Paul R. Krugman discovered that Japanese manufacturers have a greater likelihood of importing component parts than either foreign or American firms (*Business Week* 1991: 118). Correspondingly, a 1992 US Customs audit of Honda automobiles exported from Canada to the US has raised serious concerns about the ambiguity of the rules of origin under the FTA and the extent to which these vehicles meet the 50 percent Canada-US content requirement for low-tariff entry. Revisions to the rules of origin in NAFTA, touched on above, attempt to address these concerns.

CONCLUSION

North American auto manufacturers are faced with an international environment in which they are being consistently challenged by foreign producers in terms of both quality and price. Increased interaction between foreign producers and domestic consumers has led to a substantial lessening of market share for the leading US manufacturers. The industry restructuring that has been necessitated by these developments has been both extensive and painful. Indeed, the process is continuing with the closure of inefficient plants and the reduction of excess capacity. All of the Big Three North American automakers have at one time or another teetered on the edge of insolvency, and some continue to do so. It remains to be seen if all will survive.

In this highly competitive environment, the industry has attempted to respond by increasing the role of technology in the manufacturing process and by entering numerous joint ventures with foreign partners. Companies have also redoubled their demands for domestic protection against "unfair" foreign competition and an end to barriers to foreign markets, particularly Japan's. Whether or not these demands are legitimate, the importance of the sector has led both state and federal governments to respond to these developments in at least two ways: first, by protection (e.g., voluntary restraint agreements); and second, by providing financial assistance to the industry in order to assist with initiatives designed to promote increases in plant efficiency, labour-force skills, and product quality (e.g., research and development and training assistance).

These activities have been significant in both scale and scope, and similar patterns can be seen across the United States. Increasing state support, coupled with the effects of recession and globalization, have led to a rise in competition between states for plant locations, and have allowed the industry to play off competitors against each other to gain increasing levels of assistance. Empirical evidence indicates that the costs of this competition to taxpayers is considerable.

The rise in subsidy programs designed to attract the industry raises increasing concerns about the ability of the GATT or other trade agreements to police this type of activity. The provisions of the Uruguay Round draft text should go some distance toward addressing these concerns; however, one should be careful not to underestimate the resourcefulness of policymakers in finding ways to circumvent even these restrictions. Within an increasingly integrated North American market, it will be necessary to be vigilant in monitoring the development of state subsidy programs and to encourage, where necessary, revision of the rules to capture practices that may confer undue competitive advantages on various producers, thereby contributing to the reduction of global and national economic welfare.

NOTES

1   Voluntary Export Restraints (VERs) are informal arrangements through which exporters voluntarily restrain certain exports—usually through export quotas—to avoid economic dislocation in an importing country and to avert the possible imposition of mandatory import restrictions.

2   Further discussion of the Auto Pact and the Canada-US FTA can be found in Chapter 10 by Jon Johnson.

3   The Canada-US Automotive Agreement brought in the 50 percent minimum-content rule. In order to qualify for duty-free entry, vehicles required a minimum Canadian or US content of 50 percent. The United States wanted to be assured that cars imported from Canada were achieving the required North American content.

4   The Illinois Industrial Training Grant Program is the Department of Commerce and Community Affairs's largest state-funded program, with annual appropriations of $30 million. The state grants are used to upgrade employees' skills in mature companies that are retooling or implementing new manufacturing technologies or processes. The Industrial Training Program also helps new and expanding Illinois industries develop a well-trained labour force by paying directly to the firm a pre-agreed portion of worker/trainee wages.

REFERENCES

Beigie, Carl E. 1970. *The Canada-US Automotive Agreement: An Evaluation*. Montreal: Canadian-American Committee.

Business Week. 1978. Why Tension Grows around VW's Plant. February: 106.

Business Week. 1991. Honda, Is It an American Car? November: 112.

Economist. 1985. August: 61-62.

Forbes. 1984. We Started from Ground Zero. March: 99.

Fulton, William. 1988. VW in Pennsylvania: The Tale of the Rabbit that Got Away. *Governing* 2: 32-71 November.

General Agreement on Tariffs and Trade (GATT). 1980. *The Agreement and Interpretation and Application of Articles VI, XVI and XXIII*: 26s/56. Geneva: GATT Secretariat.

____. 1991. *Draft Final Act Embodying the Results of the Uruguay Round of Multilateral Trade Negotiations*. UR-91-0185. Geneva: GATT Secretariat.

Godfrey, John. 1989. Exon-Florio: No, It's Not an Oil Tanker. *Financial Post*, September 9, 11:14.

Government of Canada. 1992. *Legal Text of the North American Free Trade Agreement*. Ottawa: External Affairs and International Trade. October 7.

Illinois. 1990. *Illinois' Advanced Technology Portfolio*. Illinois Technology Challenge Program. Awards for FY 1990 and FY 1991: December.

Leidy, Michael P. 1991. Quid Pro Quo Restraint and Spurious Injury: Subsidies and the Prospect of CVDs. For the *Conference on Analytical and Negotiation Issues in the Global Trading System*. Ann Arbor, Mich.: University of Michigan. October.

Lind, Nancy S., and Elder, Ann H. 1986. Who pays? Who benefits? The case of the incentive package offered to the Diamond-Star automotive plant. *Government Finance Review* 2,6: 19-23.

Milward, H. Brinton, and Newman, Heidi Hosbach. 1989. State Incentive Packages and the Industrial Location Decision. *Economic Development Quarterly* 3,3: 203-22.

Willig, Robert D., and Dutz, Mark A. 1987. US-Japan VER: A Case Study from a Competition Policy Perspective. The costs of restricting imports, the automobile industry. Paris: Organization for Economic Cooperation and Development.

7 REGULATING THE AMERICAN AUTOMOBILE INDUSTRY:

Sources and Consequences of US Automobile Air Pollution Standards

Dennis J. Gayle

INTRODUCTION

The automobile industry is pivotal to America's economy because of the size of its direct labour force, the magnitude of its purchases from other major sectors, and the level of consumer demand for individual transport in the United States.[1] It is also a pre-eminent global industry, characterized by wide geographic dispersion, well-developed international trade, extreme demand fluctuations, rapid technological change, large corporations, frequently strong unions, and interested governments. By 1980, more than forty-five nations produced or assembled automobiles. Without exception, large automobile companies seek competitive advantage in global competition by coordinating complex networks of internal as well as external activities, which are dispersed worldwide. Meanwhile, governments seek to share in industry profits, develop or maintain national champions, and influence corporate strategy. Both home and host government taxes, regulations, and subsidies affect relative capital costs.

Social regulation has become increasingly significant in its cumulative effects on the international automobile industry. Within the United States, three categories of social regulation impact on the automobile industry: air-pollution standards, safety standards, and fuel-economy regulation. These regulations are promulgated under: the Clean Air Act Amendments of 1990, administered by the Environmental Protection Agency; the Motor Vehicle Information and Cost Savings Act of 1972 and the Energy Policy and Conservation Act of 1975, which are administered by the Secretary of Transportation; and the National Highway Traffic and Motor Vehicle Safety Act of 1966, administered by the National Highway Traffic Safety Administration.

The second section of this chapter explores the structure of the US automobile industry, further setting the stage for an examination of the sources and consequences of American automobile air pollution standards between 1970 and 1990. The third section details the requirements of the Clean Air Act Amendments of 1970, 1977, and 1990, and assesses the extent to which related regulations have been implemented. As the conclusion indicates, given the US automobile sector's substantial financial and employment losses since 1985, as well as broadening public support for environmentalism, and deepening Japanese penetration of the North American market, these standards will become increasingly demanding, contested, and internationalized in future, most immediately within the context of the North American Free Trade Agreement (NAFTA).

THE STRUCTURE OF THE AMERICAN AUTOMOBILE INDUSTRY

Since 1973, the US automobile industry has evolved within an environment that has been increasingly characterized by internationalization, intra-industry alliances, declining domestic demand, expanding overseas markets, and intensified market differentiation. Japanese and European imports had claimed over 15 percent of the US automobile market by 1973, using effective appeals to customers on the grounds of performance, styling, technology, and economy. Even so, in 1978, General Motors (GM) was still selling nearly half of all cars purchased in the United States. Indeed, GM earned a record $3.5 billion on $63 billion in sales during that year. However, in 1980, Japanese car production overtook American automobile output for the first time. This coincided with a US automobile industry crisis, as evidenced by frequently announced plant closings, layoffs, sagging sales, and import penetration.[2]

It is well-known that the 1981 Voluntary Restraint Agreement, under which Japan limited its automobile shipments to 1.8 million cars each year, was intended to allow US carmakers time to update their model lines. To be sure, between 1983 and 1988, GM, Ford, and Chrysler combined recorded increased profits of 30 percent per annum, the best of any US industry. However, the quotas produced shortages, which drove Japanese automobile prices up by a mean $2,500 and domestic cars up by a mean $700 before the close of 1985. General Motors' strategy of redesigning every one of its factories—at an estimated cost of $40 billion—to emphasize high-quality smaller cars was countered by lower gasoline prices and a surge in consumer demand for larger cars. At the same time, the quota system encouraged the establishment of foreign-owned automobile factories in the United States.

General Motors, Chrysler, and Ford responded to the continuing internationalization of the US auto industry in four main ways. First, instead of dealing with component suppliers on the basis of relative price only, the Big Three began to create stakeholder alliances by encouraging in-plant access, technical contacts, and exchanges of ideas with companies involved in areas such as broaching,[3] machine tools, furnace design, and computers. Suppliers such as Cummins Engine, Colt Industries, and Arvin Industries became more intimately involved in automobile production and design than ever before, as was the case in both Japan and Europe. At the same time, the GM Components Group sold $30 billion in products and employed 230,000 people worldwide. In 1989, 12 percent of such sales were made to competing international manufacturers. By 1988, automobile manufacturers were commonly setting broad standards while suppliers performed the design and development work, taking responsibility for complete automotive systems (*Economist* 1988: 22). Similarly, in October 1989, General Motors and Chrysler Corporation agreed to combine the operations of their Muncie, Indiana and Syracuse, New York manual transmission plants, respectively, into a company called New Venture Gear. During the same month, GM, Ford, and Chrysler launched a joint research project intended to reduce tailpipe emissions and develop alternative fuels.

This opportunistic alliance represented an unprecedented change in governance structure in that the Big Three US auto companies had never worked together in any aspect of manufacturing.[4] By January 1991, the Big Three had also formed a battery venture, with assistance from the US Department of Energy and utility companies, to improve the range and performance of electric vehicles. Additionally, in May 1991, they agreed to work together on high-speed multiplexing, intended to improve electronic-control performance (Stertz 1991: B1).

Second, product rationalization has become an increasingly important goal. For instance, at General Motors, designers cut the number of parts in a pickup truck by 46 percent and engineers reduced the component total in the 1991 Buick Park Avenue's bumper to 44 from 108 in the 1990 model, thus contracting assembly time from ten to five minutes. Similarly, Ford product planners are re-examining the product development process in an effort to cut costs by 20 percent without having an affect on new product or equipment orders. Ford executives have also re-evaluated the link between quality and customer service at other corporations outside the industry, such as Xerox and McDonalds. Chrysler has already cut costs by $3 billion and plans to sell several assets, while developing a new range of mid-size cars, as well as a now popular four-door Jeep. Chrysler President Robert Lutz contends that his attempts to decentralize authority and decision-making have led to better as well as more rapid decisions (White and Stertz 1991: B1, B9).

Third, the Big Three effectively stopped making entry-level cars and attempted to retool all their mid-range models (*Economist* 1988: 20). Market segmentation became fashionable, driven in part by the efforts of manufacturers to achieve economies of scope, as well as scale.[5] As slow sales forced the closing of at least nine car and truck assembly plants, in 1989 American automobile manufacturers began to target smaller and smaller niches, producing low-volume units with high-profile features. For example, Ford's Chevrolet Lumina APV or Aerostar XL Wagon, Chrysler's Jeep Cherokee Laredo or Plymouth Grand Voyager, GM's Oldsmobile Bravada or GMC Suburban are all pickup trucks and utility vehicles that have been marketed much like sports cars. In 1990, Chrysler sold several thousand luxury minivans, and the Jeep Cherokee was an outstanding success as an export to Brazil in particular, among other Latin American countries.

Fourth, cross-national corporate arrangements have continued to proliferate in the automobile industry. For instance, major international component companies, such as Germany's Bosch in electronics and Britain's GKN or America's Eaton in transmissions, are developing human and dedicated asset specificity, while creating component alliances that encourage single sourcing by reducing labour costs and inventory requirements. Meanwhile, in 1989 Ford purchased 15 percent of Britain's leading luxury carmaker, Jaguar PLC for $2.5 billion and negotiated "close cooperation" with Sweden's Saab Scania AB, while also planning a further $2.5 billion joint venture to build minivans in Portugal with Germany's Volkswagen.

In addition, US automakers courted Japanese joint venture

partners. The February 1983 agreement between GM and Toyota to co-produce a small automobile at GM's Fremont plant in California was prototypical. At the New United Motors Manufacturing Corporation (NUMMI), which produced both the Geo Prizm and the Corolla, Toyota provided management expertise, appointing both the CEO and the president, while GM appointed half the board of directors.[6] Toyota began to build compact pickup trucks on a second assembly line at this plant in September 1991 (White and Templin 1991: A2). This allowed Toyota to avoid a 25 percent US tariff levied on its imported trucks, while also facilitating further market segmentation.

When Chrysler sold half its interest in Mitsubishi Motors Corporation for some $310 million net in September 1989, both companies emphasized their intention to continue their cooperative relationship, including a jointly operated plant in Normal, Illinois. GM's John F. Smith commented: "Business arrangements will prove much more effective in bringing foreign automobile companies to manufacture in the US than any legislation ever could. The forces of the marketplace...have a way of inducing desirable results much faster and more effectively than any law...because everyone stands to benefit from cooperation" (Smith 1983: 25). Ironically, just as GM was closing five automobile assembly plants in December 1987, Toyota was opening an auto production facility in Georgetown, Kentucky and Honda was announcing plans to expand its US operations with a plant in East Liberty, Ohio.

New strategic alliance systems continue to emerge within the automobile industry, altering corporate governance structures in sometimes ironical ways. For instance, in 1990 the Toyota Motor Corporation discovered that Bumper Works, a small pickup-truck bumper manufacturer in Danville, Illinois, could only deliver this component at relatively high prices, with an unacceptable defect ratio. Toyota's response was to dispatch a team of manufacturing experts to Bumper Works to conduct a crash course in the Toyota Production System. One year later, productivity at Bumper Works had improved by 60 percent, and the average number of defects had been reduced by 80 percent (White 1991b: A1).

Toyota's efforts to provide training to a component supplier improved specific human assets as well as dedicated assets, while creating a novel stakeholder alliance. Bumper Works is now shipping bumpers to Fremont, California, for the Toyota pickups built at the GM-

Toyota joint venture plant. Some of Toyota's rivals will also benefit as Bumper Works implements a new contract with Isuzu Motors' Indiana plant, while making overtures to GM, Ford, and Chrysler. At the same time, General Motors Corporation is pursuing legal charges that Toyota has been dumping minivans in the United States, even as GM sends hundreds of engineers to Fremont for training in the Toyota Production System.

Indeed, cross-national corporate arrangements are not immune to serious disagreements over issues such as management and funding. For example, General Motors Corporation, which has developed four joint venture operations with South Korea's Daewoo Group since 1982, has indicated that quality problems, labour disputes, and notable agency losses might lead to the dissolution or substantial alteration of this opportunistic alliance (White 1991c: A4).

More Japanese than domestic American companies now assemble automobiles in the United States, and Japan's Honda was the fourth largest producer of cars in the country by 1988. In that year, Japanese cars built in America, together with imported models, accounted for about a quarter of the US market, while GM (34.8 percent), Ford (19.8 percent) and Chrysler (9.4 percent) remained concerned at their declining market shares (*Economist* 1988:10).[7] Indeed, in 1990, Japan's largest single US investment consisted of the Toyota Motor Corporation's $800 million expansion of its wholly-owned facility in Georgetown, Kentucky (*Japan Times* 1991a: 18). By the 1990 model year, Honda was leading all US automobile manufacturers in productivity, with 95 cars per hour, while keeping labour costs roughly 10 percent below those of GM, Ford, and Chrysler. In 1989, the average annual earnings of autoworkers at the US facilities of Honda, Toyota, and Mazda were estimated at $32,000, compared with over $36,000 at GM, Ford and Chrysler (Jackson 1990: 2). During January-June 1991, Honda Motor Corporation sold 399,120 vehicles in the United States, replacing Chrysler (361,870 vehicles) as the third largest American automaker (*Japan Times* 1991b: 16). The diagnoses of Detroit's continuing decline have ranged from fat instead of lean manufacturing, union work rules, management's short-term vision, departmental parochialism, and consumer demand for "life style" rather than "socioeconomically suitable" cars (Drucker 1991: A18).[8]

If consumer preferences have altered, several developments have also softened domestic vehicle demand during the past ten years. The average yearly growth rate of the driving-age population slowed dramatically in the 1980s, from nearly 2 percent per year to only about 0.8 percent per year. Meanwhile, the rate of increase in the number of US households also decelerated, and motor vehicle purchase growth was further dampened by a more moderate inflow of women into the labour force. Additionally, there has been a substantial drop-off in the replacement demand for vehicles (Bryan and Martin 1991). In 1970, only 16 percent of US passenger cars were at least nine years old. This compared to over 35 percent of such automobiles in 1989, as total car and light truck sales declined from a high of 15.5 million units in 1986 to an annual rate of 5.7 million units in January 1991 (Koretz 1991: 12). Where the Chrysler Corporation made a net profit of $38.5 million in 1990, the Ford Motor Company earned $860.1 million (while accumulating a negative cash flow of $3.1 billion), and General Motors reported a net loss of almost $2 billion. In response, at the end of February 1991, the three automakers announced plans to lay off 38,950 autoworkers, with the closure or partial closure of 17 assembly plants because of slow sales and model changeover (*Miami Herald* 1991a: C1). GM's 1990 loss was the largest annual loss ever for the company, and the first time GM had posted a loss for a full year since 1980. The company's losses in North America eliminated $2.4 billion in profits from overseas operations, including a record $1.9 billion profit from GM Europe.

Similarly, Ford's overseas automotive operations experienced a loss of $124 million during the fourth quarter of 1990, after earning profits totalling $281 million one year earlier (White and Templin 1991: A3). During the 20 years through 1989, Ford was a high-earnings leader of the European automobile industry with an 11.2 percent market share; in 1990, profits suddenly plunged by 88 percent (Melcher and Templeman 1991: 48). Meanwhile, within the Japanese market, sales of American cars expanded by 147 percent during 1990 to a total of 28,602 vehicles, accounting for 8 percent of the imported automobile market.

This growth in Japanese market share was propelled by the contin-ued strength of the yen relative to the dollar, more effective advertis-ing campaigns, and Japan's tax reform of April 1989, which removed a 23 percent levy on large-engine models. Where GM sales in Japan grew by 21 percent, Ford Motor Company (Japan) Limited sales increased by 27 percent, and Chrysler Japan Limited posted a 47 percent gain (Takahashi 1991: 1, 17). The eight Japanese transplant automobile factories cut back exports from Japan (where such factories were running at full capacity amid a labour shortage) rather than US output, owing to the associated public-image implications (Treece, Woodruff and Miller 1991: 21). As combined output at Chrysler, Ford, and General Motors sank to its lowest level since 1958, the seven Japanese manufacturing companies owning or operating these factories planned to build 7.1 percent more cars in the April-June 1991 period than a year earlier (Patterson 1991: 1). At that point, the Japanese automobile companies had secured almost 36 percent of the US market, compared with 31 percent in 1989.

THE CLEAN AIR ACT AMENDMENTS OF 1970, 1977, AND 1990

Congressional concern with air quality and automobile emissions in the United States was first evidenced in the 1960s by the 1963 Clean Air Act, which was amended with the passage of the 1965 Motor Vehicle Air Pollution Control Act. This followed hearings conducted by the Special Subcommittee on Air and Water Pollution of the US Senate Committee on Public Works, which found that automobile exhaust was responsible for some 50 percent of the national air pollution problem (US Senate 1964: 3). The 1967 Air Quality Act, which preceded the 1970 Clean Air Act, was based upon a regional approach implemented by the National Air Pollution Control Administration (NAPC).

This legislation provided that NAPC would issue "criteria documents" for specific pollutants and that the governors concerned would file letters of intent within 90 days, declaring that state standards would be established in each case. The 1967 Air Quality Act was a disaster because it lacked a firm data base for setting reasonable standards, given technological feasibility and economic costs (Jones 1975: 69, 123). More than two years after this legislation was enacted, no criteria documents had been issued, and no state had established a full set of standards or adopted an implementation plan to control any pollutant (Middleton 1971: 304-307; Edelman 1971: 321-326). By January 1969, the Department of Justice had vainly charged the automobile industry with conspiracy to delay the implementation of pollution-control technology (National Research Council 1982: 81).

The Environmental Protection Agency (EPA) was created by the Nixon Administration on December 2, 1970, by bringing together almost 6,000 employees from 15 government programs located in the Departments of Health, Education and Welfare, Agriculture, and the Interior. Under the 1970 Clean Air Act, the EPA was required to propose primary national ambient air quality standards to protect public health, accompanied by secondary standards intended to safeguard public welfare, within 30 days after passage of the Act. Congress mandated specific motor vehicle standards, which projected that hydrocarbon, carbon monoxide, and nitrogen emissions would be reduced by 90 percent from the average levels observed in 1968 automobiles. The hydrocarbon standard specified was 0.41 grams per mile by 1975. In the case of carbon monoxide, the 1975 requirement was 3.4 grams per mile. The nitrogen oxide criterion was 0.4 grams per mile by 1976.

Congress chose to legislate automobile emission standards directly in 1970, largely because public opinion had begun to coalesce in favour of such action.[9] At the same time, industry executives appeared unwilling to implement voluntary emission reductions, although automobiles were the single largest pollution source in terms of overall emissions weight, and despite the widely publicized link between such emissions and smog generation within the Los Angeles air basin. Such representatives tended to adopt an obstructionist perspective, successfully deploying a range of arguments against emissions controls, partially because import penetration of the US automobile market was just beginning to gather force when the 1970 Clean Air Act Amendment was promulgated.

In response to the language of this Act and the context of its passage, regulators adopted a combination of technology-inducing and non-regulatory styles.[10] General Motors, Ford, and Chrysler each sought to minimize transaction costs on the basis of a traditional calculus of assets.[11] For instance, during the hearings conducted by the Senate Committee of Public Works in August 1970, a representative of the Automobile Manufacturers Association declared that manufacturers could not meet the legislation's targets on the basis of current technology and foreseeable advances. Similarly, a Ford Motor Company spokesman stated that, if the proposed standards were adopted, "technology as we know it today would not permit us to continue to produce cars after January 1, 1975" (US Senate 1970: 1571, 1576, 1604).

A Sun Oil Company lobbyist also commented: "I still firmly believe that the reduction of automotive emissions will be most effectively achieved by Federal specification of allowable emissions, leaving industry free to apply its ingenuity and resources to meet these targets" (US Senate 1979: 1660, 1663). The 1977 Clean Air Act Amendments extended the deadline for 90 percent reduction in automobile emissions of unburned hydrocarbons to 1980, and of carbon monoxide to 1981. Discretionary authority was delegated to the EPA administrator under this legislation to delay the achievement of carbon monoxide and nitrogen oxide standards for up to two years, if the required technology proved unavailable, taking into account factors such as cost, "drivability," fuel economy, and the impact on public health (Davis et al. 1977: 1-103).

At the same time, Congress directed the Environmental Protection Agency to file economic as well as employment impact statements with all new regulations. States were required to implement, by the end of 1982, compulsory inspection and maintenance programs in areas unable to demonstrate compliance with primary air-quality standards for ozone and carbon monoxide. This placed the regulatory burden directly on individual vehicle owners. General Motors, Ford, and Chrysler responded, in part, by the use of retarded spark timing to control hydrocarbons and carbon monoxide, as well as by the installation of exhaust gas recirculation to control nitrogen oxides. These measures reduced the average fuel economy of 1974 models by about 10 percent, compared with 1970 models.

By 1975, automobile manufacturers had persuaded the US Court of Appeal for the District of Columbia to order EPA Administrator William Ruckelshaus to delay implementation of the 1970 legislation on the grounds that economic factors should be given greater weight (Quarles 1976: 198). In 1977, Congress eventually agreed to postpone the original hydrocarbon and carbon monoxide standards until the 1980 model year, while the nitrogen oxide criterion was raised to 2.0 grams per mile through 1980, and 1.0 grams per mile thereafter.[12] President Reagan's Task Force on Regulatory Relief, which was created on January 22, 1981, was instrumental in promoting the revision and elimination of much environmental regulation.[13] The effect of this activity was compounded by cuts of over 20 percent in the EPA's overall budget, and more than 30 percent in the agency's enforcement budget, which were proposed by the Reagan Administration during 1981-83 (Andrews 1984: 73-74).

By 1982, hydrocarbon (30 percent), carbon monoxide (76 percent) and nitrogen oxide (5 percent) levels in the United States were all above those stipulated by the Clean Air Act Amendments (Crandall et al. 1986: 95). There was significant support for the final version of the 1990 Clean Air Act in Congress, which, after extensive lobbying, passed this legislation by majorities of 401-to-25 (House) and 89-to-10 (Senate) on October 27, 1990. The single most important congressional ally of the automobile manufacturers, Representative John Dingell, together with other Michigan Democrats, such as Chief Deputy Whip David Bonior and Chairman of the Education and Labour Committee William Ford, won a provision that left it uncertain until the year 2000 whether additional tailpipe controls, making car exhausts 99 percent (rather than 97.5 percent) cleaner than pre-1970 models, would be required, at an approximate marginal cost of $5.6 billion.

During the congressional debate, Senate Majority Leader Mitchell (Democrat) commented, in a naturally partisan statement, that air pollution caused 50,000 premature deaths each year and cost an estimated $40 billion in lung care and lost productivity (Thomma 1990: 16A). Although President Bush had proposed less stringent tailpipe emission standards and had suggested no reformulated gasoline or fleet requirements, the White House had gone beyond the final bill in proposing that automobile manufacturers produce at least one million vehicles per year powered by methanol or other clean-burning alternatives, for sale in America's nine smoggiest cities by 1997. This proposal was eventually rejected as a result of the concerted efforts of oil industry lobbyists.[14]

The President continued to oppose a clause of the bill that provided $250 million over five years in special unemployment benefits to workers displaced by this legislation, without signalling a veto. Despite White House calculations that by 2005 the 1990 Clean Air Act would cost industry up to $25 billion each year, which is more than the estimated annual total of $32 billion now spent on air-pollution controls, President Bush declared the Act to be an important milestone in preserving and protecting America's natural resources. This legislation covered five key areas: acid rain, smog-related pollutants, automobile tailpipe emissions, industrial emissions controls, and the domestic production of chlorofluorocarbons, carbon tetrachloride, as well as methyl chloroform—three chemicals widely used in air conditioners, refrigerators, and foam insulation.

The Environmental Protection Agency estimates that the first round of automobile tailpipe emission controls, to be implemented between 1994 and 1998, could increase the average sticker price of a car by $100 (Thomma 1990: 16A). At the same time, gasoline producers will be required to alter their refining recipes so as to include oxygenates designed to yield cleaner burning gasoline. This would incur substantial research and development costs. For instance, Atlantic Richfield expects to spend $1 billion during 1991-1996 to meet California emissions standards, which are expected to be even more stringent than the federal requirements. These will take effect in the Los Angeles basin in late 1992 (Rose 1991b: A3).

Figure 1 summarizes the principal provisions of the 1990 Clean Air Act, while Figure 2 details the 96 American cities and surrounding communities with the worst ozone smog problems, as well as their

Figure 1

Summary of Automobile-Related Provisions
of the 1990 Clean Air Act

1. Nitrogen oxide tailpipe emissions shall be reduced by 60 percent and hydrocarbon emissions by 35 percent (starting with 40 percent of all cars sold in 1994) in all cars manufactured by 1998. Benzine and formaldehyde emissions from cars or fuel shall be controlled, following further EPA study.

2. Tailpipe standards shall be maintained for ten years or 100,000 miles.

3. Warranties shall last eight years or 80,000 miles for catalytic converters and electronic diagnostic equipment, and two years or 24,000 miles for all other pollution control gear.

4. Special nozzles on gasoline pumps to reduce fumes during refuelling required in almost sixty smoggy areas across the United States; fume-catching canisters to be phased-in on new automobiles, as of 1995.

5. Beginning in 1995, all gasoline sold in America's nine smoggiest cities shall be cleaner-burning reformulated gasoline, which cuts nitrogen oxide and hydrocarbon emissions by 15 percent, rising to 20 percent by 2000.

6. Fleets of ten or more automobiles in America's twenty-four smoggiest cities shall run 80 percent more cleanly than 1990 automobiles, whereas trucks shall be 50 percent cleaner. These requirements may be delayed by up to three years, if technological constraints make compliance impossible.

7. By model year 1996, automobile manufacturers must begin producing at least 150,000 cars and light trucks annually under a California pilot program designed to launch vehicles that can run on non-gasoline fuels, such as natural gas and methanol.

respective deadlines for meeting the standards established by the Environmental Protection Agency. The effective implementation of automobile tailpipe emission controls will be increasingly at issue within the set of 71 cities and communities categorized as "marginal" or "moderate," given their respective deadlines of November 1993 and November 1996. It is also notable that the 1990 Clean Air Act Amendment contains a significant "new source" bias: at a time when over 35 percent of US passenger cars are at least nine years old, the legislation includes no used-car standards, except for requiring that automobile pollution-control systems should remain essentially intact during the first 50,000 miles of use.

Following the enactment of the 1990 Clean Air Law, Ronald Boltz, Chrysler's Vice President for Product Strategy and Regulatory Affairs, commented that the Chrysler Corporation should be able to continue fielding its entire lineup: "It's a lot easier to meet the standards on lightweight automobiles with small engines than heavy automobiles with big engines." However, Michael Schwartz, Manager of Emission Control Analysis and Planning at the Ford Motor Company remarked that the new regulations could force the company to discontinue selling sections of its full-sized pickup truck line (such as the F150), and perhaps even some cars with eight-cylinder engines (*Wall Street Journal* 1990a: A7).

Automobile industry lobbyists intensified their activities and continued to promote particular interpretations of the legislation. For example, Big Three lobbyists pressed for 1989 to be selected as the base year from which improvements in automobile emissions are to be measured. This approach was ingenuous, given the relatively high emission-control standards that had already been achieved by their Japanese competitors at that time, compared to GM, Ford, and Chrysler. Also, the legislative language requires the development of newly formulated gasolines that emit 15 percent fewer hydrocarbons and other toxic fumes than a 1990 model automobile, leaving unresolved the issue of which particular model. In an effort to shape new fuel regulations, which were expected to be announced by California in late 1991, Atlantic Richfield revealed that it had developed a gasoline as clean burning as methanol.[15]

By 1990, in partial response to public opinion, the "clean air" proposals emerging from both the White House and Congress were clearly premised on a technology-forcing orientation. This approach led to positive results. For instance, following six months of intense

Figure 2

Clean Air: Target Cities

The 96 cities and surrounding communities with the worst ozone smog problems and their deadlines for meeting federal standards:

CLASS: EXTREME
DEADLINE: NOV. 2010

Los Angeles

CLASS: SEVERE
DEADLINE: NOV. 2007

Baltimore
New York, nearby N.J.
   and Conn.

DEADLINE: NOV. 2005

Chicago, nearby Ind.
   and Wis.
Houston
Milwaukee
Muskegon, Mich.
Philadelphia, nearby N.J.,
   Del. and Md.
San Diego

CLASS: SERIOUS
DEADLINE: NOV. 1999

Atlanta
Bakersfield, Calif.
Baton Rouge, La.
Beaumont, Tex.
Boston, nearby N.H.
El Paso, Tex.
Fresno, Calif.
Hartford, Conn.
Huntington, W.Va.,
   nearby Ky. and Ohio
Parkersburg, W.Va.,
   nearby Ohio
Portsmouth, N.H., nearby
   Maine
Providence, R.I.
Sacramento, Calif.
Sheboygan, Wis.
Springfield, Mass.
Washington, nearby Md.
   and Va.

CLASS: MODERATE
DEADLINE: NOV. 1996

Atlantic City, N.J.
Bowling Green, Ky.
Charleston, W.Va.
Charlotte, N.C., nearby S.C.
Cincinnati, nearby Ky. and
   Ind.
Cleveland
Dallas
Dayton-Springfield, Ohio
Detroit
Grand Rapids, Mich.
Greensboro, N.C.
Jefferson County, N.Y.
Kewaunee County, Wis.
Knox County, Maine
Louisville, Ky., nearby Ind.
Memphis, Tenn., nearby
   Ark. and Miss.
Miami
Modesto, Calif.
Nashville, Tenn.
Pittsburgh, Pa.
Portland, Maine
Raleigh-Durham, N.C.
Reading, Pa.
Richmond, Va.
Salt Lake City
San Francisco-Oakland
   San Jose
Santa Barbara, Calif.
Smyth County, Va.
St. Louis nearby Ill.
Toledo, Ohio
Visalia, Calif.
Worcester, Mass.

CLASS: MARGINAL
DEADLINE: NOV. 1993

Albany, N.Y.
Allentown, Pa., nearby
   N.J.

Altoona, Pa.
Birmingham, Ala.
Buffalo, N.Y.
Canton, Ohio
Columbus, Ohio
Erie, Pa.
Essex County, N.Y.
Evansville, Ind. nearby Ky.
Fayetteville, N.C.
Greenbrier County, W.Va.
Greenville-Spartanburg, S.C.
Hancock County, Maine
Harrisburg, Pa.
Indianapolis, Ind.
Johnson City-Kingsport-
   Briston, Tenn.
Johnstown, Pa.
Kansas City, Mo.-Kans.
Knoxville, Tenn.
Lake Charles, La.
Lancaster, Pa.
Lewistown, Maine
Lexington, Ky.
Lincoln County, Maine
Manchester, N.H.
Montgomery, Ala.
Norfolk, Va.
Owensboro, Ky.
Paducah, Ky.
Poughkeepsie, N.Y.
Scranton, Pa.
South Bend, Ind.
Stockton, Calif.
Sussex County, Del.
Tampa, Fla.
Waldo County, Maine
York, Pa.
Youngstown, Ohio-Sharon,
   Pa.

negotiations between oil refiners, environmentalists, ethanol and methanol producers, automobile manufacturers, and state and federal regulators, it was agreed in August 1991 that, by January 1995, the oil industry would invent and market a gasoline that emits at least 15 percent fewer toxic emissions (Rosewicz 1991:A2).[16] William Rosenberg, Assistant Administrator for Air at the Environmental Protection Agency, also declared that oxygenated gas should be available within the 41 metropolitan areas with the worst carbon monoxide emissions in 1992, reducing such emissions by one-fifth, at an approximate cost of five cents per gallon (*Miami Herald* 1991c: 7A).

In March 1991, the chairmen of GM, Ford and Chrysler met with President Bush to discuss the costs of implementing the 1990 Clean Air Act Amendment and successfully elicited a renewed promise not to accept an average fuel economy increase from 27.5 to 40 miles per gallon by the year 2001, as proposed by Democratic Senator Richard Bryan (Nevada). In a comprehensive joint letter to US Trade Representative Carla Hills, which was concerned with the negotiations to create the North American Free Trade Agreement, the three automakers also demanded that, in the interests of promoting automobile industry integration and trade enhancement across North America, harmonized regulations, standards, and testing procedures should be established (*Inside US Trade*, 1991). Chrysler Chairman Lee Iacocca sought new restrictions on Japanese automobile imports, with less success. The three automobile industry executives also met with Federal Reserve Chairman Alan Greenspan in an effort to encourage further interest rate reductions. Similarly, in late April 1991, 45 members of Congress arrived in Detroit—on aircraft hired by the Big Three—to meet with corporate and United Automobile Workers union executives for two days of technology displays, crash tests, new model previews, and factory tours (White 1991a: 1).

However, congressional representatives from states such as Kentucky, Ohio, and Tennessee, where transplant automobile factories have been able to provide employment for appreciable numbers of voters, have increasingly counteracted representatives who remain allied to the Big Three automobile companies. Ironically, this trend has been reinforced by the efforts of Chrysler, Ford, and GM to cut employment costs substantially and to "right size" their labour forces, in direct contradiction to the Japanese emphasis upon the development of a stable team, as exemplified by the Toyota Production System. Yet intense competition among the Japanese transplants, particularly between Toyota and Honda, whose worldwide net profits tumbled by over 6 percent during the year up to March 1991, may have increased interest in credible intra-industry commitments to limit opportunism and pool resources where practicable (*Economist* 1991a: 79-80).

By September 1991, GM, Ford, and Chrysler had poured more than $10 million into the Coalition for Vehicle Choice through their Washington, DC, trade association the Motor Vehicle Manufacturers Association, which is staffed by more than 50 employees. Senator Bryan's average fuel economy legislation has been targeted by the Coalition for Vehicle Choice, which includes a number of associations that depend upon heavy vehicles, such as the American Farm Bureau Federation and the Livestock Marketing Association (Abramson 1991: A14). Eventually, this lobbying group may also be used to promote favoured interpretations of the 1990 Clean Air Act Amendment.

To be sure, the basic declaratory premises adopted by the EPA's Office of Air and Radiation, in developing implementation principles for the Clean Air Act Amendments of 1990, were not particularly threatening from a corporate perspective: related regulations, they state, "should apply market-based approaches, and other innovative strategies, with the objective of achieving and maintaining a healthy environment, while supporting strong economic growth and sound energy policy" (EPA 1991). Indeed, White House officials have argued that the high annual cost of the Clean Air Act to industry justifies an unprecedented degree of involvement in drafting even the finest details of new clean-air rules.

For instance, White House economists and Energy Department officials reportedly pressured the Environmental Protection Agency to greatly weaken a key June 6, 1991, draft rule under the Clean Air Act that was directed at the electricity industry such that power plants would avoid up to $5 billion in pollution-control costs (Rosewicz 1991: A10). As long as Congress is willing to engage in "speculative policy augmentation,"[17] the Executive continues to lean toward traditional responses that emphasize corporate concerns with regulatory costs, immediate technological constraints, and maintaining net profit flows, as articulated by President Reagan's 1981 Executive Order Number 12291. In this spirit, the President's Council on Competitiveness, chaired by Vice-President Quayle, has inserted a provision into clean-air regulations that would allow polluters to increase their emissions, unless state authorities object within seven days (Epstein 1991: A4).

To recapitulate, automobile air pollution standards are important because such standards raise complex issues of technical feasibility, socioeconomic impact, regulatory style, industry response, and
international trade negotiation. All modern internal combustion engines
function with varying degrees of inefficiency, generating exhaust that
includes carbon monoxide, nitrogen oxide, particulates and hydrocarbons, which also evaporate from the fuel tank and carburetor,
particularly after engines are turned off. An estimated 10 percent of
all gasoline consumed evaporates into the air. Several arguments can
be made against emissions controls on the grounds of decreased fuel
economy, reduced reliability and product quality, as well as increased
repair charges (Crandall et al. 1986: 27-28; Lave 1981: 893).

In addition, the reduction of one gasoline component that generates a particular kind of toxic emission may increase the output of
other unwelcome emissions.[18] It has also been asserted that automobile emission control is regressive, in that low-income households pay
the largest share of control costs (Harrison 1976: 128-130; Tietenbaum
1985: 94-96). To be sure, an objective epidemiological approach must
first measure an index of air pollution then specify one or more human
health effects of such pollution, while demonstrating an incontro-
vertible relationship between identified causes and effects. However,
there has been abundant evidence since the late 1960s that automobile air pollution is associated with the alteration of important phys-
iological functions, such as lung ventilation, oxygen transport, and
ocular adjustment to light (Stern 1968: 548). Furthermore, recent
research has indicated that the standard automobile inspection proce-
dure developed by the Environmental Protection Agency, which
measures carbon monoxide levels while cars are idling, substantially
underestimates toxic emissions, which are sharply increased during
motion (*Economist* 1990:64).[19]

On the other hand, companies such as AT&T, Polaroid, Reynolds
Metals, and Union Carbide have been able to reduce costs as a result
of compliance with environmental standards.[20] W.R. Grace has developed catalytic converter prototypes that are battery heated and thus
begin to function before vehicles are warmed up, which would significantly reduce the cost of current exhaust requirements if proven viable
(*Wall Street Journal* 1990b). Similarly, initial tests of a prototype elec-
tro-processor, developed in Norway, indicate increased fuel efficiency
as well as an approximately 20 percent reduction in carbon dioxide

emissions (*News of Norway* 1991: 16). By 2003, at least 10 percent of each automobile company's sales in California will be subject to a zero-emission standard. Nine other states, including New York, are adopting similar requirements. This technology-forcing approach will create a growing market for electric cars, such as Clean Air Transport's LA301, which will be marketed at about $25,000, or twice the cost of a comparable conventional model (*Economist* 1991b: 80). As battery production technologies develop, the operating efficiencies and costs of such automobiles will naturally decline.

CONCLUSION

The US automobile and oil industries successfully fought proposed legislation intended to tighten car emission standards between 1977 and 1989 because corporate executives in these sectors were able to deflect unwanted regulatory initiatives by obstructionist action, opportunistic alliances, and favourable evoked set responses. By 1990, when the latest Clean Air Act Amendments were legislated, the continuing internationalization of the US automobile industry, as well as the increasing popularity of environmentalist concerns, had led to significantly altered transaction cost assessments within the industry, more accommodative action, and new stakeholder alliances. Similarly, altered political calculations within Congress, somewhat reluctantly accompanied by the White House, encouraged the emergence of new regulatory behaviour patterns. Corporate attitudes were somewhat schizophrenic: the marketing executive who worried about pollution control costs at the office might find that environmentalism expressed his immediate interests as a new suburban homeowner almost perfectly (Sullivan 1984: 36-37).

As their foreign units began to comply with European and Japanese air pollution standards, seven prime factors cumulatively altered Big Three perspectives concerning the possible benefits of new intra-industry partnerships and the need to develop more opportunistic attitudes toward government regulation: (1) economic policy was more and more cross-pressured by aggressively articulated ecological concerns in every advanced industrial country; (2) hydrocarbon, carbon monoxide, and nitrogen oxide levels exceeded those mandated by the 1970 and 1977 Clean Air Act Amendments; (3) Japanese and European competition in the United States increased in intensity; (4) consumer preferences altered; (5) domestic vehicle demand softened; (6) foreign markets remained relatively buoyant; and (7) technological change suggested new potentials for cost reduction as a result of compliance with air pollution standards.

In turn, the substantial changes in US automobile air-pollution standards that have been impelled by the 1990 Clean Air Act Amendments will influence automobile performance standards in both Canada and Mexico, given the US-Canada Free Trade Agreement and the North American Free Trade Agreement. A substantial degree of integration already exists between the automobile industries of the United States and Canada, as well as between the United States and Mexico, particularly in the engine and drive-train component subsectors. Further integration implies harmonized regulatory requirements. Automobile air-pollution standards and corporate average fuel-economy criteria represent US social regulations that will necessarily impact on negotiated performance standards. Given the pivotal nature of the automobile industry, governments, manufacturers, and unions involved in the interpretation of NAFTA will continue to contest standards that affect their competitive advantages.

By the end of the twentieth century, the automobile companies that survive and succeed will be those most responsive to customer concerns, including least-cost emission compliance, driven by articulated public opinion, competition, and technological opportunity. Such responsiveness means more sophisticated product rationalization and market segmentation: smaller production runs, shorter model life cycles, more flexible production systems, as well as more highly skilled and motivated labour forces. Survival and success will also require wide-ranging participation in stakeholder alliances and strategic partnerships, predicated upon continuing mutual benefits. Tactical trade-offs abound. However, automobile companies that do not adapt to these requirements will probably exist only in international business history in the year 2000.

NOTES

¹ The automobile sector generates more employment opportunities than any other sector in the United States. The Motor Vehicle Manufacturers Association (1989) reported that, in 1988, the industry's overall labour force included almost four million workers, while US customers purchased an estimated 15.4 million cars, vans, and light trucks. Meanwhile, the industry's purchases from other major sectors, such as steel, aluminum, electronics, plastics and rubber totalled some $40 billion, representing almost 60 percent of factory gate unit costs. Across America, about 100 million cars and pickup trucks leave for work each weekday morning, and Americans drove some 2.1 trillion miles (the equivalent of 300 round trips to Pluto) during 1989. Nearly 34 percent of the oil consumed in the United States was used to fuel the nation's automobiles. General Motors ($26.02 billion) and Ford Motor Company ($23.80 billion) constituted two of the world's largest public companies, in 1988 market values.

² Under the Chrysler Corporation Loan Guarantee Act of 1979, the US federal government found itself providing Chrysler with a $1.5 billion loan guarantee, contingent upon the achievement of internal savings amounting to $1.43 billion. Chrysler remained on the brink of bankruptcy, losing some $3.3 billion between 1979-1981. Meanwhile, Ford was furiously cutting costs.

³ Broaching is a process in which functional holes in an automobile chassis are shaped and enlarged.

⁴ Opportunistic alliances may be exemplified by joint business ventures with the goals of technology transfer, market access, or both, whereas stakeholder alliances involve complementary coalitions with groups such as suppliers, customers, and employees, on which a corporation depends.

⁵ The phrase "economies of scope" is normally applied to production configurations where manufacturers can profit from building related products, or variants of the same product, simultaneously (see Teece 1980: 223-248).

⁶ At NUMMI, the Toyota Production System was implemented. This included seven points: kaizen or continuous improvement; kanban, or cost reduction through just-in-time inventory delivery; development of full human potential; building mutual trust; developing team performance; treating every employee as a manager; and providing a stable livelihood for all employees. Although NUMMI was very successful, GM was reluctant to incorporate such techniques across the corporate horizon (see Keller 1989: 134-144).

[7] In the automobile industry, production efficiency can be achieved at annual output levels ranging from 200,000 to 400,000 units. This means that an individual firm with no more than a 6 percent market share in 1987 should have been able to reap all significant economies of scale.

[8] Drucker contends that Alfred Sloan's segregation of the automobile market into four or five socioeconomic groups continues to influence production and marketing decisions at Ford, Chrysler, and GM. In contrast, their Japanese competitors plan long-range for life-style markets, designing parts so that they can be combined in any number of ways, despite the considerable increase in tool and die costs required, and the need to organize functions such as engineering and manufacturing on the basis of company-wide teams.

[9] For instance, see Gallup International (1970: 8), where the reduction of air and water pollution was regarded as second only to crime reduction by 53 percent of the respondents polled. Additionally, Earth Day (April 22, 1970) was a tremendous success, involving thousands of well-televised demonstrations across the country.

[10] In the case of a "technology-inducing" style, regulators encourage specific corporations to see that technological innovation is in their competitive interests. A "non-regulatory" style involves the application of non-traditional techniques, such as subsidized research and development or tax credits, to implement regulatory objectives (see Poole, Jr 1982).

[11] Transaction-cost economics examines ways in which interpersonal and interinstitutional corporate costs may be minimized by the creation of complex contracts, which assign transactions to governance structures in a discriminating manner.

[12] These standards were roughly equivalent to those adopted in 1989 by European and Japanese governments. Within the European Community, the Council of Ministers agreed on new automobile exhaust standards in June 1989. This agreement, which was to be fully implemented by the end of 1992, specified a maximum of 19 to 22 grams per test cycle for carbon monoxide, and 5 to 5.8 grams per test cycle for a combination of hydrocarbons and nitrogen oxide. It was also provided that up to 85 percent of the cost of fitting a catalytic converter could be subsidized under voluntary national schemes (see European Communities 1990: 46-47). Meanwhile, the Japanese Environment Agency has submitted proposed legislation to the Diet, in response to public concern with nitrogen dioxide emissions from diesel trucks and buses. Between April and September 1991, 1,454 people reportedly suffered ill effects during the 121 days

when photochemical smog alerts were declared (see *The Japan Times*, 1991d: 4).

[13] This Task Force was established to implement President Reagan's Executive Order No. 12291, which required a benefit-cost analysis for all major new regulations. At the core of this Order were the stipulations that "regulatory action shall not be undertaken unless the potential benefits to society for the regulation outweigh the potential costs to society," and that "agencies shall set regulatory priorities with the aim of maximizing the aggregate net benefits to society, taking into account the condition of the particular industries affected by regulations, the condition of the national economy, and other regulatory actions contemplated for the future."

[14] A 1991 California Clean Air Law mandates that 2 percent of any given manufacturer's automobile sales within the state should release zero emissions by 1998, with this ratio rising to 10 percent by 2003. In response, Toyota Motor Corporation has created a division with the duty of developing marketable electric cars and vans as soon as possible. Meanwhile, at Nissan, 1991 spending for electric vehicle development increased by 30 percent, compared to 1990.

[15] By removing olefins and sharply reducing sulfur, ARCO was able to reduce nitrous oxide and carbon monoxide emissions by more than a third. Since the new gasoline, called EC-X (Emission Control Experimental) would cost 16 cents per gallon more than current gasoline products owing to the expenditure of several million dollars in research and developments costs during 1989-1991 and the need to scrap and rebuild refinery capacity, Atlantic Richfield indicated that it would only manufacture EC-X in commercial quantities if ordered to do so by the California state government.

[16] Under this agreement, the oil industry will not count already achieved reductions in gasoline evaporative emissions, but will be allowed to average batches of gasoline, in order to meet the target.

[17] A phrase coined by Jones (1975: 175-176; 274-275) to describe the process by which, as a result of mounting public pressure, legislators may escalate proposals and enact laws that are admittedly beyond the immediate capabilities of target industries or agencies.

[18] For instance, a December 1990 test of 29 different formulations of gasoline at GM and Ford laboratories in Michigan indicated that the reduction of aromatics could yield both lowered hydrocarbon and increased nitrogen oxide emissions, while reduced olefins yielded both decreased nitrogen oxide and expanded levels of carbon monoxide. These results also varied with model year. However, by mid-1991, Mitsubishi Motors Corporation and Honda Motor Corporation had blunted some of the arguments against

such standards by unveiling new "lean-burn" engines yielding more than a 20 percent increase in fuel economy, along with unchanged levels of nitrogen oxide emissions.

[19] This research was conducted by Donald Stedman (University of Denver) for the state of Illinois. He found that many new automobiles emitted higher levels of carbon monoxide than well-tuned, older models. In one case, for example, a 1934 Chevrolet was well within modern emission limits, using measurements obtained by shooting an infrared beam through automobile exhausts as cars drove by.

[20] For instance, in the case of AT&T, a redesigned circuit board cleaning process eliminated the use of ozone-depleting chemicals, while slashing annual cleaning costs by $3 million. And when Reynolds Metals replaced solvent-based ink with water-based ink in packaging plants, this reduced toxic emissions by 65 percent and saved $30 million in pollution-control equipment.

REFERENCES

Abramson, Jill. 1991. Car Firms Kick Lobbying Effort into High Gear in Bitter Fight Over Fuel-Economy Legislation. *Wall Street Journal*, September 20.

Andrews, Richard N. L. 1984. Economics and Environmental Decisions, Past and Present. In *Environmental Policy under Reagan's Executive Order: The Role of Benefit-Cost Analysis*, ed. V. Kerry Smith. Chapel Hill and London: The University of North Carolina Press.

Breyer, Stephen. 1982. *Regulation and Its Reform*. Cambridge, Mass: Harvard University Press.

Bryan, Michael F., and Martin, John B. 1991. Realignment in the U.S. Motor Vehicle Industry, *Economic Commentary*, Federal Reserve Bank of Cleveland, June 1.

Crandall, Robert W.; Gruenspecht, Howard K.; Keeler, Theodore E.; and Lave, Lester B. 1986. *Regulating the Automobile*. Washington, DC: The Brookings Institution.

Davis, Christopher; Kurtock, Jeffrey; Leape, James P.; and Magill, Frank. 1977. The Clean Air Act Amendments of 1977: Away from Technology Forcing? *Harvard Environmental Law Review* 2 : 1-103.

Drucker, Peter F. 1991. The Big Three Miss Japan's Crucial Lesson. *The Wall Street Journal*, June 18.

Economist. 1988. Closer to the Customer: A Survey of the Motor Industry. October 15.

Economist. 1990. An Infrared Pollution Solution. July 7.

Economist. 1991a. Honda Loses Its Way. September 14.

Economist. 1991b. Volting along the Freeway. November 16.

Edelman, Sidney. 1971. Air Pollution Abatement Procedures under the Clean Air Act. In *Environmental Law and Policy.* ed. James E. Krier. Indianapolis: Bobbs-Merill.

Epstein, Aaron. 1991. Council led by Quayle under fire. *The Miami Herald*, September 9.

European Communities. 1990. *Environmental Policy in the European Community*, pp. 46-47. Luxembourg: Publications Office.

Gallup International. 1970. *The Gallup Opinion Index*. Report # 60, June.

Harrison Jr., David. 1975. *Who Pays for Clean Air: The Costs and Benefit Distribution of Federal Automobile Emission Controls*. Cambridge, Mass: Ballinger Publishing Company.

Inside US Trade (Special Report). 1991. Text of Automakers' NAFTA Recommendations. September 23.

Jackson, Kathy. 1990. Transplant Wages Will Rise to Match any Gains at Big Three. *Automotive News*, July 2.

Japan Times. 1991a. March 4-10.

Japan Times. 1991b. May 20-26.

Japan Times. 1991c. July 15-21.

Japan Times. 1991d. December 16-22.

Jones, Charles O. 1975. *Clean Air: The Policies and Politics of Pollution Control*. Pittsburgh: University of Pittsburgh Press.

Keller, Maryann. 1989. *Rude Awakening: The Rise, Fall, and Struggle for Recovery of General Motors*. New York: William Morrow and Company.

Koretz, Gene. 1991. This Generation Gap Could Jump-Start Detroit. *Business Week*, March 4.

Lave, Lester. 1981. Conflicting Objectives in Regulating the Automobile. *Science* 212, May 22.

Miami Herald. 1991a. March 1.

Miami Herald. 1991b. July 11.

Miami Herald. 1991c. Cleaner Air, Gas Rules Endorsed. August 17.

Melcher, Richard A., and Templeman, John. 1991. Ford of Europe is Going in for Emergency Repairs. *Business Week*, June 17.

Middleton, John T. 1971. Summary of the Air Quality Act of 1967. In *Environmental Law and Policy*. ed. James E. Krier. Indianapolis: Bobbs-Merill.

Motor Vehicle Manufacturers Association. 1989. Impact of the Motor Vehicle Industry upon the US Economy. Washington, DC.

National Research Council, Commission on Engineering and Technical Systems. 1982. *The Competitive Status of the US Auto Industry: A Study of the Influence of Technology in Determining International Industrial Competitive Advantage*. Washington, DC: National Research Council.

News of Norway. 1991. Vol. 28, 2, March.

Patterson, Gregory A. 1991. Big Three US Car Output to Sink to a 33-Year Low. *Wall Street Journal*, April 11.

Poole, Jr., Robert F., ed. 1982. *Instead of Regulation: Alternatives to Federal Regulatory Agencies*, Lexington, Mass: Lexington Books.

Quarles, John. 1976. *Cleaning Up America*, Boston: Houghton Mifflin.

Quinn, Jr., Dennis Patrick. 1988. *Restructuring the Automobile Industry: A Study of Firms and States in Modern Capitalism*. New York: Columbia University Press.

Rose, Frederick. 1991a. Atlantic Richfield Company is Winning the West by Breaking the Mold. *Wall Street Journal*, August 7: A1, A7.

_____. 1991b. Gasoline Refiners Languish in California. *Wall Street Journal*, June 28.

Rosewicz, Barbara. 1991a. Oil Industry Signs Accord for Gasoline that Burns Cleaner to be at Pumps by '95. *Wall Street Journal*, August 19.

_____. 1991b. Memos Show White House's Heavy Hand in Formulation of Clean-Air Proposal. *Wall Street Journal*, July 22.

Schlesinger, Jacob M. 1991. Japan Car Firms Unveil Engines Lifting Mileage. *Wall Street Journal*, July 30.

Smith, Jr., John F. 1983. Prospects and Consequences of American-Japanese Company Cooperation. In *Automobiles and the Future: Competition, Cooperation and Change*. ed. Robert E. Cole. Ann Arbor, Mich.: Center for Japanese Studies, University of Michigan.

Stern, Arthur C. 1968. *Air Pollution*. New York: Academic Press.

Stertz, Bradley A. 1991. In a U-Turn from Past Policy, Big Three of Detroit Speed into Era of Cooperation. *Wall Street Journal*, June 28.

Sullivan, Julie, ed. 1984. *The American Environment*. New York: The H.W. Wilson Company.

Takahashi, Kazuko. 1991. American Automakers Find Increasing Success in Japan. *Japan Times*. February 25-March 3.

Teece, David J. 1980. Economies of Scope and the Scope of the Enterprise. *Journal of Economic Behavior and Organization* 1,2.

Teitenbaum, T.H. 1985. *Emissions Trading: An Exercise in Reforming Pollution Policy*. Washington, DC: Resources for the Future Inc.

Treece, James B.; Woodruff, David; and Miller, Lowry. 1991. Japanese Carmakers Are Coddling their US Kids. *Business Week*, March 4.

Thomma, Steven. 1990. Congress OKs First Clean-Air Act Since '77. *Miami Herald*, October 28.

United States Environmental Protection Agency (EPA), Office of Air and Radiation. 1991. *Implementation Strategy for the Clean Air Act Amendments of 1990*. Washington, DC: EPA.

United States Senate, Committee on Public Works. 1964. *Steps Towards Clean Air*. 88th Congress, Second Session, October.

_____. 1970. Committee on Public Works, Subcommittee on Air and Water Pollution, Hearings. *Air Pollution*. 91st Congress, Second Session.

Wall Street Journal. 1990a. Toward Cleaner Air: The Shape of the New Law. October 20.

Wall Street Journal. 1990b. Industrial Switch: Some Firms Reduce Pollution with "Clean" Manufacturing, and Also Cut Costs. December 24.

White, Joseph B. 1991a. Besieged Big Three Court Congress, but their Joint Effort May be in Vain. *Wall Street Journal*, April 25.

____. 1991b. Japanese Auto Makers Help US Suppliers Become More Efficient. *Wall Street Journal*, September 9.

____. 1991c. GM May End Auto Venture with Daewoo. *Wall Street Journal*, September 10.

____, and Stertz, Bradley B. 1991. Crisis is Galvanizing Detroit's Big Three. *Wall Street Journal*, May 2.

White, Joseph B., and Templin 1991. Toyota Begins Producing Compact Pickup Trucks in US. *Wall Street Journal*, September 6.

8 PUBLIC POLICY AND CANADIAN AND AMERICAN AUTOWORKERS:

Divergent Fortunes

Charlotte Yates

Negotiations between Canada, the United States, and Mexico for a North American Free Trade Agreement (NAFTA) are the latest in a series of policy challenges confronting and reshaping the Canadian and US auto industries. Since the third quarter of 1979, the North American auto industry has undergone massive restructuring in response to the dual pressures of increased international competition and saturation of consumer markets for automotive vehicles. As North American automakers have scrambled to restore their own fortunes in the world auto market, the Canadian and US governments have found themselves under pressure to preserve existing automotive capacity and create an environment attractive for future investment.

Broadly speaking, two different sets of policy initiatives can be discerned over the years spanning 1979 to 1991. The first set of policies were ad hoc protectionist responses to the 1980-82 economic recession. They were aimed at shoring up the fortunes of existing auto plants and buying time for bewildered North American automakers. The second set of policies, first embarked upon by US President Reagan and in Canada only after the 1984 Conservative election victory, were long range and informed by a commitment to the virtues of the free market. By reducing the role of the state in the economy and negotiating free trade, first between Canada and the United States and then with Mexico, governments hoped to restore the forces of competition and private initiative that would chart the course of restructuring.

Regardless of the similarity in Canadian and US policy responses to the auto industry crisis, this paper argues that their impact on, and the response of, auto unions in these two countries has been quite different. The Canadian United Automobile Workers Union (UAW) benefitted from the first set of policies, which ensured jobs and thus strengthened the union's bargaining position with employers. This enhanced strength translated into greater political clout, which the Canadian UAW used to exert greater influence over auto policy. In contrast, American autoworkers were the losers as the US government linked the first set of auto policies to the negotiation of concessions from workers. In accepting and selling these concessions to its members, the UAW was seriously weakened both in its capacity to bargain (and win) on behalf of its members and in its credibility amongst its members.

The second set of policy initiatives thus confronted unions in fundamentally different strategic positions. Based on its new-found strength, the Canadian UAW (after 1984 the Canadian Autoworkers Union [CAW]) fought against policy initiatives based on restoring the market. Canadian union leader, Robert White, was at the forefront of Canadian mobilization against free trade, arguing instead for an industrial policy that would encourage the nationally integrated development of Canadian industry. Although this fight was lost with the 1988 passage of the Canada-US Free Trade Agreement (FTA), the union has until very recently been able to protect itself at the collective bargaining table. In contrast, the American UAW was so severely weakened by the crisis of the early 1980s, that it has been fighting a rearguard action ever since. Rather than proposing alternative directions for the economy, the UAW has sought influence on restructuring through cooperation with North American automakers. Market policies combined with the union's internal problems have undermined the UAW's position in the workplace and opened up the opportunity for companies to bypass the UAW.

Since this chapter focuses on the impact of state policy on auto unions and the divergent fortunes of Canadian and American unionized workers in the 1980s, it seems appropriate to make clear the basis on which the benefits to unions are evaluated. Union and corporate interests are different. Hence policies that benefit corporations by ensuring profitability or access to new markets, or alter the labour market in general, may or may not benefit unions. Rather, unions evaluate the costs and benefits of policies based on their impact on union members and/or the union organization itself. The chief advantages sought by unions through either collective bargaining or public policy are:

1. Improved wages and benefits to members;

2. The maintenance or expansion of the number of jobs available;

3. Progress on issues of quality of working life;
4. Preservation of union organization and the capacity to act in the workplace; and
5. Enhancement of the labour movement's political influence and/or power.

Under current economic conditions, unions often find that they cannot proceed on all the above fronts at once, and instead must trade off one benefit for another. Regardless of these constraints, policies that negatively affect any one of these objectives can be seen as harmful to the union or unions in question. It is on the basis of the above criteria that this paper evaluates auto policy effects on Canadian and American auto unions.

THE AUTO PACT: THE SOURCE OF STRENGTH

It is impossible to fully understand the impact of policy in the 1980s on Canadian autoworkers without first understanding the effects of the Auto Pact on the Canadian auto industry and its unions. As early as the 1920s, the Canadian auto industry was dominated by American manufacturers. Having jumped over the 35 percent tariff barrier to produce for the Canadian market, American firms took over independent Canadian automakers and established a branch-plant industry. While lucrative for the companies, the profile of the Canadian industry was distorted owing to serious inefficiencies caused by a small market, short production runs, and duplication of plants and products. These problems, combined with corporate practices of making costly annual model changes, meant the industry was prone to accentuated boom and bust cycles, which made employment unstable. Workers in both Canada and the United States faced annual periods of extended layoff with loss of wages. These problems persisted even after World War II, when consumer demand for automobiles exploded. Throughout the 1950s, the auto industry was plagued by downturns, the most notable of which occurred in 1951, 1954, and 1957-61 (Beigie 1970: ch.1; Bladen 1962: ch. 2 & 3).

By the late 1950s, the problems in the Canadian auto industry were compounded by lagging investment and a growing inflow of European vehicles. There was little the union could do at the collective bargaining table to protect its members from these problems, and the Canadian UAW mounted a lobby to pressure government for some sort of corrective action. Canadian autoworkers were divided over their proposed solutions to auto industry problems. Left-wing militants and nationalists argued in favour of policies that would increase levels of national ownership and encourage the efficient production of a few vehicle models aimed at the Canadian market. The Canadian UAW leadership, supported by the international union, favoured greater integration of the US and Canadian industries so that economies of scale could be achieved. This would require assurances of investment and jobs in Canada.

Under pressure from the union and other groups, the Conservative government under Prime Minister Diefenbaker took the first step toward addressing the problems of the auto industry. Diefenbaker appointed Vincent Bladen to head up a Royal Commission to study the industry. The Commission's report, made in 1961, recommended that the government introduce Canadian-content regulations in exchange for removal of duties on auto imports (Bladen 1962: ch. 6). The government hesitated to follow Bladen's recommendations. Instead, in 1963, it introduced a duty remissions scheme that depended on the achievement of certain levels of Canadian content in vehicle and parts exports. Within the year, the US government responded to this policy with threats of countervailing duties on Canadian imports. Before tensions increased further, President Johnson and then recently elected Liberal Prime Minister Pearson worked out the Automotive Agreement (henceforth referred to as the Auto Pact), which was signed in 1965 (Beigie 1970: 38-39).

The Auto Pact consisted of two parts and established conditions for duty-free trade between Canada and the United States in most new automotive products. The first part consisted of an agreement between the two governments, which laid out specific conditions under which freer trade in the Canadian and American automotive sectors could be established. While the government of the United States interpreted this agreement as bilateral in nature, the Canadian government interpreted the Auto Pact in multilateral terms. Manufacturers already producing in Canada were allowed duty-free import of vehicles and parts used in assembly from anywhere in the world, as long as the operating companies met certain Canadian content and production conditions. The second part of the agreement consisted of the "letters of undertaking" from vehicle manufacturers to the

Canadian government. In these letters, the corporations agreed to a specific formula for increasing the value-added in Canada (Macdonald 1989: 10-11).

Automakers moved quickly to integrate the Canadian and US auto industries, with each corporation choosing a slightly different strategy of integration. In the first few years of the agreement, all signs pointed to its great success in rejuvenating the Canadian auto industry. From 1965 to 1970, Canada's automotive exports boomed, resulting in a trade surplus up to 1970 (Government of Canada 1989: Table 5.2). In these same years, Canada increased its percentage share of North American production of motor vehicle units from 7.1 percent in 1965 to 12.6 percent in 1970 (Government of Canada 1989: Table 3.1). This was at a time when overall sales of motor vehicles in Canada and the United States dropped (Government of Canada 1989: Table 1.1, 1.2). Finally, automakers consistently recorded higher levels of Canadian value-added (CVA) than the required minimum established by the Auto Pact. Although the decade of the seventies showed some troubling signs for the auto industry, such as a persistent trade deficit with the United States, the overall impact of the trade agreement on the Canadian industry was positive. The Auto Pact had a lesser effect on the US auto industry. Although it likely shifted a proportion of future investment away from the United States toward Canada, it did not result in massive shifts of production from one country to the other.

Beyond general economic improvements to the Canadian auto industry, the Auto Pact altered the profile of the Canadian industry. Although Canada never had a high proportion of research and development or national managerial control over branch-plant operations, the proportion decreased once the Auto Pact took effect. Research and development and managerial control were centralized in the United States (Macdonald 1980: 6). Foreign ownership in the parts sector dramatically increased as companies adjusted to the Auto Pact and began producing more parts in-house.

The Auto Pact's impact on employment was complex. In the months immediately following the agreement, when corporations adjusted their operations, thousands of US and Canadian autoworkers were laid off. In Canada, labour productivity rose as a result of efficiencies associated with economies of scale. New employment possibilities also rapidly expanded. Between 1964 and 1967, employment in the Canadian auto industry increased by 20.9 percent (Beigie

1970: ch. 7). Corporate decisions to concentrate assembly rather than manufacturing operations in Canada meant that most new jobs created were semi- or unskilled. Skilled job opportunities in Canada were further reduced under the Auto Pact by the relocation of parts manufacturing or parts sourcing to the United States and the rationalization of corporate engineering and design capacities (Macdonald 1980: 57-81). Although both the US and Canadian governments introduced transitional assistance benefit programs to help autoworkers adjust to restructuring, the Canadian plan was of limited value because it required that Canadian workers exhaust their privately negotiated supplementary unemployment benefit plans before qualifying for government assistance.

Although the extensive layoffs due to restructuring inflicted hardship on some autoworkers and created tensions within the UAW, Canadian autoworkers clearly benefitted from the Auto Pact. More jobs were available for workers. The Canadian UAW thus expanded in size, which, in turn, enhanced its bargaining strength. Integration of the industry and associated labour productivity gains also provided the union with a basis for reducing the wage gap between Canadian and US workers, which until the late 1960s equalled 30 percent. By 1970, the UAW had negotiated nominal wage parity between Canadian and American autoworkers. This put more money in the pockets of Canadian autoworkers. Finally, the Auto Pact transformed the Canadian UAW's relationship with the federal government by allowing it greater access to government officials and more regular input into auto policy for the duration of the 1960s (Yates 1988: ch.6).

The effect of the trading agreement on US autoworkers was less tangible. Although the US government soon blamed Canadian safeguards under the Auto Pact for adversely affecting the US trade position and investment possibilities, the American UAW was silent about any possible negative impact of the Auto Pact on US autoworkers. The International UAW's support for wage-parity demands suggested, however, that the union was planning for a future in which the Auto Pact, combined with higher American wages, might make the United States a less attractive place for auto investment.

Although US-Canada tensions over the Auto Pact and, in particular, over Canadian safeguards, heightened over the next ten years, the Auto Pact remained the centrepiece of auto policy for both countries throughout the 1970s (Moroz 1985: Table 1). Only in the face of declining auto industry fortunes toward the end of the decade did governments in either Canada or the United States embark on new auto-policy initiatives.

RESPONDING TO THE ECONOMIC CRISIS, 1980-84

Throughout the 1970s, when inflation plagued the economy and wage restraints were imposed on workers by Canadian and US governments, autoworkers, especially Canadian ones, fared quite well. Demand for automotive vehicles remained buoyant. Wages increased an average of 10 percent per year, and benefits were improved, including the addition, in 1979, of paid educational leave for workers.[1] Moreover, although 1975 wage-restraint legislation represented an attack on the right of unionized workers to bargain collectively, workers in Ontario made some real legislative gains in the late 1970s. New health and safety legislation gave workers the right to refuse unsafe work, and the automatic dues check-off became a legal requirement in all new collective agreements. Meanwhile, in the US, labour laws and the restrictive certification practices of the National Labour Relations Board were increasingly becoming obstacles to unions (Goldfield 1987: 182-89).

The bubble burst in 1979 when Chrysler announced its imminent collapse. The auto industry had been living on borrowed time and had hidden from the harbingers of gloom who insisted that rising imports, heightened demand for small efficient vehicles, and saturation of the consumer market were problems endemic to the industry. As Chrysler teetered on the brink of bankruptcy, the Canadian and US economies, along with other advanced industrialized countries, plunged into recession. The auto industry suffered from heightened international competition and a weakened consumer market. Japanese imports captured between 25 percent and 30 percent of the Canadian and US domestic markets. North American producers seemed incapable of retrieving their lost market share, however, as they failed to compete in the small car market, produced more expensive and poorer quality vehicles, and were slow in getting new models onto the market. Short-term corporate solutions consisted of closing and/or relocating plants and demanding concessions from workers.

As plants were boarded up, auto industry unemployment skyrocketed. Between 1978 and 1981, Canada and the United States saw respective 12.6 percent and 26.1 percent declines in automotive production employment (US-Canada Automotive Agreement Policy Research Project 1985: 29). Automakers, autoworkers, and their communities demanded government action to prevent the wholesale collapse of the industry. Neither the Canadian nor the US governments had the experience, the will, or the state machinery to respond with a comprehensive industrial policy (MacLennan 1985: 21-57). Instead, the federal and state/provincial governments in both countries fought the brush fires of recession with ad hoc policies aimed at temporarily shoring up the fortunes of North American producers.

Many of the policies introduced in the United States and Canada were similar. Both federal governments loaned money in 1980 to the ailing Chrysler Corporation to stave off imminent bankruptcy. When, in 1981, the United States negotiated a two-year voluntary cap on Japanese imports to the United States, Canadian government officials sought similar restrictions on Japanese imports into Canada. While less successful than their American counterparts, Canadian officials negotiated a one-year accord that reduced auto imports by 6 percent.[2] Annual export restraints were renegotiated in both countries until 1985 and 1986, when the last US and Canadian deals expired respectively. Other short-term policies intended to bolster the industry included the Ontario government's decision in 1980 to remove the 7 percent provincial sales tax on all unsold 1979 vehicles (*Canada and the World* 1980: 8-9).

Canadian and US governments also competed with one another for auto investment through the use of incentives. This practice had begun in the mid-to-late-1970s, when auto corporations made clear their intention to invest $58 billion in capital spending for the production of small, fuel-efficient vehicles (Leyton-Brown 1979-80: 171). The Canadian, Ontario, and Quebec governments competed with American state and local governments with offers of grants, tax breaks, and infrastructural improvements for companies willing to invest.[3] Companies such as Ford took advantage of this bidding war and exacted greater and greater concessions from government (Leyton-Brown 1979-80: 170-178).

Once it became clear that Japanese automakers were planning to invest in North America, Canadian and US governments turned their attentions to wooing these investors. The Americans seemed to have the initial edge in these appeals, owing to the greater economic and political capacity of the US government to pressure the Japanese, as well as the Japanese firms' apparent, though mistaken, belief that investment in the United States would meet both Canadian and American concerns. Honda and Nissan were the first to announce investments in the United States. They were followed shortly thereafter by other foreign automakers. In fear of losing out on this investment, the Canadian government added new incentives. Especially important to luring Japanese and German investment were the tariff remissions programs, which were first introduced in Canada in 1975 but greatly expanded in the early 1980s. Although there were at least four different tariff remission orders, these orders generally allowed companies to import parts or vehicles duty free if the company met either Canadian value-added or export requirements (Macdonald 1989: 13). These remission orders rankled the US government and threatened to become a major thorn in bilateral relations. Regardless, the Canadian government risked US displeasure as the remission orders, in combination with import quotas, succeeded in attracting Japanese investment, while also benefitting the troubled Canadian parts industry (Macdonald 1989; Laver 1984).

Despite the similarity in Canadian and US policy responses to the auto industry crisis, some important differences altered the impact of policy on the autoworkers in these two countries. The election of Ronald Reagan in 1980 signalled a shift to the right in US foreign and domestic policy. Determined to re-establish the vitality of the market, which, according to Republicans, would increase competition and ultimately boost the economy, the Reagan government announced its intention to cut government spending and deregulate the economy. Part of this agenda included attacking the position of unions, which were perceived as having forced wages too high and interfered with managerial strategies to restructure.

In contrast, the Liberal Party won the 1980 Canadian federal election on a mildly nationalist platform that appealed to Canadian concerns of foreign domination of the economy and the need for Canada to reassert control over the economy. The Canadian auto industry's status as a branch-plant industry limited the degree to which national control could be imposed on this industry. Nonetheless, the Liberals declared their intention to gain Canada's fair share of research and development, investment, and jobs. Although not a pro-union strategy, such a nationalist platform promised to benefit workers.

In contrast to Reagan's determination to further shift the burden of responsibility for social welfare onto the individual, the Liberal government remained committed to the provision of basic benefits and, in particular, to the national health insurance scheme. Government-funded medicare, combined with the Liberal's decision to allow the devaluation of the Canadian dollar to approximately US $0.75, resulted in relatively lower labour costs in Canada.

Government policies thus made Canada an attractive place for auto investment. This became clear once the recession began to ebb in 1983. Within the first six months of 1984, Honda announced its plans for a $100 million assembly plant in Alliston, Ontario; General Motors (GM) declared its intention to invest $255 million to modernize a St. Catharines engine plant; and American Motors Corporation unveiled its partnership with the federal and Ontario governments, under which $764 million would be spent on a new assembly plant in Brampton (Laver 1984). These were shortly followed by Toyota's decision to build an assembly plant in Cambridge, Ontario, GM's billion-dollar investment in the Oshawa Autoplex, and GM's joint venture with Suzuki to build a new assembly plant in Ingersoll, Ontario.

Although Canadian autoworkers opposed many of the policy tools used by the federal government, especially money spent on incentives, Canadian autoworkers benefitted from many government policies. This contrasted with the experience of their American counterparts, who found themselves under attack by governments. One of the most telling examples of the differential impact of Canadian and US policy on autoworkers comes from an examination of the negotiations and terms of the Chrysler loan of 1980. Reagan and his supporters were opposed to bailing out corporations. Nonetheless, the threat of a Chrysler bankruptcy and its potentially disastrous impact on the US economy forced the US government to agree to the Chrysler loan, but with two conditions. Chrysler had to: (a) secure loans from other countries, most notably Canada, and (b) negotiate further monetary concessions from its workers. This policy made it impossible for the American UAW to resist Chrysler's request for concessions, even though the union had already recently negotiated wage give-backs to the corporation. Moreover, there were no guarantees that these concessions would save the jobs of US autoworkers making the sacrifices. Both workers and union lost from these policies. Workers lost wages and, in many instances, also failed to save their jobs. The UAW, in accepting and selling the concessions to its workers, opened the door to further concessions and eventually found itself confronted with mounting membership discontent.

Quite different were the conditions and effects of the Canadian loan. Canadian negotiations with Chrysler were headed by nationalist Herb Gray, a Windsor MP. Gray insisted that the Canadian UAW be involved in loan negotiations, a position which stemmed both from Gray's electoral need for autoworker support and from the Canadian UAW's mounting political power. So determined was Gray to involve Canadian UAW Director, Robert White, in the negotiations that he flew the entire government and Chrysler delegation to Winnipeg for meetings, where White was involved in a Canadian Labour Congress convention (White 1985). The Canadian UAW made it clear that, without guarantees of jobs, it would not support the loan. After intense political negotiations, the Ontario and Canadian governments granted Chrysler a loan—in exchange, however, for guarantees of investment in Canada. Investments ultimately meant more jobs. In contrast to the US experience, the Chrysler loan strengthened the position of the Canadian UAW by guaranteeing more jobs and increasing the union's leverage at the bargaining table. In turn, the Canadian UAW used its renewed position of strength to resist further concessions.

This momentary advantage of the Canadian over the American UAW became more pronounced as the recession of the 1980s deepened. Despite great odds against success, the Canadian UAW faced a more favourable government and decided to resist all further concessions demanded by North American automakers. This brought the Canadian branch of the union into conflict with its international parent, whose leadership found itself unwilling and unable to resist further concessionary demands. Thus, American autoworkers, under pressure from both their union and governments, negotiated massive wage concessions. The UAW insisted that, through cooperation with North American automakers, workers would survive. As jobs continued to be lost in spite of their sacrifices, American autoworkers became disenchanted with their union, thus further weakening its ability to bargain effectively. Meanwhile, Canadian autoworkers mounted a massive campaign to resist concessions and fought against plant closures. In the absence of government insistence upon concessions, the Canadian UAW was able to mobilize resistance to many corporate demands. Consequently, Canadian auto wages were higher than those in the United States, and master and pattern bargaining were largely maintained.[4] The Canadian UAW quickly became the darling of the media and one of the most powerful unions in Canada.

Differential government policies and divergent union responses to corporate demands for concessions had the combined effect of steering the Canadian and US sections of the UAW onto different strategic paths. Canadian autoworkers and their union benefitted in terms of jobs and organizational strength from the cumulative effect of government policies, such as incentives, the lower value of the Canadian dollar, and the governing Liberal party's nationalist rhetoric, which lent credibility to the Canadian UAW's fight against multinational corporations. The union emerged from the economic crisis strong in the workplace and politically powerful. Robert White became the voice of hope and an economic alternative for the entire labour movement. The union was now in a position to negotiate some of the terms of corporate restructuring, thus ensuring a place for itself in the future.

The culmination of the UAW's new-found power came in 1983, when Robert White was made the first union leader to co-chair a major task force on the economy. The 1984 report of the Task Force on the Canadian Motor Vehicle and Automotive Parts Industry recommended an extension of the Canadian content regulations of the Auto Pact to all foreign carmakers with a certain volume of investment and production in Canada.[5] Supported by all the major automakers and the independent parts suppliers, this recommendation, derived from Canadian UAW proposals for a comprehensive automotive industrial policy, represented a major victory for the UAW. The real victory would come, however, if the union could pressure the government into implementing this recommendation. The union thus mounted a massive mobilization campaign in support of the Task Force.

While Canadian autoworkers were basking in success, the American UAW was deeply troubled. At first glance, it seemed to be bearing up under the strain of economic pressure. Having chosen to accept concessions and cooperate with automakers to save the industry, the American UAW acquired various trappings of power. It was given representation on the Chrysler Board of Directors and made joint presentations with management to government. However, the very basis of UAW power—i.e. membership support—was crumbling, as workers resented negotiated concessions that reduced their wages without granting them security. Many American autoworkers distrusted the union's cooperation with management and accused UAW leaders of selling out their interests. Internal union opposition caucuses emerged to challenge the incumbent leaders and the direction in which they were steering. When these developments were combined with the more severe long-term effects of the recession, such as plant closures and continuing high unemployment, the American UAW was in a vulnerable position. The situation was made worse as the anti-labour climate persisted in the United States with the appearance of right-to-work states and the success of non-union southern states in wooing investment and jobs away from their unionized northeastern counterparts. American autoworkers were pitted against each other in bids to keep their plants open. Amidst this disarray, the American UAW was paralyzed (Herzenberg 1991: ch. 6; Slaughter 1983: 58-65).

The divergent Canadian-US autoworker strategies produced increasing tensions within the International UAW. The last straw came during 1984 negotiations with General Motors, when it became clear that the American UAW leaders were willing to cooperate with management to force Canadian autoworkers to conform with US collective bargaining patterns. The result was the splitting of the International UAW and the creation of a new Canadian Autoworkers Union (CAW). Round one of auto industry restructuring was over.

"TO MARKET, TO MARKET...": FROM RECOVERY TO RECESSION

Until 1984, the Canadian and US governments had pursued quite different paths to economic recovery. The result was intense competition for investment and growing tensions between the two countries. These tensions diminished when, in 1984, the Liberal Party was defeated in its bid for re-election, and the Conservative Party, under the leadership of Brian Mulroney, won a massive majority. Like the US government under Ronald Reagan, the Mulroney government committed itself to restoring the primacy of market forces by reducing the role of the state in the economy. This would entail slashing social programs and deregulating industry. Although the government professed a desire to consult with unions in seeking an acceptable solution to Canada's economic woes, by allowing a steady rise in unemployment, government policy had the effect of disciplining workers through the market.

Philosophically, the Conservative government seemed less interested than the Liberals in protecting the Canadian auto industry and more committed to letting the market determine the fate of the industry. In reality, however, the Conservative government, under intense pressure from a number of different sources, continued in the short term to pursue protective measures designed to give North American automakers more time to restore their fortunes in the world market. Thus, in 1985, Conservative Industry Minister Sinclair Stevens negotiated one more year of import quotas with Japan in the hope that these would force Japanese carmakers to invest in Canada. This contrasted with the US government's decision to allow quotas to end after the last agreement expired in March, 1985 (Clark 1985: 26). The ad hoc use of incentives also continued in both countries, despite government declarations that competition must determine industry survival. When faced, in 1987, with the possible closure of the Ste. Thérèse General Motors' assembly plant, and in consideration of the Conservative Party's electoral dependence on Quebec, the Tories agreed to join with the Quebec government in granting GM $200 million of interest-free loans and tax benefits (*Financial Post* 1987: 8).

Other than these ad hoc interventions in the auto industry, the Conservative government showed little initiative in the area of auto policy. Recommendations from the 1984 federal Task Force died with the Conservative victory as expanded Canadian-content regulations would mean greater, rather than lesser, government regulation of industry. Although cuts in government spending on unemployment insurance and health care augured poorly for workers, the mid-1980s boom of the Ontario economy, and the auto industry in particular, masked the impact of these changes on workers. Instead, autoworkers won substantial gains at the collective bargaining table. When they were not concentrating on winning back some of the ground lost in the early 1980s, their energies were focused on building their new national union.

This relative calm was shattered in 1986 when the federal government announced its commitment to a free trade agreement with the United States. Through such an agreement, the market could be expanded and greater opportunities for Canadian business secured. An FTA became the centrepiece of Conservative policy and the answer to Canada's future in the restructured world economy. The response amongst unions and a host of interest groups, including social welfare, women's, arts, and anti-poverty groups, was immediate opposition to this vision of Canada's future. Fearing that free trade would result in the loss of Canada's cultural identity, social welfare programs, and industrial base, an anti-free trade coalition called the Pro-Canada Network was formed. This group argued in favour of an industrial policy that would help rationalize the economy through strategic state intervention. The state would encourage the development of "winning" Canadian industries, help the adjustment of workers and communities dependent on non-competitive industries, and sustain and expand social welfare and cultural programs that had long made Canada distinct from the United States. Canadian politics and public life revolved around the free trade debate between business groups and the Pro-Canada Network. Very quickly, the Canadian Autoworkers Union became a key player in the anti-free trade coalition with its president, Robert White, a visible and articulate spokesperson for the group.

The FTA had a special significance for Canadian autoworkers as it threatened to undermine, if not end, the Auto Pact. This policy had long been identified by the union as crucial to the survival of the Canadian auto industry and autoworkers' jobs. The threat to the Auto Pact thus galvanized the union into action. Autoworkers feared that plants would be closed, investments would dry up, and jobs would be lost once Canadian safeguards were removed. Their concerns were shared by many Canadian parts makers, who feared more intense competition from low-cost producers and a possible loss of business as more parts were sourced from the United States (SCEAIT 1988: 59). Although the government repeatedly proclaimed its intention to leave the Auto Pact alone, this promise, along with ones to preserve Canada's social welfare programs, seemed hollow in the face of the government's commitment to competition and a free market.

Despite a considerable popular mobilization against free trade, a Conservative electoral victory in 1988 gave the government a mandate to finalize the already negotiated free-trade agreement. The autoworkers had lost in their struggle to prevent the FTA. A new era of auto policy was about to begin.

Chapter 10 of the FTA lays out a ten-year plan for the transformation of auto policy under free trade. Although Auto Pact safeguards are theoretically maintained, the incentives for fulfilling the commitments to Canadian content and Canadian production/sales ratios are all but destroyed with the planned elimination of auto tariffs by 1998.[6]

Once the 9.2 percent tariff is removed, automakers will no longer have to earn duty-free status by meeting Canadian production and content requirements. The only remaining enticement to meeting Auto Pact safeguards comes from the ability of automakers covered by the Auto Pact to import duty-free parts from third countries if they meet Canadian production and content requirements (Macdonald 1989: 10). Beyond changes to the Auto Pact, the FTA also eliminates the Canadian government's ability to use duty remission orders to encourage Japanese auto investment. Having lost many of the current and anticipated advantages of investing in Canada, Japanese automakers may choose to make future investments outside of Canada. To make matters worse, the policy tools that had secured the Canadian auto industry and its workers a better future would no longer be available to Canadian governments.

Along with the FTA, the Canadian government has pursued a policy of radically reduced government spending, especially in the areas of health care and education. Furthermore, the government has pursued a policy of re-valuation of the Canadian dollar, thus increasing the price of Canadian-made goods and of Canadian labour. These policy changes have eroded Canadian autoworkers' current labour cost advantage over their American counterparts, leaving them open to more direct competition from US plants for work. This problem has been aggravated over the past ten years by the American UAW's inability to negotiate decent wage increases for its membership and its willingness to cooperate with employers at any cost.

Examples of such direct competition are already emerging. In June 1991, General Motors announced that the state-of-the-art Oshawa Autoplex would have to compete for work with two other plants in the United States. The plant that offers the corporation the best and most effective production package will be awarded a new line of cars to assemble; the losers will face plant closure. This threat was made in spite of GM's recent investment of billions of dollars to modernize the Oshawa plant. If Oshawa autoworkers thought that such investments would deter GM from closing the Oshawa plant, they had only to look at the experience of Saab in Sweden, in which General Motors has recently acquired 50 percent ownership. After investing massive amounts of capital in a new plant at Malmö, GM announced that the plant would close in 1991—only two years after it was opened— apparently due to high labour costs and low productivity (Prokesch

1991: B3). The lesson was clear to Canadian autoworkers. After initial opposition to GM's strategy, the Oshawa CAW local agreed to cooperate with Oshawa management to create an attractive package that would win the new line of cars. As of January 1992, they seem to be losing out to their US competitors.

In addition to the competitive pressure on many Canadian autoworkers, the CAW has found many of its members in the parts industry permanently laid off as plants close to relocate to Mexico or the southern United States, where labour is cheaper. For those workers left on the assembly line, pressures have increased to intensify work by adding a third production shift and taking on more overtime so that plants can run continuously for a 24-hour period. With little room to manoeuvre, the CAW has agreed for the first time in its or the Canadian UAW's history to negotiate a third shift on the assembly line.

Although recent government policies threaten to hurt both Canadian autoworkers and their union, the CAW has so far retained its strength in the workplace and at the bargaining table. It used its collective bargaining strength in 1990, to protect autoworkers from the worst effects of restructuring. In September 1990, after a week-long strike at Ford, the CAW established a new agreement. In addition to substantial wage increases, the agreement contained sweeping job and income security provisions for workers dislocated as a result of industry restructuring. As the union made clear, if the government was unwilling to protect workers through universal programs, unions would take it upon themselves to force employers to become responsible for the impact of restructuring on autoworkers (Galt 1990: A1, A6). In so doing, the CAW continued its long postwar tradition of securing a future for its workers in the private sphere of collective bargaining.

CONCLUSION

The future of the Canadian auto industry, and hence of Canadian autoworkers, remains unclear. The negotiation of the North American Free Trade Agreement opens a bleaker future for the auto industry and its workers. With Mexican labour paid approximately US $ 2.45 per hour, compared to the $16.60 and $21.80 (US) per hour paid to Canadian and US autoworkers, respectively, the downward pressure on Canadian and American wages is likely to increase (*Ward's* 1990:

262). Moreover, free trade is likely to accelerate the already rapid relocation of many Canadian and American auto and parts plants to Mexico.

At the same time, various corporate strategies, such as the implementation of just-in-time production (JIT), may have the effect of encouraging geographical concentration of parts plants around existing and new auto plants. Barring the unlikely closure of all major auto plants in southern Ontario and the northeastern United States, it is possible that JIT will reinforce parts makers' commitment to production in this region. Finally, it is possible that the combined productivity and education levels of Canadian workers may continue to make Canada an attractive place to invest auto monies. Nonetheless, Canadian and American autoworkers have entered a decade of uncertainty. With the persistence of low consumer confidence in a North American economic recovery, as well as the real threat of overcapacity, many plants are going to become idle. How seriously the Canadian and US auto industries suffer as a result of this crisis relies as much on union strategy and government policy as it does on corporate decision making.

NOTES

[1] Wages are measured as average weekly earnings in the manufacturing sector between 1971 and 1981 (Courchene 1989: 73, Table 1).

[2] It seems that, although imports were reduced by 6 percent, due to inventory in Canada before the deal was signed, the Japanese share of the Canadian vehicle market actually increased in 1981-82 (Whittington 1981: 44).

[3] For discussion of various incentives offered to auto companies, see Leyton-Brown (1979-80: 171); Mair, et al. (1988); and Chapter 6 by Plumstead, Russell, and Stuewe.

[4] Master bargaining refers to a process whereby one master contract is negotiated to cover many plants owned by the same company so that workers' wages, benefits, job classifications, etc., are the same across the various plants. Pattern bargaining refers to the collective bargaining process whereby the contract gains won with one company are used as a pattern for negotiations and contracts with other companies. Patterns may be negotiated from one company to another or even from one sector to another. Both master and pattern bargaining were entrenched in the North American auto industry in the 1950s and greatly enhanced union power as they prevented whipsawing and allowed common strike action. For these reasons, the Canadian UAW fought hard and largely succeeded in preserving these practices. In the United States, the UAW allowed the devolution of collective bargaining to the local plant level, thus losing the organizational strength associated with master and pattern bargaining. On the emergence of these structures in Canada, see Yates (1988). On the US auto industry, see Katz (1985). On divergence of Canadian and American practices in the 1980s, see Holmes and Kumar (1991: Table 3).

[5] The content regulations themselves would have stayed virtually the same, although the proposed levels of Canadian content would gradually increase. The big change proposed by the Task Force was that all vehicle makers who sold a certain volume of vehicles in Canada would be required to make binding investment and production commitments parallel to those required under the Auto Pact (Lavelle and White 1983: 106-107).

[6] For more in-depth discussion of the effects of the FTA on the Auto Pact, see Chapter 10 by J. Johnson.

228 DRIVING CONTINENTALLY

REFERENCES

Beigie, Carl. 1970. *The Canada-US Automotive Agreement: An Evaluation*. Quebec: Canadian-American Committee.

Bladen, V.W. 1961. *Report of the Royal Commission on the Automotive Industry*. Ottawa.

Canada and the World. 1980. 45, April: 8-9.

Canadian UAW. 1969. *Brief on the Canada-US Auto Pact*. December.

Clark, Marc. 1985. A Standoff on Car Quotas. *Macleans* 98, July 15: 26.

Courchene, Melanie. 1989. Wages, Productivity and Labour Costs Reference Tables. The Current Industrial Relations Scene in Canada, 1989. Kingston: Queen's Industrial Relations Centre.

Financial Post. 1987. Where will aid to business stop? Editorial, April 6: 8.

Galt, Virginia. 1990. Ford, CAW reach deal. *Globe and Mail*, September 22: A1, A6.

Goldfield, Michael. 1987. *The Decline of Organized Labour in the United States*. Chicago: University of Chicago Press.

Government of Canada. 1990. *Statistical Review of the Canadian Automotive Industry: 1989*. Ottawa: Department of Supply and Services.

Herzenberg, Stephen. 1991. Towards a Cooperative Commonwealth? Labour and Restructuring in the US and Canadian Auto Industries. PhD thesis, Department of Economics, MIT. May.

Holmes, J., and Kumar, P. 1991. Labour Movement Strategies in the Era of Free Trade: The Uneven Transformation of Industrial Relations in the North American Automobile Industry. Unpublished paper. Kingston: Queen's University. May.

House of Commons. Standing Committee on Finance and Economic Affairs (SCEAIT). 1988. *Report on the Canada-US Free Trade Agreement*. Ontario Trade Review, Vol. 1. Toronto: Queen's Printer for Ontario.

Johnson, Jon R. 1992. The Effect of the Canada-US Free Trade Agreement on the Auto Pact. Chapter 10, this volume.

Katz, Harry. 1985. *Shifting Gears: Changing Labour Relations in the US Automobile Industry*. Cambridge, Mass.: MIT Press.

Lavelle, Pat, and White, Robert. 1983. *An Automotive Strategy for Canada*. Report of the Federal Task Force on the Canadian Motor Vehicle and Automotive Parts Industry to Honourable Edward Lumley, Minister of Industry Trade and Commerce. Ottawa: Minister of Supply and Services.

Laver, Ross. 1984. Ontario's Billion Dollar Auto Win. *Macleans* 47, June 25: 40.

Leyton-Brown, David. 1979-80. The Mug's Game: Automotive Investment Incentives in Canada and the United States. *International Journal* 35: 170-84.

MacDonald, N.B. 1980. The Future of the Canadian Automotive Industry in the Context of the North American Industry. Science Council of Canada, Working Paper No. 2.

____. 1989. Will the Free Trade Deal Drive a Gaping Hole through the Auto Pact? *Policy Options*, 10,1: 10-17.

MacLennan, Carol. 1985. Political Response to Economic Loss: The Automotive Crisis of 1979-82. *Urban Anthropology* 14 : 21-57.

Mair, Andrew; Florida, Richard; and Kenney, Martin. 1988. The New Geography of Automobile Production: Japanese Transplants in North America. *Economic Geography*, 64, October: 352-73.

Moroz, Andrew. 1985. Canada-US Automotive Trade and Trade-Policy Issues. In *Canada-US Trade and Investment Issues*. Toronto: Ontario Economic Council.

Plumstead, Janice; Russell, Brian R.; and Stuewe, David. 1992. The North American Automotive Industry: State Government Response to a Changing International Environment. Chapter 6, this volume.

Prokesh, Steven. 1991. Volvo's experiment on brink of failure. *Globe and Mail*, July 9: B1-B3.

Slaughter, Jane. 1983. *Concessions and How to Beat Them*. Detroit: Labour Notes Publication.

US-Canada Automotive Agreement Policy Research Project. 1985. *The US-Canada Automotive Products Agreement of 1965: An Evaluation for its Twentieth Year*. Lyndon B. Johnson School of Public Affairs, Policy Research Report: #68.

Ward's Automotive Yearbook, 1990. Detroit: Ward's Publishing.

Whittington, Les. 1981. Toyota Quota. *Macleans* 94, June 15: 44.

White, Robert. 1985. Interview. December 31.

Yates, Charlotte. 1988. From Plant to Politics: The Canadian UAW 1936-1984. PhD thesis, Carleton University, Political Science.

9 STRATEGIC MANPOWER POLICIES AND INTERNATIONAL COMPETITIVENESS:

The Case of Mexico

Glen Taylor

The North American automobile industry is in transition from a pattern of production and trade dominated by bilateral relations with the United States to a multilateral pattern in which Asian, European, South American, and North American trading partners all play a role in a more globally integrated industry. It is essential that production-sharing and trading partners, such as Canada, the United States, and Mexico develop a policy framework to guide the development of the North American automotive industry within a global context.

The automobile industry embodies many of the dimensions of modern industrial life—good and bad. It is the basis for an independent mass mobility that has shaped the lifestyles of industrialized countries. It is a major employer and links many underlying product and process technologies spanning a wide range of supplier industries. It is also inextricably linked to international friction on trade, investment, labour, and environmental policies.

The complex policy issues surrounding this industry need to be seen in the context of broader social, environmental, and economic development patterns. Wealthy industrial countries are rapidly "demassing" their economies to slow the rate of pollution and resource degradation. The shift to a knowledge-based economy as the main source of productivity improvement opens the possibility of renewed global growth based on progressively less wasteful resource use on the part of industrialized countries. The efficient use of materials and labour, including innovations that eliminate the need for materials and labour altogether, is rapidly becoming the main source of wealth. Poor countries like Mexico cannot realistically expect to close the gap with rich countries by selling their raw resources or their unskilled labour. This development strategy may already be economically and ecologically unacceptable to wealthy countries, where cheap labour and cross-boundary pollution generate heated political opposition.

The challenge for poor countries is to find a new and more effective route to develop their economies. Failure to shift from resource- and labour-intensive production methods threatens to create an insurmountable and widening gap between rich and poor countries. The gap can only be closed by achieving productivity gains, which, in turn, depend on continuous improvement in the utilization of human and natural resources. Industrial and less-industrialized countries have an unparalleled degree of common interest in reversing the destabilizing impact of widespread underemployment and poverty.

The basis for a new international development policy must be to increase productivity in order to increase living standards. This is, in essence, the strategy employed by the successful Asian countries:

> What these countries did was quite new. They took an American invention of World War II—it was called "training" and it enabled the US during the war years to change pre-industrial, unskilled people into efficient, high-productivity workers—and turned their unskilled and low-wage people rapidly into highly productive but still low-wage workers whose output could then compete in the developed markets (Drucker: 1988).

The example of South Korea here is instructive:

> Between 1965 and 1988, South Korea's gross domestic product soared from $3 billion to $171 billion.... Almost 40 percent of South Korea's high school graduates now go on to more than 200 technical colleges and universities. The government spends one-fifth of its budget on education, and businesses invest heavily in worker management and training. South Korean companies also provide training to their suppliers more routinely than other developed and developing countries do. In essence, South Korea created comparative advantage by investing in education. The same path lies open to other developing countries and companies (Austin 1991: 135).

This is not meant to suggest that Japan, Korea, or Singapore are model societies. Many aspects of Asian social and political systems are inconsistent with western political culture. The notable contribution of Asian strategies is their emphasis on facilitating development processes. Rather than acting as the locus of control for decisions, governments act in a supporting role, helping to build public-private links and developing institutions and infrastructures needed for human resource development. In this context, strategic manpower issues act as both a link to and a test of the effectiveness of other policy sectors. When faced with issues of North American economic integration we need to ask what impact economic integration will have on human resource development under competing trade regimes.

THE SALINAS SEXENIO

Following the 1988 elections, the new Mexican president, Carlos Salinas de Gortari began to redefine the course of Mexico's political and economic development policies, emphasizing privatization and export-led economic development through increased links to the global economy. Unlike in Canada, where most of the business community supports free trade, Mexico's business managers continue to expect active assistance from the government (Austin 1991). Despite considerable opposition from labour unions and many industrialists, Salinas privatized state-owned companies, lowered import restrictions, eliminated many foreign-ownership restrictions, modified local content rules, and reduced government subsidies.

The Institutional Revolutionary Party (PRI) has traditionally relied on organized labour for support. The most influential union, the Mexican Workers' Confederation (CTM), in turn, had helped enforce a long-standing policy of wage restraint in Mexico at or below the level of productivity increase in the economy. By the end of the 1970s, this relationship was in serious trouble. Inward-focused development policies were not generating sufficient economic growth to keep pace with a rapid increase in population. Income fell in real terms as well as in relation to the earnings of private owners of capital. Divisions within the business community became more sharply defined as some industrialists geared their operations to international competition, while most continued to look to the PRI for support and protection.

The inward-looking policies that stabilized the political system in Mexico for thirty years are being discarded. The implicit social contract that existed between the PRI and the CTM is slowly dissolving as the PRI realigns both its economic strategy and Mexico's political culture toward an uncertain future (Roxborough 1988; Weintraub 1990).

Mexico is struggling to get back on its feet after weathering an extremely difficult decade. The collapse of oil prices in the early 1980s, the steep devaluation of the peso, followed by massive capital flight and an inability to service Mexico's large foreign debt, all combined to create a precipitous drop in living standards. This set the stage for radical changes in the national power structure, including strong support for eliminating the corruption that had become a feature of the authoritarian political system. Politically, the PRI has not made bold strides toward democratization. Rather, Salinas has decided to put economic liberalization ahead of democratic reform. If the economic reforms fail, the political situation in Mexico is likely to become very unstable. This gives the United States a high stake in the outcome. At the very least, a free trade agreement would contribute to political stability in Mexico and help avert a tidal wave of migrant workers from flooding the southern United States in the 1990s.

Salinas worked to consolidate the changes introduced in Mexico's foreign economic policy earlier in the 1980s. Mexico joined the General Agreement on Tariffs and Trade (GATT) in 1986 and signed two bilateral trade agreements (a subsidy-countervailing duty agreement signed in 1985 and a broad "framework" agreement signed in 1987). This latter agreement provided the basis to negotiate a number of specific sub-agreements on textiles, steel, beer, and other products (Weintraub 1990). The NAFTA negotiations between Mexico, the United States, and Canada represent another step in a lengthy process of realigning the Mexican economy. The risk to Salinas and the PRI is that it will take time for the sacrifices imposed during the 1980s and 1990s to generate any net benefits.

THE COMPETITIVENESS OF LOW-WAGE MEXICAN INDUSTRY

The negotiation of NAFTA between two rich countries and one poor country has sparked fears that employers in the United States and Canada will shift production to Mexico. The adjustment problems Canada has experienced under the Canada-US Free Trade Agreement (FTA) have made Canadians particularly sensitive to the risks of widespread unemployment in an open trading environment. Many blame the FTA for current difficulties, including high unemployment and a substantial exodus of jobs and employers in 1990 and 1991. Even without NAFTA, Mexico's border industrialization program has attracted a large, rapidly growing number of US and Canadian manufacturers. To evaluate the risks inherent in a new trade agreement, it is necessary to come to terms with the competitive implications of integrating two relatively wealthy countries and one very poor country.

As noted above, following the collapse of the Mexican economy in the early 1980s, a sharp devaluation of the peso and an austerity program were imposed. By 1989, nearly 75 percent of all Mexican households earned less than three times the Mexican daily minimum wage of US $3.68 (EIU 1990). In the automotive industry, wages declined during the 1980s, falling below Korean wage levels and on a par with wages in Brazilian auto manufacturing (See Figure 1).

The poorest Mexicans have suffered a disproportionate loss of income. The inequity of income distribution is one of the reasons cited as an obstacle to Mexico's development as an industrial country (Fajinzylber 1990). This is a characteristic Mexico shares with most other Latin American countries and one that distinguishes Latin America from the majority of Asian countries, which have achieved impressive gains in industrialization in the last ten years.

Manufacturing accounts for roughly one-quarter of Mexico's GDP and employs about one-fifth of the work force (EIU 1990). Between 1940 and 1980, Mexican industrialization was promoted by government policies for import substitution and upgrading of raw resources, such as textiles from cotton and steel from iron ore. Since 1980, government policy has shifted more toward the promotion of exports. During this latter period, the growth of the *maquila* (in-bond processing) industries has been a dominant aspect of Mexican industrialization.

By early 1990, there were 1,795 *maquiladoras*, employing 437,000 people (see Table 1). Although the vast majority of the maquiladoras are located along the border with the United States, a growing number are located in the interior regions of Mexico (223 by the end of 1989). These firms account for over 70 percent of foreign investment in Mexico, providing mainly US-based firms in a wide range of industries with cheap processing labour and easy access to the US market (EIU 1990). The labour force is comprised mainly of women, and labour turnover rates as high as 200 to 300 percent per year have been sustainable so long as jobs require only minimal training and a

Figure 1

**Manufacturing Hourly Direct Pay
(Canadian $)**

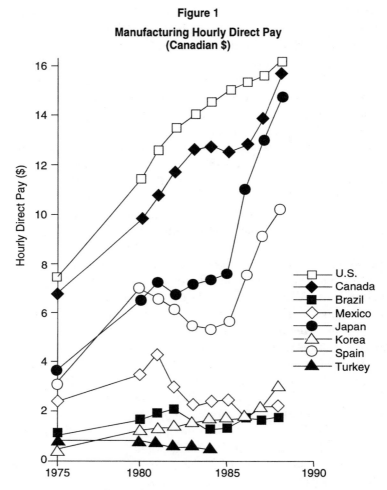

Sources: Automotive Parts Manufacturers' Association.
The Mexican Auto Industry: A Competitor for the 1990s.
Table III-20.

large pool of unemployed labour is available. Both of these conditions are changing as training needs rise in response to the increased technological requirements of the maquiladora (George 1990).

The vast majority of maquila plants ship components in-bond into Mexico, assemble them, and then reship them as finished products. The maquila concept was initially promoted in 1964 as a means of developing "twin plants" along the border. The US manufacturer would

Table 1

Profile of the Maquiladora Industry vs. Automobile Related Maquiladoras, 1984-88

	Entire Maquiladora Industry			
	1984	1986	1988	Average Yearly Rate of Growth
Value-Added (Mns of $US)	1,120	1,290	1,570	10.0%
Employment	202,100	268,400	361,800	19.8%
Plants	722	987	1,450	25.2%
	Auto Industry			
	1984	1986	1988	Average Yearly Rate of Growth
Value-Added (Mns of $US)	194.9	304.4	486.7	37.4%
Employment	29,378	49,048	77,502	40.1%
Plants	51	78	129	38.2%

Sources: INEGI/Asociación Mexicana de la Industria Automotriz.
Automotive Parts Manufacturers' Association.
The Mexican Auto Industry: A Competitor for the 1990s.
Table 4-5.

establish two plants, one on either side of the border, with the US management group in control of both operations. The US plant would be the main facility for capital-intensive production and the Mexican plant would perform the labour-intensive tasks. Border industrialization would thus involve "coproduction" based on a division of labour reflecting the comparative advantage of US capital and management and Mexican labour. In actual practice, relatively few plants have located along the US side of the border, preferring instead to ship components greater distances. Although there is some clustering of plants on both sides of the border, the "twin plant" concept did not become the dominant pattern of production (Grunwald and Flamm 1985).

The principal value-added in the maquiladora is the unskilled labour required to assemble components. The maquiladoras have been an important source of income for Mexican workers and their dependents. One estimate is that each maquiladora worker supports as many as seven other people (Martinez 1978). The strategy of the maquila does not, however, seem to be tied to the economic or social advancement of the work force. On the contrary, expansion in border assembly operations is based on the preservation of as wide a gap as possible between wages in Mexico and wages in the United States (Grunwald and Flamm 1985; Young 1986). There is little visible effort to upgrade the level of value-added in the maquiladoras beyond labour-intensive assembly operations. Rather than initiating a process of sustained development leading to higher living standards, higher levels of value-added, and a stronger infrastructure of Mexican suppliers, maquila assembly plants tend to accomplish exactly the reverse: Mexico is locked in a perpetual state of economic stagnation and dependency (Forbes 1984; Young 1986) in which there is an equilibrium based on low wages, low value-added, and unskilled labour.

The maquiladoras have grown in number, employing more people and providing income to more Mexicans and their dependents. Yet they do not appear to be contributing much toward economic and social development. Businesses in the maquila industries incorporate few Mexican components, and only negligible technological capability has been transferred either to Mexican-owned firms or to the Mexican labour force. The maquiladoras operate within an enclave where there is a sharp separation between the foreign business and local Mexican interests. Training and technology transfer are kept to a minimum, which perpetuates dependency on foreign firms for skills, technology, components, and capital.

The close proximity between related US and Mexican plants is a mixed blessing. It provides Mexico with an advantage over Asian competitors, who must ship their products from greater distances. So long as continued dependence on US managerial and technical specialists continues, there is little incentive to transfer these strategic capabilities. Japanese maquiladoras engage in significantly more training than their North American counterparts, if only because they cannot jump in their cars and drive down to the Mexican border from their offices in Japan every time there is a production problem (Tiersten 1989).

In 1989 the Mexican government stepped up efforts to integrate maquiladora firms into the Mexican economy by exempting their local suppliers from value-added taxes (VAT) and by allowing them to sell up to half their output in Mexico. It is too early to know the results. Since the in-bond producers are already exempt from VAT on goods assembled for re-export, this new provision is really aimed at the expanding Mexican market. So long as the incomes of the vast majority of Mexicans stagnate, these tax incentives are unlikely to produce substantial results. Nor do they directly impact on the ongoing dependence on US technical capability.

GOVERNMENT POLICIES TO PROMOTE THE AUTOMOBILE INDUSTRY

Mexico has initiated a series of policies aimed at increasing Mexican exports (see Table 2). The automobile industry has figured prominently in Mexico's economic planning for several decades. The Salinas government has changed tactics in promoting the industry by reducing restrictions to accelerate integration into a rationalized North American production system. The latest government decree on the industry provides more latitude to the private sector and the marketplace to decide on a division of labour for North American production, although several of the decision variables are strongly influenced by governmental policy. To build a more fully integrated industry, Mexico has instituted policies that encourage automobile manufacturers and their suppliers to establish production clusters deep in Mexico's northern industrial states.

Mexican automotive trade shifted from a deficit to a surplus as domestic demand plunged by approximately 60 percent following steps to severely retrench the economy in 1982. In 1990, the surplus was US $1.6 billion in automobiles and US $2.2 billion in auto parts (see Figure 2). The government decree of 1983 had a dramatic impact on the industry. Over half of the improvement in the trade balance was the result of the collapse of domestic demand in Mexico following the implementation of the government austerity program and another 34 percent was due to increased export sales of engines. Only 2 percent of the increase was due to higher levels of vehicle exports and 6 percent from higher levels of domestic content.

The 1989 decree appears to have two main aims:
1. To institutionalize a trade surplus in motor vehicles; and
2. To build an extensive Mexican parts industry.

The degree to which Mexico succeeds in its efforts to increase exports will also be influenced by US and Canadian regulations and

Table 2

Summary of Regulations and Decrees by the
Mexican Government to Promote the Automobile Industry

(1) 1962 Decree

Finished vehicles cannot be imported into Mexico.
Local content must reach 60 percent of direct cost of production.
Foreign raw materials require permits.
Each firm has a maximum production limit.
Auto parts firms cannot be owned by the assemblers and must have 60 percent
Mexican capital.

(2) 1969 Regulation and 1982 Decree

Assemblers are encouraged to export.
Production limits set in 1962 are modified.
Exports are used as a benchmark to determine production levels.

(3) 1977 Decree

Exports are required as a condition of producing in Mexico.
Assemblers are required/permitted to rationalize production.
Manufacturers must generate employment.
Development of the border region is encouraged.
Government support is offered to Mexican-owned parts suppliers.
The Inter-Secretariat Commission is created to oversee the industry.
An annual foreign exchange budget is set for the assemblers.

(4) 1983 Decree

An effort is made to decrease imports.
Local content requirements are set at 55 percent for 1986 and 60 percent
for 1987.
The trade deficit is to be reduced through increases in local content instead
of through exports.

(5) 1989 Decree (effective November 1990)

Further liberalization of rules for foreign companies.
Further rationalization of production.
Assemblers can import 15 percent of their Mexican sales if they maintain a
positive trade balance.
Assemblers must export five cars for every four that they import.
Local content requires that 36 percent value-added (narrowly defined) must be
purchased from domestically-owned suppliers and 36 percent must be
domestically produced.

Sources: Bennett and Sharpe (1985).
           APMA (1990).

Figure 2

Change in Auto Related Trade Balance 1981-1986

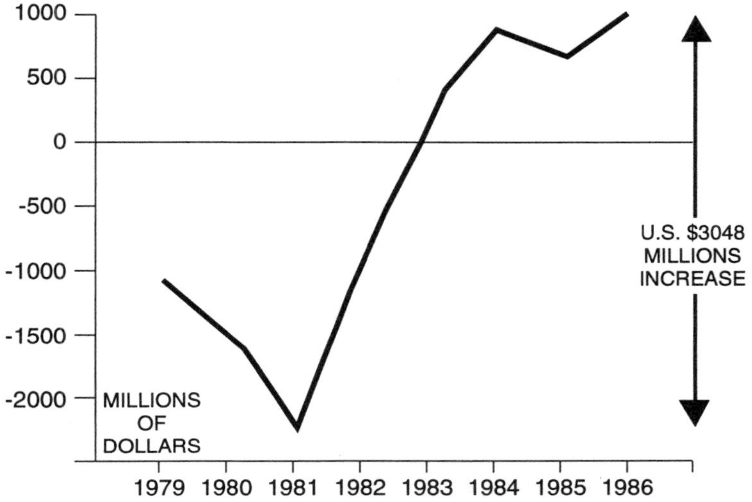

Source: Automotive Parts Manufacturers' Association.
The Mexican Auto Industry: A Competitor for the 1990s.

existing trade agreements. The Corporate Average Fuel Economy (CAFE) regulations in the United States require "domestically" produced cars (those with more than 75 percent North American content) to meet or exceed an average of 27.5 miles per gallon.[1] This rule was first introduced to curtail the importation by Ford, General Motors, and Chrysler of Japanese vehicles. It is in Mexico's interest to have its Mexican-produced cars included as part of the domestic North American fleet under the CAFE rules. This will permit greater rationalization of vehicle production with smaller, more fuel-efficient vehicles likely to be produced in Mexico. Alternatively, fuel-inefficient vehicles may be produced in Mexico, or produced with Mexican parts, to ensure that they are not counted as part of the domestic fleet. Under existing "rules of origin," an automotive part is considered foreign or domestic on an all-or-nothing basis. Such a definition makes it very difficult to determine how much domestic content a car contains. It also leads to elaborate gamesmanship. A shift of large niche car production to Mexico could lead to a greater loss of jobs in Canada and the United States, since these vehicles typically require more labour hours to build (Moskal 1991).

NAFTA includes a "rules of origin" provision that has set a domestic-content requirement of 62.5 percent, to be implemented in two stages over eight years. North American producers hope this provision will prevent Japanese manufacturers operating in Mexico from using Mexico as a back-door to the North American market. The Japanese might be inadvertently compelled to invest more heavily in Mexico.

THE MEXICAN QUALITY MOVEMENT

Low labour costs alone are unlikely to be sufficient to attract major automotive investments. The global structure of the auto industry is increasingly responsive to labour productivity and quality. This places greater emphasis on the degree of work force flexibility and the skills and competencies of the work force. Labour costs, per se, cannot be compared without also taking into account the quality of the labour force and other factors affecting productivity. "In the context of new best-practice production systems, the location of production in low-wage economies for export either of whole autos or of the major components therein is an unlikely outcome of the restructuring process" (Hoffman and Kaplinsky 1988: 288).

The diffusion of "lean production" from Japan to North America has been the subject of extensive research (Womack et al. 1990; Hoffman and Kaplinsky 1988). The breathtaking speed with which the Japanese established more than a dozen assembly plants in North America, not to mention the hundreds of suppliers who followed them from Japan, proves that the Japanese are serious about transferring their production system (Wolf and Taylor 1991). The question for Mexico is whether to follow the strategy of mass-producing standardized, relatively low-quality, low-priced products or to become a major site for lean-production and product/process innovation. If Mexican motor vehicle production could match the labour productivity of the Japanese (measured in labour hours per vehicle), it would help to open the Mexican market and would probably ensure deep penetration of the broader North American market.

Many of the ingredients for a conversion of Mexican manufacturing to lean production are already in place or are taking shape (Shaiken 1991):

1. Assemblers with experience in implementing lean production;
2. A parts supply infrastructure capable of supporting high-quality, just-in-time production of parts in relatively small lots (as distinct from small scale);
3. A skilled and literate work force capable of, and willing to, work in a flexible, team-based production system.

Nearly all of the major automobile producers now have experience in implementing lean production. Ford's Hermosillo plant is an indication of the degree of success Mexico can achieve in terms of quality and productivity. "At this greenfield site, Ford applied what it had learned from Mazda in building a Mazda-designed car.... Mexican workers embraced lean production with the same speed as American workers at the Japanese transplants in North America and at Ford's own US and Canadian plants" (Womack et al. 1990: 265). The missing ingredient at the Hermosillo plant is the lack of a suitable supplier infrastructure. A small but significant number of maquiladora operations have also implemented flexible-production strategies, including the use of advanced production methods, computerized technologies, and flexible work organization (Wilson 1990). By allowing more flexibility in meeting the requirements for local content and by promoting exports, the Mexican government has targeted one of the two missing links in its lean-production system. Now the only questionable ingredient is the learning capacity of the work force.

STRATEGIC MANPOWER DEVELOPMENT POLICIES

The relationship between education, employment, and economic development is complex. Data on educational attainment in Mexico is sparse and sometimes contradictory. One study of economic development in a northern border region of Mexico, Ciudad Juarez, which is home to a large number of maquiladoras, found that educational attainment reflected economic status. Children from poor families were far more likely to be required by circumstances to leave school, even in their pre-teen years, in order to work and contribute to subsistence level family incomes (see Table 3). The conclusion drawn is that, barring economic improvement among the poor, the formal education system

Table 3

Educational Attainment

Country	Year	Age Group	No School	First Level Incomplete	First Level Complete	Second Level	Post Secondary
Canada	1980	25+	2%	14%	9.5%	37%	37%
Mexico	1981	25+	34%	31%	17%	12%	5%

Source: International Science and Technology Data Update.
National Science Foundation, Special Report NSF 89-307.
Directorate for Scientific, Technological and International Affairs.

cannot meet the needs of people living in this region. "Nonformal education may be more appropriate for building the skills of the labour force in response to the requirements of the labour market" (George 1986: 127). It is left to the employer and/or the community to find some way of providing continuing education, extension courses, and technical training to a population that has received minimal, if any, formal education.

For those who are fortunate enough to have received a formal education, there appears to be widespread underemployment (George 1986; Lagana and Galan 1990). Educational requirements may exist for maquiladora employment, but the criteria for employment are often "little more than stereotypes in the heads of (male) managers regarding female dexterity and docility" (George 1986: 135). Indeed the work force of the maquila factories has been primarily young females. Women under 25 and entering the work force for the first time are the largest segment of the maquila work force (Grunwald and Flamm 1985). There has been little support in the literature for the contention that non-Mexican assemblers transfer marketable skills to the work force, aside perhaps from inculcating a set of values suitable to surviving the working conditions in a low-wage industrial factory. On the contrary, a number of scholars have noted the lack of skill development resulting from the maquiladoras, despite the requirement in Mexican law that these plants provide training to their assembly workers (George 1986).

In a recent speech on free trade with Mexico, a prominent Canadian Liberal politician, Paul Martin Jr., warned that Canada would have to come to grips with its declining competitiveness. Noting that

Canada is negotiating with Mexico on the assumption that Mexico will get the low-wage jobs while Canada enjoys the high-wage jobs, Martin was quoted as saying, "we don't have the highly trained people to make the transition." The article goes on to say that "the Mexicans are already graduating four times as many engineers as Canada and with a free trade agreement will make an enormous push into high tech industries" (Crane 1991).

Data comparing Canada and Mexico indicate that Mr. Martin may be entirely right and yet wrong on this issue. There is substantial evidence that the Mexican government has placed, and will continue to place, a high level of importance on education. It is not enough to spend money on higher education, however. The high percentage of research and development (R&D) monies spent in higher educational institutions points out one of the great weaknesses of the Mexican economy. Mexico does not have sufficient resources in terms of teachers or money to train students abroad to be a direct threat to Canada or the United States in most of the high-tech industries. Where Mexico is developing this ability, it is almost entirely in conjunction with multinational companies that have formed public-private partnerships. This supports the assertion that Mexico's competitiveness vis-à-vis Canada is improving. It is important to note, however, that Mexico's R&D dollars are still largely absorbed by the agricultural and resource extraction sectors (see Table 4).

There is substantial variation in the pattern of research and development spending. The United States spends the bulk of its public R&D

Table 4

Total Expenditure for the Performance of Research and Experimental Development in the Private Sector by Branch of Economic Activity

	Agriculture	Extractive Industries	Manufacturing	Transportation Communications
Canada	–	4.0	76.6	8.7
Mexico	22.6	19.1	10.1	1.2

Source: International Science and Technology Data Update.
          National Science Foundation, Special Report NSF 89-307.
          Directorate for Scientific, Technological and International Affairs.

money on defence. This expenditure is offset to some extent by the relatively high level of R&D spending conducted by the US private sector. Canada spends relatively more on industrial development, which is, ironically, concentrated in public-sector spending. Mexico directs a far higher percentage of its limited resources to the advancement of knowledge, and yet lacks the private sector organizations needed to fully capitalize on new knowledge. Canada has a far higher level of per capita Gross National Product (GNP) and spends a much higher percentage of its GNP on research and development than does Mexico. Despite Canada's having more money to spend and its spending a higher percentage of its GNP on R&D, Mexico has had more research technicians and support personnel, in absolute numbers, engaged in R&D than Canada (see Table 5). The area where Mexico turns out to be weakest is in the absolute number of engineers—only half as many as in Canada. A large portion (53 percent) of engineering effort expended in Mexican universities is in the natural sciences, presumably in support of R&D in agriculture and resource extraction.

There is some anecdotal evidence that the technological sophistication of the maquiladoras has been rising. This has created demand for more skilled technical and managerial workers. The rising level of demand for skills has created economic pressure on firms to undertake legitimate training programs as a matter of self-interest (Grunwald and Flamm 1985; Tiersten 1989). Training costs can run as high as 15 percent of payroll costs (Tiersten 1989). Ironically, this cost is due, in part, to the extraordinary levels of annual employee turnover that result from paying low wages, and then hiring replacements who need a week or two to get used to working in a factory for the first time.

Table 5

Personnel Engaged in R&D

	Scientists & Engineers	Technicians	Auxiliary Personnel
Canada (1985)	37,853	21,497	17,635
Mexico (1984)	16,679	29,467	22,826

Source: International Science and Technology Data Update.
National Science Foundation, Special Report NSF 89-307.
Directorate for Scientific, Technological and International Affairs.

The demand for engineers is partly driven by the number of computer and electronics firms that have located in Mexico. For these companies, low-wage assembly is not the primary reason for establishing a Mexican base of operations. The main difference between these plants and the maquiladoras is that they interact more intensely with other elements of the Mexican economy. They engage in research and product development and enter into public-private partnerships with the Mexican government. To date, these plants have focused on making improvements on designs created elsewhere, but, as they gain expertise and experience, there is increasing pressure to move into higher levels of technical innovation as well. A Semiconductors Technical Centre has been created to design and develop application-specific super-conductors and computer boards (Fretz 1989). This centre, which is financially backed by IBM and the Mexican government, is helping to fill the shortage of highly skilled engineers by training undergraduate, master's, and PhD level engineers. The centre is part of Mexico's National Educational Plan, released in November 1989. The plan calls for the creation of a national committee to review research projects to be carried out by advanced students, to connect research projects with private-sector production, and to direct studies to suit the needs of the nation's development priorities. It also encourages universities to raise funds by loaning researchers to the private sector and by petitioning the private sector to pay for grants in order to enable students to pursue advanced degrees (Fretz 1989).

In many of the firms that have decided to partially automate, direct-labour training problems are replaced by indirect-labour shortages, and the need to push employees to seek more formal education in order to attain higher-level analytical and research skills training. This group includes engineers, computer technicians, and managers. While, in many of these plants, the skilled employees are mainly foreigners on loan to the maquiladoras, in a growing number of cases, the declining ratio of foreign-to-Mexican employees shows that there is substantial upward mobility for the Mexican work force. For example, at General Electric's Mexican operation, the ratio of Mexican-to-US employees is 99-to-1 (Tiersten 1989). Mexican employees under these circumstances are likely to be highly motivated by career advancement possibilities.

Elements of government policy in Mexico are aimed at increasing the supply of skilled, trained, educated, and/or experienced workers for Mexican industry. By subsidizing education in engineering and management disciplines, the Mexican government is establishing the foundations for a sustainable competitive advantage in engineered products. This combination of training and low labour costs could pose a much greater challenge to Canadian industry than is generally recognized. The development of strategic manpower policies is a critical issue in determining future international competitiveness. In the short term, however, Mexico's educational needs cannot be met primarily through formal, publicly financed education. Informal education, including job-specific training, as well as a wide array of analytical and interpersonal skills that are transferred to employees during the full implementation of total quality management, is an essential part of worker education.

CONCLUSIONS AND IMPLICATIONS

Competitiveness in the North American automobile industry has become a function of training, education, and flexibility. It cannot be taken for granted that Canada will enjoy an advantage in adopting lean production, as recent experience in Mexico suggests that all of the elements are present to permit the rapid diffusion of the necessary managerial, organizational, and employee learning skills. This preparedness to learn, combined with public-private cooperation and a more liberal trade regime, will make it virtually impossible to prevent Mexico from developing into a fully integrated competitor and trading partner.

> In other words, the location decision to produce in Mexico is likely to be far more sensitive to differences in wages and productivity than to changes in tariffs. In particular, a major question would seem to be how rapidly Mexican labour productivity can be improved.... Raising productivity requires improvements in education and in Mexico's industrial infrastructure. If Mexico can improve its productivity, it should be in a very strong position to compete either under the current regime or in a free trade agreement (Wonnacott 1991: 111).

Canada has a significant lead over Mexico in every respect. Low Mexican wages are less of a threat to Canadian jobs than low Canadian productivity growth.

Although a trilateral free trade agreement will be a watershed in North American economic development, it is more likely to affect the pace of the transition within North America than the direction. A slow transition will not help North America to maintain its position as a leader among the world's major regional trading areas. It is easy to forget that the economic stagnation of Central and South American countries has already been very costly to the developed countries. Economic stagnation means that resources and opportunities are being wasted. The transition should be managed, but it should not be delayed.

NOTES

[1] For a more detailed discussion of the CAFE regulations, see Chapter 7 by Dennis Gayle.

REFERENCES

Austin, James E. 1991. The Boundaries of Business: The Developing Country Difference. *Harvard Business Review* 69, July-August: 134-37.

Automotive Parts Manufacturers' Association of Canada (APMA). 1990. *The Mexican Automotive Industry: A Competitor for the 1990's.* Toronto: September.

Baker, Stephen. 1991. The Mexico Pact: Worth the Price? *Business Week*, May 27: 32-35.

Bennett, Douglas, and Sharpe, Kenneth. 1985. *Transnational Corporations versus the State: The Political Economy of the Mexican Auto Industry.* Princeton, NJ: Princeton University Press.

Bennett, Mark. 1986. *Public Policy and Industrial Development: The Case of the Mexican Autoparts Industry.* Boulder, Colo.: Westview.

Booz, Allen, and Hamilton Inc. 1990. *A Comparative Study of the Cost Competitiveness of the Automotive Parts Manufacturing Industry* in North America. Toronto: March 26.

Brothers, Dwight S., and Wick, Adele E. 1990. *Mexico's Search for a New Development Strategy.* Boulder, Colo.: Westview Press.

Business Week. 1991. The Friends of Carlos Salinas. July 22.

Clark, Kim, and Fujimoto, Takahiro. 1991. *Product Development Performance: Strategy, Organization, and Management in the World Auto Industry.* Boston: Harvard Business School Press.

Crane, David. 1991. Mexican free trade pact could act as spur. *Toronto Star*, September 1.

Cypher, James. 1990. *State and Capital in Mexico: Development Policy Since 1940.* Boulder, Colo.: Westview Press.

Darling, Juanita. 1991. Top Mexican firms look forward to trade. *Toronto Star*, July 15: D1.

Drucker, Peter F. 1988. Low Wages no Longer Give Competitive Edge. *Wall Street Journal*, March 16: 30.

Economist Intelligence Unit (EIU). 1990. Mexico Country Profile. London: The Economist Intelligence Unit.

Fatemi, Khosrow. 1990. *The Maquiladora Industry: Economic Solution or Problem?* New York: Praeger.

Fajinzylber, Fernando. 1990. *The Unavoidable Restructuring in Latin America.* Durham: Duke University Press.

Forbes, D.K. 1984. *The Geography of Underdevelopment.* Baltimore: Johns Hopkins University Press.

Fretz, Deirdre. 1989. Wanted: Engineers. *Mexico Journal*, November 13: 25-26.

Gayle, Dennis J. 1992. Regulating the American Automobile Industry: Sources and Consequences of US Automobile Air Pollution Standards. Chapter 7, this volume.

George, Edward Y. 1986. Human Resources and Economic Development in Ciudad Juarez. In *The Social Ecology and Economic Development of Ciudad Juarez*, ed. Gay Young. Boulder, Colo.: Westview Press.

____. 1990. What does the Future Hold? In *The Maquiladora Industry: Economic Solution or Problem?*, ed. Khosrow Fatemi. New York: Praeger.

Grunwald, Joseph, and Flamm, Kenneth. 1985. *The Global Factory: Foreign Assembly in International Trade*. Washington, DC: The Brookings Institution.

Hayes, Robert, Wheelright, Steven C., and Clark, Kim. 1988. *Dynamic Manufacturing: Creating the Learning Organization*. New York: Free Press.

Hoffman, Kurt, and Kaplinsky, Raphael. 1988. *Driving Force: The Global Restructuring of Technology, Labour and Investment in the Automobile and Components Industries*. Boulder, Colo.: Westview Press.

House of Representatives. 1991a. Joint Hearing before the Subcommittee on Labour-Management Relations and the Subcommittee on Opportunities of the Committee on Education and Labor. Washington, DC: April 30.

____. 1991b. (Economic Impact of the Mexico Free Trade Agreement.) Hearing Before the Task Force on Economic Policy, Projections and Revenues of the Committee on the Budget. Washington, DC: May 14.

International Labour Office. 1991. Social and Labour Bulletin. Geneva: International Labour Office, Quarterly Publication No. 2, June.

Lagana, Antonio, and Galan, Mauricio. 1990. Highly Educated Labour Surpluses and Educational Planning in Developing Countries: A Case Study of Mexico. *Canadian Journal of Development Studies* XI, 1.

Martinez, Oscar J. 1978. *Border Boom Town: Ciudad Juarez Since 1848*. Austin: The University of Texas Press.

Moskal, Brian. 1991. Viva Mexico: South of the Border is Becoming a Haven for Impressive Auto-Related Manufacturing and Quality Consciousness. *Industry Week*, September 16: 61-62.

Philip, George. 1988. *The Mexican Economy*. London: Routledge.

Roxborough, Ian. 1984. *Unions and Politics in Mexico: The Case of the Automobile Industry*. New York: Cambridge University Press.

Schonberger, Richard J. 1990. *Building a Chain of Customers: Linking Business Functions to Create the World Class Company*. New York: Free Press.

Shaiken, Harley. 1991. The Universal Motors Assembly and Stamping
    Plant: Transferring High-Tech Production to Mexico. *The Columbia
    Journal of World Business* 26, 2. Summer: 125-37.

Story, Dale. 1986. *Industry, the State and Public Policy in Mexico.*
    Austin: University of Texas Press.

Tiersten, Sylvia. 1989. Mexican maquiladora plants present a catch 22.
    Electronic Business, November 27: 17-18.

US Department of Labour, Bureau of International Labour Affairs.
    1989-90. Foreign Labour Trends: Mexico. American Embassy,
    Mexico City.

Weintraub, Sidney, ed. 1986. *Industrial Strategy and Planning in
    Mexico and the United States.* Boulder, Colo.: Westview Press.

_____. 1990. *Transforming the Mexican Economy: The Salinas Sexenio.*
    Washington, DC: National Planning Association.

Wilson, Patricia Ann. 1990. The New Maquiladoras: Flexible Production
    in Low-Wage Regions. In T*he Maquiladora Industry: Economic
    Solution or Problem?* ed. Fatemi, Khosrow. New York: Praeger.

Wolf, Bernard M., and Taylor, Glen. 1991. Employee and Supplier
    Learning in the Canadian Automobile Industry: Implications for
    Competitiveness. In *Foreign Investment, Technology and Economic
    Growth,* ed. D. McFetridge. Calgary: The University of Calgary
    Press.

Womack, James P.; Jones, Daniel T., and Roos, Daniel. 1990. *The
    Machine that Changed the World.* New York: Rawson Associates.

Wonnacott, Ronald J. 1991. Mexico and the Canada-US Auto Pact.
    The World Economy 14, March 1: 103-11.

Young, Gay, ed. 1986. *The Social Ecology and Economic Development of
    Ciudad Juanz.* Boulder, Colo.: Westview Press.

10 THE EFFECT OF THE CANADA-U.S. FREE TRADE AGREEMENT ON THE AUTO PACT

Jon R. Johnson

S ince 1966, trade in automobiles and original equipment parts between Canada and the United States has been governed by the Auto Pact.[1] The Auto Pact was signed on January 16, 1965, and came into force on September 16, 1966. On January 1, 1989, the Canada-US Free Trade Agreement (FTA) came into effect. The FTA devotes an entire chapter to trade in automotive goods. The relationship between the Auto Pact and the FTA provisions respecting automotive goods has been fertile ground for confusion ever since.

CONFLICTING VIEWS

At a trade policy conference in 1991, one speaker stated that the FTA has not affected the Auto Pact. Later in the program, another speaker stated that the FTA has "gutted" the Auto Pact. How could two knowledgeable people draw such diametrically opposed conclusions? The purpose of this chapter is to review the Auto Pact and the provisions of the FTA respecting automotive goods, and to describe the effect that the FTA automotive provisions have had on the Auto Pact.

While the "Auto Pact" is the 1966 agreement entered into by the governments of Canada and the United States, Canadians also use the expression "Auto Pact" to refer to Canada's automotive duty remission programs, based on principles contained in the 1966 agreement. Used one way, the expression "Auto Pact" means the 1966 agreement. Used the other way, the "Auto Pact" is a policy instrument. The effect of the FTA on the "Auto Pact" depends upon which way the expression is used. This chapter will consider the effect of the FTA on the "Auto Pact," both as the 1966 agreement and as a policy instrument. Unless otherwise indicated, the expression "Auto Pact" in this paper means the 1966 agreement.

The impact of the FTA on the Auto Pact is that US obligations have been subsumed under the FTA. The sole practical effect of this inclusion is that, to receive duty-free treatment, automotive goods entering the United States from Canada must now satisfy the FTA rules of origin rather than the Auto Pact origin test. Canadian Auto Pact obligations are unaffected by the FTA.

The effect of the FTA on the Auto Pact as a policy instrument is that the incentive for vehicle manufacturers in Canada to meet Auto Pact requirements has been weakened and further extension of the Auto Pact prohibited.

ASYMMETRICAL AUTO PACT OBLIGATIONS

The Auto Pact resulted in duty-free movement of new vehicles and original equipment (OEM) parts, northbound and southbound, between Canada and the United States.[2] However, the basis for granting duty-free treatment has been completely different on each side of the border. The asymmetrical nature of the Auto Pact is the key to understanding the effect of the FTA upon it.

The asymmetrical nature of the Auto Pact reflects the different policy objectives of the US and Canadian governments regarding the automotive industries in their respective countries at the time the Pact was signed. From the US perspective, the Auto Pact was a sectoral free trade arrangement (Wonnacott 1987: 9) permitting the three major US automobile manufacturers to rationalize their Canadian and US operations. From the Canadian perspective, the Auto Pact was a market-sharing arrangement (Wonnacott 1987: 9) that, while compatible with rationalization, ensured that a certain share of the North American[3] automotive industry remained in Canada.

US AUTO PACT OBLIGATIONS

Eligibility for duty-free treatment of southbound vehicles and OEM parts under US Auto Pact obligations,[4] depended[5] upon origin. To qualify for duty-free treatment under the Auto Pact, new vehicles and

OEM parts imported from Canada had to satisfy an Auto Pact-prescribed value test.[6] If the test was satisfied, the goods qualified as "Canadian articles."

Goods eligible as "Canadian articles" were identified in the then applicable Tariff Schedule of the United States[7] (TSUS) on a line-item by line-item basis. New vehicles that were "Canadian articles" received duty-free treatment. Parts that were "Canadian articles" received duty-free treatment if they qualified as "original motor-vehicle equipment."[8] To so qualify, the item had to be imported by a "bona fide motor-vehicle manufacturer in the United States" and be intended for use as original equipment in the manufacture of a motor vehicle in the United States. A "bona fide motor-vehicle manufacturer" was defined in the TSUS[9] as a person producing no fewer than fifteen complete motor vehicles in the United States during the previous twelve months and with capacity in the United States to produce ten or more complete motor vehicles per forty-hour week.

The "bona fide motor-vehicle manufacturer" concept is not in the Auto Pact. Annex B of the Auto Pact merely stipulates that parts be imported "for use as original equipment in the manufacture of motor vehicles." However, to be a "bona fide motor-vehicle manufacturer" requires qualifications that could hardly be described as performance criteria.

CANADIAN AUTO PACT OBLIGATIONS

Canada's Auto Pact obligation to admit new vehicles and OEM parts duty-free rests upon a completely different principle. Eligibility for duty-free treatment is based not on the good's origin but on fulfilment by the importing manufacturer of performance criteria.

A manufacturer of automobiles, buses, or specialized commercial vehicles is eligible to import new vehicles and OEM parts if, during the twelve-month period ending July 31 (an "Auto Pact year") in which the imports are made:

a. The ratio of net sales value of vehicles produced in Canada to vehicles sold for consumption in Canada is equal to at least the greater of 75-to-100, or the corresponding ratio for the manufacturer, for the period from August 1, 1963, to July 31, 1964 (the "Auto Pact base year"); and

b. The Canadian value-added (CVA) of the vehicles produced by the
   manufacturer in Canada is no less than the CVA of the vehicles
   produced by it in Canada during the Auto Pact base year. CVA is
   defined[10] as the aggregate for an Auto Pact year of a number of
   defined categories of manufacturing costs.[11]

These are the so-called Auto Pact safeguards. While the Auto Pact
introduced free trade in new vehicles and OEM parts, the safeguards
were designed to ensure that a certain portion of North American
vehicle and parts manufacturing took place in Canada. While the
manufacturer was free to supply the Canadian market from either
domestic or US production, the volume of sales the manufacturer
could make in Canada was linked to the volume of its Canadian
production. The CVA requirement was designed to ensure that Canadian
production amounted to more than mere assembly. The Canadian
side of the Auto Pact was originally carried into effect by the Motor
Vehicles Tariff Order, 1965. This was superseded by the Motor Vehicles
Tariff Order, 1988 (MVTO 1988).[12]

The only manufacturers producing vehicles in Canada during the
Auto Pact base year were the Canadian subsidiaries of the three major
US automakers—General Motors (GM), Ford, and Chrysler—as well as
Volvo, a Swedish manufacturer. Given that the Auto Pact criteria are
tied to the Auto Pact base year, these are the only manufacturers in
Canada entitled to import vehicles and OEM parts duty-free under the
Auto Pact.

There are two critical points about the Canadian Auto Pact obligations. First, if the importing manufacturer meets the Auto Pact qualifications, it does not matter from where the new vehicles or OEM parts
originate or from where they are imported.[13] Second, notwithstanding that the Auto Pact is an agreement between the United States and
Canada, the nationality of the manufacturer is irrelevant. As a corol-
lary, under the Auto Pact, new vehicles and OEM parts imported into
Canada from the United States by an importer that is not a qualifying manufacturer are not entitled to duty-free treatment, regardless of
how much Canadian or US content they may contain.

AUTO PACT STATUS

The US Auto Pact obligation to admit vehicles and OEM parts imported
from Canada duty-free was inconsistent with the GATT most-favoured-

nation principle.[14] Accordingly, the United States applied for and was granted a GATT waiver.

The Canadian representative argued before the GATT Working Party considering the US application that Canada did not need such a waiver because the Canadian Auto Pact obligation to allow duty-free treatment applied to new vehicles and OEM parts imported from anywhere by qualifying manufacturers, thereby making it consistent with the GATT most-favoured-nation principle. The Canadian representative stated that the Canadian government was willing to qualify any manufacturer, regardless of nationality, that started manufacturing vehicles in Canada and met criteria analogous to the Auto Pact requirements.[15] The Working Party did not comment on the Canadian reasoning, so, presumably, they accepted it.

Following the granting of the GATT waiver, the Canadian government began assigning company-specific duty remission orders to any automotive manufacturer that could meet production-to-sales and CVA requirements similar to those in the Auto Pact.[16] The terms of the individual remission orders vary. The CVA requirement is sometimes expressed in terms of maintaining CVA at least as great as that in a base year. Other remission orders provide that the manufacturer must maintain CVA that is at least a prescribed percentage of its cost of production or sales.[17] The production-to-sales ratios generally increased from the Auto Pact ratio of 75-to-100 to one-to-one.

Strictly speaking, the Auto Pact applies only to manufacturers operating in Canada during the Auto Pact base year. However, the performance criteria for granting duty remission to later manufacturers are based on Auto Pact safeguards. Upon meeting the criteria, such manufacturers are said to have attained "Auto Pact status." Canada's use of Auto Pact principles as the basis for a policy instrument for encouraging development in a critical industrial sector resulted in the expression "Auto Pact" acquiring the second meaning described at the beginning of this paper.

American Motors (now owned by Chrysler) was not manufacturing vehicles in Canada during the Auto Pact base year and was not a qualifying manufacturer under the Auto Pact. American Motors received Auto Pact status through one of these company-specific duty remission orders. CAMI, a joint venture between General Motors and Suzuki, received Auto Pact status just before the FTA came into effect. The other companies that attained Auto Pact status were, for the most part, small specialty vehicle manufacturers. While Toyota, Honda, and Hyundai were the beneficiaries of other duty remission programs, none was granted Auto Pact status.

THE US AGENDA

The Canadian practice of encouraging industrial development by waiving duty on the fulfilment of performance requirements has generally been regarded by the United States as improper subsidization. The original trade dispute that led to the negotiation of the Auto Pact was over such a program. While Canada regarded the Auto Pact safeguards as permanent, the United States viewed them as transitional measures that would disappear when the Canadian industry had adapted to the duty-free environment (Wonnacott 1987: 11). While suggestions were made in the United States from time to time that Canada should be pressured into dropping the safeguards, no serious steps were taken to achieve this objective and the Auto Pact safeguards continued in force. This acquiescence may have occurred because the only significant beneficiaries of the Auto Pact in Canada were major US corporations.

A number of events made US acquiescence to the continuation of the Auto Pact safeguards improbable. Duty-free imports into Canada from third countries[18] under the Auto Pact increased dramatically, with the result that firms in third countries, as well as US firms, were benefitting from the Auto Pact. Canada initiated a new automotive duty remission program that waived duty based on the CVA in exports.[19] Japanese and Korean firms became major players in the North American automobile market and a serious competitive threat to the US industry. Toyota, Honda, and Hyundai established operations in Canada under a "production-based" duty remission program, which allowed duty remission based on CVA in Canadian production. Each of these manufacturers was working toward and, in due course, would receive Auto Pact status. Once this occurred, Japanese, Korean, and US firms operating in Canada would utilize the transitional Auto Pact safeguard provisions to their advantage. All these events shaped the US automotive agenda during the FTA negotiations.

PROVISIONS OF THE FTA

The relationship between the FTA and other agreements to which Canada and the United States are party is set forth in FTA Article 104. This article affirms existing rights and obligations of Canada and the United States to each other under other agreements, but provides that, unless otherwise stated, the FTA prevails if there is an inconsistency between another agreement and the FTA. The sole reference to the Auto Pact in the FTA appears in Article 1001, which is not an operative provision and does not alter the rule in Article 104. Accordingly, while the FTA affirms the rights and obligations of Canada and the United States under the Auto Pact, the FTA prevails to the extent that its provisions are inconsistent with Auto Pact provisions.

THE FTA AND US AUTO PACT OBLIGATIONS

FTA Articles 401.1 and 401.4 and the US Tariff Schedule set forth in FTA Annex 401.2 (US Tariff Schedule) have the effect of incorporating the US Auto Pact obligations into the FTA, with one significant modification. FTA Article 401.1 binds the United States not to increase any existing duty or introduce any new duty on goods originating in Canada. FTA Article 401.4 binds the United States to continue to admit duty-free all items originating in Canada that are designated as being in Staging Category "D" in the US Tariff Schedule.

The various categories of "motor vehicles for the transport of persons or articles"[20] are set forth in headings 8702 through 8704 of the US Tariff Schedule. All these goods fall within Staging Category "D." Under FTA Article 401.4, the United States is obliged to continue to admit these goods duty-free, provided they originate in Canada. Under FTA Article 301, to originate in Canada, goods must satisfy the rules of origin set forth in Chapter 3 of the FTA.

The concepts of "original motor vehicle equipment" and "bona fide motor-vehicle manufacturer" are carried into the US Tariff Schedule in a note at the beginning of Chapter 87. The language mirrors that contained in the TSUS, except that the reference to "Canadian article" in the TSUS has been replaced by language requiring that the item originate in Canada under the FTA rules of origin.[21] Goods which may qualify as "original motor vehicle equipment" are identified through-out the US Tariff Schedule on a line-item by line-item basis. Take, for example, sealed beam lamp units under US tariff item 8539.10.00. If this item is "original motor vehicle equipment," the Staging Category is "D." FTA 401.4 obliges the United States to admit a sealed beam lamp unit duty-free if it originates in Canada under the FTA rules of origin and is imported as "original motor vehicle equipment."[22]

The one obvious inconsistency[23] between the FTA and the Auto Pact is in the determination of origin. To be eligible for duty-free treatment under the Auto Pact, goods had to satisfy the test set forth in the Auto Pact. Under the FTA, goods must satisfy rules of origin different from, and inconsistent with, the Auto Pact test. Because of FTA Article 104, the rules of origin imposed by the FTA prevail. Therefore, the single effect of the FTA on US Auto Pact obligations has been to substitute the FTA rules of origin for the Auto Pact test.

The obligations of the United States in the FTA to grant duty-free treatment to vehicles and OEM parts are independent of the Auto Pact and do not depend on its continued existence. If the Auto Pact were terminated, the US FTA obligations to accord duty-free treatment would continue in force.

COMPARISON OF ORIGIN UNDER THE AUTO PACT AND THE FTA

Whether the effect of the FTA on US Auto Pact obligations has been significant depends on how much the FTA rules of origin differ from the Auto Pact test. The conventional wisdom when the FTA was signed was that the FTA test was tougher to meet than the Auto Pact test. In fact, the two tests are based on completely different approaches, and it is not possible to make a general statement that one is tougher to meet than the other. Degrees of relative "toughness" will vary from item to item. Whether the FTA regime is tougher than the Auto Pact regime will also depend on how the FTA rules of origin are ultimately applied by the respective customs officials of Canada and the United States. These are questions of interpretation that are still in a state of flux.[24]

The Auto Pact test operates by comparing the appraised customs value of the goods being imported into the United States with the aggregate value of imported materials (other than materials imported from the United States) contained in those goods. The value of the imported materials is their value when entering at a Canadian port of entry, excluding any landing cost or Canadian duty. If the aggregate value of the imported materials does not exceed 50 percent of the appraised value of the goods, the test is satisfied.

In determining the origin of goods containing materials or submaterials imported from third countries,[25] the FTA rules of origin require that the production of the goods results in the imported materials or submaterials[26] undergoing a prescribed change in tariff classification. The prescribed changes in tariff classification are set forth in the Rules in FTA Annex 301.2.[27] For a number of goods, in addition to undergoing the prescribed change in tariff classification, a value test must also be satisfied. The "direct cost of processing"[28] the goods plus the "price paid" by the producer for originating materials must equal at least 50 percent of the "direct cost of processing" plus the "price paid" by the producer for all materials.

Most automotive parts are not subject to the FTA value test. Consider, for example, the sealed beam lamp unit referred to above. Unless the imported materials contained in a sealed beam lamp unit produced in Canada are parts,[29] the FTA value test does not apply.[30] Origin will be determined solely on the basis of the production of the sealed beam lamp unit, resulting in the tariff classification of all imported materials changing in the prescribed manner. Domestic[31] value-added will result from producing the sealed beam lamp unit, but satisfying the test is not tied to the amount of domestic value-added. The amount of domestic value-added required will be whatever amount is necessary to achieve the change in tariff classification.[32] Determining origin solely by reference to a change in tariff classification follows a completely different approach from the Auto Pact test, and it is not possible to make any general statement about which is easier and which is tougher.

All motor vehicles are subject to the FTA value test,[33] as are some important components, such as spark ignition engines.[34] However, the FTA value test is not sufficiently akin to the Auto Pact test to be able to make general statements about which is tougher. The basis for saying that the FTA value test is tougher than the Auto Pact test is that the FTA definition of "direct cost of processing" excludes a number of significant costs, such as general and administrative expenses, as well as profit. The Auto Pact test is based on the US customs appraised value of the goods being imported, which, in turn, is based on the price charged by the exporter. In that price, the exporter would, in normal circumstances, be recovering general and administrative expenses and including a profit. The effect of the Auto Pact test is to count general and administrative expenses and profit as domestic value-added. As these items are excluded from the FTA value test, if other things were comparable, the FTA value test would be tougher to meet.

However, other things are not comparable. The Auto Pact and FTA tests are comparable only in the simple situation in which a producer uses solely imported materials and wholly domestic materials. The Auto Pact test treats the price of the imported materials as non-domestic and everything else as domestic, including the price paid for the wholly domestic materials and the producer's general and administrative expenses and profit. As with the Auto Pact test, the FTA value test would, in this situation, treat the price paid for the imported materials as non-domestic and the price paid for the wholly originating domestic materials as domestic. General and administrative expenses and profit are excluded from both the numerator and the denominator in calculating the FTA value test, making the 50 percent result harder to achieve.

Consider an automobile manufactured in Canada containing an "intermediate material," such as an engine, which the automobile manufacturer purchases from a supplier in Canada or the United States. Suppose that the engine contains submaterials imported from third countries. Under the Auto Pact test, the landed cost of all imported materials contained in the engine would be treated as non-domestic. Under the FTA value test, the origin of the engine is determined by applying the FTA rules of origin to the engine as if the engine were the item being imported from the United States into Canada, or vice versa. If the engine passes the test (and is therefore "originating"), the entire price of the engine counts as domestic, notwithstanding the fact that it contains imported submaterials. These imported submaterials are counted as domestic, whereas, under the Auto Pact value test, they would not be. If the engine fails the test, and is therefore not "originating", its entire price is treated as non-domestic, even though the engine may contain domestic materials and may have been assembled by domestic labour.[35]

The Auto Pact test excludes all imported materials. Everything else is included. The FTA value test identifies imported submaterials as domestic if they are incorporated into intermediate materials that are "originating". The FTA value test bars domestic value-added included in intermediate materials that are not "originating". The rules by which the origin of most intermediate materials is determined (such as the sealed beam lamp unit discussed above) are based solely on prescribed changes in tariff classification and not on any measurement of value. The manufacture of a complex item of equipment, such as an automobile, will involve many intermediate materials, so the simple model described above does not reflect reality.

Given that the FTA value test operates on a completely different basis from the Auto Pact test, except in the most simplistic of circumstances, it is not possible to draw a ready comparison between the two. The FTA value test may be harder to satisfy. On the other hand, it may not be. Given that the customs authorities on each side of the border are just beginning to come to terms with the FTA value test, and given that the first customs audits are just being completed, it is too early to tell. Since this paper was first written, US Customs completed its audit of Honda and issued several rulings to which the Canadian government took strong exception. The contentious issues in these rulings have been resolved in the new North American Free Trade Agreement (NAFTA)[36] rules, which are briefly described below.

THE FTA AND CANADIAN AUTO PACT OBLIGATIONS

The FTA affects Canada's obligations respecting automotive goods in two ways. First, automotive goods originating in the United States will be admitted duty-free after January 1, 1998, without regard to the Auto Pact safeguards. Second, Canada may no longer confer Auto Pact status on manufacturers.

1. ELIMINATION OF DUTIES

The effect of FTA Articles 401.1 and 401.2 and the Tariff Schedule of Canada set forth in FTA Annex 401.2 (Canadian Tariff Schedule) is to oblige Canada to admit automotive goods originating from the United States duty-free after January 1, 1998, and at progressively diminishing rates of duty until then, regardless of whether the importer is a manufacturer meeting the Auto Pact safeguards.

The Canadian Tariff Schedule sets out a base rate[37] of duty and a staging category[38] for each good. All motor vehicles covered by Canada's Auto Pact obligations, and most parts, fall within staging category "C."[39] FTA Article 401.2 requires that duties on goods in staging category "C" be eliminated over ten equal annual stages.[40] The base rate in the Canadian Tariff Schedule on all motor vehicles covered by the Auto Pact is 9.2 percent. The duty for these motor vehicles originating from the United States is 5.5 percent for 1992, and will be 4.6 percent in 1993, 3.6 percent in 1994, and so on, declining to zero in 1998. Origin is determined in accordance with the FTA rules of origin.

2. NO FURTHER EXTENSION OF AUTO PACT STATUS

FTA Articles 405.1 and 405.2 prohibit the introduction of new programs waiving customs duties that are contingent upon fulfilment of performance requirements[41] and require that existing programs of this kind be eliminated by January 1, 1998.[42] The MVTO 1988, and the duty remission orders by which Auto Pact status has been granted, all fall within this description. FTA Article 405.4 provides that the elimination requirement does not apply to the MVTO 1988 or to duty remission orders conferring Auto Pact status, which, at the time the FTA was signed, had been, or were about to be, granted.[43] However, under FTA Article 1002.1, Canada may not grant Auto Pact status to new manufacturers nor may it extend the duration or expand the extent of any existing order. While the duty-free treatment of imports of new vehicles and OEM parts by qualifying manufacturers may continue indefinitely, Canada may no longer qualify any new manufacturer.

3. CANADA'S AUTO PACT OBLIGATIONS INDEPENDENT FROM FTA

While the MVTO 1988 may be a duty remission program for Canada's automotive industry, it is also the means whereby Canada's obligations under the Auto Pact are carried into effect. General Motors Canada is able to import vehicles and parts from the United States and elsewhere duty-free into Canada because Canada is fulfilling its Auto Pact obligations through the MVTO 1988. The FTA permits the MVTO 1988 to continue in perpetuity, but there is no obligation under the FTA that it be continued. The Canadian Auto Pact obligation to accord duty-free treatment to goods (imported by manufacturers such as General Motors Canada) that comply with the Auto Pact safeguards, while affirmed by FTA Article 104.1, has not been incorporated into the FTA and continues to arise exclusively from the Auto Pact. If the Auto Pact were terminated, Canada would have no obligation under the FTA to maintain the MVTO 1988.

THE FTA HAS NOT AFFECTED THE AUTO PACT

This statement was set forth at the beginning of this chapter as one of the conflicting views of the effect of the FTA on the Auto Pact. Is the statement correct or not? The answer depends on how you look at it.

The US obligations under the Auto Pact clearly have been affected by the FTA. While the obligation to allow duty-free treatment continues, the basis for the duty-free treatment depends upon the imported goods satisfying a different rule of origin. For the statement to be correct, this difference would have to be seen as technical only, and not one of substance. It cannot be categorically stated that the FTA rules of origin impose a tougher test than the Auto Pact. At this stage, it is too early to tell. However, the FTA rules of origin clearly constitute a substantial departure in approach from the Auto Pact test.

From a technical point of view, Canadian Auto Pact obligations have been unaffected by the FTA. If the Auto Pact is viewed as the agreement that was entered into by the United States and Canada in 1966 and one considers as minimal the indirect effects on the Auto Pact safeguards flowing from duty elimination, the statement is correct. If the Auto Pact is seen as a policy instrument to encourage automotive production in Canada by granting duty remission upon fulfilment of performance requirements, then the FTA has had the effect of preventing further expansion of the program. Because of the FTA, Auto Pact status can never be granted to manufacturers such as Honda, Toyota, and Hyundai.

THE FTA HAS "GUTTED" THE AUTO PACT

Critics of the FTA, particularly those associated in one way or another with the automotive industry, allege that the FTA has "gutted" the

Auto Pact. The expression "gutted" is taken to mean "having made the Auto Pact safeguards ineffective."

The FTA clearly provides an alternative means for importing motor vehicles and parts from the United States duty-free. Following January 1, 1998,[44] a manufacturer such as General Motors Canada will have a choice of complying with the safeguards and importing such items duty-free under the Auto Pact, or ignoring the safeguards and importing such items duty-free under the FTA solely by ensuring that they satisfy the FTA rules of origin. Theoretically, manufacturers like GM, Ford, and Chrysler could withdraw from Canada altogether and supply the Canadian market for their motor vehicles from their US plants. The Auto Pact safeguard prescribing the sales-to-production ratio was designed to ensure that this would not happen.

It can be argued that the Auto Pact safeguards are no longer necessary because Canada's automotive industry is now at least as efficient as that of the United States. While this may be so, such an argument does not respond to the question of whether the FTA has removed or seriously weakened the incentives to comply with the Auto Pact safeguards. Therefore, one can assume for the moment that the safeguards continue to be important.

Whether or not the FTA has "gutted" the Auto Pact depends first upon whether the scenario of US-owned manufacturers (GM, Ford, and Chrysler) pulling their manufacturing operations out of Canada and supplying the Canadian market from their US plants is realistic. If this is a plausible scenario, then the FTA has "gutted" the Auto Pact. Given the vast investments each of these manufacturers has in Canada, coupled with the relative efficiency of the Canadian operations of each, there would have to be a fairly cataclysmic series of events occurring in Canada for this scenario to unfold. Assuming that these manufacturers continue to manufacture automobiles in Canada, what incentive will there be to comply with the Auto Pact safeguards, given that the duty saved on imports from the United States will be nil following January 1, 1998?

GM, Ford, and Chrysler import a considerable volume of parts each year from third countries, and, based on current duty rates, the duty these manufacturers save annually by complying with the Auto Pact safeguards is considerable.[45] The real incentive to comply with Auto Pact safeguards following duty elimination under the FTA will be to save duty on imports of vehicles and parts from third countries.

The fact that such companies as General Motors, Ford, and Chrysler have the ability in Canada to import vehicles and parts from third countries duty-free puts them at an advantage over producers in Canada such as Honda, Toyota, and Hyundai.

Duty payable as a result of failure to comply with the Auto Pact safeguards has, hitherto, been a formidable sanction. By eliminating duty on motor vehicles and parts imported from the United States, this sanction has been weakened. However, the question as to whether the Auto Pact has been "gutted" depends upon whether elimination of duties under the FTA means that a significant sanction has been replaced by an ineffective sanction or whether a draconian sanction has been replaced by a sanction that is merely significant. Applying draconian sanctions against major manufacturers can be counterproductive.[46]

Following duty elimination under the FTA, the effectiveness of a sanction applied to an automotive manufacturer that is entitled to Auto Pact benefits, but that does not meet the safeguards, will depend on two variables: the volume of the manufacturer's third-country imports, and the rates of duty applicable to those imports. The effectiveness of the sanction will ultimately depend upon factors influencing those variables. Multi-country sourcing trends in the automotive industry should increase third-country imports, although there will be a limit on the volume of third-country parts that an automotive manufacturer in Canada can use and still satisfy FTA rules of origin (for its US exports) and CVA requirements.[47] However, there will be downward pressure on rates of duty for several reasons. Rates of duty will fall with the completion of the Uruguay Round. For reasons described below, the FTA elimination of duty drawback will create pressures in Canada to harmonize duty rates with lower US rates.

POSITION OF NON-AUTO PACT MANUFACTURERS

As indicated above, one effect of the FTA is that Canada may no longer confer Auto Pact status on automotive manufacturers. Prior to the FTA, all manufacturers were either covered by the Auto Pact or an Auto Pact status remission order, or had the opportunity to attain Auto Pact status. Following the FTA, there are two classes of automotive manufacturers in Canada: there are those covered by the Auto Pact itself or an Auto Pact status remission order, and those that are

not covered and never will be. The major non-Auto Pact manufacturers are Honda, Toyota, and Hyundai. One effect of the FTA on the
Auto Pact has been to alter the position of these manufacturers vis-à-
vis that of Auto Pact manufacturers such as GM, Ford, and Chrysler.

1. EXPORTING FROM CANADA TO THE UNITED STATES

As US obligations to admit vehicles and parts imported from Canada
duty-free have depended, both under the Auto Pact and the FTA, solely
on goods satisfying an origin requirement, Auto Pact and non-Auto
Pact manufacturers continue to be in the same position, relative to
each other, respecting exports to the United States. The only change
has been from the Auto Pact test to the FTA rules of origin, and the
change applies to both. The FTA value test will apply to exports from
Canada of any automotive manufacturer, whether it be General Motors,
Ford, Chrysler, Honda, Toyota, or Hyundai.

The one significant implication of the FTA for non-Auto Pact
manufacturers exporting from Canada flows from the FTA elimination of duty drawback after January 1, 1994. As of this date, neither
Canada nor the United States will be permitted to waive or refund
duty paid on materials imported from third countries and incorporated into goods exported to the United States (in Canada's case) or to
Canada (in the case of the United States).[48] Most Canadian production
of non-Auto Pact manufacturers is exported to the United States.
Accordingly, the relief provided by drawback of the relatively high
duties on imported parts and components is significant. Following
the elimination of duty drawback, this relief will no longer be available.
While non-Auto Pact manufacturers currently receive a degree of duty
relief under production-based duty remission orders, these must be
eliminated by January 1, 1996.[49]

The elimination of duty drawback is not a problem for Auto Pact
manufacturers. So long as they comply with the Auto Pact safeguards,
they can import items from third countries duty-free under the Auto
Pact. The elimination of duty drawback following January 1, 1994, will
provide an additional incentive for Auto Pact manufacturers to continue
complying with the Auto Pact safeguards.

2. EXPORTING FROM THE UNITED STATES TO CANADA

Duty elimination under the FTA will not have the same significance for US affiliates of Auto Pact manufacturers as for US affiliates of non-Auto Pact manufacturers. The FTA simply provides US affiliates of Auto Pact manufacturers with an alternative means of securing duty-free access for vehicles exported to Canada. The US affiliates of non-Auto Pact manufacturers will, under the FTA, receive duty-free access to the Canadian market, which they previously did not have. Prior to the FTA coming into effect, vehicles and parts exported by US affiliates of non-Auto Pact manufacturers from the United States into Canada were subject to duty.[50] With the FTA, the duty will be phased out by January 1, 1998. Vehicles and parts exported by US affiliates of non-Auto Pact manufacturers from the United States to Canada will enter Canada duty-free after January 1, 1998, and at progressively diminishing rates of duty prior to that date, provided they satisfy the FTA rules of origin.

The elimination of duty drawback under the FTA will affect US affiliates of Auto Pact and non-Auto Pact manufacturers equally. For both, US duty will be paid on parts imported from third countries and, following January 1, 1994, no refund of the duty will be allowed upon exportation of vehicles to Canada.

3. OVERALL EFFECT

Prohibition of further granting of Auto Pact status eliminates a potential incentive for non-Auto Pact manufacturers to expand Canadian operations or use Canadian-produced parts. Duty elimination under the FTA, however, could act as an incentive for the affiliates of non-Auto Pact manufacturers to expand US operations to serve the Canadian market. The elimination of duty drawback under the FTA will act as an incentive to source parts in North America as opposed to third countries, but, for FTA rules of origin purposes, these parts can be sourced in the United States as well as in Canada. Elimination of drawback will act as a disincentive for non-Auto Pact manufacturers to expand Canadian operations because of the relatively higher rates of duty imposed in Canada on imported parts and components. The Canadian government could neutralize this disincentive by reducing duty rates on these items to US levels. However, by so doing, the incentive for Auto Pact manufacturers to comply with the Auto Pact safeguards would be weakened. Alternatively, the Canadian government could introduce a duty remission program based on criteria other than fulfilling "performance requirements," directed specifically at non-Auto Pact manufacturers. However, if the United States could demonstrate that such a program adversely affected US based manufacturers such as General Motors, Ford, or Chrysler, the program would have to be eliminated or expanded to include these manufacturers.[51] If these manufacturers had to be included in such a program, the incentive to comply with the Auto Pact safeguards would disappear altogether.

AUTOMOTIVE PARTS MANUFACTURERS

Canadian automotive parts manufacturers have been the beneficiaries of the Auto Pact safeguards. The production-to-sales ratio has ensured that manufacturers such as GM produce a certain number of motor vehicles in Canada. The CVA requirement has provided a powerful incentive to source parts in Canada. To the extent that the FTA has made ineffective the incentives for Auto Pact manufacturers to comply with these requirements, the FTA has undermined the position of the parts producers. As indicated above, the validity of this concern depends upon factors affecting the amount of duty on imports of third country automobiles and OEM parts that can be saved by Auto Pact manufacturers complying with Auto Pact safeguards.

The FTA has prevented the extension of Canada's automotive duty remission program to manufacturers such as Honda, Toyota, and Hyundai. As a result of not receiving, or being capable of receiving, Auto Pact status, these manufacturers will not have the same incentive to source parts in Canada as do Auto Pact manufacturers. FTA rules of origin requirements for these manufacturers' exports to the United States can be met just as easily with US-produced as with Canadian-produced parts.

Has the FTA created an incentive for parts manufacturers to transfer operations from Canada to the United States? For the most part, it has not. A parts producer supplying OEM parts to an Auto Pact manufacturer such as GM Canada could have supplied the manufacturer from the United States just as easily prior to the FTA coming into effect as after. The parts would have entered Canada duty-free in either case. However, the FTA does open an opportunity for a parts producer that supplies OEM parts to a non-Auto Pact manufacturer to supply the Canadian operations of the manufacturer with US-produced parts on a duty-free basis following January 1, 1998, and at progressively diminishing rates of duty up to that time.

While OEM parts produced by Canadian automotive parts manufacturers for the US market continue under the FTA to enter the United States duty-free, the rule of origin has changed. As the FTA rules of origin impose only a prescribed change in tariff classification requirement on most parts, the FTA rule for many manufacturers may be easier to meet. Even if as much domestic effort is required to meet the prescribed change in tariff classification as to meet the Auto Pact test, establishing that a change in tariff classification has occurred does not require the accounting effort that must be expended to satisfy a value test. It is unlikely that many Canadian automotive parts manufacturers are demonstrably worse off as a result of the change from the Auto Pact test to the FTA Rules of Origin.

If the FTA rules of origin impose a tougher test on Auto Pact manufacturers than does the Auto Pact test, automotive parts manufacturers in the United States and Canada should benefit, at the expense of automotive parts manufacturers in third countries. As indicated above, it is too early to tell whether or not the FTA rules of origin are tougher.

Automotive parts manufacturers in Canada and the United States will benefit, at the expense of third country parts manufacturers, from the elimination of duty drawback following January 1, 1994, although the benefit in Canada will be less clear. On the one hand, duties on automotive parts are higher in Canada than in the United States, so the incentive for domestic vehicle assemblers to shift from third-country to Canadian or US parts will be stronger in Canada than in the United States. On the other hand, Auto Pact manufacturers complying with Auto Pact safeguards already import parts from third countries into Canada duty-free, and will be, to this extent, unaffected by the elimination of drawback.

CONCLUSION

As the Auto Pact is asymmetrical, so the effects of the FTA upon it are asymmetrical. The only significant change on the US side is in the rules of origin. While the FTA test may or may not be tougher than the Auto Pact test, it is more complex and its effect is, as yet, uncertain.

The FTA affects the Canadian industry in two ways. First, once fully implemented, Canadian manufacturers will be able to import vehicles and parts from the United States without complying with Auto Pact safeguards. The only incentive to comply with Auto Pact safeguards after duty elimination under the FTA has been completed, will be the duty saved on third-country parts and components. While increases in third-country sourcing will strengthen this incentive, the lowering of rates of duty as the result of the Uruguay Round, and pressures arising from the elimination of duty drawback, will work in the opposite direction. Second, Canada cannot confer Auto Pact status on any more manufacturers, with the result that there are now two classes of manufacturers in Canada: those with Auto Pact benefits, and those that can never attain such benefits. Canada can no longer use the Auto Pact type of policy instrument to attract new automotive investment or to encourage non-Auto Pact manufacturers to expand their Canadian operations. Automotive investment in Canada will be left more to pure market forces than was previously the case.

The NAFTA negotiations have now concluded among Canada, the United States, and Mexico, and an agreement scheduled to go into effect on January 1, 1994 has been initialled. NAFTA permits the Auto Pact and the Auto Pact duty remission orders to continue, and maintains the status quo in prohibiting the extension of "Auto Pact status" to new manufacturers. Mexico's Automotive Decree,[52] which operates very differently from the Auto Pact, is to be dismantled in stages and will be completely eliminated by January 1, 2004. The Mexican automotive industry is already being integrated into the North American, but full integration is not possible under the Automotive Decree in its present form. By eliminating the Automotive Decree, NAFTA will set the stage for full integration. Unlike the Automotive Decree, the Auto Pact is consistent with an integrated North American automotive industry.

NAFTA will eliminate duties on all automotive goods traded between Canada and Mexico by 2004, with earlier elimination for a number of items. As roughly one-half of non-US automotive goods imported into Canada are Mexican, NAFTA will further reduce the incentive for Auto Pact manufacturers to comply with the safeguards.

NAFTA will alter the basis for duty-free entry of automotive goods into the United States by replacing the FTA rules of origin with new and more stringent rules for automotive goods. The version of the NAFTA value test applicable to passenger vehicles and small trucks and buses will eliminate roll-up by tracing and counting as non-originating the duty-paid value of all materials incorporated into a vehicle, if they are imported under specific tariff headings. In this respect, this test resembles the old Auto Pact value test, although enforcement by US Customs is likely to be much more rigorous. The test is based on a net-cost concept that includes a wider range of non-material costs than the FTA value test. However, the threshold percentage of 50 percent will be increased to 62.5 percent in two stages over eight years. The version of the NAFTA test applicable to specialty vehicles and large trucks and buses is similar to the other test in its treatment of non-material costs, but permits roll-up on all materials except engines and transmissions. Engines and transmissions are broken down into specified parts and sub-assemblies, and each non-originating part or sub-assembly counts against the manufacturer, even if the engine or transmission is originating. However, there is no roll-down effect if the engine or transmission is non-originating. The threshold percentage for these vehicles will ultimately be 60 percent, with a similar phasing-in period. As each of these tests is calculated very differently from the FTA value test, a direct comparison between the threshold percentages cannot be made.

The NAFTA origin rules resolve a number of problems that arose under the FTA test, but may create new problems. For example, cost allocation will probably be more contentious with the net-cost concept (which starts with all costs and eliminates certain cost categories) than with the production-cost approach under the FTA. The multiple forms of the value test for automotive goods will be coupled with tracing and layers of complexity. How effectively NAFTA rules work in practice will depend largely on whether the "Uniform Regulations" that the parties are currently drafting are precise and workable.

NAFTA will postpone the elimination of duty drawback for goods traded between Canada and the United States until January 1, 1996. This will simply delay by two years the choices described above facing the Canadian government. After January 1, 1996, NAFTA will permit drawback of Canadian duty paid on materials up to the amount of the US duty paid on the finished good. Based on the current differential between the Canadian rate on parts (9.2 percent) and the US duty on vehicles (2.5 percent) a non-Auto Pact manufacturer in Canada may, depending on its circumstances, have little incentive to comply with the rules of origin.

Auto Pact manufacturers in Canada will receive benefits in the form of duty remission that cannot be made available to manufacturers in the United States or Mexico. So long as Canadian costs remain competitive with US and Mexican costs, the Auto Pact will act as a positive incentive for vehicle manufacturers to continue their Canadian operations. However, if Canada becomes the high-cost producer in the North American automotive market, the incentives provided by the Auto Pact will not be sufficient to offset market pressures to shift vehicle assembly and parts production to more cost-effective locations in the United States or Mexico.

NOTES

[1] The formal title of the Auto Pact is the *Agreement Concerning Automotive Products between the Government of Canada and the Government of the United States of America.*

[2] Tubes and tires are excluded from the Auto Pact. Aftermarket parts are not covered by the Auto Pact.

[3] Unless otherwise indicated, "North America" means Canada and the United States only.

[4] The provisions of the Auto Pact were carried forward in the United States by the *Automotive Products Trade Act of 1965,* Pub.L.No. 89-283, 19 USC 2001 et seq.

[5] The past tense is used in respect of US Auto Pact obligations because these obligations have been subsumed in the FTA. The present tense will be used in respect of Canadian Auto Pact obligations because these have been unaffected by the FTA.

[6] The test is set forth in paragraph (3) of Annex B of the Auto Pact.

[7] The Tariff Schedule of the United States (TSUS) referred to is the US tariff schedule in effect at the time that the FTA was signed at the beginning of 1988. See 19 USC 1202. The term "Canadian article" was defined in TSUS General Headnote 3(d)(ii). The TSUS was not based on the Harmonized System. The TSUS was superseded by the Harmonized Tariff Schedule of the United States (HTSUS) at the beginning of 1989. The HTSUS is based on the Harmonized System and carries forward the provisions set forth in the Tariff Schedule of the United States contained in FTA Annex 401.2. The Tariff Schedules in FTA Annex 401.2 are based on the Harmonized System.

[8] Defined in headnote 2, Part 6B, Schedule 6 of the TSUS.

[9] See TSUS, headnote 2(c), Part 6B, Schedule 6.

[10] See Section 2(1) of the Motor Vehicles Tariff Order, 1988, SOR/88-71.

[11] By letters of intent, the Canadian subsidiaries of the major US producers agreed to increase levels of CVA to specified levels by the end of the 1968 model year (Chayes 1968: 326-8).

[12] SOR/88-71 31 December, 1987.

[13] Subject only to the requirement that goods from the country from which they are imported be entitled to the benefit of the Most-Favoured-Nation Tariff. This includes most countries in the world. See Schedule III of the

Customs Tariff for a list of the countries entitled to Canada's Most-Favoured-Nation Tariff.

[14] As set forth in Article I of the General Agreement on Tariffs and Trade (GATT).

[15] BISD, Thirteenth Supplement, 114-15.

[16] The obligations could not be identical with those in the Auto Pact because none of the companies to which such duty remission orders was granted was producing automobiles in Canada during the Auto Pact base year.

[17] The prescribed percentage is frequently 40 percent. Sometimes it is 60 percent and, occasionally, some other percentage.

[18] Third countries are countries other than the United State or Canada.

[19] The recipients of these "export-based" duty remission orders are listed in Part Two of FTA Annex 1002.1.

[20] This is the language used in Annex B of the Auto Pact.

[21] The note at the beginning of Chapter 87 of the US Tariff Schedule is carried forward in the subdivision (c)(iii)(A) of General Note 3 of the HTSUS, with slight changes in wording. The expression "Canadian article" is re-introduced in paragraph (1) of this subdivision and means an article originating in Canada in accordance with the FTA rules of origin. The expression "original motor vehicle equipment" and "bona fide motor-vehicle manufacturer" are defined in paragraphs (2) and (4) respectively.

[22] If this item is not to be used as "original motor vehicle equipment," the current US rate of duty for such an item originating in Canada is free for use in a civil aircraft and, in 1992, 1.8 percent for any other use. As the item, for any use other than as "original motor vehicle equipment" or in a civil aircraft, is in Staging Category "C," final tariff elimination will not be complete for this item until January 1, 1998.

[23] There is one other potential inconsistency. It is possible that the line item identification of items eligible for treatment as "original motor vehicle equipment" in the US Tariff Schedule may omit some items identified in Annex B to the Auto Pact. If items have been omitted, the provisions of the FTA would prevail. This does not seem to be a practical concern.

[24] Since this paper was first written, a Chapter 18 binational panel decided that non-mortgage interest on loans to finance the acquisition of plant and equipment is included in the "direct cost of processing." See FTA Panel re Article 304 of the FTA, reported in 5 TCT 8118.

[25] The FTA rules of origin are the same for both Canada and the United States, and it does not matter whether a material or submaterial comes from Canada or the United States. Goods produced in Canada from US materials will nonetheless originate in Canada, and vice versa.

[26] The prescribed change in tariff classification must also be met by any material produced in Canada or the United States that contains imported submaterials and would not meet the FTA rule of origin applicable to it.

[27] The prescribed changes in tariff classification are expressed in terms of chapters, headings, and subheadings of the Harmonized System, which is used by both Canada and the United States. The chapter is the first two digits of a tariff item, the heading is the first four digits, and the subheading is the first six digits. Canadian and US numbering is identical down to the six digit subheading level.

[28] This expression is defined in FTA Article 304 as costs directly incurred or that can be reasonably allocated to the production of goods, with some specific inclusions and exclusions.

[29] That is, parts falling under a Harmonized System parts heading or subheading. If a sealed beam lamp unit (which falls under Canadian or US tariff schedule subheading 8539.10) is assembled from imported parts falling under parts subheading 8539.90, Rule 4 of FTA Annex 301.2, Rules, Section XVI, would apply. The required change in tariff classification is from a parts subheading (in this case 8539.90) to a heading which is not a parts subheading (in this case 8539.10). In addition, this rule requires that the FTA value test be satisfied.

[30] A sealed beam lamp unit falls under subheading 8539.10 in both the Canadian and US tariff schedules. The applicable rules are set forth in FTA Annex 301.2, Rules, Section XVI. Unless the imported materials are parts, Rules 1 and 2 apply, neither of which prescribes the FTA value test.

[31] The expression "domestic" is used to mean Canadian or US.

[32] Suppose, for example, that the glass envelope for making the bulb contained in the unit is imported from a third country. Under both the Canadian and US tariff schedules, the glass envelope falls under tariff heading 7011. The sealed beam lamp unit falls under tariff heading 8539. Rule 2 under FTA Annex 301.2, Rules, Section XVI, requires that there be change from one heading (other than a parts heading, which heading 7011 is not) to another heading. As a result of the production process, the glass envelope (originally under heading 7011) will be part of a sealed beam lamp unit, which falls under heading 8539. The change in tariff classification required

by Rule 2 will have been satisfied, at least with respect to the imported glass envelope.

[33] The motor vehicles covered by the Auto Pact fall under headings 8702 to 8704 inclusive in both the Canadian and US tariff schedules. The applicable FTA rule of origin is Rule 4 in FTA Annex 301.2, Rules, Section XVI.

[34] Spark-ignition reciprocating or rotary internal combustion engines fall under 8407 in both the Canadian and US tariff schedules. The applicable FTA rule of origin is Rule 3 in FTA Annex 301.2, Rules, Section XVII. Interestingly, diesel engines, which fall under heading 8408 in both tariff schedules, are not subject to the FTA value test unless the imported components fall under a parts heading such as 8409.

[35] The Guidelines published by Revenue Canada, Customs and Excise on the FTA Rules of Origin indicate that a similar approach would be followed in respect of intermediate materials manufactured in house by the manufacturer. See Memorandum D11-4-12, paragraphs 38(b), 39 and 40. It is not clear that this concept of internal roll-up is supported by the actual wording of the FTA value test. While US Customs accepts that the internal roll-up concept does exist, the approach taken is much more restrictive than that of Revenue Canada. See US Customs ruling CLA-2:R:C:M 000131 JLV, dated December 12, 1991. The internal roll-up issue is explicitly covered in the new NAFTA rules of origin, which are briefly discussed below.

[36] North America in this context means Canada, the United States, and Mexico.

[37] The base rate of duty was the most-favoured-nation rate in effect at the time that the FTA was signed at the beginning of 1988.

[38] The staging categories in the Canadian Tariff Schedule do not necessarily correspond to those in the US Tariff Schedule. Because US Auto Pact obligations are covered in the US Tariff Schedule on a line-item by line-item basis, while Canadian Auto Pact obligations are based on an entirely different principle, there is no correlation at all between Canadian and US staging categories for automotive goods. For automotive goods, the US staging category is "D," while, for the most part, the Canadian staging category is "C."

[39] Some special-purpose motor vehicles are designated as staging categories "A" and "B." See Canadian Tariff Schedule heading 8705. None of these would have been covered by Canada's Auto Pact obligations.

[40] Under FTA Article 401.2, customs duties on goods designated as staging category "A" were eliminated on January 1, 1989. Goods designated as

staging category "B" are to be eliminated in five equal stages from 1989 to 1993, with complete elimination occurring by January 1, 1994.

⁴¹ The principal beneficiary of these types of programs, besides the automotive industry, has been the textile industry. The expression "performance requirement" is defined in FTA Article 410, and clearly includes a requirement to maintain a certain level or percentage of domestic content. As to whether maintaining a production-to-sales ratio is a "performance requirement" this might be debated.

⁴² FTA Articles 1002.2 and 1002.3 contain, respectively, specific requirements respecting the elimination of export-based duty waivers and production-based duty waivers for automotive goods. Export-based duty waivers cease to apply to exports to the United States following January 1, 1989 and must be completely eliminated by January 1, 1998. The production-based duty waivers must be eliminated by January 1, 1996.

⁴³ The exception in FTA Article 405.4 applies to waivers granted the manufacturers listed in Part One of FTA Annex 1002.1. Part One lists Canadian manufacturers that have qualified for duty remission under the Auto Pact or "comparable arrangements" or that would reasonably be expected to qualify by the 1989 model year. The "comparable arrangements" are the various individual remission orders that have been or are to be granted, including conditions for remission of duty comparable to the conditions in the Auto Pact. The expression "model year" means a twelve-month period commencing on August 1 and ending on the following July 31. The 1989 model year is the twelve-month period ending on July 31, 1989. To qualify, a manufacturer must have achieved or must achieve the CVA and production-to-sales ratio requirements that apply to it in any model year up to and including the 1989 model year. Most of the manufacturers listed in Annex 1002.1 had already qualified at the time that the FTA was signed. One manufacturer that had not qualified was CAMI Automotive Inc., a joint venture between General Motors and Suzuki. CAMI Automotive Inc. did achieve Auto Pact status in the 1989 model year. Footnote 1 to Annex 1002.1 contains rules of succession for remission orders. Essentially, if control of a recipient business passes to a manufacturer of motor vehicles that is not a listed recipient and the fundamental nature, scope, or size of the business is significantly altered, the recipient ceases to be entitled to remission of duty.

⁴⁴ Note that the duty applicable on a motor vehicle imported under the FTA in the years immediately prior to 1998 will be very low. The duty will be 2.7 percent in 1995, 1.8 percent in 1996, and 0.9 percent in 1997. The effectiveness of duty on imports from the United States of new vehicles

and OEM parts, as a sanction to ensure compliance with the Auto Pact safeguards, will steadily erode as January 1, 1998 approaches.

[45] In 1988, Paul Wonnacott estimated the volume to be about $3 billion annually and the duty saved annually to be $300,000,000 (Wonnacott 1988: 7-8).

[46] Paul Wonnacott is of the view that the threat of duties on imports from third countries may be a more effective sanction because to have invoked the larger sanction available before the FTA came into effect would have been ruinous to a manufacturer. The analogy is drawn with inhibitions on the use of nuclear as opposed to conventional weapons (Wonnacott 1988: 9-10).

[47] The need to meet the US Corporate Automotive Fuel Economy (CAFE) requirements for "domestic" automobiles may also impose a limitation on the volume of third-country imports that can be incorporated into a manufacturer's Canadian-produced vehicles, although in some circumstances manufacturers have found it advantageous to have fuel-inefficient vehicles classified as non-domestic for CAFE purposes (see also Chapter 7 by Gayle).

[48] See FTA Article 404.

[49] See FTA Article 1002.3.

[50] Note that non-Auto Pact manufacturers could, if they wished, import vehicles from their US affiliates within the limits of the production based duty-remission programs. However, such imports would limit their ability to import duty free from Asia. Under the FTA, provided that FTA rules of origin are satisfied, the ability of such US affiliates to export to Canada will not be limited.

[51] See FTA Article 405.3.

[52] Decree for the Development and Modernization of the Automotive Industry ("Decreto para el Fomento y Modernización de la Industria Automotriz") December 1989.

REFERENCES

Chayes, Abram. 1986. *The International Legal Process: Materials for an Introductory Course.* Boston: Little, Brown, and Company.

GATT. 1965. Basic Instruments and Selected Documents (BISD). Thirteenth Supplement.

Gayle, Dennis J. 1992. Regulating the American Automobile Industry: Sources and Consequences of US Automobile Air Pollution Standards. Chapter 7, this volume.

Wonnacott, Paul. 1987. *US and Canadian Auto Policies in a Changing World Environment.* Toronto: C.D. Howe Institute and Washington, DC: National Planning Association, July.

____. 1988. The Canada-US Free Trade Agreement. *Trade Monitor,* No. 2, March.

11 ALTERNATIVE APPROACHES TO NORTH AMERICAN FREE TRADE AND THE AUTO INDUSTRY

Murray G. Smith
Ronald J. Wonnacott

INTRODUCTION

In the negotiation of free trade with Mexico, there were several possible outcomes, each with different implications for the auto industry. These various outcomes can be grouped into some broad options as follows:

1. A trilateral North American Free Trade Agreement (NAFTA);

2. A bilateral US-Mexico Free Trade Agreement alongside the present Canada-US Free Trade Agreement (FTA); and

3. A pair of US-Mexico and Canada-Mexico bilaterals along with the present Canada-US Free Trade Agreement.

THE CURRENT FORMAT: A TRILATERAL NORTH AMERICAN FREE TRADE AGREEMENT (NAFTA)

The objective of the negotiations was to create a trilateral NAFTA—an open market with a combined GNP of more than US $6 trillion and with annual trade in goods and services between its members exceeding US $270 billion. Such an agreement, moreover, sets the stage for further moves toward a free-trading hemisphere from the Beaufort Sea to Cape Horn.

Under such an expanding free trade agreement, each country, such as Canada, through partnership with the US, will expect:

1. Gains from free trade with the United States, *augmented by*

2. Later, additional gains from free trade with new partners, such as Mexico, as each signs into the expanding regional arrangement.

In the case of a Canada-Mexico-US trilateral NAFTA, what will be the implications for the auto industry of duty-free trade in all directions? Since such trade already exists between Canada and the United States, the major change would be in their trade with Mexico.

From the Mexican point of view, all producers (and consumers) in that country will get imports from the United States or Canada duty free. At present, this privilege only goes to *maquiladora* firms. However, NAFTA will mean the end of this program as it now exists, since the maquiladora is essentially a form of duty drawback and duty drawback is not permitted once a free trade agreement is implemented.[1] Specifically, these firms in Mexico will no longer be able to acquire duty-free imports from Japan and other fourth countries (at least on automotive equipment eventually destined for Canada or the United States). This disadvantage, however, will at least be partially offset by the duty-free access of these firms exporting to the Canadian and US markets. This is not as important as it might seem, however, since exporters in Mexico already face a substantially reduced US tariff due to US tariff items 806 and 807 or the Generalized System of Preferences (GSP) (which they sometimes switch back and forth between).

Automotive producers in Mexico also enjoy a zero tariff on most exports to Canada—namely, on exports to Auto Pact firms, because these firms qualify for duty remission under Canada's Auto Pact safeguards. About 90 percent of Canada's imports of automotive parts and components from Mexico enter duty free. Moreover, Auto Pact firms may import finished vehicles duty free.

From the US point of view, firms and consumers will benefit from lower-cost duty-free inputs from Mexico (an advantage which, as already noted, is reduced by the fact that 806/807 or GSP treatment already applies to these goods). In addition, US exporters will get duty-free access to all Mexican firms, not just to those in the maquiladora program.

The benefit of lower cost inputs will also accrue to Canadian exporters. A second benefit for Canada will be duty-free access to Mexican supplies which, in automotive equipment, is less important than in other goods because, as noted above, Auto Pact producers in Canada already get duty-free access to these imports.

A key issue in NAFTA negotiations for US and Canadian automotive operations was the timetable for elimination of the Mexican automotive decrees. Although there has been some liberalization of the Mexican automotive decrees, which impose import licencing and mandate trade balancing for each auto firm producing in Mexico, the decrees are still a potent non-tariff barrier to the export of automotive parts or finished vehicles to Mexico from either the United States or Canada. What is especially important for Canadian automotive operations in NAFTA, whether they are engaged in vehicle assembly or parts production, is that, whatever the specific transition provisions for elimination of Mexican import licencing in the automotive sector, they will have the same degree of access to the Mexican market as US operations.

The elimination of the Mexican automotive decrees and import licencing poses challenges for the existing operations who have predicated investment on a highly protected market and for foreign auto producers who do not have assembly capacity in Mexico. What the Big Three proposed in the NAFTA negotiations was a fast phase-out of the automotive decrees applied to the five firms with assembly operations in Mexico—the Big Three plus Nissan and Volkswagen—and a phase-out over a much longer time frame of automotive decrees on auto producers who do not presently have assembly facilities in Mexico.

Equivalent access to the growing and highly protected Mexican market is important for Canada because of bilateral trade opportunities and because of the implications for investment and plant location. Presently, Canada has a large trade imbalance with Mexico in the automotive sector; exports are about $100 million and imports are about $1.8 billion. Liberalization of the Mexican automotive market will open significant opportunities for exports of auto parts and assembled vehicles from Canada. Since Canada has virtually no barriers on exports from Mexico and projections for the Mexican automotive market suggest that demand growth will be rapid (see Scheinman, Chapter 13), the bilateral Mexico-Canada trade imbalance should be reduced as NAFTA is implemented.

Although NAFTA will have important direct implications for bilateral trade between Mexico and Canada, the indirect implications for investment decisions and the location of production could be much more significant. Whether auto firms are considering new investment or making retooling and retrenchment decisions, equivalent access to the Mexican market with US operations will be important to the competitive position of Canadian operations.

The rules of origin in NAFTA for automotive products are also an important issue. There have been differences between Canada and the United States over the interpretation of the automotive rules of origin under the present Canada-US Free Trade Agreement. Rules of origin under NAFTA that are more restrictive than the Free Trade Agreement could pose difficulties for transplant operations, which already have difficulty meeting the current rules of origin. These difficulties may be partly, or fully, offset through clarification of the rules of origin for automotive products.

A HUB-AND-SPOKE FORMAT IF CANADA HAD LEFT THE NEGOTIATIONS

If Canada had withdrawn from the NAFTA talks, the United States and Mexico would have been left to sign their own bilateral agreement. Consequently, the United States would have become a trading hub, with separate bilateral free trade agreements with Mexico and Canada. In such a system of two overlapping free trade areas, each US partner would have achieved essentially the same gains from bilateral trade with the US as stated at the beginning of this paper. However, each partner would not have realized the full gains of free trade with other partners; indeed, it might even have incurred losses, as the US went on to sign bilaterals with new spoke partners.

To illustrate: if the United States, with its Canadian bilateral agreement now in place, had signed a bilateral agreement with Mexico, Canada could not have achieved the free-trade benefits of free access to the Mexican market. Instead, Canadian access would have been diminished because of the discrimination it would have faced in the Mexican market in competition with regard to US products, which alone would have had the advantage of free entry into that market. This discrimination would have been a problem for Canada, even if Mexican external barriers to Canadian goods did not increase. But such Mexican barriers on Canadian goods would doubtlessly have increased since the United States, in its bilateral negotiations with Mexico, would have required Mexico to end maquiladora duty-free privileges to Canadian (and other third-country) exports, at least on products eventually destined for the United States. Another problem Canadian firms would have faced is that they would not have gotten the benefits of less expensive duty-free Mexican inputs that would otherwise have made them more competitive in world markets. Instead they would have had to face stronger competition in North America and elsewhere from US firms that would have been able to acquire these low-cost inputs.

The more spoke bilateral agreements the United States were to add, the wider the discrimination and the greater the consequent erosion of gains a US partner would have to face. It is even conceivable that a partner's initial gains from its own bilateral free trade agreement with the United States would be more than offset by second-stage costs down the road, leaving it worse off than before this process began. On the other hand, it is possible that its second-stage costs would be more than offset if the analysis is broadened to take into account the indirect spillover benefits it might receive by increasing its exports into the more prosperous markets of each new spoke. But regardless of whether an existing partner would benefit or lose overall once these second-stage effects were taken into account, one conclusion remains: it would benefit more from an expanding free trade agreement.

What would happen to the US hub as it added new spoke partners? It would acquire the benefits of free trade with each new spoke; in particular, it would gain from an expanding domain of preferences in each spoke market in competition with all other spokes. These preferences, based on the fact that the United States alone would have free trade with all spoke countries, would provide it with a substantial advantage in attracting investment. This scenario can be seen from another point of view: any free trade agreement provides a location advantage to participating countries. In a hub-and-spoke system, the United States alone would fully realize this advantage, because it alone would be participating in all the free trade bilaterals.

As an example of the special set of preferences the United States would enjoy, a spoke bilateral agreement with Mexico would give the United States preference in the Mexican market in competition with Canada. At the same time, its bilateral agreement with Canada would give it preference in the Canadian market in competition with Mexico. As the United States added more spoke bilaterals, it would benefit from more and more of these preferences. But in comparison with a free trade agreement, any such US gain would almost surely come at even greater expense to its bilateral partners; the reason being that a hub-and-spoke system, with its remaining trade restrictions and hence lower level of efficiency, would be expected to generate less total income than an expanding free trade agreement.

Why then would there be any new applicants for spoke status—that is, new countries seeking bilateral agreements with the United States? One answer is that a prospective new-spoke country may, of course, be short-sighted, seeing only the immediate benefits of free trade with the United States but not the subsequent build-up of costs. There is, however, a more fundamental reason why such a country might be willing to say yes, why it would have an incentive to do so even if it could foresee fully the accumulating costs and, indeed, even if it were in the special situation in which these costs, down the road, would exceed its initial free trade gains. The reason is that, essentially, all the new spoke's decision would do is give it the benefits of free trade with the United States. If it said yes, it would get these benefits; if it said no, it would not. It would have to face the costs of being discriminated against as the United States went on to add new spokes, whether or not it decided to participate in this process.

What would this sort of a hub-and-spoke development mean for the auto industry, compared to a full trilateral NAFTA? The answer, in most but not all respects, is the hub-and-spoke problems facing other industries, as just described. As in other industries, auto exports from Canada would be discriminated against in the Mexican market due to remaining Mexican restrictions against third countries; thus the United States would become the preferred supplier of vehicles and parts to the Mexican market. Moreover, as in other industries, Canadian auto producers would also be at a disadvantage in competing with US producers in the US market or, for that matter, in any other market, because Canadian producers would not benefit from duty-free Mexican supplies. However, this disadvantage would apply only to non-Auto Pact producers in Canada. Thus, a hub-and-spoke system would have a unique effect on the auto industry alone because there would be one group of producers in Canada—Auto Pact producers, whose number has already been fixed by the Canada-US FTA—that would not suffer from US competition because they would also get duty-free access to Mexican supplies. Thus, non-Auto Pact producers in Canada would be at a disadvantage in competing with producers in the United States or with Auto Pact companies in Canada.[2] This disadvantage would add to the problem (described in the Box) that these transplants will face, in any case, in 1994 (now 1996) from their loss of duty drawbacks under the Canada-US FTA. This is a problem that Auto Pact companies would not face, because of their permanent duty-free access to imports from everywhere. However, both the transplants and the Big Three assembly operations would still face Mexican tariffs for exports from Canada and they might also face discriminatory phase-out of the Mexican import-licencing restrictions.

THE COMING PROBLEM FOR TRANSPLANTS IN CANADA, AND HOW TO DEAL WITH IT

Regardless of the trading regime that may develop in the Americas, the 1989 Canada-US Free Trade Agreement will eventually put transplant producers in Canada at a disadvantage vis-à-vis Auto Pact producers since the transplants will lose their duty remissions and duty drawbacks.[3] One way of dealing with this problem is for Canada to unilaterally reduce its most-favoured-nation (MFN) tariff on imports from the current level of about 9 to 10 percent to the US level of about 2.5 percent. Then transplants such as Honda or Toyota would pay the same 2.5 percent duty on imports from third countries such as Japan, whether they located in Canada or the United States. The problem is that this tariff reduction would diminish the incentive for Auto Pact companies to continue to satisfy Auto Pact safeguards, since their only incentive for doing so is the remission of this Canadian duty on imports from third countries. Thus, this policy would reduce their incentive from the present $200 to $300 million in duty saved to $50 to $100 million.[4] Would this be enough?

This question would cause concern if the Auto Pact companies were now producing near safeguard levels, implying that safeguards were keeping production up. However, since 1981, the Big Three have been producing far beyond their safeguard levels. For example, 1990 production of passenger vehicles in Canada was about 60 percent above the safeguard level. (The excess production of trucks and buses was even greater.)

Production in excess of the other operative safeguard—Canadian value-added (CVA)[5]—was a less dramatic, but still substantial, 20 percent, as it had been for each of the previous two years. Indeed, production in each year since 1982 has exceeded this safeguard by 20 to 50 percent, with the exception of a 10 percent excess in 1987. This excess production implies that the safeguards have not been binding and that production has been taking place in Canada because it is judged a good place to produce.[6] Insofar as the safeguards have not been keeping production up, there are no grounds for excessive concern that a reduction in the incentive to meet them would lead to substantially reduced production.

This situation apparently opens up the possibility for Canada to unilaterally improve its otherwise deteriorating location attraction for transplants by reducing its MFN tariff on automotive equipment. It also illustrates more generally how a free trade agreement puts pressure on the more protective partner to liberalize its trade with third countries.

In short, one disadvantage of the transplants in Canada that are not Auto Pact members is their lack of access to duty-free imports from Mexico. This drawback would be eliminated under NAFTA, but such transplants would remain in a hub-and-spoke system, which might, however, be modified by the type of action described in the Box. A similar disadvantage would apply to Canadian consumers of Mexican cars brought into Canada by non-Auto Pact companies, or brought into Canada by Auto Pact companies that would be able, as a result of less competitive pressure, to charge a higher price.

Down the road, another potentially important disadvantage of a hub-and-spoke system, compared to a trilateral one, is that the less efficient hub-and-spoke configuration would yield substantially lower income levels, hence lowering demand for autos in North America. This lower potential income is likely to apply even to the United States, the apparent special beneficiary of a hub-and-spoke configuration.[7] The hub-and-spoke system would not only fail to achieve the gains from trade and economies of scale that could be achieved through an expanding free trade area, but would also likely lead to higher average excess capacity in the industry and less efficient investment. There are also foreign policy reasons why the United States would eventually judge a hub-and-spoke arrangement to be inferior. In comparison to a free trade agreement, a hub-and-spoke trading system would allow the United States, already the dominant country with the highest income in the hemisphere, to benefit at the expense of its trading partners, thus giving the charge of exploitation so often levelled at the United States a degree of credibility that it does not now deserve.

CLOSING THE HUB-AND-SPOKE SYSTEM WITH A CANADA-MEXICO BILATERAL

It would appear that the disadvantage of a hub-and-spoke system of two bilaterals overlapping on the United States could be overcome by closing the system with a third bilateral between Canada and Mexico. While such an initiative would tend to reduce certain disadvantages, it would remain inferior to a full trilateral free trade agreement for several reasons. For example, without some degree of enforced consistency required by a trilateral agreement, the three bilaterals would almost certainly involve greater inconsistencies (e.g., more restrictions left on trade across some borders than others) that would distort trade and reduce potential income. Another example is the rule-of-origin problem that would remain in a three-bilateral system. To illustrate, suppose there is a NAFTA with a 50 percent rule of origin. Goods with 25 percent US content, 25 percent Mexican content, and zero Canadian content would enter Canada from Mexico duty free because of their 50 percent Canadian-Mexican-US content. But such goods would not enter Canada from Mexico duty free if there were instead a three-bilateral system including a Canada-Mexico bilateral with a similar 50 percent rule of origin; these goods could not enter Canada duty free because they would have only 25 percent Canadian-Mexican content.

This problem cannot be resolved by a redefinition of rules of origin by Canada and Mexico in their bilateral negotiation. To simulate a trilateral free trade agreement with three bilaterals requires that the United States redefine its rules of origin as well. In short, a NAFTA could not be simulated by three bilaterals alone. In the last analysis, agreement among all three is required, at least in some respects. Moreover, the best, but far from guaranteed, possible outcome from such an extended set of bilateral pairs of negotiations would be the more consistent and coherent trilateral free trade agreement they could have negotiated in the first place. The more likely outcome will be a series of trade and investment disputes among the three countries.

Thus, the message is simple: Canadian participation was crucial to ensure that the negotiations with Mexico remained on the trilateral track.

CONCLUSION

There are significant potential gains for all three countries from integration of the automotive industry on a North American basis. By removing barriers to trade and investment and by creating a more predictable environment for North American commerce, NAFTA will stimulate investment and economic growth. The shift to "lean production" means that there are economies of scope in the form of a network of supplier relations and the process of model development, as well as economies of scale in production and assembly. These economies of scope and scale increase substantially the gains made from expanded trade in this sector. Building on the Canada-US free trade agreement, and based on the restructuring that has already occurred, firms based in North America will become more competitive with offshore rivals.

The preferred option for Canada was a full trilateral NAFTA. The gains from NAFTA could be especially significant in stimulating investment, production, and employment at the Big Three operations in Canada. A separate US-Mexico bilateral agreement alongside the present Canada-US free trade agreement would have been disadvantageous to Canada and would have led to recurring tensions over automotive trade and investment.

ADDENDUM: THE AUTOMOTIVE SECTOR IN NAFTA

The specific trade rules for rules of origin, duty drawback and other aspects of NAFTA in the automotive sector were a central focus of concern during the trilateral negotiations. The United States pressed for a restrictive rule of origin for trade in automotive products under the trilateral free trade agreement. If the goal was to limit trade diversion, it is puzzling why the United States, with a current tariff of 2.5 percent on automotive products, would be concerned about the rules of origin for automotive products, because the potential incentives for trade diversion or trade deflection are extremely limited with such a low MFN US tariff. The situation is somewhat different with light trucks, which have a 25 percent tariff. A greater US concern was apparently that Mexico, rather than the United States, would attract new Japanese and other fourth-country investments, i.e., that Mexico would become a low-wage platform for assembling Asian cars and shipping them duty free into the US, a precedent the United States does not want to have established prior to the possible accession of a whole series of other low-wage Latin American countries. It is evident that the economic impact and political clout of the automotive sector is such that the rules for this sector will receive great scrutiny in Congress. Political sensitivity in the United States has been heightened by the prolonged recession in the North American automotive market and the closing of production facilities by the Big Three.

The NAFTA negotiations over automotive rules of origin were influenced by trade disputes between Canada and the United States. Bilateral disputes over whether certain vehicle manufacturers are meeting the rules of origin under the FTA have important implications for the companies involved and will influence the perceptions of third-country investors under the existing Canada-US FTA and now the North American Free Trade Agreement.

Complicated technical issues are involved in the disputes about the Canada-US FTA over whether vehicles manufactured by the GM-Suzuki joint venture and the Honda subsidiary meet the FTA rules of origin. The key issue in each case is whether there is sufficient value-added occurring in Canada and the United States for the vehicles to qualify for duty-free trade under the FTA. Customs administration and legal interpretation of customs law are arcane issues, as was illustrated by a sudden ruling in the late 1970s that light trucks assembled in the United States were not transformed sufficiently to avoid paying the 17.5 percent US duty.

Rules of origin became a lightening rod for protectionism under the Canada-US FTA as well as in the NAFTA negotiations. These protectionist pressures were stimulated by the lingering recession in the US economy and the disputes between Canada and the United States over the interpretation of FTA rules of origin. For example, the audit of Honda by the US Customs Service of the Treasury raises complicated issues. One of the issues involves the administration of roll-up or roll-down. Under this approach, if major components such as the engine are deemed to meet the FTA rule of origin, then all of the value of the engine counts toward the required 50 percent direct cost of manufacturing; in other words, the engine is rolled-up. On the other hand, if the engine is deemed not to meet the FTA rule of origin, then it is rolled-down. Roll-up versus roll-down is a key issue in the Honda dispute.

One of the unusual aspects of the US customs rulings on Honda was that the substantial US value-added to the engines was not counted, but the small proportion of the value attributed to purchased components was counted toward the direct cost of manufacturing (Palmeter 1992). Since the value-added for engines machined and assembled by Honda in Ohio was excluded by a technicality, the Honda Civics assembled in Alliston, Ontario, were judged not to qualify for duty-free entry into the United States. As an illustration of the technical complexity of rules of origin, one of the issues is the non-arms-length relationship between the US and Canadian Honda subsidiaries and the interpretation of the FTA by US Customs.

Some of the technical issues involved in automotive rules of origin were the subject of an arbitration panel under Chapter 18 of the Canada-US FTA. This binational panel ruled unanimously that Canada's interpretation permitting the deductibility of different types of interest charges was correct.

NAFTA sought to resolve these technical problems for automobiles through more detailed rules of origin, but the quid pro quo was tracing the imported content of components and increasing the rules-of-origin requirements. Many of the technical problems in the FTA rules of origin were addressed in the NAFTA negotiations. For example, NAFTA contains alternatives to the controversial roll-up process that should be more easily administered by the governments. In addition, NAFTA arrangements include a new mechanism to develop common interpretations of rules of origin, which is aimed at limiting the scope for unilateral interpretation of these rules by the national customs authorities. This appears to be a useful innovation, but it remains to be seen whether this mechanism and the new definitions of rules of origin can stand the rigours of legalistic deconstructionism that dominate the US conduct of trade relations at the present time.

Mexico and Canada resisted restrictive rules of origin in the automotive sector, in part because of concerns about their impact on existing Japanese assembly plants and on new automotive investment by offshore firms. This issue and those relating to the Mexican automotive decree and duty drawback were among the most contentious in the negotiations.

The clarification of rules of origin in NAFTA to a net cost basis apparently offsets a higher content number than the 50 percent direct cost of manufacturing in the Canada-US FTA, but the equivalent percentage is debatable. Under NAFTA, the content requirement will stay at 50 percent for four years, rise to 56 percent for four years, and then increase to 62.5 percent after eight years. The latter number is more restrictive than the existing requirements under the Canada-US FTA, notwithstanding the redefinition of rules of origin for automotive products. In order to cushion the impact on new investment, new automotive production facilities qualify for 50 percent North American content for five years.

It is customary in free trade areas to eliminate duty drawbacks on imported components that are subsequently exported duty-free to free trade partners. (If this were not done, a special advantage would be provided to small FTA partners, who could offer Japanese transplants the privilege of acquiring duty-free the imported components used in their cars exported to the large US market. A Japanese transplant producing and selling in the US would get no such privilege.) Thus, duty drawbacks were scheduled to be eliminated by January 1, 1994, in the Canada-US Free Trade Agreement. For Canada, full duty drawback was extended for two years in NAFTA. Mexico obtained a seven-year transition period before its duty drawback (or, more precisely, the roughly equivalent in-bond maquiladora privilege in Mexico) disappears under NAFTA. What is retained permanently is a device to eliminate the payment of double duty. Goods not meeting the NAFTA rules of origin will continue to receive drawback. If, for example, Canadian exporters do not meet the NAFTA rules of origin and have to pay a US tariff, they will still be allowed duty drawbacks on their imported components (or relief from the US tariff, whichever is less). Thus, they do not have to pay both a Canadian duty on their components and a US duty on their exports. This removes a potential anomaly under the Canada-US FTA.

In addition to the rules of origin for preferential tariff access, the other key issue for border measures under NAFTA was the coverage of quotas and import licences. In principle, all such quantitative restrictions should be eliminated, but there were pressures to retain, at least for a considerable period, many of these quantitative restrictions. For example, Mexico is phasing out its import licencing and trade balancing requirements under the 1989 Automotive Decree over ten years, but the phase-out favours the five automobile manufacturers in Mexico (the Big Three, Nissan and Volkswagen) that have already made investments under the existing Mexican automotive decrees. On the other hand, in Canada the protective Auto Pact safeguards remain, although their practical impact has now been reduced for a number of reasons, most notably the fact that production in Canada is well in excess of these safeguard levels. NAFTA also provides Mexican automotive assembly operations the right to qualify as a North American Producer under the CAFE rules. (Canadian vehicles were already included, but at the option of the manufacturer, who could choose whether the vehicle was to be treated as "imported" or "domestic" for CAFE purposes, as long as the vehicle met the separate rule of origin under CAFE regulations).

APPENDIX A: WHAT DID THE 1989 CANADA-US FTA DO TO THEIR 1965 AUTO PACT?[8]

While the FTA did not "gut" the Auto Pact, as was sometimes claimed, it did have some effects on autos shipped each way across the border:
1. On imports from Canada into the United States, the Auto Pact's rule of origin was replaced by the new free trade agreement rule of origin. It is not clear that this represented a big change since, in some cases, the content requirement was more stringent under the Auto Pact, while in other cases it has been more stringent under the free trade agreement.
2. On imports into Canada, Auto Pact members must be distinguished from non-Auto Pact companies operating in Canada.

AUTO PACT COMPANIES

Duty remission remained unchanged on all imports by Auto Pact companies meeting Canadian safeguard requirements. However, the duty remission on imports from third countries (of about $300 million a year) will become the only incentive for Auto Pact companies to meet the safeguards; the previous additional incentive of duty remission on imports from the United States will disappear as import duty disappears under the free trade agreement. In short, there will be no duty and no incentive to get relief from it by complying with the safeguards.

The Auto Pact companies were given a second option: to import duty free by satisfying the free trade agreement's rule of origin. But as long as Auto Pact companies have large imports from third countries, they will use Auto Pact duty remissions that cover these imports from third countries (whereas the free trade agreement's rule of origin does not).

Thus, the incentive to meet the Auto Pact safeguards remains, although the penalty for not meeting the safeguards is only a "conventional bomb" (i.e., loss of duty remission on imports from third countries only), rather than the previous "atomic bomb" (loss of duty remissions on imports from the United States as well). Is this conventional-bomb deterrent less effective? Not so, according to Paul Wonnacott, who argues that an atomic bomb is less effective because everyone knows that, in the last analysis, you will find it almost impossible to drop it (1988: 9-10). In the Auto Pact analogy, it would have been almost impossible to reimpose duties on all imports of the Auto Pact companies, since it would risk driving them right out of Canada.

NON-AUTO PACT COMPANIES

Companies such as Volkswagen, Hyundai, and the Japanese transplants were substantially affected by the free trade agreement. Their incentive for locating in Canada was reduced for three reasons:
1. Their duty remissions were immediately ended or eventually ended by 1996;
2. Their duty drawbacks are to be ended in 1994 (extended to 1996 under NAFTA); and
3. Canada could no longer offer them the incentive of eventual Auto Pact status. (Only CAMI was able to qualify at the last moment, but now that door has been permanently closed.)

The Box in the text describes the policy that could be used to deal with these disincentives and, at least in terms of trade policy, remove the deterrent against transplants deciding to locate in Canada rather than in the United States.

NOTES

[1] The Canada-US FTA requires the elimination of duty drawbacks by 1994. Under NAFTA, these were extended to 1996. Mexico sought a fifteen-year transition period before drawbacks or maquiladoras would be eliminated.

[2] For those non-Auto Pact producers with duty-remission privileges not abolished by the FTA—i.e., those based on production or on exports not to the United States—there would be only a partial disadvantage until these privileges expire.

[3] Auto Pact companies will face no such problem, since the Auto Pact and Chapter 10 of the FTA have left them with their duty remissions, and therefore they have no need for duty drawbacks. (Whereas a duty drawback is provided on a component imported by, say, Honda and incorporated into an exported vehicle, a duty remission applies to items imported by, say, Honda, whether or not they are re-exported).

[4] The incentive for Auto Pact companies in Canada to meet the safeguards was, originally, duty remission on any imports. As the Canadian tariff on imports from the United States is phased out in the FTA, and no duty will therefore be left to remit on these imports, this incentive will become duty remission on imports from third countries—an incentive that has recently been in the $200-$300 million per annum range.

[5] Strictly for simplicity of exposition, the term "safeguard" is used for the CVA requirement, even though it is less binding than the vehicle assembly safeguard, for reasons given in the next footnote.

[6] Some production above safeguard levels is to be expected in a world of: (i) lumpy invested capital (i.e., if a plant is to be built, it must be a large one); (ii) cyclical swings in auto sales that do not necessarily coincide in the two countries; and (iii) no prior knowledge of how a new model produced in Canada will be received in the marketplace. This means that prudent companies must plan production somewhat above the safeguard level—although nothing like the present observed 50 or 100 percent margin in vehicle assembly. It may also be concluded that the 20 percent excess in CVA is well above that prudently required because this is a far less binding requirement. Specifically, the companies can run much closer to the CVA safeguard level because there is no explicit penalty attached to violating it. The reason is that this safeguard did not appear in the treaty itself, but in letters of commitment by the auto companies to the Canadian government. Their legality has never been tested, and it would be difficult and risky for the Canadian government to take action against a company that

was unexpectedly in violation one year, if it had been well above this safeguard in previous years and planned to be in succeeding years. For example, CVA of the Big Three and 15 other smaller Auto Pact producers fell 12 percent below the safeguard level in 1980. However, the Canadian government took no formal action because of the expectation that these producers would increase their investment. That expectation was confirmed: by 1982, the companies that, regardless of the legality of this commitment, appeared to take it very seriously, were exceeding their CVA safeguard by 52 percent.

In addition to these vehicle assembly and CVA safeguards, there were two others also built into the Auto Pact. But because these were defined in absolute terms, they have long since ceased to be effective.

[7] Reasons for this paradoxical conclusion are given in Wonnacott (1991: 37-42 and 64-69).

[8] For more detail on this issue, an excellent source—and one drawn on in this Appendix—is Chapter 10 by Jon Johnson.

REFERENCES

Palmeter, David. 1992. The Honda Decision: Rules of Origin Turned Upside Down. In *The Free Trade Observer*. Special Edition. Toronto: CCH Canada Limited.

Wonnacott, Paul. 1988. The Canada-US Free Trade Agreement. Toronto: C.D. Howe Institute, *Trade Monitor* 2, March.

12 CONTINENTAL INTEGRATION AND THE FUTURE OF THE NORTH AMERICAN AUTO SECTOR

Stephen Herzenberg

INTRODUCTION

The auto industry, like most manufacturing in North America, stands poised between two quite distinct futures. In one—a high-wage, high-skill scenario—the auto industry throughout North America would enjoy rapid productivity growth, help develop and deploy new technology, and provide a positive example of work-force skill development, of cooperation between assemblers and suppliers, and of organizational practice generally. In a second—a segmented industry scenario—high productivity, new technology, and human resource development would be confined to portions of the operations of major assembly companies and first-tier suppliers. Even in this industry core, the weakness of worker representation and high levels of work intensity would partially undermine worker commitment to performance improvement. Outside the core, competition would be driven more by a search for low wage, non-union workers.

This chapter argues that state regulation will play a critical role in determining which scenario most closely describes the future of the North American auto sector. A segmented future is more likely if state regulation—in the United States and, through its influence, in North America as a whole—remains guided by ideological commitment to free markets and free trade, departing from this commitment only for crudely protectionist concessions to short-term political pressure. A skill-based auto industry development path, on the other hand, would require an integrated set of trade, investment, technology, and labour policies. In two complementary ways, these state policies would channel marketplace competition in economically and socially construc-tive directions: by fostering worker skill development and auto parts company technical capacity, without which dynamic development is impossible; and by limiting low-wage competition and short-term cost pressures that now threaten the labour-management and assembler-supplier cooperation that is essential to innovation and productivity improvement. While few of the state policies discussed here are included in the North American Free Trade Agreement (NAFTA) signed in December 1992, most of them are consistent with NAFTA and could be adopted through a supplementary auto-sector parallel agreement.

This chapter is divided into three sections. The second section describes the two scenarios for the future of the North American auto industry at greater length. Section Three describes trade, investment, technology, and labour policies intended to institutionalize high-wage, high-skill competition. These policies include the negotiation of a Japan-North America Auto Pact (JNAAP) that would require the major Japanese producers to achieve specified North American assembly-to-sales ratios and local content levels. The proposals here also include transitional production safeguards for each country in North America, common North American investment policies toward Japanese auto firms, the establishment of "North American Works Councils" that would facilitate labour-management information exchange and consultation at the continental level, and a "continental improvement factor" that would raise Mexican wages, over time, to US and Canadian levels. The conclusion to the paper considers the prospects for policies along the lines proposed here, given the content of NAFTA and the election of a Democrat to the presidency of the United States.

THE NORTH AMERICAN AUTO INDUSTRY: TWO SCENARIOS

Between 1950 and 1980, major auto assemblers in North America competed with one another by trying to lower the unit cost of standardized products using mass-production technologies. Within auto plants, production workers performed minutely divided, repetitive tasks, and managers retained broad authority to run the shop. Assemblers had arms-length relations with suppliers. Governments in the United States and Canada played a limited role in industry development. Since 1980, the growing North American market share of Japanese producers and changes in the technology and organization of production have destabilized the labour-management, assembler-supplier, and business-government relations that grew up with, and supported, traditional mass production.

Some analysts believe that the current transformation of the auto industry, despite a socially costly transition period, will ultimately benefit North America by leading to the replacement of mass production by the "lean production" system developed in Japan (Womack et al. 1990). Lean production was the outcome of Japanese auto assemblers' defeat of independent unions in the 1950s and of Toyota's efforts to adapt the mass-production techniques pioneered by Henry Ford to a protected market context in which model runs numbered in the thousands rather than hundreds of thousands. The end result was that the Japanese learned how to achieve the scale economies of continuous-flow mass production at much lower volumes (Cusumano 1985). Japan's consolidation of enterprise unionism and keiretsu assembler-supplier relations also created a production system in which workers, managers, and suppliers cooperated with productivity and quality improvement and with the development of new products adapted to customer tastes and designed for "ease-of-manufacture." By developing and using the collective knowledge of those involved in production, and because its strengths are well suited to the global market fragmentation and volatility of the last fifteen years, Womack et al. (1990) conclude that lean production has enabled Japanese producers to establish a position of increasing dominance within the global auto industry.

Their analysis of Japanese production methods, and their claim that these methods require locating assembly plants, suppliers, and product and process development close to one another and to the market, lead Womack et al. (1990) to argue that North America would benefit from the diffusion of lean production. Such diffusion, they believe, will ultimately happen as a result of market forces; that is, until US producers complete their adoption of lean production, Japanese firms will increase their market share because of the superior performance of lean production. Whatever the steady state market shares of Japanese and US-based firms in the industry, Womack et al. (1990) maintain that each will develop fully integrated lean production systems in North America, including locally based design and research and development (R&D) centres, and regionally concentrated supplier networks. The result will be higher productivity and quality, rising wages, more rewarding jobs for production and white-collar workers, prosperity for auto-producing regions, better products and value for North American consumers, and balanced trade with the Asian lean-production system. Womack (1991b) suggests that Mexico could contribute to the transfer of lean production to North America—and to balancing trade between the Asian and North American blocs—by producing small cars (which are now imported from Asia) within a lean-production system located in northern Mexico.

Contrary to the optimistic predictions of Womack et al. (1990), empirical evidence points toward a second, less economically and socially desirable outcome of the current restructuring of the North American auto industry. The central features of this segmented, low-wage, low-skill scenario are described below (data cited are from Herzenberg 1991):

1. Rapid labour productivity growth and labour-management coop-eration would be limited to permanent employees of major assem-bly company operations and some first-tier suppliers. Outside these "islands of automation," firms would compete by combining tradi-tional mass production with a search for low wages. As a result, productivity in suppliers would grow only slowly.

Despite the efforts of North American auto parts firms to learn Japanese organizational practices in the 1980s, slow productivity growth among auto suppliers has been the aggregate tendency. From 1978 to 1989, for example, real value-added per production-worker-hour in the US automotive parts and accessories industry [Standard Industry Classification (SIC) 3714] declined by 0.1 percent annually. In the US automotive stamping (SIC 3465) and engine electrical equipment (SIC 3694) industries, real value-added per production-worker-hour in the same period rose by only 1.3 percent annually. These figures compare with 6.7 percent in the automotive assembly industry (SIC 3711).

2. Overall auto industry productivity growth would decline as the share of total industry employment accounted for by high productivity growth assembly companies declines.

Indicative of this possibility, from 1978 to 1989, the number of production workers in US assembly plants declined from 45 to 38 percent of total production worker employment in the US motor vehi-cle and equipment industry (SIC 371). In the same period, as low productivity parts production accounted for more of total employ-ment—and despite the 6.7 percent annual growth of assembly plant value-added—the annual growth rate of real output per production worker in the SIC 371 slipped to 2.7 percent.

3. Constrained by low productivity growth and by intense competition based on price and labour costs, real wages in independent parts suppliers—which averaged $9.43 per hour in 1989 in the United States (60 percent of assembly company wages) but were much lower in some firms and have been falling at over 1 percent annually since 1978—would continue to fall in real terms.

4. Real hourly wages at assembly firms would remain high relative to suppliers but, as from 1978 to 1989 in the United States, would not increase in real terms.

5. Within the relatively high-wage, lean-production plants of assembly companies, high productivity would result partly from high levels of work intensity. In the 1980s in the United States, the advent of lean production contributed to reported increases in injury rates and lost workdays due to injury of over two-thirds.

6. As a result of adversarial North American labour-management traditions, Japanese assemblers' reluctance to train workers who may then leave the firm, and the low engineering intensity of production taking place in North American plants of Japanese firms, competitiveness in North American auto assembly companies would depend less on work-force skill and labour-management cooperation than in Japan.

7. Due to North American suppliers' attempts to combine low wages with traditional mass production and to the import of engineering and design-intensive products from Japan, competitiveness in North American suppliers would also rely less on product and process engineering, cooperation with assemblers, and work-force skill development than in Japan.

8. The low productivity and limited engineering and design capabilities of the North American auto and allied (e.g., machine tool) industries would lead to a continuing North American trade deficit in engineering-intensive parts, in high profitability specialty vehicles, and in capital equipment for auto plants.

9. Driven by greenfield Japanese investment and US firms' relocation to low-wage areas, the restructuring of the North American auto industry would impose substantial social costs on workers and communities in traditional auto-producing regions in the United States, Canada, and Mexico.

In sum, as well as the vision of a revitalized industry built on geographic concentrations of assembly and parts production (Womack et al. 1990), the restructuring of the North American auto industry could produce an industry characterized by greater labour market segmentation than the Japanese auto industry but less innovative capacity and collective learning.

IMPLICATIONS FOR NORTH AMERICAN TRADE, INDUSTRIAL AND LABOUR POLICY

With the North American auto sector poised between two quite distinct futures, the critical policy question is whether state regulation can help to push the industry toward a more skill-intensive and less segmented future. This section outlines a regulatory regime designed to achieve this goal.

The state policies outlined here are likely to be controversial in at least two respects. First, they include proposals for managed auto sector trade between North America and Japan, and for a measure of temporary trade management within North America. These proposals are predicated on the view that "lean producers" can be forced to produce locally in proportion to their market sales without sacrifices in efficiency. Thus, while some past trade management—although not the US-Canada Auto Pact—may have come at the expense of consumers, this need not be the case with trade management in the auto industry today.

Second, the proposals here concern not only the trade regulations that have dominated the NAFTA auto debate, but also trilateral investment regulation, technology diffusion, and labour policies. The need for policies in these areas stems from the fact that trade management alone is unlikely to prevent short-run cost pressure in North America from consolidating low-wage competition in suppliers and from weakening reliance on worker skills and cooperation in assembly plants. Only if mutually reinforcing trade, investment, technology, and labour policies are pursued, and if complementary policies are pursued at the level of the labour market as a whole, will the policy options outlined here have a decisive influence on the dominant business strategy and labour market structure in the North American auto sector of the twenty-first century.

NORTH AMERICAN TRADE RELATIONS WITH JAPAN

The historical origins of the North American auto sector trade deficit with Japan and its likely continuation at high levels (McAlinden et al. 1991) have little to do with free trade and the global allocation of production based on the principle of comparative advantage. From the 1950s to the 1980s, the Japanese auto industry developed its lean-production methods under the protective umbrella of a series of government regulations: import prohibitions, high tariffs, cumbersome customs procedures, safety and emissions standards that acted as non-tariff barriers, restrictions on foreign investment, and domestic taxes that shifted demand toward the products of domestic manufacturers (Cusumano 1985: 23-26). Combined with a protected home market, the quality levels and product diversity achieved by the Japanese production system led in the 1970s and 1980s to a massive Japanese trade surplus in automotive products.

While they developed their highly successful production methods in a particular market and cultural context, Japanese assemblers have now demonstrated that they can achieve quality and productivity levels in North America that are similar to those in Japan (Womack et al. 1990). Traditional North American assemblers have also improved quality and productivity, in part by adopting organizational practices pioneered by Japanese producers. Despite a reduction in the comparative advantage of producing vehicles and parts in Japan, however, two non-market factors may prevent the elimination of the North American trade deficit in automotive products. First, remaining Japanese non-tariff barriers—primarily Japanese assemblers' control over distribution channels and parts sourcing decisions—are likely to keep exports from North America out of Japan, even when these are cheaper and competitive on non-price terms. Second, and more important, Japanese producers are unlikely to transfer assembly or parts production to North America in proportion to their North American sales because keeping production in Japan helps them maintain job security and promotion opportunities for Japanese employees and ensure profits for Japanese suppliers.[1] In recent congressional testimony, Womack himself came around to the view that, without state intervention, the auto trade deficit would remain large because "[lean] production, once set up in one place, has no tendency to migrate" (Womack 1991a).

While the benefits gained by Japanese employees and suppliers from exports to North America reinforce the commitment to performance improvement that serves the long-term efficiency of the Japanese industry, these same exports lead to layoffs, work intensification, and cut-throat supplier competition that threatens the long-run productivity and quality of the North American industry.[2] In sum, the trade deficit with Japan deprives traditional US, Canadian, and Mexican auto producers of the market share they need to institutionalize employee and supplier commitment to performance improvement in North America.

On grounds of efficiency, reciprocity, and economic self-interest, the preceding discussion suggests that there is a case for regulating trade between Japan and North America in the global auto industry. The United States, Mexico, and Canada all stand to benefit from a joint decision to negotiate measures that would reduce their collective auto sector trade deficit with Japan.[3]

To date, most discussion of how to ensure that NAFTA encourages auto and auto parts production within North America has been framed in terms of what "rule of origin" auto products should have to meet to obtain duty-free access to the US, Mexican, and Canadian markets. Consistent with this, the NAFTA requires North American content that rises, over time, to 62.5 percent for cars and light trucks and 60 percent for other vehicles and parts.

There is little reason to believe, however, that this rule will significantly reduce either the US or the North American auto trade deficit with Japan. Nor does this rule prove a strong inducement to produce high value-added components or to develop dynamic regional concentrations of auto production in North America. Given the 2.5 percent US tariff for finished cars and many auto parts (parts are assessed the car tariff upon exit from US foreign trade zones), the US market could still be served with little penalty by wholly non-North American cars and parts or by Mexican products that do not meet NAFTA rules of origin. Moreover, while import of high Asian content Mexican products is possible under current trade rules, it might be more likely after NAFTA, as a result of deregulation in Mexican auto parts investment rules (see below) and increased confidence in the institutional and political stability of Mexico.[4] In sum, NAFTA rules of origin will not prevent US and Canadian auto-dependent regions from being squeezed by the production of labour-intensive parts, moderate complexity parts, cars, and light trucks in Mexico and by the production of high value-added components and cars in Japan and Europe.

A more effective approach to increasing vehicle and parts production in North America would follow past European Community (EC) and Canadian policies. Although no written agreement has been made public, the EC approach combines import limits and local content requirements. Through 1998, the Japanese import share is restricted to roughly 16 percent of the market (OTA 1991). Disagreement exists over whether Japanese vehicles assembled within Europe or the United States will be counted as part of the Japanese share. With regard to content, the three largest Japanese transplants (Nissan, Toyota, and Honda, all in the United Kingdom) are committed to achieving 80 percent content levels within two to three years after startup, which compares to US content levels of around 50 percent in plants that have been operating an average of about five years (OTA 1991).

Canada's approach under the Canada-US Auto Pact differs from the EC's in two respects. First, the Auto Pact includes a net corporate content requirement as opposed to a content rule that applies to each vehicle. Second, rather than restraining finished vehicle imports, Canada requires each company covered under the Auto Pact to meet a specified ratio of vehicles assembled in Canada to sales in Canada. Net corporate content and assembly-to-sales ratios give corporations additional flexibility because they allow them to satisfy the requirement by increasing exports as well as by lowering imports.[5] A required assembly-to-sales ratio of about one-to-one and a high net content rule in North America would encourage Japanese companies to both expand exports from North America to Japan and Europe, and to reduce exports from Japan to the US.[6]

Determining the appropriate assembly-to-sales and content ratios in a possible Japan-North America Auto Pact, and the length of any phase-in period, would require extended discussion among assemblers, suppliers, unions, and governments in each North American country. Since the Japanese companies' actual 1991 assembly-to-sales ratio in North America was about one-to-two, Japanese companies would presumably favour a long phase-in period before the assembly-to-sales ratio approaches one-to-one. US assembly companies and their workers would prefer a more rapid rise toward one-to-one so that the Big Three, at least temporarily, regain market share before the Japanese companies expand their North American production capacity. An increase in Big Three market share would help major US companies meet (and extend) their job security guarantees to United

Auto Workers members and reduce excess capacity in the North American industry. A rapid rise to one-to-one might also prompt Japanese companies to form additional joint ventures with the Big Three or buy Big Three plants. Japanese operation of existing (or "brownfield") facilities rather than new capacity would reduce the social costs of industrial restructuring. US suppliers and their workers would also advocate a rapid rise toward a one-to-one assembly-to-sales ratio, which would increase the market share of their traditional customers (the Big Three) and encourage Japanese companies to follow a brownfield parts sector strategy. Mexico might prefer a ratio that approaches one-to-one before substantial weakening of its trade balancing laws: the combination of trade balancing laws and a Japan-North America Auto Pact might prompt substantial small car assembly investment in Mexico so that companies can satisfy both regulations at once.

The appropriate content level in a Japan-North America Auto Pact might be closer to 80 percent than the 60 percent in the US-Canada Auto Pact. As illustrated by Canadian experience under the Auto Pact, a 60 percent net content level does not guarantee that large amounts of high value-added production and research and development will take place within a region. As in the case of a high assembly-to-sales ratio, a rapid rise to a content requirement of 80 percent would increase utilization of existing parts sector capacity instead of new investment. To reach 80 percent quickly, Japanese firms would have to give more business to existing US parts suppliers and/or form joint ventures to revitalize existing facilities.[7]

A Japan-North America Auto Pact would not require modifying NAFTA; it could be done in a parallel agreement between North America and Japan. Such a pact could be made consistent with the General Agreement on Tariffs and Trade (GATT) in one of two ways: through informal agreements with Japan that cannot be challenged in GATT; or by negotiating with Japan *and* the Europeans, leading to a GATT waiver, and establishing a stable framework for interbloc auto trade over the next several decades.

In exchange for the benefits of a JNAAP, the US and Canadian governments should consider requiring that traditional North American assembly and supplier companies make domestic investment and training commitments. In the United States, the Steel Voluntary Restraint Agreement (VRA), established in 1984 and re-authorized in 1989, provides a precedent for this. To counter low-wage pressures and help create dynamic industrial networks of suppliers in Ontario and auto-producing US states, portions of investment and training commitments could be channelled to sectoral human resource and technology diffusion institutions. A number of such institutions were created in the 1980s in some north-central US states and in Ontario (Herzenberg 1991: 35).

TRADE REGIMES IN NORTH AMERICA

Trade Balancing and Content Rules. One of the primary explicit goals of the NAFTA negotiations was the liberalization of auto trade in North America. In the short run, US-based producers and the US government saw the liberalization of Mexican rules as likely to lead to the use of excess US capacity to ship vehicles and some parts south. While the draft agreement does liberalize existing trade rules in North America, however, it also grants Mexico and Canada significant transitional protection over the first decade of the agreement.

In particular, the Mexican trade balance rule falls from the current 100 percent to 80 percent in 1994, and to 55 percent in 2003. The share of purchased parts that assembly plants must buy in Mexico falls from the current 36 percent to 34 percent in 1994, and to 29 percent in 2003. For Mexico, gradual liberalization is critical to prevent further deterioration in its trade balance and foreign exchange position. It is also necessary to increase the links among advanced northern assembly plants, the nearby parts plants they have spawned, and the *maquiladoras*, and to peacefully manage the transition to more productive labour and assembler-supplier relations in existing plants serving the domestic market. A gradual phase-out of Mexican trade restrictions was also favoured by the Big Three, who feared that complete and immediate liberalization would enable firms without Mexican operations, such as Honda and Toyota, to compete away oligopoly profits in Mexico and establish operations more efficient than those previously set up in compliance with local-content, trade-balancing, and licencing rules.

Canada's transitional protection consists of the grandfathered performance commitments made by the Big Three upon signing the Canada-US Auto Pact. In their dialogue with the Canadian government during the NAFTA negotiations, Canada's Automotive Parts Manufacturers' Association and the Canadian Autoworkers Union had actually sought new domestic content provisions that could be extended to Japanese producers. These industry participants felt that such a rule would help ensure that the Canadian industry is not decimated by a rush of auto parts investment to Mexico.

Given that the integrity of its own parts industry is also in question, the United States could have sought some form of reciprocal transitional protection in NAFTA. Since it did not, the possibility exists that major suppliers will lose interest in building dynamic agglomerations of parts producers and instead focus new investment on Mexico. In the context of negotiations over a JNAAP, the new US Administration might re-examine the need for US safeguards similar to the content rules that will remain in place in Canada and Mexico. With regard to the operations of US producers, a transitional US content safeguard rule would be unlikely to constrain sourcing decisions. Its impact would fall on Japanese producers as well as provide the psychological reassurance to states and auto-parts investors that efforts to improve performance in the US remain critical.

US Corporate Average Fuel Economy (CAFE) Laws. After a ten-year period in which individual companies may choose whether their Mexican operations qualify as "domestic" or "foreign" under US CAFE laws,[8] NAFTA makes Mexico part of the domestic US industry for CAFE purposes. Under CAFE laws, both the domestic (defined as 75 percent or more US content) and foreign fleet of each manufacturer must meet specified miles-per-gallon averages. Mexico sought inclusion as part of the US domestic fleet, which already includes Canada, so it could assemble small cars that the Big Three cannot produce profitably in the United States. These cars will be most in demand in the Mexican market (Womack 1991b). In the context of a JNAAP, this CAFE change would almost certainly provide Mexico with substantial small-car production, including modest Honda and Toyota starter plants, without reducing total US and Canadian production. Without a JNAAP, designating Mexico as part of the domestic US industry for CAFE purposes might precipitate the gradual movement to Mexico of the small cars now made unprofitably in the United States, without any guarantee of compensating production coming back to the United States from Asia.

Tariff Reductions. NAFTA eliminates US tariffs on cars immediately, and reduces the US light truck tariff from 25 percent to 10 percent immediately and to zero over the subsequent five years. Mexican car and light truck tariffs are eliminated over a period of ten and five years, respectively. The most controversial part of the tariff-reduction package for the United States is the rapid reduction in the US light truck tariff. In the medium term, Womack (1991b) expects this change to make Mexico the preferred location for entry-level light trucks in North America. As with incorporating Mexico into the United States domestic fleet for CAFE purposes, the impact on the US of eliminating light truck tariffs depends on whether a JNAAP is implemented simultaneously to reduce net imports of Japanese vehicles and parts. If not, the movement of truck investment to Mexico will place further downward pressure on employment and parts demand in the United States.

INVESTMENT REGIMES

The two critical issues in this area concern the liberalization of existing Mexican investment restrictions and whether, as in the area of trade policy, North America should consider new and common investment regulations.

Liberalization of Mexican Investment Restrictions for US and Canadian Auto Parts Firms. In the past, foreign ownership restrictions were regarded as necessary to technology transfer and long-term Mexican development. Today, investment liberalization is expected to facilitate technology transfer to Mexico more than impede it. Consistent with this view, the Mexican government agreed in NAFTA to permit "NAFTA investors" to make investments of up to 100 percent in Mexican "national suppliers" of parts, and up to 49 percent in other automotive parts enterprises, the latter increasing to 100 percent after five years.

Together with trade-balancing and local-content rules, the transitional restriction on foreign ownership of non-national suppliers will channel some new investment to existing firms with deep roots in Mexico. As in the US and Canada, however, additional measures to encourage firms to invest in training and technology may be necessary to restructure the Mexican auto parts industry into integrated networks of dynamic firms. Along these lines, it could be argued that, in exchange for the right to own 100 percent of their Mexican operations, US and Canadian firms should contribute to training and technology consortia in Mexico that serve Mexican-owned as well as foreign firms. Requiring contributions based on investor nationality, however, would violate the NAFTA principle of "national treatment". If they did apply across the industry, NAFTA does not rule out measures such as a training payroll tax or mandated contributions to industry-wide industrial extension and research institutes.[9]

North American Regulation of Japanese Auto Industry Investment. Liberalization of investment regulations governing the Mexican auto industry could prompt concentrated investment in Mexico by Japanese auto suppliers that currently have more financial resources and less excess capacity than their US and Canadian counterparts. While such investment might transfer some Japanese technology and organizational practices to Mexico, it could also lead to layoffs and increases in short-term and low-wage pressure on established North American suppliers.[10] It could also increase the use of Japanese capital equipment and components in Mexican auto operations. Finally, Mexican openness to Japanese auto investors could intensify competition throughout North America to attract greenfield Japanese plants through local and regional subsidies.

The possible drawbacks of a liberal policy toward Japanese auto investment in Mexico and North America as a whole suggest a need for discussions about whether continental investment regulation could increase the benefits of Japanese foreign direct investment (FDI). The following range of policy options should be considered, all of which stop short of a limit on Japanese market share that would reduce pressure on North American producers to improve their own performance: (1) limits on new investment when excess capacity reaches high levels, and promotion instead of Japanese investment in existing facilities; (2) the establishment of discipline on subsidies for new investment; (3) a requirement that Japanese investors contribute to sectoral skill-development and technology-diffusion institutions that help move North American suppliers generally down a high-wage, high-skill path; and (4) common regulation of the use of Japanese nationals in the North American operations of Japanese investors. At managerial levels, and for an extended transition period, one could argue that allowing unrestricted use of Japanese nationals promotes the diffusion of Japan's superior organizational practices (Womack 1991b). Some US evidence, however, suggests that Japanese auto firms rely on Japanese nationals for long periods, even at first line supervisory and non-supervisory skilled positions (Herzenberg 1991). This could retard the transfer of Japanese organizational practices as well as deny North Americans significant numbers of good jobs.

INDUSTRIAL RELATIONS[11]

Institutionalizing high-wage, high-skill development in the auto industry will require transcending the Taylorism and adversarial labour-management relations that characterized unionized North American mass producers before the rise of Japanese competition. Despite the critical significance of industrial relations to the future dynamism of the auto industry and the North American economy in general, the Salinas, Bush, and Mulroney administrations opposed making labour questions an explicit part of NAFTA negotiations. Opposition to discussing labour matters in NAFTA stemmed first and foremost from the Mexican government's desire for autonomy as it manages the complex restructuring of Mexico's corporatist state-labour relations. The dilemma in this restructuring is that the governing party in Mexico remains dependent on the traditional labour movement to contain wage demands, to limit opposition to privatization and other aspects of economic restructuring, and to provide political support; at the same time, the Mexican government sees much of the traditional labour movement as an obstacle to the modernization of workplace relations.

While the reason for excluding labour matters from the NAFTA talks is not hard to understand, institutionalizing labour-management cooperation throughout North America should be facilitated by explicit negotiation on labour issues. In the United States and Canada, the failure to address labour issues could have several undesirable consequences: it might heighten fear of the movement of production to Mexico and create a new obstacle to the development of trust between workers at the Big Three and their employers; it might reinforce managerial efforts to expand lean production in the north of Mexico, where unions so far have little shop-floor presence, in the process reducing managerial willingness to accept more negotiated and sustainable forms of cooperation in the United States and Canada; finally, the absence of measures to harmonize Mexican wages upward over time could increase southern flows of auto-parts investment by firms that see Mexico as a permanent low-wage site.

In Mexico, despite the sensitivity of the topic, negotiation over labour issues could help manage critical tensions in the modernization of industrial relations. The most fundamental tension in Mexico concerns workers' desires for more accountable union representation. In the north of the country, this issue has arisen when workers at modern, CTM-organized plants have perceived their union as unwilling to support demands for wages that more closely match their "world-class" productivity. In the centre of the country, the issue of union representation arose at the Ford Cuautitlan plant, where workers sought more effective representation against the work pace and managerial freedom in a reorganized, leaner workplace.

After the implementation of NAFTA, disputes over wages in high productivity Mexican plants and over the terms of work reorganization in older plants may recur as the Mexican industry expands and is rationalized. Resolving these conflicts through negotiations with democratically elected representatives is more likely to produce a stable system of labour-management cooperation—and satisfy US and Canadian public opinion—than state or official union reprisals against representatives with rank-and-file support. Moreover, two features of the auto industry in Mexico—the considerable presence of independent unions in the centre of the industry and these unions' acceptance that labour relations must be made more "flexible"—suggest that giving more autonomous unions the space to act could turn the auto industry into a model of "modernized" industrial relations.

The rest of this section makes three tentative proposals that might facilitate management of the labour-management tensions discussed above, thereby leading to a stable, high-skill, high-productivity continental auto industry. The first of these ideas, the establishment of North American Works Councils, could be incorporated into a parallel agreement on labour issues. Progress toward the negotiation of the second and third proposals, regarding wages and work hours, might also be possible in a parallel agreement.

North American Works Councils. In Europe, the 1992 single market has been accompanied by a proposal from the European Commission to establish "European Works Councils" in companies that employ more than 1000 EC workers or more than a hundred workers in two or more countries of the Community. Employers would provide funding for works councillors and management representatives to meet once a year, or more, if the need arises (BNA 1991). In the North American auto industry, the creation of "North American Works Councils" at major multinational auto companies would have two major benefits. First, regardless of how worker representatives were selected, the contact between US, Canadian, and Mexican workers would likely increase the space within Mexico for independent union leaders to negotiate the consensual modernization of Mexican industrial relations. They would be further aided if, as has been argued in Europe, works councillors were elected in a secret ballot. Second, the establishment of North American works councils might lay the groundwork for negotiation over the harmonization of Mexican, US, and Canadian labour standards.

Continental Wage Rules. The most critical labour standards issue in the North American auto industry is wages. At some point over the next decade or so, establishing in Mexico a counterpart to the "annual improvement factor" (AIF) and cost-of-living adjustment (COLA) clauses negotiated between the United Autoworkers (UAW) and the major auto assemblers in the post-World War II United States and Canada might help raise Mexican wages toward US and Canadian levels (Herzenberg 1991: 16).[12] With a "continental improvement factor" (CIF) and COLAs written into major auto assembly contracts in Mexico, Mexican real wage increases would be fixed at an annual percentage rate.

There should be no illusion that such continental wage rules would quickly equalize Mexican, US and Canadian wages: assuming a 40 percent appreciation of the peso, a ten-to-one initial wage ratio, and a 4 percent difference in the growth of US and Mexican wages, it would take 36 years for Mexican wage levels to reach US levels. The length of time that wage increases in Mexico will take to equalize wages with the United States and Canada is one reason that extended transitional safeguards may be necessary for the United States and Canada. What a CIF might do is partly remove the contentious issue of wages from annual negotiations in major assembly companies, increase shop floor peace by giving Mexican workers confidence that they would share in the benefits of productivity growth, and ensure that wage competition in Mexico does not prevent the expansion of aggregate demand. These are the kinds of benefits that were provided by the AIF and COLA in the United States following the shop floor turbulence and prolonged wage strikes during and after World War II.

Continental wage rules might also stabilize bargaining in smaller firms by establishing a target wage increase that is considered both affordable and fair to workers. Over the long term, a higher-wage, high-skill path for the North American auto industry might consist of sectoral wage agreements in Ontario, Quebec, several regions in the United States, northern Mexico, and the area near Mexico City, plus negotiated links between the wages in each regional agreement. Legislation that could facilitate the creation of regional industry-wide wage agreements (such as those that limit low-wage competition and are a key feature of West German industrial relations) exists in both Mexico (article 404 of the Federal Labour Law) and Quebec (the Quebec Decree System), and has recently been debated in Ontario.

Shorter Work Time. Given that increases in productivity in major auto assembly companies will likely exceed output growth, the total number of hours worked in such companies is likely to decline. With average annual work hours remaining constant, lower total hours would mean lower employment and reduced promotion opportunities. It would thus make it more difficult for employers to institutionalize worker cooperation. Shorter work time, on the other hand, would create additional employment and promotion opportunities in all three countries of North America. Competition among national labour markets, however, could prevent the United States, Mexico, and Canada from achieving the shorter work time incrementally, even if it would benefit all three countries. Continental negotiations might solve this "prisoner's dilemma" and enable each country to shorten work time in the auto sector without suffering a competitive disadvantage. Shorter work time in the auto industry might set a precedent for other industries or for continental legislative standards. General reductions in working time are likely to be an essential ingredient of continental efforts to reduce unemployment and promote environmentally sustainable development.[13]

NORTH AMERICA'S CHOICE: HIGH SKILLS OR LOW WAGES [14]

This paper argues that the North American auto industry faces a choice between a low-productivity, low-wage future that continues to exclude most workers and suppliers from efforts to improve performance, and a high-skill future that fosters the development and use of worker and supplier knowledge to improve productivity, quality, and adaptability. While the North American auto industry made substantial progress in the 1980s toward the development of institutions that foster a high-skill, high-productivity path, the changes in management structure, industrial relations, sourcing practices, and network-building among suppliers remain fragile. While the institution-building of the 1980s offers a clue as to what a high-productivity, high-skill path would look like in the North American auto industry, it leaves open the possibility that such an approach will be confined to assembly companies and to a declining share of industry employment. This would leave the majority of North American autoworkers competing based on wage levels in traditional mass production or lower-wage labour-intensive operations.

In the context of the transformation taking place, the NAFTA by itself, which simply liberalizes trade and investment regulations, could push the North American auto industry in the wrong direction. Increased awareness of the possibility of locating in Mexico could reinforce the tendency of US and Canadian suppliers to emphasize low-wage strategies and, in the process, undermine attempts to diffuse skill development and new managerial practices beyond the assembly company core. In the Big Three themselves, the threat or fact of relocation to Mexico could exacerbate worker suspicions stemming from major employment reductions and cripple the development of labour-management cooperation.

On the other hand, modifications to the existing agreement, primarily through supplemental agreements, could still make NAFTA a vehicle for instigating a progressive and dynamic restructuring of the North American auto industry. To accomplish this, it is argued in this chapter, NAFTA and a package of supplemental agreements would have to initiate the development of mutually reinforcing trade, investment, and industrial relations policies that directly and indirectly foster the development of workers' skills and the technical capacities of auto suppliers. The state policies proposed here include: adoption of managed trade between Japan and North America; establishment of intra-continental production safeguards for each North American country; the development of common policies toward Japanese auto and auto parts investment in North America; and a series of measures intended to harmonize Mexican, US and Canadian labour standards (through gradual increases in Mexican standards rather than lowering of US and Canadian standards).

As of this writing (mid-November 1992), the prospects for a continental auto policy similar to that proposed here are hard to predict. The current NAFTA incorporates none of the measures proposed here, particularly due to the free-trade and laissez-faire philosophies of the outgoing Bush Administration in the United States. While the Clinton administration is committed to NAFTA, it is more sympathetic to the idea of managed trade, labour concerns, and to the notion that government has a role to play in fostering skill development and industrial dynamism. At the very least, given the economic and political logic behind continental managed trade with the Japanese, the new administration is likely to express a willingness to contemplate supplementary talks with Mexico and Canada about something like a JNAAP or a Japan-Europe-North America auto agreement. Over the longer term, moreover, it is hard to imagine economic integration with Mexico proceeding without continued discussion of labour standards harmonization.

The process of economic integration in North America offers a rare opportunity to rethink old assumptions, to evaluate a range of institutional and policy options that span the historical experience of all three countries, and to focus on the long term. This opportunity is particularly needed in the United States, where laissez-faire ideology, parochial (imperial) instincts that inhibit learning from other countries, and short-term political horizons have all inhibited the process of coming to terms with recent changes in the global and regional economy. As we collectively search for institutional arrangements that reconcile our economic and social priorities, the automobile industry may play a central role in guiding North America toward new understandings about the role of workers, the state, and employers in industrial and social development.

NOTES

The views expressed in this chapter are those of the author and do not necessarily reflect those of the US Department of Labor.

[1] Even in a relatively tight national labour market such as Japan's, enterprise unionism and keiretsu assembler-supplier relations make shrinking production at Japanese companies costly to their employees and major suppliers. This is because workers and suppliers that switch employers or major customers enter their new situation with a status and security inferior to the new company's pre-existing workers and long-standing suppliers.

[2] The notion that market share is critical to long-term productivity growth is consistent with the kinds of themes that have recently been formalized by the "new trade theory" (Krugman 1987). This body of theory suggests that "strategic trade policy" sometimes benefits a country by enabling it to gain a larger share of oligopoly profits or to increase its share of industries in which "dynamic externalities" are significant. Implicit in the text of this chapter is the idea that both these motivations and an even more important third one—the endogenous dependence of employee and supplier effort (creative and physical), and thus of productivity growth, on wage growth, employment security, and career opportunities—lie behind Japanese corporate practices that amount to a strategic trade policy.

[3] Consistent with his revised view that market forces will not eliminate the North American trade deficit with Japan, Womack now argues that the auto trade imbalance with Japan should be dealt with directly (Womack 1991a).

[4] See Morici (1991) for a general argument about why rules-of-origin are not sufficient to ensure US-Mexico coproduction after NAFTA and would leave the window open for Asia-Mexico coproduction, posing a serious threat to the US industrial base and to US workers' living standards.

[5] Net content also allows companies to produce some vehicles with low domestic content, as long as they compensate by exporting significant parts and vehicles and/or by assembling other vehicles with very high domestic content. One danger of a net content rule in the case of trade with Japan is that North American firms would export low value-added, low profitability parts and vehicles to Japan while importing engineering-intensive parts and vehicles from Japan. Some of the investment proposals below would help overcome this danger by fostering the technical capacities of North American suppliers. A more direct approach would be the Mexican one of identifying "critical components" that must be produced within North America.

[6] A variant of two current Mexican regulations—a trade-balancing (or near-trade balancing) rule combined with finished vehicle import restrictions—would operate like the JNAAP described in the text, except that the import restriction would not give Japanese companies the flexibility to choose between lowering vehicle imports from Japan and increasing exports from North America.

[7] One question in implementing a JNAAP would be whether companies that met its performance requirements would get duty-free access to the North American market. Such tariff elimination would probably meet Canadian opposition because it weakens the last benefit for Auto Pact producers to meet US-Canada Auto Pact performance requirements—duty remission on imports from third countries that are later exported (Holmes, Chapter 2).

[8] For a discussion of CAFE regulation, see Chapter 7 by Gayle.

[9] US and Canadian workers and unions may consider ideas for promoting the dynamism of the Mexican auto parts sector as a threat. In practice, such measures—and analogous measures in other parts of the Mexican manufacturing and agricultural sectors—would facilitate broad-based development in Mexico and protect US and Canadian workers by permitting real appreciation of the Mexican peso. The biggest danger for US and Canadian workers in advanced firms is that Mexican development remains unbalanced and restricted to high-tech plants of major multinationals. In this case, low productivity growth, labour surplus, and low wages in the less-developed bulk of the Mexican economy would continue to act as a drag on wages in high-tech firms and prevent real exchange rate appreciation.

[10] One reason greenfield investment reinforces low wage pressure in the United States is that new firms have much lower health and pension costs than established firms with older work forces and high retiree-active employee ratios (Howes 1991). This is less of an issue in Mexico and Canada, where health care is funded through payroll taxes or general revenues.

[11] The discussion here is based on Herzenberg (1991), which draws heavily from the work of Kevin J. Middlebrook and Harley Shaiken. See also US Congress 1992, Ch. 4, especially pp. 81-86.

[12] For more on the origins and functions of the AIF, see Katz (1985:14-22).

[13] Increasing investment in human resource development, particularly in auto-parts firms, is also critical to institutionalizing a high-wage, high-skill North American auto industry. Although a continental agreement on training might encourage the necessary investment, human resource

development can, for the most part, be dealt with effectively at the national level. Therefore, it is not discussed here.

[14] The title of this section is adapted from the report of the Commission on the Skills of the American Workforce, *America's Choice: High Skills or Low Wages!* (CSAW 1990). That bipartisan and multi-constituency report made a general argument about the US economy as a whole that parallels the argument about the US auto industry presented here.

REFERENCES

Bureau of National Affairs (BNA). 1991. *Daily Labour Report* 133, A-5 and 115, A-9.

Commission on the Skills of the American Workforce (CSAW). 1990. *America's Choice: High Skills or Low Wages!* Rochester, N.Y.: National Center on Education and the Economy, June.

Cusumano, Michael A. 1985. *The Japanese Automobile Industry: Technology and Management at Nissan and Toyota.* Cambridge, Mass.: Harvard University Press.

Gayle, Dennis J. 1992. Regulating the American Automobile Industry: Sources and Consequences of U.S. Automobile Air Pollution Standards. Chapter 7, this volume.

Herzenberg, Stephen A. 1991. The North American Auto Sector on the Eve of Continental Free Trade Negotiations. Washington, DC: Bureau of International Labour Affairs, US Department of Labour. Discussion Paper 38, July.

Holmes, John. 1992. From Three Industries to One: Towards an Integrated North American Automobile Industry. Chapter 2, this volume.

Howes, Candace. 1991. The Benefits of Youth: The Role of Japanese Fringe Benefit Policies in the Restructuring of the US Motor Vehicle Industry. *International Contributions to Labour Studies* 1: 113-32.

Katz, Harry C. 1985. *Shifting Gears: Changing Labour Relations in the US Automobile Industry.* Cambridge, Mass.: MIT Press.

Krugman, Paul. 1987. Is Free Trade Passé? *The Journal of Economic Perspectives* 1,2. Fall: 131-44.

McAlinden, Sean P.; Andrea, David J.; Flynn, Michael S.; and Smith, Brett C. 1991. *The US-Japan Automotive Bilateral Trade Deficit.* Ann Arbor: The University of Michigan Transportation Research Institute. Report No. UMTRI 91-20, May.

Middlebrook, K. 1989. Union democratization in the Mexican automobile industry: a reappraisal. *Latin American Research Review* 24, 71-93.

Middlebrook, K. 1991. The politics of industrial restructuring: transnational firms' search for flexible production in the Mexican automobile industry. *Comparative Politics* 23,3: 275-97.

Morici, Peter. 1991. *Trade Talks with Mexico: A Time for Realism.* Washington, D.C.: National Planning Association.

Office of Technology Assessment (OTA). 1991. *Competing Economies: America, Europe, and the Pacific Rim.* Washington, DC: Congress of the United States, OTA. October.

____. 1992. *US-Mexico Trade: Pulling Together or Pulling Apart?* ITE-545. Washington, D.C.: US Government Printing Office. October.

Prestowitz, Jr., V. Clyde; Cohen, Robert B.; Morici, Peter A.; and Tonelson, Alan. 1991. *The New North American Order: A Win-Win Strategy for U.S.-Mexican Trade.* Washington, DC and Lanhan, Maryland: Economic Strategy Institute and University Press of America, Inc. October 15.

Shaiken, H., and Herzenberg, S. 1987. *Automation and Global Production: Automobile Engine Production in Mexico, the United States and Canada.* Center for US-Mexican Studies, University of California. San Diego: Monograph Series 26.

Womack, James. 1991a. Testimony before the Joint Economic Committee of the US Congress. December 10.

____. 1991b. A Positive Sum Solution: Free Trade in the North American Motor Vehicle Sector. In *Strategic Sectors in Mexican-US Free Trade,* eds. M. Delal Baer and Guy F. Erb. Washington, DC: The Center for Strategic and International Studies and the US Council of the Mexico-US Business Committee.

Womack, James; Jones, Daniel T.; and Roos, Daniel. 1990. *The Machine that Changed the World.* New York: Rawson Associates.

World Bank. 1990. *World Development Report 1990: Poverty.* Oxford: Oxford University Press.

13 CORPORATE STRATEGY, GLOBALIZATION, AND NAFTA:

Mexico's New Role

Marc N. Scheinman

INTRODUCTION

This chapter examines the rapid growth of the Mexican automotive industry since 1986 from the perspectives of corporate strategy and positioning and their impact on production, sales, and trade. Mexico's significance in these areas has been enhanced by the country's growing integration into the globalization strategies of the major vehicle and components producers and by the negotiation of a North American Free Trade Agreement (NAFTA) with the United States and Canada. However, Mexico's emerging role is not simply the reflection of structural changes in automotive competition. In addition, pervasive political and economic liberalization have provided a much more attractive operating environment for the multinational automotive players.

Above all, then, it is this combination of industry-specific and external environmental factors that is transforming Mexico and thrusting it abruptly onto centre stage as one of the few newly industrializing countries (NICs), other than South Korea and perhaps Brazil, that will be an international force in the highly competitive automotive industry of the 1990s.

The chapter's major argument is premised on the assumption that Mexico will be the fastest growing North American market in the 1990s. Strong increases in automotive production and consumption will be accompanied by impressive technological gains and plant modernization. The net result of these changes will be to furnish the US Big Three vehicle producers primarily, but also others such as Volkswagen and Nissan, with crucial domestic and export sales opportunities. The same is true for major component manufacturers, which will also integrate Mexico into their North American operations.

The chapter is divided into three sections. The first provides situational analysis of Mexico from 1986 to 1990, with special attention given to the devastating effects of government regulation (i.e. the Automotives Decrees) on the international competitiveness of the automotive industry. The second focuses on the changing structure of the industry during the same period and emphasizes how the leading vehicle producers have altered their strategies in order to gain new competitive advantages, particularly through exports to the United States. The third section provides a forecast of Mexican sales through 1994 and projections through 2000. The further internationalization of the Mexican industry under NAFTA is also examined.

Before presenting the major arguments and supporting data, it would be helpful to briefly review recent trends in North American automotive competition and market development, particularly in the United States.

BACKGROUND

After years of being relegated to the sidelines, Mexico has emerged as the big growth market in North America for the 1990s, especially with respect to car and truck sales. While NAFTA will spur this expansion, the real groundwork was established in the 1980s, when global competition between US and Japanese vehicle producers in North America intensified and Mexico became an increasingly important source of high-quality vehicles exported into the booming US market. Subsequently, the turnaround of the Mexican economy under the bold policies of today's incumbent, President Carlos Salinas de Gortari, has ignited extraordinary domestic growth in the automotive industry.

This resurgence in Mexico's market could not have come at a better time for the US Big Three, since Mexicans normally consume about three times as many Fords, Chryslers, and General Motors (GM) vehicles as Nissans (the only Japanese manufacturer currently producing in Mexico). By contrast, the United States in the early 1990s is mired in deep recession. To make matters worse, the Japanese name-brand cars produced at US transplants, along with imported vehicles from Japan, continue to gain market share despite the recession.

This trend of rapidly growing Japanese penetration into the US market began in the mid-1980s when the Japanese began to replicate their leading edge management and production systems in the United States through the installation of transplants. These transplants were a direct response to American-imposed Voluntary Export Restraints (VERs) on Japanese-built cars, a response that the Big Three had supported.

The success of the transplants has nullified any benefit that the Big Three manufacturers could have expected to gain from the export quotas, which began in 1981 and are still in effect. Although the current quota is 2.3 million cars, the Japanese do not fully utilize this allocation because of rising sales from their new US assembly facilities. For example, in 1990 they imported 1.9 million units but sold more than one million US-transplant-produced vehicles. In other words, at present, about one in every three Japanese vehicles sold in the United States is produced domestically, and, by the mid-1990s, this proportion will increase to one in two.

Japan's dual-sourcing strategy for the American market—imports supplemented by domestic production—has been resoundingly successful. During the first eight months of 1991, Japanese penetration of the light vehicle market, which includes cars and light trucks, reached record levels as US sales of Japanese-owned or managed companies (import + transplant sales) accounted for 31.6 percent of total US sales in this category. In unit terms, this amounted to sales of 2.18 million of the 5.9 million vehicles sold in the January-August selling period.

The magnitude of this achievement in corporate strategy has resulted in fresh, new Japanese investments in production facilities at precisely the moment when the US Big Three are being forced to close some of their older plants. These events are unequivocal indicators that market-share battles among North American vehicle producers (traditional US Big Three and Japanese transplants) in the 1990s are very likely to be even more feverish than in the 1980s, as the manufacturers confront the problem of industry overcapacity.

This is where Mexico's future role begins to emerge. In the past it was considered primarily a source of cheap labour. With this in mind, the US automotive manufacturers invested heavily in *maquiladora,* or in-bond, plants that assemble mostly American-made components for re-export to the United States. They did so because US tariffs are assessed only on the Mexican value-added. The prolonged economic crisis in the 1980s transformed Mexico into a low-cost, highly efficient production site. By 1989, the cost of direct labour in automotive-related maquiladoras was one-third the South Korean rate ($1.50 vs $4.50 per hour, including benefits).

However, Mexico's experiments in world-class manufacturing began and ended with these maquiladoras in the 1980s. These plants were 100 percent foreign-owned subsidiaries and, consequently, exempt from the very restrictive domestic laws that severely limited foreign investment and ownership. Since the prevailing Mexican development model was import substitution, which was designed explicitly to protect local industry, it is easy to understand why the much more efficient and internationally competitive maquiladoras were required to export virtually all of their production so they would not compete directly with the less efficient domestic firms. It was not coincidental that, while the maquilas boomed and provided an export-led growth model, the rest of Mexican industry languished throughout most of the decade. For instance, in 1987, domestic passenger car sales reached a nadir, less than half what they had at their zenith only six years before in 1981 (154,152 vs 340,363 units, respectively). Between 1982 and 1986, the halving of Mexico's domestic market for cars and trucks produced losses that amounted to $1.5 billion for the five leading manufacturers (Chrysler, Ford, GM, Nissan, and Volkswagen).

In the absence of a sustained domestic recovery the Mexican government, for the first time, began to focus on export development and the establishment of internationally competitive industries. What this would amount to was the systematic dismantling of their crippling import substitution regime and the opening of the economy to foreign trade and investment. In August 1986, Mexico entered the General Agreement on Tariffs and Trade (GATT) and quickly, unilaterally, lowered its maximum tariffs to 20 percent and eliminated many barriers to foreign investment.

By the end of 1989, in the midst of strong economic growth and foreign investment and the lowest inflation rate of the decade (20 percent), Salinas publicly targeted the automotive industry as the key to Mexico's future internationalization plans, announcing the country's fifth and most liberal automotive decree. The timing was perfect. Mexico was about to achieve its second consecutive year of 20 percent plus growth in domestic vehicle sales, while exports continued their ascent as well. It was the beginning of a new Mexico, which, for the 1990s, will provide vehicle and components manufacturers with domestic and export opportunities that only a few years ago were unimaginable.

The size of the opportunity can only be glimpsed partially now, but the view is sufficiently clear to indicate that, some time between 1996 and 1998, Mexican vehicle production will probably surpass Canada's, and so will its domestic sales of cars and trucks. Between 1990 and 1995, total Mexican vehicle sales (domestic and export) will double to approximately 1.7 million, and it is very likely that by the year 2000 this figure will double again to approximately 3.5 million units. Given such an optimistic outlook for Mexico, which contrasts sharply with much more modest Canadian and American growth expectations, it is hardly surprising that the US Big Three view Mexico as one of their most powerful competitive weapons against the Japanese in North America and that, since they are the dominant players in Mexico now, they sought, under NAFTA, to protect their competitive advantage in Mexico from Japanese encroachment.

SITUATIONAL ANALYSIS

DEMAND/ECONOMY

1986 ended on a bitter note for the Mexican economy: inflation soared to almost 106 percent, after hovering around 60 percent for the previous two years, and overall economic growth for the year, as measured by gross domestic product (GDP), declined 7 percent. The surge in consumer prices wiped out hopes of any imminent economic recovery, despite modest GDP growth in 1984 and 1985 of 1.4 and 0.4 percent, respectively. The recession that began in 1982 persisted.

Perhaps no indicator reflected Mexico's dejected circumstances better than the depression in motor vehicle sales. From the vantage point of domestic consumption, 1986 sales of 258,825 units represented 45.3 percent of the 1981 record of 571,013. However, what was especially noteworthy and hopeful for the industry that year was the increasing role of exports. For the fifth consecutive year, export sales grew impressively. The 72,429 vehicles sold abroad in 1986 accounted for 21.9 percent of total sales (331,254 units), whereas, in 1981, in the midst of an economic boom, they represented a meagre 2.5 percent (14,428 vehicles) of industry sales (585,441), while domestic consumption boasted 97.5 percent of that bullish vehicle market.

Viewed in growth terms, these results were even more impressive. In contrast to domestic vehicle sales, which declined by 54.7 percent during the 1981-86 period (or at a yearly rate of 10.9 percent), export sales grew by 402 percent for these years (or at an annual rate of 80.4 percent), albeit from a minimal base. The significance of the trend was not only unmistakable, but planned for by Mexican government officials, who had begun to alter the cumbersome regulatory framework that had been constraining the automotive industry. These dramatic increases in exports accelerated even faster during the subsequent 1986-90 period, initially, as a result of the boom in the US market and slower growth in Mexican vehicle sales. For example, from 1986 to 1990, exports grew by 282.2 percent, or at a rate of 70.6 percent annually. In unit terms, they increased from 72,429 to 276,859 vehicles, a record that was 41.3 percent higher than the previous one established only the year before in 1989. On the other hand, sales of domestic cars and trucks grew by only 112.6 percent during the same years, or at a yearly rate of 28.2 percent. Although 550,306 vehicles were sold in Mexico in 1990, that number, which included 5,376 imported cars, minivans, and sports utility vehicles, still did not match the 1981 record year of 571,013.

Total industry sales, thanks largely to export growth, reached 827,165 units in 1990, a new record. For that year, exports comprised 33.5 percent of all vehicles sold, an indication that exports will contribute even more to industry growth in the 1990s under NAFTA.

REGULATORY FRAMEWORK/DECREES

The operating rules for the automotive industry have been implemented through a series of five presidential decrees, the first of which was issued in September 1962, and the last in December 1989. Although the specific details of each have varied, their basic objectives have remained constant, namely, to balance the often conflicting interests of the foreign-owned vehicle producers with those of the domestically-owned parts and components manufacturers, while simultaneously attracting foreign investment and avoiding balance-of-payments deficits.

Until 1983 and the announcement of the fourth decree, the Mexican government had tightly regulated the number of models that the motor vehicle companies could produce, as well as the minimum local content that they had to source from the domestic supplier industry. Furthermore, in the name of import substitution and domestic market growth, vehicle imports had been prohibited for two decades.

Yet, by 1983, the government, vehicle producers, and suppliers became desperate over the steep declines in domestic sales that had begun in 1982. In response to these dramatic changes in market behaviour, the de la Madrid administration loosened some of the government's traditional industry restraints. Under its aegis, the new decree allowed the vehicle companies to produce an additional line of passenger cars if they were targeted for export. And even more important, while it stipulated that 60 percent of a domestic vehicle's content had to be sourced locally (on a cost-of-parts basis), for exports the proportion of local content was reduced to only 30 percent.

Subsequently, the government provided other incentives to encourage the car manufacturers to establish state-of-the-art export plants in Mexico. In the context of government-business relations, this concept was radical, as previous Mexican decrees had ensured the impossibility of ever building such plants since there was never any interest in exports, but only in domestic production and sales.[1]

In addition, the very high local-content requirements for domestic vehicles and the relative smallness of the Mexican market precluded the achievement of economies of scale and world-class competitiveness. However, these constraints would not inhibit exports, which in the absence of domestic demand, would now have to be the anchor for sales growth. The new North American consumers of the Mexican-built vehicles would provide a true test of Mexico's ability to compete in international markets because the Americans would demand much more exacting standards than the Mexicans.

Ford was the first to respond positively to the Mexican government's overtures with its announcement in January 1984 that it was investing $500 million to build a new plant in Hermosillo, dedicated exclusively to export production of Mercury Tracers and Ford Escorts (Escort production began in 1990). The factory, which came on-stream in 1987, has provided the entire industry with a powerful demonstration of what can be achieved in Mexico: Hermosillo has transformed Ford into Mexico's leader in vehicle exports. Subsequently, others, such as Nissan and Volkswagen, emulated Ford when they publicized $1 billion investment plans in 1990 to spur exports through new production facilities, but only after the Salinas government had further liberalized the industry's regulations and provided them with significant, if temporary, forms of protection.

In spite of the 1983 decree's tendency toward deregulation, crucial impediments to manufacturing in Mexico remained, the most important of which prevented foreign-owned components companies from gaining majority control, and maintaining performance and local-sourcing requirements for vehicle producers, while prohibiting them from importing cars or trucks. Each of these obstacles made it difficult for the global automotive players to rationalize their Mexican production.

At the end of 1989, Salinas indicated that he was prepared to remove some of these restraints in order to jump-start the Mexican economy by attracting larger infusions of foreign investment in capital-intensive and technologically driven industries in which Mexico could produce internationally competitive products. To Salinas and Mexican business executives alike, the automotive industry became the key to Mexican development, because it was the most globally sophisticated. But even more important was the fact that many of the most important international automotive producers were already in Mexico and were prepared to expand Mexico's role in their North American operations.

The 1989 decree offered the vehicle manufacturers specific incentives, but carefully balanced liberalization measures with protective devices. For the first time in decades, vehicle imports were permitted, but only on a limited scale (15 percent of domestic sales for the 1991 and 1992 model years, and 20 percent for 1993 and 1994). In order to qualify for even these limited quotas, each manufacturer had to maintain a positive trade balance and compensate for the imports by satisfying stiff export requirements. For every dollar value of imported new cars, the producer had to export $2.50 for the 1991 model year, $2.00 for the 1992 and 1993 model years, and $1.75 for the 1994 model year.

The nature of these reforms indicated that the 1989 decree was a very delicate balancing act, but most importantly, it displayed the adeptness of the new Mexican government at negotiating with some of the world's most powerful multinational corporations. Nowhere was this approach more apparent than in the section of the decree that regulated the import of subcompact cars. Since Nissan and Volkswagen had both pledged to invest $1 billion in Mexico during Salinas' regime, as a quid pro quo, the government prohibited the import of precisely the same, entry-level cars that they produced until 1993, when the first output from their new plants should be available to meet any possible new competitors in the Mexican market.

The 1989 decree was also notable for reducing local-sourcing requirements to 36 percent of the total value-added for passenger cars and 40 percent for trucks. However, for the first time since 1962, vehicle producers were free to select their suppliers and to produce as many lines as they wanted. Moreover, components companies were able to obtain 100 percent control over their Mexican subsidiaries through the establishment of special financial trusts.

The 1989 decree and the previous one have already had a profound impact on the automotive industry. Aside from attracting unprecedented amounts of foreign investment, they established the foundations for NAFTA negotiations by creating a very positive business climate. The surges in domestic and foreign demand for Mexican-built vehicles have whetted the appetites of global car and truck manufacturers, who believe their Mexican operations are capable of furnishing them with competitive advantages in international markets. But they are also convinced that, in addition to these much-publicized export opportunities (to the United States), the growth potential of the Mexican market, itself, cannot be ignored.

TECHNOLOGY

To date, despite these dramatic changes, the Mexican automotive industry is just entering a period of sustained growth in which domestic sales will finally surpass the record established in 1981. Subsequent to 1991, motor vehicle growth for both the domestic and export markets will reach new heights as Mexico is fully integrated into the North American operations of the US Big Three. However, before the Mexican subsidiaries of these powerful multinationals can achieve strategic advantages within the newer and much more highly competitive domestic and international markets, large investments in state-of-the-art technology are required. Given the strong growth projections for the 1990s, these infusions in capital-intensive projects have already begun.

In the past, because the domestic market alone never reached 600,000 units, it was difficult for Mexico's five leading vehicle producers to rationalize their production to competitive international standards.

The limited size of Mexico's market meant that at best a vehicle producer could count on selling 145,000 units, while at worst only 34,000. And these figures combined sales of both cars and trucks. Since each manufacturer offered at least two different models, and frequently three or four, it was impossible for any of them to achieve economies of scale, which normally require minimal production runs of 100,000-150,000 units per model.

Equally important, the government's import substitution model made it impossible for the vehicle producers to financially justify investing in the latest technology for their Mexican subsidiaries. Sourcing major components and parts from a highly protected local supplier industry translated into higher production costs and lower quality standards. Consequently, vehicles assembled in Mexico for domestic consumption were not competitive by international standards. The exceptions to this rule, of course, were those products that were destined for export and subject to minimal government regulation. It is not shocking to learn that the plants responsible for manufacturing such products as the Mercury Tracer and Ford Escort utilized the latest, most sophisticated technology, while the manufacturing facilities that supplied the domestic market were at least a decade behind. The same was true for the production of motors for export, where the amount of local content was approximately one-third of the 60 percent mandated for the domestic market. These incentives encouraged the major vehicle producers, but especially General Motors, to use its very modern Ramos Arizpe plant as an export platform to the United States.

From 1982 to 1990, 10.5 million motors were exported from Mexico, or an average of almost 1.2 million annually. General Motors' share of these engines, mostly four-cylinders, was a dominant 37.9 percent.

COMPETITION/DOMESTIC

In 1990, the five major vehicle producers in Mexico—Ford, Chrysler, General Motors, Volkswagen, and Nissan—accounted for 96.8 percent of domestic sales. In unit terms, this translated into 532,872 of the 550,306 total, which includes the purchases of 5,376 imports. In 1990, cars accounted for almost two out of every three vehicle sales (64.1 percent). Trucks, on the other hand, totalled 34.9 percent of vehicle purchases.

The five leading vehicle producers manufacture commercial trucks (below 3,500 kg GVW), light trucks (3,501-5,000 kg GVW), and cars. There are other vehicle assemblers that restrict their production to heavy trucks, truck tractors, and buses, although their output is relatively small and will not be discussed until the last section of the chapter.

Volkswagen dominated the 1990 domestic passenger car market, largely as a result of its leadership in the popular car segment (subcompacts), which is the largest and fastest growing one in Mexico. Cars in this segment are the least expensive, and represented 61.2 percent of total 1990 car sales. Volkswagen's sedan, or Beetle, was the best-selling model of its subcompacts, with sales of 84,245. Nissan's Tsuru placed a close second, with sales of 79,945. Although Nissan also finished second in overall car sales, it trailed Volkswagen by a wide margin, as did Chrysler, which placed third. The 1990 market share leaders and their rankings are compared with their 1986 figures in Table 1.

In the category of truck sales, General Motors changed positions with Volkswagen. GM overwhelmed all others in commercial/light truck sales. In 1990, it finished with a commanding 32.1 percent on sales of 61,188 units. Volkswagen, which led in car sales, was by far the poorest truck performer, with a segment share of only 5.4 percent. Chrysler and Ford battled over the second position, which Chrysler eventually won, but both were far behind General Motors. The truck competitors and their market positions are illustrated in Table 2.

It is important to note that the 1990 market share positions of the individual companies were virtually identical to their 1986 rankings

Table 1

Car Market Share Leaders, by Company, 1986 & 1990

| | Rank | | Share | |
	1990	1986	1990	1986
Volkswagen	1	1	38.2%	34.1%
Nissan	2	2	22.8%	26.9%
Chrysler	3	3	14.9%	14.9%
Ford	4	4	14.9%	14.9%
General Motors	5	5	9.2%	6.9%

Source: Asociación mexicana de la industria automotriz (AMIA) and the author's own calculations.

Table 2

Truck Market Share Leaders, by Company, 1986 & 1990

	Rank		Share	
	1990	1986	1990	1986
General Motors	1	2	31.9%	21.5%
Chrysler	2	3	20.5%	20.0%
Ford	3	1	19.3%	22.0%
Nissan	4	4	16.8%	18.0%
Volkswagen	5	5	5.3%	10.6%

Source: AMIA and author's calculations.

for both car and truck sales. The one difference was that Ford was the truck leader in 1986, but only by a hair, as it edged General Motors by 0.5 percent, while Chrysler was only 1.5 percent behind, in third place. By 1990, GM had left these other two US manufacturers far behind. The very significant difference between 1986 and 1990 Mexican vehicle sales was the tremendous expansion in market size. During the years 1986 to 1990, Mexican car purchases skyrocketed at a 29.9 percent annual growth rate, while truck sales increased a little more slowly, at a yearly speed of 24.2 percent.

COMPETITION/EXPORTS

As fast as domestic car sales increased, exports grew even faster, at the meteoric rate of 130.4 percent annually, from 1986 to 1990. Truck exports actually declined at an average yearly rate of 4.1 percent. However, trucks have never played as crucial a role as passenger cars. In 1990, for example, truck shipments comprised only 9.7 percent of vehicle exports. On the other hand, 249,921 of the 276,859 vehicles exported in 1990 were cars (90.3 percent). From the vantage point of passenger-car and total exports (cars + trucks), a new record has been established every year in the period under examination.

With the completion of its Hermosillo plant expansion in 1990, Ford charged into first position with a 35.4 percent share of car exports. Chrysler was a distant second, with a 22.1 percent share. Yet, Chrysler, the perennial leader in truck exports, once again finished first with a 75.6 percent share of the 26,938 units exported. All of its export vehicles were RamChargers.

Table 3

Car and Truck Export Leaders, by Company, 1986 & 1990

	Company	Rank		Share[a]	
		1990	1986	1990	1986
Car	Ford	1	5	35.4%	0.0%
	Chrysler	2	2	22.1%	38.5%
	Volkswagen	3	4	18.5%	0.2%
	General Motors	4	1	16.4%	46.4%
	Nissan	5	3	7.5%	14.8%
Trucks	Chrysler	1	1	75.6%	89.4%
	Nissan	2	2	24.4%	10.0%

a. Share figures do not add up to 100 percent due to smaller manufacturers whose numbers are not included here.

Source: AMIA and author's own calculations. Annual Round-up Issues.

The 1990 car and truck export leaders are compared with those of 1986 in Table 3.

As could have been predicted, the rapid growth in domestic and export vehicle sales has begun to change the structure of the industry and the bases of competitive advantage. The success of the last five years will attract new entrants, while the old players will have to re-create their corporate strategies with these new competitors in mind. One thing is certain: the Mexican automotive industry of the 1990s will be much more complex and competitive than that of the 1980s. To get a better understanding of what these novel configurations will look like, it would be helpful to: analyze industry structure in terms of the changing face of competitive rivalry; look at the relationship between the different vehicle manufacturers and their suppliers; and examine the relevance of NAFTA as a source of opportunity, as well as an entrance barrier.

INDUSTRY STRUCTURE AND CORPORATE STRATEGY

RIVALRY AMONG COMPETITORS

The modernization of the automotive industry has enabled the vehicle manufacturers to craft new strategies in which exports play a crucial role in the marketing mix. By contrast, in the past these decisions were almost entirely domestic ones and were restricted to allocating production between cars and trucks.

Today, some of the fastest growing and most successful companies (e.g., Ford, which, in 1990, ranked second in total vehicle sales) sell more Mexican-assembled passenger cars in the United States and Canada than in the local market but target all of their truck production to Mexican consumers. On the other hand, a firm such as Nissan, which ranked second in domestic-market penetration for 1990, was reduced to fourth place in total vehicle sales, barely nosing out the last place finisher, GM, because of a weak export program.

In other words, in today's industry, export production has become an increasingly important source of competitive advantage, which the US Big Three have utilized far more extensively than either Nissan or Volkswagen. This growing export importance, mostly in cars, is revealed

Table 4

Export Contribution to Total Sales, by Company and Product, 1986 & 1990

| Rank | Company | Percentage | | | |
| | | 1990 | | 1986 | |
		Domestic	Exports	Domestic	Exports
1	Volkswagen				
	Cars	70.4	24.2	84.3	0.1
	Trucks	5.4	0.0	15.5	0.0
2	Ford				
	Cars	29.4	49.7	48.1	0.0
	Trucks	20.9	0.0	51.9	0.0
3	Chrysler				
	Cars	31.4	33.0	30.4	17.0
	Trucks	23.5	12.2	21.1	31.1
4	Nissan				
	Cars	58.3	13.6	62.2	8.6
	Trucks	23.4	4.8	24.7	4.5
5	General Motors				
	Cars	24.1	30.5	22.4	36.9
	Trucks	45.5	0.0	40.7	0.0

Source: AMIA and author's own calculations.

dramatically in Table 4, which compares the ratio of exports-to-total sales in 1986 and 1990.

The impact of these corporate strategy changes on an individual company's total sales is further clarified when export sales and rate of growth are examined in terms of their contributions to total sales between 1986 and 1990. For example, in 1990, Ford was the company with the highest export-to-total sales ratio (49.7 percent) and the most exports (88,604). During the entire 1986 to 1990 period, Ford's total sales growth averaged 84.7 percent annually, or more than twice the industry benchmark (40.2 percent). The immediate and tangible consequences of Ford's leading export drive was that it catapulted the firm from a last place finish (fifth) in 1986 total sales to second in 1990. At the same time, Nissan, the second leading company in 1986 total sales, dropped to a very distant fourth in 1990, as it finished last in exports. However, Chrysler, the leader in total market share and exports in 1986, plummeted to third place in 1990 total market share, and second in exports. Yet, unlike Nissan, Chrysler's loss of position was not due to low export levels, but rather to the larger increases of Volkswagen and Ford. Chrysler's 1986 to 1990 export growth rate of 18.3 percent was the slowest, trailing the industry yearly average of 70.6 percent by more than 50 percent.

These total market share differences between 1986 and 1990 are detailed in Table 5. The figures include both car and truck sales.

Table 5

Total Market Share Position and Growth, 1986 & 1990

| Company | 1990 | | 1986 | | 1990/1986 |
	Unit Sales	Share	Unit Sales	Share	Change/Yr
Volkswagen	191,308	23.1%	65,063	20.5%	48.5%
Ford	178,108	21.5%	40,591	12.8%	84.7%
Chrysler	167,666	20.3%	91,006	28.7%	21.1%
Nissan	138,117	16.7%	69,636	22.0%	24.6%
General Motors	134,532	16.3%	50,643	16.0%	41.4%

Addendum: Comparative yearly growth rates, 1986-1990

Average yearly growth rate in export sales:	70.6%
Average yearly growth rate in total sales:	40.2%
Average yearly growth rate in domestic sales:	28.2%

Source: AMIA and author's own calculations.

VEHICLE SUPPLIER RELATIONS

While it is unmistakable that the automotive industry has been powered by export growth, and that exports are among the most effective sources of competitive advantage, export growth has also put increasing stress on vehicle supplier relations. In the past, when the government tightly enforced very high local-content rules and vehicle exports were not yet a critical part of automotive strategy, the vehicle manufacturers had much less control over quality standards, and economies of scale were simply out of the question. Now, however, export plants are measured by competitive international standards and are clearly the most efficient ones in the country.

This focus on international standards has put enormous pressure on the suppliers to produce in much larger volumes and at more competitive prices. Currently, Ford has about two hundred suppliers, of which sixty are certified as Q-1, the firm's highest international quality designation. The challenge for Ford is to help elevate all its suppliers to this level during the next few years so that the company can further increase its Mexican competitive advantages. This challenge, of course, is not limited to Ford: all the other manufacturers must confront it, directly. They do not want to be left behind.

Not all the Mexican suppliers are capable of meeting the new demands of global competition because they are too small and under-capitalized. As a result of more liberal investment rules, some important local producers are being acquired by foreign firms, which are infusing the businesses with capital and state-of-the-art technology. The largest Mexican suppliers, many of which are already joint venture partners with powerful US firms, can and are responding to the profound changes in industry dynamics, but it is not easy. For the few very large companies that are often members of conglomerates, such as Grupo Spicer, Grupo Condumex, and Grupo Tebo, integration in the North American market is moving at a blistering pace. The most important auto parts exports are motorparts, bodies, transmissions, suspensions, clutches, and brakes.

The impact of this internationalization process on vehicle supplier relations is revealed in the recent trade figures. By 1990, Mexico exported $5.8 billion in auto parts and components to the United States and ranked as its third leading foreign supplier. According to the Banco de México, the central bank, and the INEGI (the national statistics agency), $3.9 billion of the total exports were shipped from maquiladoras. Still, only $910 million of this figure was comprised of Mexican value- added, which means that about 77 percent of the total value was sourced outside Mexico, mostly in the United States. Of the remaining $2 billion, $1.3 billion were for motor exports, while the final $677 million was for miscellaneous parts.

It is important to observe that exports from the maquiladoras, mostly 100 percent wholly-owned subsidiaries of US companies, have grown three times as fast since 1986 as exports from Mexican-owned firms (if maquila growth is evaluated in value-added terms only). In other words, the maquilas are competing with the Mexican-owned firms. From 1986 to 1990, exports from the automotive-related maquiladoras grew at an average yearly rate of 45.2 percent, from $310 to $910 million, while similar exports from the Mexican-owned industry grew by 15.7 percent annually, from $940 million to $1.5 billion.

Even if maquila factories are excluded from export calculations and considered separately, as Mexican analysts prefer, the loss of leverage among the Mexican suppliers is obvious. For instance, 1990 exports from the Mexican suppliers comprised only 33 percent of the automotive industry total ($4.6 billion)—vehicles and parts—compared with 41.4 percent of the 1986 total ($2.3 billion). What a difference between this situation and the one that prevailed in 1981! At that time, when vehicle exports were irrelevant to a booming and highly protected domestic market, the Mexican-owned suppliers accounted for 70.6 percent of the industry's exports.

MEXICO'S NEW ROLE UNDER NAFTA

TRADE/INVESTMENT

By the time NAFTA negotiations began in June 1991, it was already clear to auto industry specialists that Mexico was in the midst of a very rapid growth cycle that was especially strong in North American trade. At the end of 1990, Mexico accounted for 12.9 percent of all US auto parts imports, trailing only Japan (33.1 percent) and Canada (27.9 percent). In dollar terms, these imports amounted to $4.4 billion, according to the United States International Trade Commission (USITC).

From the perspective of both absolute and relative growth, components imports from Mexico increased briskly during the period from 1986 to 1990. In dollar terms, these imports grew at a yearly rate of 17.3 percent, while Mexico's share of the total US auto parts import market increased by 2 percent over the 10.9 percent share of 1986. By sharp contrast, the value of auto parts imports from Canada grew by an average of less than 1 percent each year, but Canada's share of the US market declined by more than 9 percent during those same years. The big story, however, was that, by 1990, cars exported from Mexico represented 5.5 percent of total US passenger car imports, or some 216,000 units. For the 1986 to 1990 time frame, US car imports from Mexico grew by almost 104 percent per year, while imports from Canada were flat, increasing by 1.2 percent annually. In unit terms, these 1990 imports were only about 58,000 higher than in 1986.

Mexico's penetration of the US vehicle market is more impressive still when measured against its three major NIC competitors—South Korea, Brazil, and Yugoslavia. In 1986, Mexico accounted for 17 percent of US passenger car imports from the four NICs, but four years later tripled its share to 50.2 percent. While imports from Mexico increased by almost 104 percent from 1986 to 1990, those from South Korea, its closest competitor, grew by less than 5 percent, from 169,000 to 201,000 units. Imports from Brazil grew rapidly, from 3,000 to 10,000 cars, or at a yearly rate of 58.3 percent, but gave no indication of challenging Mexico's position. On the other hand, after a promising start, imports from Yugoslavia have nearly disappeared in same the period, from 36,000 to 3,000 passenger car sales.

These remarkable gains by Mexico in North American positioning, through exports and expanding domestic sales, have also set the stage for strong US export growth in Mexico among auto parts firms. From 1986 to 1990, these American-based firms increased their exports to Mexico, from about $1.9 billion to more than twice that amount or $4.3 billion in 1990. These achievements set the stage for the NAFTA negotiations and made it certain that new entrants would begin establishing production facilities in Mexico in the not-too-distant future. But they will be playing catch-up against companies that are already established and expanding their capabilities to meet the challenges of the 1990s.

Among the players now in Mexico, Mercedes-Benz, for one, has announced recently that it is investing $325 million, in order to double its truck production, and is planning to assemble a limited number of luxury cars in Mexico for export, beginning in 1993. And Ford has publicized a $700 million investment in its Chihuahua motor plant, where it will begin to produce 500,000 four-cylinder engines for export in 1993. The Chihuahua plant will be closed for two years in order to enable the company to retool and double its yearly output, which will supply 20 percent of the company's North American needs for the next generation Topaz and Tempo models. Over the past decade, Ford has invested $2.8 billion in its Mexican operations.

Nissan and Volkswagen, too, are now in the midst of doubling their production, particularly for export, so they can utilize their Mexican facilities more effectively than in the past. During the Salinas years, 1989 to 1994, Mexico will receive at least $4 billion in new foreign investment that will transform the country's automotive structure, as it becomes possible for vehicle manufacturers to achieve real economies of scale, for the first time.

SALES FORECAST

From 1990 to 1994, domestic sales of passenger cars will increase from 352,608 to 675,996, or at a rate of 22.9 percent per year, while truck sales will grow somewhat more slowly, from 196,127 to 293,808, or by 12.5 percent annually. Total domestic sales, which include cars and trucks, will increase from 550,306 to 969,804 units during the period, for an average yearly growth rate of 19.1 percent. This forecast is detailed on a yearly basis in Table 6.

Exports during the 1990 to 1994 period will grow slightly faster, at a rate of 19.7 percent per year, from 276,859 to 495,371. Total

Table 6

Domestic Sales Forecast, 1990-94

	Cars	Trucks	Total
1990	352,608	196,127	548,735
1991	396,311	226,777	624,088
1992	478,194	246,154	724,348
1993	566,319	269,994	836,313
1994	675,996	293,808	969,804

Source: AMIA.

Mexican automotive sales will therefore increase from 827,165 to 1.465 million units, or at a yearly rate of 19.3 percent. For 1995, total sales will reach 1.7 million unit sales. In other words, the size of the industry will have doubled in five years, from 1990 to 1995.

Although it is difficult to forecast beyond the middle of the decade, it is not difficult to envision Mexican industry sales doubling again by 2000, but this development awaits the announcement of the corporate strategies that will emerge now that NAFTA has been signed.

NEW ENTRANTS

The enormous promise of the Mexican automotive industry is attracting considerable interest among vehicle producers that are not currently manufacturing in Mexico. Honda has intimated that it is preparing to enter the Mexican market, although it is now only manufacturing motorcycles and parts in its Guadalajara plant. Toyota, too, is a natural, and when they have had time to consider the details of NAFTA, they may make public their future plans.

There is no question that the vehicle producers currently in Mexico did everything in their power to convince the NAFTA negotiators to establish strict entry barriers against newcomers to Mexico so that they could protect the capital investments they have already made. On the other hand, the potential new entrants, particularly those with US subsidiaries, such as Honda and Toyota, argued that they should be treated equally as North American businesses. The differences that emerged concerned minimum local or, more precisely, regional content rules. Although the Canada-US Free Trade Agreement was used as a model, the 50 percent FTA local content necessary to qualify for tariff-free treatment appeared too low (by about 10 percent) to many industry analysts.

The phasing out of duties on automotive imports from Mexico will take ten years. Even if Japanese firms such as Honda were to establish themselves in Mexico, they could probably well afford to pay the 2.5 percent duty assessed on US passenger car imports. The 25 percent tariff on minivans is quite another problem and will be more difficult to resolve.

As important as tariff barriers are as impediments to the further integration of Mexico into the US Big Three's North American operations, non-tariff barriers are even more powerful obstacles. Of primary interest to the foreign vehicle assemblers were: the removal of minimum Mexican content rules, the elimination of restrictions on foreign investment and imports, and the phasing out of performance requirements for export.

These are all complex problems, but the magnitude of the Mexican opportunity is one not to be lost. With the signing of NAFTA, Mexico has the opportunity to present North American manufacturers with growth figures not attainable in the United States or Canada.

CONCLUSION

Even without NAFTA, Mexico would be the fastest growing automotive market in the 1990s. Although NAFTA is scheduled to be implemented beginning in 1994, it is important to speculate on what would happen in the absence of such an agreement. The best estimate would be that sales might be hurt by 2 to 3 percent annually, which is minimal given the projected growth of the Mexican Motor Vehicle Manufacturers and, according to this author, who maintains that the growth rate will average 20 percent per year between 1990 and 1994.

In addition to the domestic boom, Mexican production will play an increasingly important role in export production for the US and Canadian markets. By the year 2000, such shipments may well reach about 1.5 million units. Finally, Mexico will also serve as an important supplier to other Latin American markets, such as Chile and Venezuela, as free trade agreements multiply.

NOTES

[1] Recall that in 1981 vehicle exports comprised only 2.5 percent of total Mexican unit sales.

REFERENCES

Asociación mexicana de la industria automotriz (AMIA) / Monthly and yearly bulletins.

Interviews with automotive executives.

14 THE MEXICAN AUTOMOTIVE INDUSTRY IN THE NAFTA NEGOTIATIONS

Miguel Angel Olea

INTRODUCTION

This chapter analyzes the North American Free Trade Agreement (NAFTA) negotiations from the standpoint of the interests of Mexican auto parts suppliers. Unfortunately, this group was not successful in obtaining everything it wanted in the negotiations. However, the aim of this analysis is to help explain the sector's point of view with regard to the different elements of the NAFTA negotiation process, starting from a medium-term outlook on the auto parts industry in Mexico. The first part of the chapter sets out the context for the North American automobile industry at the regional level. The second part establishes the positions that the main participants in the industry took regarding the negotiations. Finally, the third part presents an analysis of the significance of the industry's position in the negotiating process.

THE CONTEXT OF THE NORTH AMERICAN AUTOMOBILE INDUSTRY

The US and Canadian automobile industries are undergoing a process of structural change to adjust to the new world-wide conditions of competition in the sector. The reorientation of manufacturing processes to "lean production" introduced by the Japanese companies, and the redefinition of market share that has gone hand-in-hand with it, involve a complete revolution in the design, manufacturing, and marketing of motor vehicles.

Lean production, which involves an interdisciplinary effort in the design and engineering phases of automobile production, flexible manufacturing, just-in-time inventories, and total quality, requires a relationship between assembly plants and suppliers that is synergistic and collaborative. The trend is to reduce and integrate the number of suppliers to assembly plants and to give them greater responsibility in design, product engineering, and the maintenance of high standards of quality.

In the United States and Canada, this revolution in the industry has taken place as a result of reduced competitiveness and loss of market share both at the world-wide and domestic levels, particularly for the three main companies, General Motors (GM), Ford, and Chrysler. In the last thirty-five years, Japan's share in world production of vehicles rose from less than 1 percent to over 30 percent. In the US market, imports of Japanese and European vehicles amount to more than 30 percent of total sales, without counting vehicles produced and marketed in the United States by Japanese off-shore plants.

The changes in competitive conditions and in comparative advantage between producers have had a considerable impact on the North American automobile industry. In the United States alone, recent results in the operations of the Big Three show how hard pressed they are in their own markets. Their financial decline is explained, for the most part, by the fall in demand for vehicles in their domestic and foreign markets. While the US companies are projecting shut-downs and layoffs, Japanese companies are programming increases in production.

The US firms' loss of competitiveness is explained to a great degree by the difficulty the assembly plants and suppliers have experienced in adjusting to the changing conditions of demand and to the extensive segmentation of markets that the Japanese producers have brought about. Even the European firms, which traditionally were dominant in the luxury car end of the market in the United States, have seen their position threatened by Honda, Toyota, and Nissan's new luxury models.

The natural tendency of the Big Three in the United States will be to gradually move into flexible lines, greater integration with suppliers, emphasis on quality and design—things-gone-right (TGR)—and service to consumers. In order to compete in a radically different market, these firms will have to redefine their products and processes within a very limited time horizon, seeking the best alternatives on a world-wide level.

Over the last four years, important developments in the industry have modified the view of Mexico's role in the face of this strategy of repositioning and changes in production technology at GM, Ford, and Chrysler. On the one hand, disillusionment about operations in Southeast Asia, due to rising exchange rates, higher wages, and unstable quality and services, have brought down the potential of this area for producing low-cost compact and subcompact cars. On the other hand, the development of industrial and production conditions in Mexico have enhanced the auto industry's potential. Assembly plants in Mexico, in spite of being obsolete for the most part, have achieved world-class quality levels.

Particularly outstanding is the case of the Ford plant in Hermosillo, which is considered to be the second in the world as far as quality is concerned, exceeded only by Mercedes-Benz in Germany. It is well above the quality coefficients found in Japanese and US plants. This factory has demonstrated that lean manufacturing techniques can be successfully applied in Mexico. Table 1 shows quality levels in terms of defects-per-vehicle obtained in Mexican assembly plants in comparison with those in the rest of the world.

In the in-bond industry, too, lean manufacturing has been successfully implemented. A good example of this success is Packard Electric, which rose from being the most quality-deficient supplier in 1984, according to the New United Motors Manufacturing Corporation (NUMMI), to become the highest in quality in 1987. The most probable scenario for the development of the Mexican automobile industry is the trend toward setting up assembly plants using lean manufacturing practices for the production of world-class quality parts, with

Table 1

Defects per Vehicle in Mexican Automotive Plants

Plant	Defects per Vehicle
Ford, Hermosillo	0.276
Nissan, Cuernavaca	0.736
Volkswagen, Puebla	0.862
Chrysler, Toluca	0.956
Weighted Average Mexico	0.665
World-wide Optimum (Mercedes Benz)	0.261
World-wide Average	0.696

Source: Womack (1990).

a comparative advantage in costs. For the next fifteen years, Mexico will be the country with the greatest growth potential in North America, with the facilities and resources to produce, at low cost, world-class quality compacts and subcompacts, as well as low-volume full-size cars. Where the best competitive advantage will be depends on what happens regarding the CAFE regulations[1] during the NAFTA negotiations, as well as other issues.

Mexico, moreover, can become a high-potential producer of labour-intensive automobile parts and components, supplying the finished products to plants in the United States and Canada. Alternatively, Mexico could become a producer of compacts, subcompacts, and light trucks, with Mexican parts manufactured close to the final production plants. Another strong possibility is direct export of auto parts to the open market.

The evolution of the North American automobile industry is critical to defining the industry's interests vis-à-vis the North American Free Trade Agreement. The stances taken by the different segments of the auto industry during the negotiations revealed differences in their views as to what the "North American automobile industry" will become and the way to promote its interests through NAFTA.

NAFTA AND THE NORTH AMERICAN AUTOMOBILE INDUSTRY

During the NAFTA negotiations, the Automobile Group met formally a number of times to identify some basic issues and to define the mechanisms required to advance toward liberalization of the automobile market in North America. The main issues in the negotiations were:
(a) The Auto Pact between the United States and Canada;
(b) Legislation on the efficient use of fuel in the United States (commonly known as cafe);
(c) Legislation regarding the automotive sector in Mexico and performance requirements;
(d) Tariff elimination arrangements and rules of origin;
(e) Elimination of non-tariff barriers.

Even with NAFTA signed in December 1992, all of these issues are subject to change, as there are different interests at stake in regard to the framework of regulations for the industry in each of the participating countries. However, it is clear that these issues will define the structure of the North American market by necessitating guidelines for access and complementarity of the auto industry at the regional level.

THE STANCE OF THE BIG THREE

In September 1991, Chrysler, Ford, and General Motors sent a letter to US Trade Representative, Carla Hills, indicating their stances on the NAFTA negotiations. Because of the presence and profile of these three firms in the North American automobile market, and their capacity to directly influence the negotiation process, it is important to examine the implications of their stances for the future development of the industry in the region.

The Big Three consider Mexico a marginal producer (at 4 percent of the region's production) with few resources to become a large-scale competitor in the long term. The growth potential of the Mexican market, which depends to a large extent on the recovery of purchasing power, represents a major market for the current surplus capacity of North American plants. From this point of view, NAFTA is seen as an instrument to ensure that the growth of demand that takes place in the Mexican market will be capitalized by these firms to the greatest extent possible.

To this purpose, the Big Three proposed a dual (two-tier) system, in which the automobile firms that are newcomers to the Mexican market would have to accept a fifteen-year transition period for performance requirements and tariff reductions, while, for those already operating in Mexico, the liberalization of the market would be speeded up. Basically, this position is an ingenious combination of measures that would enable North American companies to capitalize, to the greatest extent possible, on the Mexican market's development potential. These are:

1. A so-called two-tier system in which the performance targets or performance requirements defined in the Automotive Decree would be done away with for finished product companies already operating in Mexico (the Big Three plus Nissan and Volkswagen), whereas, for those just entering the market, there would be a period of transition between ten and fifteen years. The system foresees the immediate elimination of tariffs for North American products.

In this Big Three scenario, the time limit contemplated is at most five years. The system would operate as follows:

(a) Change in the requirement from 36 percent to 25 percent of value-added to be generated by purchases from the Mexican auto parts industry over the total value-added for the industry, to be put into force immediately for assembly firms already operating in Mexico, and gradual reduction of this over a period of fourteen years.

(b) Change in the foreign exchange compensation to a ratio of 1-to-0.5 and its gradual elimination over the fifteen-year transition period.

(c) Immediate elimination of tariffs on products and inputs for the firms already operating in Mexico.

For firms not currently operating in Mexico:

(a) Application of the 36 percent value-added requirement for the automobile parts industry, to be applied during the same transition period (fifteen years).

(b) Application of the foreign exchange compensation as contemplated in the 1989 Automotive Decree, and with a ratio of over one-to-one, anticipating its elimination in linear fashion over the transition period.

(c) Elimination of tariffs over a longer period, namely the fifteen-year transition period, as long as rules of origin are complied with.

2. A high rule of origin (60 to 70 percent of the value-added requirement) that ensures that only companies with a North American imported component of this level will have access to zero tariffs, calculating the value-added on the basis of the value of originating

Figure 1
Performance Requirements: Value-Added Phase-Out Schedule

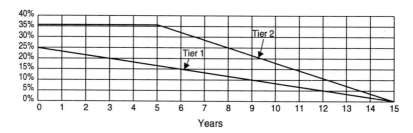

Figure 2

Performance Requirements: Foreign-Exchange Balance Phase-Out Schedule

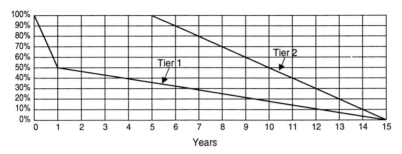

Figure 3

Tariff Elimination Schedule

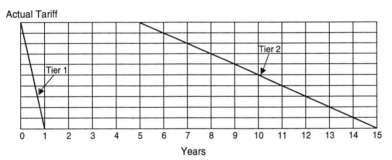

materials plus research and development expenses incurred in North America, that is, in the free-trade area.

The Big Three proposal eliminated the performance requirements for newcomers during a transition period of fifteen years, while, for companies already operating in Mexico, the requirements would quickly be done away with. Thus, the domestic market and the import market would be reserved for assembly firms already operating in Mexico, whereas the high rule of origin would make it more expensive and more difficult for non-North American companies (e.g., Nissan, Mercedes-Benz, and Volkswagen) to operate, by reducing their possibilities for extra-regional outsourcing; in certain cases, this provision would result in a reduction in their competitive potential, particularly if these companies wanted to supply part of the regional market. In

brief, this system would let the North American assembly firms operate with all the competitive advantages that derive from a reserved
market, whereas assembly firms from outside the region would be
forced to operate marginally and within an outright discriminatory
regime.

Rather than considering NAFTA a tool for exploiting possibilities and
developing new competitive advantages, the North American companies see it as a means of freezing the present situation and reserving the
Mexican domestic market for themselves. The strategy they have set
up does not even anticipate relocating plants and facilities to Mexico
from other areas outside the region to capitalize on Mexico's competitive advantage in some areas. With the exception of some isolated
statements, the North American firms already operating in Mexico
perceive the possibility of relocating further supply sources to Mexico
as a potential source of friction with US trade unions.

THE STANCE OF THE ASSEMBLY PLANTS IN MEXICO

In comparison with the position of Chrysler, Ford, and GM, the stance
taken by the assembly plants in Mexico is slightly different. Concerning
motor vehicles and light trucks, attention is concentrated on the way
in which the performance requirements set out in the 1989 Automotive
Decree will be gradually eliminated, and on the definition of the rule
of origin. The main problem for Nissan and Volkswagen, which are
also first-tier companies, will be to accomodate a rule of origin that is
highly restrictive, rather than to encourage world-class technology
and supplies.

The stances taken by the North American firms vis-à-vis NAFTA will
be reflected in their Mexican subsidiaries. They have had little difficulty persuading the two non-North American firms to agree with
them about keeping other assembly firms out. It is widely thought in
Mexico that the market would have to reach a volume of 2.5 million
units a year to have suitable economies of scale, with nearly 500,000
vehicles and an average of three models for each of the present
assembly firms.

Both the assembly firms themselves and the distributors point
out that the market is saturated with brands and models and, therefore, newcomers to the market are not welcome. This defensive posture
will be reinforced if conditions arise for setting up lean distribution

systems, without having to install assembly capacity and develop Mexican suppliers.

THE STANCE OF THE SUPPLIER INDUSTRY IN MEXICO

The Mexican automobile parts industry presents a different stance with regard to the future of the North American automobile industry. Its position is based on the concept of optimum complementarity that could exist between Canada, the United States, and Mexico, both regionally and world-wide. According to this perspective, in the medium run, Mexico presents competitive advantages that will not arise in the two former countries in the near future, thus opening up options and possibilities for lean manufacturing in the region.

With regard to the issue of excess capacity in the region, Mexican suppliers estimate a growth in the domestic market that may reach 1.5 million vehicles per year over the next three years, and 2 to 2.5 million vehicles per year in the following six years. Therefore, they also define the transition period as fifteen years, setting guidelines for opening the market as follows:

1. Maintenance of the performance requirements set out in the 1989 Automotive Decree, including foreign exchange compensation and national value-added, for a period of five years, gradually starting to eliminate them in year six, continuing until year fifteen, with a formula linked to the volume of operations. This step-by-step elimination would apply equally to firms already operating in Mexico and to newcomers.

2. Establishment of a reasonable rule of origin, with a value-added of 50 percent on the basis of manufacturing costs—as is the case between Canada and the United States under the Canada-US Free Trade Agreement (fta). The Mexican parts industry proposed a measurement of local content on the basis of "regional value-added," defined as a maximum level of allowable imports in a firm's total sales, eliminating the binary system of accounting and averaging the value-added per plant.

The combination of a reasonable transition for performance requirements and tariffs with a flexible rule of origin is, in the view of the Mexican parts industry, a more efficient formula for seeking a genuine complementarity within the region's automobile industry,

Figure 4

Performance Requirements: Value-Added Phase-Out Schedule

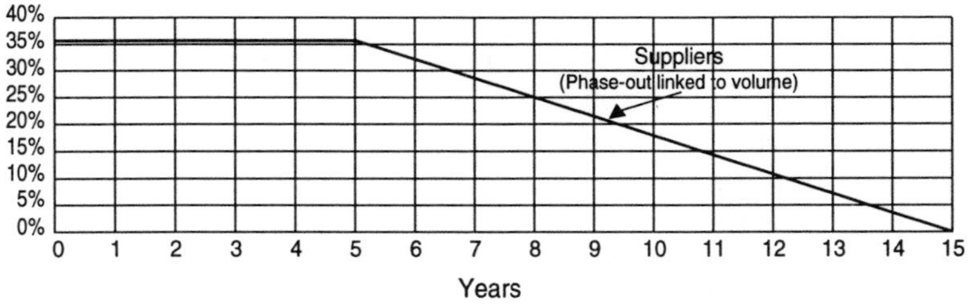

whilst promoting the interest of the firms with already established operations in Mexico. Furthermore, once the transition period is over, the terms of access for newcomers to the market will be defined without discrimination; NAFTA will be a "trade creation" mechanism instead of a "trade diversion" one.

In light of what has just been said about the Mexican auto industry, some points should be considered from the perspective of the US industry as well:

(a) The form in which the two-tier proposal is presented goes against the most elementary rules for international trade and against all the principles for setting up free-trade areas established by the gatt. It would be very difficult to justify a non-discriminatory free-trade area when there is a tool for open and frank discrimination in the automobile sector.

(b) If barriers are set up against newcomers by using the two-tier system, they will simply ignore the rule of origin and pay the 2.5 percent tariff applied to light motor vehicles on entering the United States. The low level of this differential suggests that the performance requirements set in the 1989 Automotive Decree are the best formula to guarantee that firms already in the marketplace can take advantage of the transition period to improve their competitiveness.

(c) Firms such as Toyota and Honda, which are potential newcomers, are in a better position to export to Mexico from their plants in the south of the United States than to set up assembly operations in Mexico. Suppliers of Japanese origin, since they have surplus capacity that the American market is not absorbing, will be able to do the same thing. From the Mexican point of view, the 1989

Figure 5
Tariff Elimination Schedule

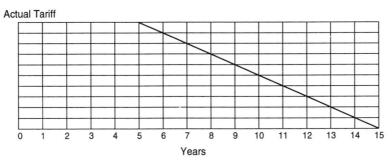

Actual Tariff

Years

Decree demands that they develop suppliers and assembly in Mexico. Otherwise, with the two-tier system and the high rule of origin, with which they already comply in the United States, the establishment of lean distributors, without any commitment to manufacture or invest, would be facilitated. This same argument applies to trucks and tractor-trucks.

THE EXPECTED IMPACT OF NAFTA ON THE MEXICAN AUTOMOBILE INDUSTRY

By gradually eliminating protection for the industry and moving toward freer trade and investment conditions, there will be substantial changes in the inputs and finished products markets. When tariff and non-tariff barriers start to be dismantled as a result of NAFTA, firms in the automobile, truck, and tractor-truck sector in Mexico will not be as flexible in their pricing policies and market penetration strategies.

For the US and Canadian industries, the opening of the market will have an impact on demand, mainly because of the effect of tariff liberalization: the 20 percent tariff on products now entering the Mexican market will gradually be reduced to zero. The Mexican automobile industry amounts to about 4 percent of the North American industry; therefore, the challenge for the US and Canada will be eventual competition from an efficient manufacturing base in Mexico, if the period of adjustment and rules of origin permit such a development.

The free import of vehicles will enable US and Canadian competitors to take part in the Mexican market and offer their different product lines in direct competition with those manufactured in Mexico. The pressure of competition in the market will be immediately transferred to profit and operating margins, thus creating a more complex environment for the firms already established in Mexico that have yet to gain economies of scale and therefore currently operate with higher unit costs.

To maintain or increase its share in the domestic market, the Mexican automotive industry will have to offer world-class prices and quality in a very short time because there will be competition from imports within five to ten years. The key factor for developing the Mexican industry's competitiveness are:

1. *Suppliers.* Assembly parts and components for autos and trucks amount to more than 85 percent of manufacturing costs in Mexico. The development of world-class suppliers, with international price and quality levels, is the most important factor in a competitive strategy. Thus, the comparative advantage of having cheap labour is lessened, due to the fact that processing (assembly) costs only account, on average, for 10 to 15 percent of manufacturing costs. The most important aspects deserving attention in supplier development are their own assembly and manufacturing cost structures, quality, supply logistics, and inventory control.

2. *Scale.* Although the production lines in the assembly industry have a high labour content, the majority of suppliers are highly capital-intensive industries and, therefore, manufacture parts and components with high degrees of operating leverage.2 In these circumstances, the operating scale becomes the most important element in order to absorb a higher level of fixed costs and raise plant profitability. Scale also constitutes the central element for bringing suppliers' unit manufacturing costs down to internationally competitive levels. In order to develop world-class suppliers, a necessary but not sufficient condition is to have substantial scale economies.

3. *Quality.* Quality and product integrity are factors that must be guaranteed within the assembly process, and not become objectives of it. Mexican industry has evolved significantly with regard to quality because of total quality programs that already form a part of the Mexican automobile industry's manufacturing culture.

4. *Supply Logistics and Inventory Control.* The high level of Mexican interest rates makes inventories a significant factor in production and distribution costs. Furthermore, the communications and transportation infrastructures is among the most critical constraints on supply logistics. These are both factors that have inhibited the industry's competitiveness in the domestic and foreign markets.

5. *Lean Production.* Integrating suppliers into lean-production systems involving flexible production lines, total quality, and just-in-time (JIT) handling of inventories makes it possible to focus the problem of competitiveness as part of a global strategy. Lean manufacturing also involves activities prior to assembly, such as engineering, design and product development, and post-production activities, for example, sales, marketing, and customer services.

The Mexican auto industry will have to redefine its position in the North American market, with the dual aim of maintaining and increasing its share in the domestic market and penetrating the North American market so as to achieve international production scales. However, in order to operate competitively in the continental free-trade arena, the first priority must be to minimize differences in comparative advantages that favour assembly plants located in the United States and Canada. To this purpose, the Mexican auto industry must attack on two fronts at the same time: first, establishing a defensive capacity in the domestic market by adjusting suppliers' and other internal costs; and second, developing an offensive capacity in the US and Canadian markets, based on a volume of operations aimed at the regional market.

CONCLUSIONS

1. Recent developments in the regional automotive industry underline the need to restructure its operations. NAFTA provides an opportunity to do so on the basis of optimal complementarity. While the US and Canadian industries position themselves in a market dominated by lean manufacturing and extensive market segmentation, Mexico is developing increasingly flexible production systems with stringent quality requirements in low-volume, low-cost operations.

2. NAFTA will induce changes in the input and end-product markets, thus putting significant pressure on assembly plants and suppli-

ers, and even on the distribution chain, to improve competitiveness and operating efficiency. The association between Canadian, US and Mexican producers could tap new competitive advantages, making the North American automotive industry more competitive at the global level, and giving it more means to regain market participation against extra-regional imports of motor vehicles and even transplant operations.

3. Thus far, the stance of the North American companies (Chrysler, Ford, and GM) suggests very different ambitions for the future of the North American auto industry. According to their stated position, NAFTA will be an instrument to secure the growth potential of the Mexican domestic market as a residual destination for the excess capacity that they have built in the United States. Mexico is considered a marginal participant in the market, and there does not seem to be any consideration given to the contribution its installed capacity could make to an optimal complementarity scheme.

4. The main issues discussed in the NAFTA negotiations were the transition period and the elimination of the open or disguised performance requirements that each party in NAFTA maintains in its respective regulatory schemes. These included the calculation of content under the Canada-US FTA, the 1989 Mexican Automotive Decree, tariff elimination schedules, CAFE, as well as the rule of origin. Other aspects of the negotiations were largely complementary to these key provisions, which will open or close access to and within the integrated North American market.

5. The Big Three were committed to a transition period of fifteen years as the minimum timeframe required to adjust to the new trade and investment environment. They also stated categorically that the used vehicle market should be excluded from NAFTA benefits. In essence, the US auto companies supported what everybody else agreed was an adequate adjustment period, during which the following should occur:

(a) The scale of operations in Mexican assembly plants has to reach levels of 2.5 million per year to attain world class manufacturing volumes. This will give each one of the five assemblers in Mexico an average of 500,000 vehicles per year, with an average of three models per firm. This will set the conditions for adjusting fixed costs to international standards.

(b) Industry costs in Mexico have to be reduced. Vehicle assembly operations in Mexico cost 10 to 15 percent more than the international standard. For heavy trucks, the spread could be as much as 20 percent. Half of this differential could be attributed to the operating scale of assemblers as well as of suppliers. In a typical vehicle assembled in Mexico, the direct material costs, which depend mainly on suppliers, represent more than 80 percent of the total manufacturing cost. Suppliers have more capital-intensive operations than assemblers; hence, the impact of operating scale is more substantial for suppliers than for assemblers.

(c) The industrial logistics and communications infrastructure will continue their modernization process, which will result in international competitiveness in distribution and commercialization costs and will allow just-in-time systems to be implemented between the different participants in the production chain.

(d) Financial costs and taxes will be harmonized with those elsewhere in North America to avoid introducing distortions in the resource allocation process and to foster optimal complementarity for the motor vehicle manufacturers at the regional level.

6. The supplier industry also advocated an approach based on the complementarity potential of the automotive industry at the regional level. It argued for a 15-year transition period in which the performance requirements contemplated in the 1989 Automotive Decree would be maintained for five years, and then begin to be phased out linearly from year six until year 15. The same treatment would be given to tariffs. The main argument for this phase-in was the need to establish a world-scale manufacturing operation among the assemblers and the suppliers, as well as the need for time for the modernization of the industrial and communications infrastructure to take place.

7. The main difference among the three parties in the NAFTA negotiations involved their radically opposed ideas about the North American auto industry and its aims for the future. From the Mexican supplier industry's perspective, the best means to foster optimal complementarity at the regional level lay in maintaining the 1989 Mexican Automotive Decree's provisions for the transition, and in designing a reasonable rule of origin, requiring at most

the same value-added as in the Canada-US FTA but simplifying its calculation and eliminating the cumbersome binary accounting procedures. In this way, firms already operating in Mexico would have enough time to adjust their operations to the new trade and investment environment and the rule of origin would balance any attempt to make Mexico an export/import platform for third countries trading with the US and Canada. It would also guarantee a flexible operation and more options for assemblers and suppliers to compete with extra-regional outsourcing.

8. Finally, it must be understood that the national interests of the Mexican auto industry in the negotiations did not concern only the opening of the Mexican market. First and foremost, the Mexican industry wanted to increase its access to the US and Canadian markets and have a transparent and fair trading environment. It sought to eliminate any obstacles to trade with these two countries, mainly those resulting from CAFE legislation and the Auto Pact, as well as tariff and non-tariff barriers. For Mexico, it was of utmost relevance to devise adequate rules concerning subsidies, countervailing duties, safeguards, and unfair trade practices, as well as to establish dispute-settlement mechanisms to ensure the permanent access of its exports to the North American market. While this paper has analyzed the general strategic issues of NAFTA from the perspective of the Mexican automotive industry, there are, of course, other issues fundamental to the negotiation process that could not be touched on here.

NOTES

The views put forward in this document do not necessarily represent the official position of the Mexican Autoparts Industry, (INA).

[1] See discussion of CAFE regulations in Gayle, Chapter 7.

[2] For an exhaustive description of this process, see Womack et al. (1990).

REFERENCES

Womack, James. 1990. Paper presented at the meeting of the Automobile Parts Manufacturers Association. Toronto. October.

Womack, James; Jones, Daniel T; and Roos, Daniel. 1990. *The Machine that Changed the World*. New York: Rawson Associates.

15 PROSPECTS FOR THE MEXICAN AUTOMOTIVE INDUSTRY IN THE CONTEXT OF A NORTH AMERICAN FREE TRADE AGREEMENT

Kurt Unger

The purpose of this chapter is to look at the major trends in the automotive industry in an international context and to assess their impact on the Mexican automotive industry. Two major concerns will be discussed: the effect of technological transformation on the international location of production; and the extent to which the export potential from Mexico under a North American Free Trade Agreement (NAFTA) should, or could, remain associated with domestic market achievements.

The Japanese organizational paradigm has dramatically altered the traditional view derived from product life cycle theory, namely, that labour-cost advantages can be gained by locating the production of a commodity, in the latter stages of the manufacturing cycle, in less developed countries (LDCs). For the most part, the successful growth of auto parts exports from a selected number of LDCs (including Mexico) in the mid-1970s seemed to indicate that we were well on our way to reaching this stage. Now the focus has shifted from the analysis of individual production cost factors to an integrated concept of efficiency that considers the whole sequence of production operations.

This Japanese organizational transformation involves using advances in electronics and materials technologies in areas ranging from design to tooling to flexible automated production systems. These new technologies seem to open up opportunities to combine the potential for increased product differentiation (to satisfy demand) with decreased economies of scale, made possible by the new flexible, automated production facilities. However, it is still necessary to take account of short-term constraints before changing the whole production system. For example, enormous investment outlays are required to replace old, outmoded plants with new plants embodying new technologies. Thus, the coexistence of both types of production will be a fact for many years. But the need to update production still affects the strategic choices of new entrants into the industry.

Recent years have seen increased state pressure on the Mexican auto industry to balance trade flows. The 1977 Automotive Decree required each final assembler to balance its automotive trade within a few years. To meet these requirements, all six multinational assemblers then operating in Mexico (General Motors, Ford, Chrysler, Volkswagen, Renault,[1] and Nissan) constructed large engine plants in the late 1970s and early 1980s to be used primarily for export production. In addition, some facilities for manufacturing wiring harnesses, seat covers, and other minor parts for export to US assembly plants were built along the US-Mexican border. Owing to the long lead times required to bring major plants on line and the pre-1982 boom in the Mexican economy, however, the short-run results of the 1977 Automotive Decree were the opposite of what had been expected: imports rose much faster than exports up to 1982.

The economic crisis of 1983 reversed this trend. From that year to the present, we have had a very different pattern of development. The Mexican motor vehicle industry is now experiencing a trade surplus for the first time. This is due to the simultaneous effect of import reductions as the domestic market remains constrained and the expansion of exports facilitated by the investments undertaken in the late 1970s and early 1980s. Both of these trends are likely to continue in the near future, though the rates observed in the past cannot be realistically expected to continue.

The prospects to continue expanding the export capacity of the industry may not be as bright in the near future. It is true that the auto industry has been the undisputed leader in manufactured exports in recent years. However, most automotive products, like many other major exports, have been showing some vulnerability since 1988 when, for a variety of reasons, the growth rate of major exports slowed. The export of automotive products will be hindered in the future by the exhaustion of installed-plant capacity, particularly the capacity for engine and parts manufacturing. This situation applies to all firms, including the Big Three.

The US multinational corporations continue to play the leading role in Mexico's automotive industry, both in exports and domestic production, in spite of the difficulties that many of these firms have been facing at home and in most other industrialized countries. The Big Three dominate Mexican exports of the most important products. They account for 96 percent of vehicles exported in 1987 and for about 80 percent of engines exported in that year. The Big Three continue to lead in the export of vehicles, mostly destined for the US market. They account for 74 percent of total vehicles exported during the first ten months of 1990—Ford at 33 percent, Chrysler at 23 percent, and GM at 18 percent. The other exporters, Volkswagon at 19 percent and Nissan at 7 percent, are less firmly oriented to exports.

In other auto parts and components, it is the same competitors that lead the export drive, though, in some cases, participating in joint ventures with domestic firms. There are, for instance, Ford and General Motors joint ventures in Carplastic, Nemak, Vitroflex, and Autopartes Condumex. However, it is crucial to note the declining trend in the growth (virtual stagnation, in fact) of these exports in 1988 and 1989, as an indication of the exhaustion of installed capacity in Mexican plants, as well as the competitive problems that most of these firms are having in the United States and elsewhere.

The exports of engines and automobiles by Chrysler, Ford, and General Motors show very clearly the importance of both economies of scale and economies of scope for plants that were designed from the beginning to serve export markets through intra-firm sales. Their parent companies in the United States, as well as Canadian subsidiaries, are the major destinations for these exports. Since exports already consume most of the installed capacity of these plants, there is not much room left for further growth in the medium run.

Additional exports could only come from new investment in export-oriented plants, a step that has not yet taken place and does not seem likely in the foreseeable future—at least, in the same magnitude as in the past. We have already shown the stagnating trend of these exports since the late 1980s as a result of both the exhaustion of installed capacity in engine-producing plants and the limited demand for exports of vehicles, given the short product lifecycle life left to most of the mature models of vehicles assembled in Mexico for export. Further difficulties may derive from the evident excess capacity world-wide, which is forcing most firms into rationalization programs on an international scale.

Another class of exports consists of auto parts produced by joint ventures between multinational assemblers and large Mexican conglomerates with, given their experience in related fields, a natural advantage in producing these parts. Among these joint ventures are relatively new manufacturers of windshields (Vitroflex), heads for engines (Nemak), plastic components (Carplastic), and wiring harnesses (Condumex). Most of these exports are distributed through intra-firm sales, though in some cases the parts are sold on open markets. Such joint ventures provide considerable possibilities for export (one can expect a significant contribution from the Mexican partner in the form of economies of scope), given the domestic supply of the basic raw materials, plus the use of installations, training schemes, and the learning obtained through experience. Growth prospects for these joint ventures require the displacement of other producers of the same parts and components, either independent auto parts producers or subsidiaries of the same multinational partner that may be in the process of restructuring in the United States and Canada. Both the multinationals' trade and industrial strategy and US trade policy will determine how much more the production of these components is allocated to low-wage countries. At any rate, it is safe to assume that the fast gains made by Mexico in the past are not going to be repeated without complaints from displaced competitors.

Is there any room to make or promote strategic choices that will enhance Mexican comparative advantage in the short run and sustain this advantage in the long term? In view of the arguments made above, I believe it is necessary to anticipate certain broad trends in the automotive industry. These trends include: a transition to an emphasis on domestic market growth over export growth, and only then the conscious development of export capacity; the need to make export capacity compatible with domestic market growth; a change to products that have export potential and will benefit from short-term technological innovations; the selection of firms most likely to survive the current period of intense international competition; and development of broader social and economic organization to promote the auto industry's selected locations.

Until recently, the development of a Mexican export capacity was seen as essential to finance the trade deficits caused by the rapidly expanding Mexican domestic market. The US and European firms creating such deficits have since been conditioned to develop an export capability in Mexico that could equalize their foreign-exchange flows. However, these firms also face similar pressures at home (as has clearly occurred for US auto producers due to Japanese penetration of their market) and these pressures will likely increase in the near future, endangering exports from many sites.

Consequently, it is no longer feasible to rely solely on the auto firms to develop a Mexican exports strategy based on their interests in the Mexican domestic market. On the contrary, Mexican authorities must anticipate and construct a more consistent, coherent, and integral export strategy in anticipation of the firms' own interpretation of the North American Free Trade Agreement and the restructuring effects that it will generate.

Many of the products exported from Mexico so far are primarily low-technology, labour-intensive, bulky items that depend on lower wage rates and lower shipping costs to compete favourably. Some of them, such as parts for engines and other steel-based parts, also have lower pollution-control costs when made in Mexico. However, this type of product will likely be affected by new production materials. Inasmuch as electronics and new materials will change the production of wiring harnesses, which are only second to engines as the most important components exported from Mexico, there is a need to identify parts, components, and subsystems that may create a dynamic comparative advantage for future Mexican production. These decisions may rest more heavily on the assembly firms themselves, but industry policy should also be geared to this purpose.

One delicate aspect of a more active state policy is the selection of projects. The selection process should include consideration of the firms involved, their competitive strategy internationally (thus, the importance of the Mexican project), and the real potential for the development of local linkages that may later diffuse technology and efficient production. Even the major auto producers have recognized the need to learn from each other, as shown by the General Motors-Toyota project in Fremont, California, and Ford-Mazda's project in Hermosillo, Mexico.

Finally, as the conditions for success listed earlier suggest, there is a need to plan and develop the whole system of linkages—backward and forward—that support an export strategy. All linkages, from the transportation system and the provision of other basic infrastructure (which call for production concentration at specific sites), to labour training, and, most important, the early development of relationships between assemblers and component suppliers, must be considered. At the international level, component producers are becoming increasingly involved in the design and development of new system components. This situation may result in a new policy that will selectively attract into Mexico some of the leading component suppliers as well.

NOTES

[1] Renault stopped assembling cars in Mexico in 1986.